TEACHING ENGLISH LANGUAGE LEARNERS

TEACHING ENGLISH LANGUAGE LEARNERS

Content and Language in Middle and Secondary Mainstream Classrooms

Michaela Colombo
University of Massachusetts Lowell

Dana Furbush
Methuen Public Schools

Los Angeles • London • New Delhi • Singapore • Washington DC

For information:

SAGE Publications, Inc.
2455 Teller Road
Thousand Oaks, California 91320
E-mail: order@sagepub.com

SAGE Publications Ltd.
1 Oliver's Yard
55 City Road
London, EC1Y 1SP
United Kingdom

SAGE Publications India Pvt. Ltd.
B 1/I 1 Mohan Cooperative Industrial Area
Mathura Road, New Delhi 110 044
India

SAGE Publications Asia-Pacific Pte. Ltd.
33 Pekin Street #02-01
Far East Square
Singapore 048763

Printed in the United States of America

Library of Congress Cataloging-in-Publication Data

Colombo, Michaela.
Teaching English language learners : content and language in middle and secondary mainstream classrooms/Michaela Colombo, Dana Furbush.
        p. cm.
Includes bibliographical references and index.
ISBN 978-1-4129-5965-0 (pbk.)

   1. English language—Study and teaching (Middle school)—Foreign speakers. 2. English language—Study and teaching (Secondary)—Foreign speakers. 3. Content-area reading. I. Furbush, Dana. II. Title.

PE1128.A2C673 2009
428.2′40712–dc22   2008026554

This book is printed on acid-free paper.

12 10 9 8 7 6 5 4 3

Acquisitions Editor:	Steve Wainwright
Editorial Assistant:	Julie McNall
Production Editor:	Astrid Virding
Copy Editor:	QuADS Prepress (P) Ltd.
Typesetter:	C&M Digitals (P) Ltd.
Proofreader:	Dennis W. Webb
Indexer:	Sheila Bodell
Cover Designer:	Arup Giri
Marketing Manager:	Nichole M. Angress

Contents

3 Culture, Adolescents, and Culturally Responsive Instruction   51

Enduring understanding: Culture shapes the way we teach and the ways in which our students learn.

4 Academic Literacy in the Content Areas 75

Enduring understanding: Academic literacy across content areas is essential to learning.

5 Planning for Enduring Understanding 99

Enduring understanding: Instruction based on enduring understandings ensures English Language Learners access to high-level content.

6   Connecting With Context: Assessments and Essential Questions   121

*Enduring understanding: Clear assessments and essential questions
provide a contextual road map for instruction.*

7   Assessing Content and Language   141

Enduring understanding: Effective assessment facilitates targeted instruction and evaluation of content and language.

8 Making Content Comprehensible   163

Enduring understanding: Grade-level content can be made comprehensible.

9 Building Academic Language   187

Enduring understanding: Academic language must be specifically addressed in content-area classrooms.

PART II: PUTTING IT TOGETHER IN CONTENT-AREA CLASSROOMS   207

Enduring understanding: The TELLiM model integrates content and language instruction for all content areas.

10 Putting It Together in the Science Classroom   213

11 Putting It Together in the Mathematics Classroom   233

Preface

English Language Learners (ELLs), the fastest-growing population in U.S. schools, are a very diverse group of students. Some ELLs have recently immigrated to the United States, while others were born and have been educated here. Although ELLs differ from one another in many ways, including homes of origin, languages spoken, previous schooling, and socioeconomic status, all of them struggle to acquire academic-English proficiency in classrooms across the United States. Effectively teaching ELLs is increasingly the responsibility of content-area teachers across grade levels.

While ELLs acquire academic English, they must also learn content. During this time, they need instruction from content-area teachers who know the concepts that must be mastered for *enduring understanding* (Wiggins & McTighe, 1998, 2005), understand the specific language required to access content and demonstrate content-area mastery, and have developed strategies to effectively convey this knowledge to ELLs. As content becomes more sophisticated in the middle and upper grades, teaching ELLs becomes increasingly complex. We have written this text to provide middle and secondary content-area teachers with the necessary knowledge base to address this challenge.

Content-area expertise is a critical starting point in teaching ELLs. This is illustrated in a story told by a colleague. Amy had been a teacher in mainstream, bilingual, and ESL classrooms, mostly in the middle grades. When she knew the content area well, Amy was an excellent teacher. Amy spoke Spanish fluently and therefore was called on to teach classes in which she lacked content-area expertise, such as secondary science and mathematics. According to Amy, she was a very mediocre teacher in these classes. This mediocrity was not the result of lack of effort. Amy spent many hours searching for traditional and electronic resources to inform her teaching, and she worked to provide the ELLs in her classrooms with content-area instruction and content-specific English. Amy learned a lot and shared this knowledge with her students, yet she was unable to provide the conceptual depth that a well-qualified science teacher would have provided.

Amy often thought about the academic advantages a content-area teacher who was also well prepared to teach ELLs could have provided to her students. Yet just as it was unreasonable to expect Amy to adequately teach science without a science background, it is equally unreasonable to think that, without adequate preparation, content-area teachers can teach both content and content-area language to ELLs. Teaching content effectively to ELLs *is* good teaching, yet it is *more than just good teaching*. It requires knowledge of linguistics, of second language acquisition, and of the role culture plays in teaching and learning. Such knowledge enables teachers to plan and deliver instruction that is relevant and comprehensible and that builds academic language. This text provides content-area teachers with the necessary knowledge in these areas.

We know that mainstream teachers want ELLs to succeed in their classrooms yet are often unsure about how to meet the needs of these students. Even teachers who understand the strengths and needs of ELLs may not know the specific strategies necessary to teach content and content-area academic language. As a result, they may feel underprepared to provide instruction to ELLs. *Teaching English Language Learners: Content and Language in Middle and Secondary Mainstream Classrooms* addresses the concerns and apprehensions of pre- and in-service teachers:

"My biggest fear," Shannon told participants in a Methods of Sheltered Content Instruction course, "is that I won't be able to teach the English Language Learners in my classes—either they won't understand me or I won't understand them."

"It is really hard to know how I am going to make American short stories comprehensible to [ELL] students, while at the same time teaching everyone else," added Laura. "We are all responsible for our students' test scores. How can I be responsible for the scores of students who don't even speak English? I mean, I want to work with the students. I'm just not sure I can do it," James remarked later in the class.

"How do I teach U.S. history without watering it down?" asked Mark, a U.S. history teacher.

These concerns about preparedness exist at a time when increasing numbers of ELLs are being placed in mainstream classrooms (Zehler et al., 2003). Regardless of the type of language development program that is provided for ELLs, most ELLs will receive instruction from a mainstream content-area teacher at some point during their education. While bilingual teachers and English to Speakers of Other Languages (ESOL) teachers are essential to the education of ELLs, the important role of the mainstream content-area teacher cannot be overlooked.

Working with mainstream teachers, we have sometimes noticed a tendency to plan and implement instruction based on what teachers perceive is accessible to ELLs rather than on the academically challenging concepts and theories that all students must learn. This approach to teaching ELLs fails to capitalize on the content-area expertise of mainstream teachers and results in teaching of overly simplified content.

In Methods of Sheltered Content Instruction, a graduate course for pre- and in-service teachers, we require content-area teachers to plan instruction based on the concepts and theories that students must know—the enduring understandings in their content areas (Wiggins & McTighe, 1998, 2005). We have searched for a text that capitalizes on the knowledge base of content-area teachers and provides an understanding of what teachers need to know in order to plan and implement effective, high-quality instruction for ELLs in their mainstream classrooms. However, we have not been able to find a text that that blends the concepts underlying teaching for enduring understanding with the key concepts of second-language acquisition and learning, culturally responsive teaching, making content comprehensible, and building academic language.

Three years ago, Michaela began to formally compile the materials she had created for the Methods of Sheltered Content Instruction course. She piloted these materials across three iterations of the Methods of Sheltered Content Instruction course; collected and analyzed participants' journals, reflections, content-area units, and lesson plans; and organized focus groups to gather comments and suggestions. She adjusted the materials in response to teachers' recommendations.

Dana has provided support services to content-area teachers who welcome ELLs into their classrooms but feel poorly equipped to meet the academic needs of these students. Frequently, these teachers have sought Dana's advice, often while passing in the hallway between classes. While Dana responds to these queries with recommendations about teaching practice or materials that may be of use, these recommendations are often temporary solutions. Mainstream teachers often lack the knowledge framework that would enable them to integrate Dana's recommendations into their instruction. *Teaching English Language Learners* provides a framework and a useful model for planning and implementing instruction: Teaching English Language Learners in the Mainstream (TELLiM). Using the TELLiM model, content-area teachers can purposefully structure, build, and present lessons that are effective for ELLs in the middle and secondary grades.

This text is meant to prepare mainstream teachers who teach ELLs while they are also teaching native-English-speaking students. It addresses some of the questions asked by many of our mainstream pre- and in-service teachers: What should I be doing that is different from what I already do? Do any of the strategies I've learned while working with other populations work for ELLs? What should all the other students in the classroom be doing while I'm helping the ELLs?

For some readers, various chapters of this text will review familiar concepts and strategies, yet provide them with slightly different ways to think about these previously studied concepts and strategies. For others, some chapters may serve as an introduction to new ideas and concepts. While teaching ELLs is more than *just good teaching*, it is definitely grounded in good teaching, and therefore, the TELLiM model and the teaching strategies we present in this text will help teachers improve instruction for many other students in the classroom.

The principles and strategies presented in *Teaching English Language Learners* are interwoven around content and language instruction for ELLs with proficiency levels ranging from early intermediate to transitioning. ELLs at these levels are most likely to benefit from the expertise of the mainstream content-area teacher. Often, however, beginner ELLs are placed in mainstream content-area classrooms, and for this reason, we have included strategies for working with beginners and for using the skills of bilingual teachers/tutors and paraprofessionals. The importance of collaborating with ESOL teachers is stressed throughout the content-area chapters.

It seems equally important to discuss what lies beyond the scope of this text. Although we provide suggestions for meeting the needs of beginner ELLs in mainstream classrooms, the suggestions are appropriate for beginners who have a solid base in their first languages—that is, ELLs who have first-language literacy. Teachers of beginners who, for myriad reasons (war, poverty, lack of opportunity), are not yet literate in their first language should consult texts that focus on the methods of instruction most suitable for this vulnerable population of students. Also, like some native-English-speaking students, some ELLs may require special education services. The strategies provided in this text may indeed be applicable to teaching ELLs with special needs. Yet other crucial topics, such as the appropriate methods of identification, testing, and placement of ELLs with special needs and broader instructional issues regarding ELLs with special needs, remain beyond the scope of this text.

TEXT ORGANIZATION

Teaching English Language Learners is a practical resource to facilitate planning and implementation of grade-level instruction in specific content areas. It is meant to be used in alignment with national curriculum frameworks and the reader's state and local content-area curriculum and ELL frameworks. The first four chapters provide readers with the necessary background knowledge to teach ELLs, Chapters 5 through 9 provide suggestions for instruction, and Chapters 10 through 13 (Part II) illustrate the implementation of instruction.

Each chapter of the text is anchored by an *enduring understanding* (Wiggins & McTighe, 1998). A list of desired learning outcomes and a selection of assessment activities are included in each chapter to provide the reader with learning guides and as a way to check for understanding.

Many chapter sections are followed by Review, Reflect, Apply activities, which prompt readers to reflect and elaborate on topics and to apply the concepts, theories, and strategies covered to their own subject areas, grade levels, and curriculum frameworks. Each chapter ends with a Resources for Further Reading section, which includes traditional and electronic resources for more in-depth study.

Chapter 1 provides an overview of the demographics of ELLs in U.S. schools and a history of the language programs that have been implemented to teach this diverse student population. Chapter 1 then explains the critical role content-area teachers play in the academic success of ELLs. The core content-area teachers we introduce are composite teachers, based on the many teachers with whom we have worked. Although they provide exemplary teaching models in science, history, English language arts (ELA), and mathematics, their methods of planning and instruction as well as their teaching strategies are transferable to other content areas such as technology, family and consumer science, and the arts.

Chapter 2 provides a working guide to commonly accepted theories of second-language acquisition as they relate to classroom practice in various content areas and introduces relevant linguistic theories.

Chapter 3 introduces the concept of culture and asks readers to think about the cultures that have shaped their experiences, perspectives, and behaviors. The chapter continues with an overview of the vast diversity in the sociocultural backgrounds, ages, schooling, experiences of immigration and trauma, and socioeconomic status of ELLs. Chapter 3 introduces three ELLs who illustrate some of the challenges of negotiating U.S. schools and classrooms. The chapter concludes with a discussion of culturally responsive teaching.

Academic literacy is the focus of Chapter 4. The chapter discusses the four domains of academic literacy: listening, speaking, reading, and writing. Chapters 5 and 6 build on the theoretical framework presented in the first four chapters and provide a structure for planning content and content-area language instruction. Chapter 5 explains how to plan instruction that will meet the needs of ELLs based on enduring understandings and clear learning outcomes. The topic of differentiation is introduced in Chapter 5. Chapter 6 establishes methods of assessment that allow teachers to measure mastery of the enduring understandings in their content areas. The chapter also shows how to frame instruction with essential questions.

Differentiating summative assessments for students with varying levels of English language proficiency and planning daily lessons with clear objectives and assessments for content and content-area language are the focus of Chapter 7.

Chapter 8 presents strategies and methods for providing comprehensible instruction to ELLs. Comprehensible materials and presentations are illustrated across various content areas. Although comprehensibility improves ELLs' access to the enduring understandings in content-area classrooms, teachers must also plan lessons that build the academic-language ability of ELLs. The building of academic language is the topic of Chapter 9.

In Part II (Chapters 10 through 13), content-area teachers demonstrate the ways in which they plan instruction and implement strategies. These chapters provide model units in science, mathematics, and ELA at middle and secondary levels. Each chapter illustrates the different strategies teachers use to make content comprehensible, build content-area academic language, and differentiate instruction. The strategies presented are transferable across content areas and middle and secondary grade levels.

Part II begins with an introductory overview of the ideas and perspectives common to the four content-area teachers. Chapters 10 to 13 feature secondary science, middle school math, secondary history, and secondary ELA, respectively. Each chapter begins with a tour of the classroom, a review of the materials the teacher has collected, reflections from the teacher, descriptions of content-area lessons, and snapshot descriptions of ELLs and other students in the classroom. Each chapter includes sample lessons focused on content and content-area language and mini lessons specifically dedicated to building language.

Profiles of ELLs with English proficiency levels from beginner to transitioning are included in the Appendix. Readers are asked to refer to these profiles in the Review, Reflect, Apply activities and in the Assessment Evidence Activities at the end of each chapter.

ACKNOWLEDGMENTS

We wish to express our appreciation of the many people who have contributed to the completion of this text. Our editor, Steve Wainwright, editorial assistant, Julie McNall, and the editing team patiently guided us through the writing, revising, and editing phases. We thank them for their suggestions and advice.

The experiences and insights of many colleagues and students have informed our teaching and learning and have enriched the content of this text. Several colleagues contributed their content-area expertise in the areas of math, science, history, and ELA, as well as their expertise in pedagogy. Thanks go to Patricia Fontaine, Regina Panasuk, and Joseph Walsh of the University of Massachusetts Lowell; to Paul Colombo and Denise Paparazzo of the Clinton Public Schools; and to Linda Perry, Lynn Turchi, Amy Halloran, Katherine Proietti, Debra Thomas, and Jim Carson of the Methuen Public Schools. We are grateful for their generous sharing of their time and expertise.

The help and suggestions of the following reviewers are also greatly appreciated: Martha Adler, University of Michigan-Dearborn; Grace Cho, California State University, Fullerton; Marilee Coles-Ritchie, Utah State University; Zohreh Eslami, Texas A&M University; Rosa Fagundes, Metropolitan State University (MN); Don Hones, University of Wisconsin, Oshkosh; Linda Lewis-White, Eastern Michigan University; Anne Walker, University of North Dakota; Solange A. Lopes-Murphy, James Madison University; Juan Rodriguez (Emeritus), University of Massachusetts Lowell; Cynthia Jacobs, University of Massachusetts Lowell; Grace Huerta, Utah State University; Martha Nyikos, Indiana University; Holly Hansen-Thomas, State University of New York, Binghamton; Jeanmarie Hamilton Boone, Pepperdine University; Irma Guadarrama, University of Houston; and Susan L. Schwartz, Methuen Public Schools.

Last, we would like to recognize Paul Colombo and Bill Furbush, who assumed many of our responsibilities as we worked on this project. We thank them for their ongoing support and encouragement.

PART I

Preparing to Teach English Language Learners

Demographics, History, and the Changing Roles of Teachers

Enduring understanding: Today's content-area teachers play an increasingly important role in the education of English Language Learners.

CHAPTER 1 OPENS WITH THE MATH EXAM, A SHORT VIGNETTE OF FOUR EIGHTH-GRADE ENGLISH LANGUAGE Learners (ELLs) and two of their teachers. The vignette illustrates the instructional challenges confronting ELLs and teachers in U.S. schools today. The intention of this first chapter is to provide a demographic and historical perspective on the education of ELLs in U.S. schools and to highlight the changing and important roles of mainstream teachers in educating ELLs. ELLs differ from one another in many ways, including language, culture, socioeconomic status, previous schooling, and background experience. This chapter provides an overview of the languages spoken by ELLs in the United States and then illustrates aspects of diversity with a profile of Fredy Solis, an eighth-grade ELL. A review of the history of U.S. language policies, which have been shaped by economic, social, and political events, provides context for discussing current programs for educating ELLs and the implications of the No Child Left Behind Act of 2001 (NCLB). Following an overview of NCLB regulations,

Chapter 1 discusses the need for high-level content-area instruction and highlights the important role of content-area teachers in facilitating such instruction. This chapter concludes by addressing the concerns content-area teachers have shared about teaching ELLs.

LEARNING OUTCOMES

The following learning outcomes (LOs) serve as a guide for Chapter 1. At the end of the chapter are assessment activities that are aligned with each LO to enable readers to check their understanding.

LO-1 Become familiar with levels of language proficiency and be able to explain the language characteristics of ELLs with varying levels of language proficiency

LO-2 Develop a basic understanding of the types of programs designed to meet the needs of ELLs and the advantages and disadvantages of each

LO-3 Identify concerns that you, as a mainstream teacher, have about teaching ELLs

LO-4 Identify the ways in which content-area teachers can inspire ELLs to become lifelong learners

---

TERMS THAT MAY BE NEW

Bilingual: The ability to communicate fluently in two languages (We have included this term because it is commonly misused to refer to ELLs who are fluent in their first language and are learning English.) For more information regarding levels of bilingualism, see Baker (2006).

Biliterate: The ability to read and write in two languages

ESOL: English to Speakers of Other Languages (may refer to a program or to the trained teacher who provides the instruction)

ELD: English Language Development (Generally used synonymously with ESOL, ELD is used to refer to a program of instruction or to the teacher who provides the instruction.)

THE MATH EXAM

Fredy, Ben, Victor, and Willy, all ELLs with intermediate English proficiency, sat in Mr. Bob Green's eighth-grade classroom working on the state-mandated mathematics exam. With 10 years of experience, Mr. Green is one of the district's most qualified mathematics teachers and is recognized for his content-area expertise. Mr. Green, however, does not teach math to Fredy, Ben, Victor, and Willy. They receive math instruction from Ms. Marcia Connolly, the middle school's ESOL teacher. Ms. Connolly is also an excellent teacher, highly qualified to teach ESOL and known for her dedication to students. Ms. Connolly is responsible for teaching core content-area subjects to ELLs in Grades 7 and 8.

Ms. Connolly works long hours to prepare science, math, and history lessons. She often meets with Mr. Green and other seventh- and eighth-grade content-area teachers before and after school. She borrows materials and asks many questions to ensure that she covers the same content-area materials with her students. Ms. Connolly has worked hard to familiarize herself with the curricula yet lacks the expertise of content-area specialists and often expresses concerns about her lack of ability to make math interesting and challenging:

> I *know* eighth-grade math. I do find, however, that whereas it seems like math teachers find a variety of ways to explain problems, processes, and mathematical operations to students, I rely heavily on the teacher's guide from the textbook publisher for instructional strategies.

Mr. Green watched Fredy, Ben, Victor, and Willy as they attempted to work through the word problems on the math exam. The ELLs searched for words in their state-allowed, word-to-word dictionaries but seemed stumped by nearly all the word problems. Mr. Green knew that the problems were difficult and that vocabulary causes barriers for ELLs. He also noticed that the four ELLs seemed to stick with one strategy regardless of its ineffectiveness.

Mr. Green's students, on the other hand, made diagrams and charts in the margins of their test booklets and used alternate strategies when the first strategy they tried did not help solve the problem. Mr. Green thought, "The language is tough enough for these students. Marcia is a great ESOL teacher. She makes the students feel comfortable and teaches them English, but she's just *not* a math teacher."

Halfway through the period, Ms. Connolly peered into Mr. Green's room and saw the four ELLs struggling.

> "Everything about this subject is difficult for them," she thought. "Bob might have been a far better math teacher for these ELLs than I, except he doesn't know anything about language acquisition, the difficulties of learning a second language for academic purposes, or the students' cultures. If only Bob had the second-language acquisition expertise to help ELLs with math, but he *doesn't*. When I mainstreamed students into his room, they were completely lost."

The unfortunate truth is that both Mr. Green and Ms. Connolly are accurate in their perceptions. ELLs must master challenging content *and* develop academic English proficiency. While they are developing English language proficiency, ELLs are held to the same academic standards as their mainstream peers, including mandatory participation in high-stakes testing which, in many states, determines high school graduation. Often, however, ELLs, who need the best instruction to succeed academically, receive instruction from teachers who are either underprepared to teach content or underprepared to teach students who are acquiring English.

ELLS IN U.S. SCHOOLS TODAY

According to the U.S. Department of Education (2006a), ELLs are the fastest growing student population in U.S. schools. From 1995 to 2005, the percentage of ELLs grew by 60.8% compared with the total growth in school population of 2.6%. ELLs are projected to constitute 40% of the school population in the 2030s (Collier & Thomas, 1999a).

As the Math Exam vignette illustrates, ELLs are double-burdened in educational settings; the current structure of many school districts often fails to meet their complex needs and to recognize and capitalize on the strengths and abilities they bring to classrooms. Based on the results of standardized tests, ELLs as a group are ranked at approximately the 10th percentile for academic achievement (Collier & Thomas, 1999a). To reach the 50th percentile, ELLs must make a gain of 15 months for every 10 months of school, for six school years (Collier & Thomas, 1999a).

Standardized testing that is designed for English speakers is, in itself, problematic for ELLs. Researchers estimate the time to develop sufficient language proficiency to access the English language within standardized tests as anywhere between 5 and 10 years (Baker, 2006; Cummins, 1984b, 2000; Thomas & Collier, 1997), yet after 10 months in U.S. schools, ELLs are mandated to participate in standardized testing that aims to measure achievement in reading and math (U.S. Department of Education, 2006a, 2006b). Under the NCLB Act, which was signed into law in 2002, ELLs and other students are tested annually in Grades 3 through 8 and once in high school (U.S. Department of Education, 2005b). Unfortunately for ELLs, this testing ultimately measures English language proficiency rather than content-area knowledge (Abedi & Dietel, 2004; Teachers of English to Speakers of Other Languages [TESOL], 2003). Additionally, tests include items that are biased in terms of assumption of cultural knowledge (history, holidays, and customs) (TESOL, 2003), and the often imposed time constraints for standardized testing may be culturally foreign to ELLs who have not participated in timed tests in their previous educational systems (TESOL, 2003).

Test results actually begin to shape educational programs and outcomes for ELLs early on in their education. On the basis of test results, ELLS are often placed into remedial programs, as though ELLs themselves (rather than the testing measures) had deficiencies that require specialists to fix (Collier & Thomas, 1999a). Collier and Thomas (1999a) explain, "The end result of much of this *well-meaning* [italics added] remedial work is that former English language learners make up the lowest achieving groups, graduating at the 10th percentile or leaving school without graduating" (para. 6). In fact, the National Education Association (McKeon, 2005) reports that the 2001 national drop-out rate for ELLs was four times that of native-English-speaking students. Currently, 22 states implement high-stakes exams as a requirement for high school graduation, and at least 4 states are planning to implement this requirement (Zabala, Minnici, McMurrer, Hill, Bartley, & Jennings 2007), which has implications for the opportunity for ELLs to obtain high school diplomas.

The educational needs of ELLs are complex. ELLs differ from mainstream students and from one another in language, culture, history, family background, and prior educational experience (Corson, 2001; La Celle-Peterson & Rivera, 1994; Spring, 2000). Figure 1.1 illustrates the first languages spoken by ELLs in the United States.

The 2000 U.S. Census indicated that 311 languages are spoken in the United States; 162 of these are immigrant languages (National Virtual Translation Center, 2007). A list of these languages is provided by the Modern Language Association (n.d). According to state-reported data for the 2000–2001 school year, speakers of Spanish are the largest percentage of ELLs in U.S.

FIGURE 1.1 ELLs by Language Group

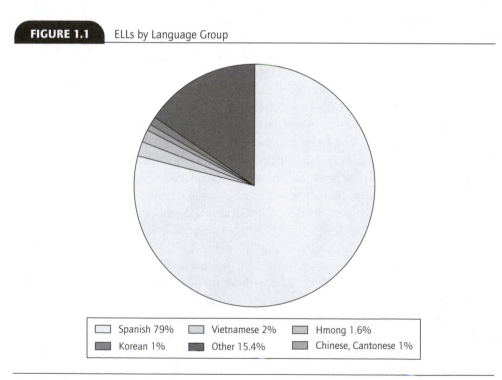

| Spanish 79% | Vietnamese 2% | Hmong 1.6% |
| Korean 1% | Other 15.4% | Chinese, Cantonese 1% |

SOURCE: National Education Association (McKeon, 2005).

TEACHING ENGLISH LANGUAGE LEARNERS

schools (79%). Vietnamese speakers represent approximately 2% of ELLs. Speakers of Hmong and Chinese/Cantonese account for 1.6% and 1.0% of ELLs, respectively, and the remaining 15.4% are composed of other language groups (McKeon, 2005). The large percentage of ELLs who speak Spanish as a first language can be misleading; these ELLs are not a monolithic group. In 2002, the U.S. Census Bureau reported that 66.9% of Spanish-speaking ELLs are Mexican American, 14.3% are Central and South American (two geographic regions comprising many different countries, cultures, and dialects), 8.6% are Puerto Rican, 3.7% are Cuban American, and 6.5% are other Hispanic (Ramirez & de la Cruz, 2002).

ELLs differ in other important ways. Some ELLs are themselves immigrants to the United States, others are children of immigrants, and still others are second- and third-generation Americans (Carrasquillo, Kucer, & Abrams, 2004; Cummins, 2000; Smiley & Salsberry, 2007). Some ELLs may be able to read and write in their first languages, whereas others have not had the opportunity to develop these abilities. ELLs may have had access to consistent grade-level content, or their formal schooling may have been interrupted due to circumstances beyond their control or the control of their families. Additionally, many ELLs have been traumatized socially, economically, and emotionally by the immigration experience (Igoa, 1995) and by the racism and prejudice they may encounter in the wider social circle (Lee, 2005).

ELLs are represented in many socioeconomic and educational levels. Beyond language, culture, socioeconomic status, education, and previous experiences, ELLs in middle and secondary grades are adolescent learners—a group whose members differ greatly in interests, developmental stages, and cognitive ability (American Academy of Child & Adolescent Psychiatry, 1999). Indeed, substantial diversity exists within the population of ELLs who attend U.S. schools.

One way, however, that we as educators seek to group ELLs for instructional purposes is by level of English language proficiency. Although proficiency in English is just one factor in the educational profile of ELLs, accurate knowledge of an ELL's English language proficiency enables guidance counselors and principals to make appropriate placement decisions. A teacher's knowledge of an ELL's language proficiency is likely to result in instruction that meets the ELL's strengths and needs. (Native-language proficiency, including reading and writing levels, which are often not measured, provides important data that can also be used to inform and improve instruction.)

The proficiency levels developed by TESOL serve as a guide for state standards and benchmarks. Individual states, however, determine the descriptors of each proficiency level. Table 1.1 is based on research in the field, proficiency guidelines from TESOL, and those of various states. The table characterizes a range of language proficiency from *beginning* to *transitioning* and provides a description of the broad characteristics within each level. Given the great diversity that exists among ELLs, the descriptions of characteristics are purposely broad. Ten profiles of ELLs, which will be used in later chapters of this text, provide greater detail of the language proficiency level of each student and are included in the Appendix. (Readers are also encouraged to review TESOL guidelines, which are found on the TESOL Web pages: www.tesol.org/s_tesol/ sec_document.asp?TrackID=&SID=1&DID=5349&CID=1186&VID=2&RTID=0&CIDQS=& Taxonomy=False&specialSearch=False)

As Table 1.1 indicates, ELLs come to U.S. schools with a wide variety of English proficiency levels (and, as one might imagine, within each level exists a range of language abilities.) This chapter began with a vignette in which Fredy Solis, an eighth-grade ELL, worked quite unsuccessfully to complete a standardized math exam. Table 1.2 provides a brief profile of Fredy and illustrates that many factors beyond English language proficiency influence Fredy's school experience.

TABLE 1.1 Four Levels of English Language Proficiency

Transitioning

These students understand social and academic content, both abstract and literal. They can use complex language structures when speaking and writing and understand such structures when listening and reading. Transitioning students can participate at grade level, though they may require clarification of certain idioms, nuances, or cultural references. These students may or may not speak with an accent.

Intermediate

Students at the intermediate level may participate in interpersonal and academic conversations, although frequent repetitions and visual cuing may be required to ensure comprehension. These students often rely on word analysis/decoding to gather meaning and therefore require more processing time than the native speaker. Writing can be focused, with supporting details; however, grammatical, mechanical, and spelling errors are often present, and students are able to correct these when editing with support. Intermediate students may or may not feel comfortable speaking in front of peers but can make contributions to the class. These students may be overwhelmed by large portions of text and/or may not trust their own comprehension. These students may or may not speak with an accent.

Early intermediate

Early-intermediate students understand interpersonal conversations and words/phrases related to school when spoken to in a slow, repetitious fashion. They use basic grammar patterns in speaking and writing and often make errors when attempting more complex language combinations. Early-intermediate students require breakdown, clarification, and visual cuing, especially when dense or multilayered information is presented. These students may appear silent when taking time to process information. They may also appear overwhelmed, distracted, or exhausted due to the high cognitive demand of the language. These students generally speak with an accent.

Beginner

A beginning student may have a command of isolated vocabulary/phrases. These students may be able to comprehend, read, write, or speak singular, highly repetitious words/phrases; however, they generally cannot produce novel language combinations. Beginners may or may not be comprehensible when speaking English, and they often respond with single words, in their native language, or with gestures. These students often pass through a *silent period*, during which time they are building language skills, even though they may not yet have the confidence to participate.

As Table 1.2 illustrates, a combination of factors tells the story of Fredy and suggests some of the strengths he brings to the classroom as well as the challenges he may confront in instructional settings. While we cannot know Fredy's level of proficiency in Spanish, we do know that his language abilities are sufficiently sophisticated to enable him to interpret and translate from English to Spanish. We also know that he can read letters from his family and respond to these in written Spanish. We know that Fredy has intermediate language proficiency, and we can see by an overview of his history that there is a lot more we need to know about him. Chapter 3 provides more information about Fredy and two other ELLs and illustrates multiple ways in which factors combine to influence the educational experiences of ELLs.

THE NEED FOR INSTRUCTIONAL PROGRAMS FOR ELLS

Sometimes teachers we have known have questioned the need for language services. Very often pre- and in-service teachers in our courses reflect on the experiences of their grandparents and

TABLE 1.2	A Profile of Fredy Solis

Fredy Solis

Age: 13

Grade: 8

Placement: Fredy was originally placed in a Sheltered English Immersion Program (described in Table 1.3) and is now mostly in mainstream content-area classes.

Time in U.S. schools: Three years
Country of origin: Dominican Republic

Prior schooling	School was in session only sporadically in the area of the Dominican Republic where Fredy was raised. As a result, Fredy has substantial gaps in his schooling.
Literacy in first language	Fredy cannot read or write on grade level in Spanish. Because he was not evaluated for native-language literacy, it is impossible to know his reading and writing levels in Spanish when he arrived in the United States in Grade 5. He has not received instruction in Spanish since his arrival.[a] Fredy speaks Spanish at home and often interprets for his father. He also translates written documents and writes letters home to his family.
Socioeconomic status	Jorge Solis (Fredy's father) is a steady worker who works overtime at the local factory as often as it is offered. He sends money home to his family in the Dominican Republic and saves to bring his family to the United States. By all accounts, life is a financial struggle for the Solis family.
Other factors	Fredy's mother and little sister are still in the Dominican Republic awaiting visas. Fredy often mentions to the guidance counselor that he misses his family and Coco, the pet dog he had to leave behind.
English proficiency level	Intermediate—Fredy has to struggle with reading and writing in English, which negatively affects his performance in content-area classes.

a. ELLs' ability to read and write in their native language positively influences their ability to read and write in English.

great-grandparents, who entered the United States with almost no English proficiency and received English-only instruction, an instructional method often referred to as *sink or swim*. As one teacher described her family history, "My grandparents worked hard, they provided for their families, *and they learned English.* They may have kept their own language but they *had* to learn English."

The passing of time, it seems, has served to rewrite our historical memories. While it has long been legend that early immigrants who received sink-or-swim instruction learned English quickly, and through hard work attained the American dream, in actuality often two or three generations passed before members of an immigrant family attained even moderate academic success and the first descendant graduated from high school (Crawford, 2004). During this time, individual ELLs suffered greatly in U.S. classrooms. It is also important to consider that the socioeconomic structures in the first half of the 20th century did not require immigrants to be fully educated in English. There were many factory and other positions in which immigrants with only minimal English proficiency could work long hours to garner sufficient wages to support their families. A historical perspective helps us understand the development of the programs that exist for ELLs today.

EDUCATING ELLS IN THE UNITED STATES: A BRIEF HISTORY

Unlike many other countries with diverse populations, including Canada, India, Switzerland, and countries within the European Union, the United States has never had a comprehensive language policy that capitalizes on the linguistic strengths of students who speak languages other than English (Crawford, 2004). That being said, most early immigrants wanted their children to maintain home languages such as German, French, and Dutch, while they learned English. As a result, some form of bilingual education was actually the norm in the United States from the 1600s until the early 1900s, when support for bilingual education began to disappear (Baker, 2006; Crawford, 2004).

The 1912 textile strike in Lawrence, Massachusetts, prompted industrialists to actively campaign to "Americanize the immigrant" (Crawford, 2004, p. 88), and soon the speaking of English became synonymous with being loyal to the United States. The Americanization (and anti-bilingual) movement continued to grow and strengthen as the United States became involved in World War I. The use of German, once a popular language in bilingual and foreign-language programs, was banned from U.S. schools. Schools adopted a sink-or-swim approach to the instruction of ELLs; instruction was provided in English, and it was believed that students who worked hard enough would *swim* and learn both content and language. During this period, immigrants continued to arrive in the United States, and members of each successive group were expected to sink or swim in their attempts to be educated. Unfortunately, many ELLs could not swim academically.

Despite the academic failure of many immigrant children, sink-or-swim policies informed classroom practice until the 1970s. While some students were exceptions who did succeed during this time, others failed miserably. Drop-out rates were high. The costs were often high even for those students who achieved academic success. Maria, a teacher with nearly 30 years' experience in bilingual education, has been a guest speaker for the *Methods of Sheltering English Content* course. Here, she explains the effects of sink-or-swim programs to pre- and in-service teachers:

> I cried every day. I began many mornings by throwing up—just thinking about school. I dreaded school where my friends and I were punished when we spoke Portuguese, the only language we understood. I felt stupid. I knew so many things, but I couldn't share them in English and I was not allowed to speak Portuguese.

Often during the question-and-answer period following Maria's talk, participants have said, "But you are *successful*. You *learned* English." Maria nods and then tells them about her friends. Each of them dropped out of school at the age of 16. It is hard not to imagine all the children who, like Maria, were traumatized by school each day during the period of sink-or-swim instruction and those children for whom school was so painful that dropping out seemed their only recourse. Yet sink-or-swim instruction remained in place. Language was and continues to be closely linked with culture and power (Cummins, 2000). Members of the dominant English-speaking culture were (and are) in a position to make decisions about educational opportunities for minority-language children—to do what was "best" for these children. While the intersection of language and power is not the topic of this text, it is important to recognize that language and power are inextricably connected and that minority-language children like Maria and other children introduced in this text confront this unequal balance of power as they work in classrooms to learn English even as their own language is largely ignored.

The unfortunate plight of many ELLs was publicized in 1970, when 1,789 Chinese-speaking students filed a law suit (*Lau v. Nichols, 1974*) against the San Francisco Public School District for its sink-or-swim educational policy. The suit claimed that these students did not understand the instruction of the classroom and were therefore denied their right to an education. In 1974, the Supreme Court (*Lau v. Nichols*) ruled that sink-or swim-instruction violated the Civil Rights Act of 1964, stating, "There is no equality of treatment merely by providing students with the same facilities, textbooks, teachers, and curriculum, for students who do not understand English are effectively foreclosed from any meaningful education."

School districts could no longer deliver the same instruction with the same materials to ELLs who did not speak or read English. The Court, however, refused to offer specific remedies, which has left decisions regarding specific programs to the states (Baker, 2006; Crawford, 2004).

TYPES OF PROGRAMS FOR ELLS

Since 1974, various types of programs have evolved in efforts to meet the educational needs of ELLs. There is no one-size-fits-all program; rather, programs can and will vary from district to district depending on the number of ELLs and languages spoken. There is, however, general agreement that programs of quality must include

- a welcoming environment for ELLs and their families and well-trained teachers and paraprofessionals who recognize and build on the strengths of ELLs and celebrate and honor the first language of ELLs (e.g., Collier & Thomas, 1999a; Crawford, 2004; Cummins, 1984b, 2000)
- acknowledgment of and value for the culture of ELLs (Au, 2006; Gay, 2000; González, Moll, & Amanti, 2005; Menken & Antunez, 2001); and
- outreach to families in culturally appropriate ways in the language of the home (Barbour, Barbour, & Scully, 2005; Moll, 1994).

Programs for ELLs are categorized along a continuum from *additive* to *subtractive*. As the descriptors imply, *additive* programs add to the language abilities of ELLs; program goals include bilingualism, biliteracy, and biculturalism. The term *subtractive* is used to describe programs that focus only on the development of English language proficiency and ignore the value of bilingualism and biliteracy. Many programs fall on the continuum between these two end points (Baker, 2006).

Although they are far from exhaustive, the programs shown in Table 1.3 represent the broad spectrum of ELL programs, from additive to subtractive. Programs are described by purpose, language of instruction, and the length of time that students remain in the program. Reading through Table 1.3, it is important to keep in mind that the additive and subtractive labels are general and may not reflect the quality of the program described. Also, additive programs such as Two-Way Immersion, Maintenance Bilingual, and late-exit Transitional Bilingual Education (TBE) require larger numbers of ELLs from the same language group and therefore may not be feasible in all districts.

TABLE 1.3 Programs for ELLs in U.S. Schools

Program	Goal	Language of Instruction	Approximate Time in Program
Two-Way Immersion	Bilingualism and biliteracy for ELLs and native-English speakers	English and native language	Generally at least six years and may continue throughout student's education
Maintenance Bilingual	Bilingualism and biliteracy for ELLs	English and native language	Generally at least six years and may continue throughout student's education
Transitional Bilingual Education (TBE), late exit	English proficiency	English and native language	Generally five years
TBE, early exit	English proficiency	English and native language	Generally not to exceed three years
Sheltered English Immersion (SEI) and/or Specially Designed Academic Instruction in English (SDAIE)	English proficiency	English	Varies—one to three years is often the norm, but this can be extended
English to Speakers of Other Language (ESOL) alone[a]	English proficiency	English	Varies depending on proficiency levels of ELLs on entry into the program

a. ESOL consists of two models: a pull-out model, in which ELLs leave mainstream classrooms for instruction, and a push-in model, where the ESOL/ELD teacher provides support within the mainstream program.

In *Two-Way Immersion* programs, ELLs who speak the same native language and native-English speakers are placed together in the same classroom and receive content-area instruction in both languages. Two-Way Immersion programs promote bilingualism, biliteracy, and academic achievement in two languages for native-English speakers and ELLs. Students generally attend these programs for at least five to six years.

Maintenance Bilingual programs are similar to Two-Way Immersion programs in purpose and outcome for ELLs. Native-English-speaking students, however, do not participate in these programs. ELLs who attend these programs actively maintain and develop their native language while simultaneously learning academic English. Again, bilingualism and biliteracy are the goals.

The primary goal of other programs for ELLs is proficiency in oral and written English. *Transitional Bilingual Education (TBE)* programs provide instruction in ELLs' native languages until ELLs have developed sufficient English proficiency to participate in mainstream classes. TBE programs are categorized as either *early exit*, in which ELLs generally exit the program after three years, or *late exit*, meaning that ELLs remain in the program until Grade 5 or 6 (Baker, 2006).

The purpose of *Sheltered English Immersion (SEI)* and *Specially Designed Academic Instruction in English (SDAIE)* programs is to help ELLs develop English for academic achievement. SEI and SDAIE programs provide ELLs with content-area instruction in English, although the teachers and paraprofessionals, who speak the language of the ELL, are generally allowed to clarify the instruction in the native language when necessary. Because the language of SEI/SDAIE programs is English, ELLs from various language backgrounds may be placed together in one classroom. SEI/SDAIE programs vary from district to district but generally consist of a teacher who is trained to both provide content in a comprehensible manner and build content-area language. Programs may also include an ESOL specialist, who provides ongoing, additional support in ELD, and/or a native-language tutor.

English to Speakers of Other Languages (ESOL) programs are typically implemented in two ways. In a traditional ESOL pull-out program, ELLs leave the mainstream classroom to receive extra support from an ESOL teacher. ESOL can also be implemented as a push-in program, in which the ESOL teacher works within the mainstream content-area classroom. Both of these ESOL options focus on developing English language proficiency within content areas and/or providing additional support with content-area assignments. The number of hours that ELLs receive ESOL support varies according to student need and resources available within the district—unfortunately, the resources available do not always meet the level of student need.

Summarizing Programs for ELLs

Two-Way Immersion, Maintenance Bilingual, and late-exit TBE programs, all of which provide ELLs with up to six years of native-language instruction and native-language literacy as they acquire academic English, are often considered to be among the more effective programs (Baker, 2006). Early-exit TBE, SEI, and SDAIE are considered to be approximately equal in effectiveness. While ongoing ESOL instruction, used in conjunction with another language development program, has the capacity to improve academic language, used alone it is often considered to be the weakest program for ELLs (Collier & Thomas, 1989). In reality, however, the variety of programs to support ELLs in U.S. schools may vary as much in quality as in underlying philosophy.

Under NCLB, all programs must meet mandated regulations, including procedures for identification, placement, assessment, and transition to mainstream classes for ELLs (Public Education Network and National Coalition for Parent Involvement in Education, 2006; U.S. Department of Education, 2005a). Table 1.4 explains the NCLB guidelines and illustrates their implementation in the testing placement, and transition of Fredy Solis. (Links to the full description of regulations and procedures, maintained by the Office for Civil Rights [U.S. Department of Education] and NCLB Action Briefs, published in a joint project of the Public Education Network and the National Coalition for Parent Involvement in Education, are included in the resource section at the end of this chapter.)

Review, Reflect, Apply

1. *Apply:* Collier and Thomas state that ELLs must make 15 months of progress for every 10 months of school time. What implications does this have for content-area instruction?

2. *Review:* Review the history of bilingual education. What were some of the major issues that ELLs encountered in public schools prior to the 1974 Supreme Court ruling that sink-or-swim instruction violated the Civil Rights Act of 1964?

3. *Reflect and apply:* The job market is much more specialized in today's economy than it was in 1974. What additional barriers might arise from a sink-or-swim educational program in today's economy?

TABLE 1.4	Procedures for Program Placement

No Child Left Behind (NCLB) Regulations	Fredy Solis
1. In accordance with NCLB, every district must have a procedure for the identification of ELLs.	1. When Fredy registered for school, he was referred to the guidance department, where the counselor completed a home-language survey with Fredy and Mr. Solis to determine the languages spoken within the Solis home as well as the languages that Fredy used to speak with parents, siblings, and friends.
2. Under NCLB, ELLs must be assessed prior to placement. States determine placement assessments that are appropriate.	2. Based on the home-language survey, the counselor determined that Spanish was the language of the home and that Fredy spoke very little English. She referred Fredy for language proficiency testing.
3. Districts are mandated to provide programs that meet the needs of ELLs.	3. The results of Fredy's assessment indicated that he needed a special program for English language development.
4. NCLB requires parental notification, including reason for placement, current level of proficiency, means of assessing proficiency, method of instruction of program, how the program will meet the child's needs and help the child learn English and meet academic achievement standards, how the program will meet the needs of the child with an Individual Education Plan (IEP), program exit requirements, and anticipated date of graduation (Public Education Network and National Coalition for Parent Involvement in Education, 2006).	4. Mr. Solis was notified within 30 days of the district's recommendation that Fredy should be placed in the district's SEI program. The letter explained that Fredy had beginning English proficiency, that the SEI program was specially designed to develop English language proficiency, and that Fredy would receive all academic subjects within the program. It further explained that Fredy would be tested annually and his father would receive these test scores and that once Fredy had achieved the level of English proficiency necessary to complete normal schoolwork in English, he would transition from the program into mainstream classes.
5. Parents must be informed of their rights to decline program services, withdraw their child from a program, and choose among programs if various programs are offered.	5. Mr. Solis was given the opportunity to accept or reject this decision.
6. Districts are required to assess language proficiency annually, report assessment results to their state, and demonstrate progress on Annual Measurable Achievement Objectives (AMAO).	6. Fredy has been assessed annually to measure his progress in listening, speaking, reading, and writing in English.
7. The Office for Civil Rights mandates ongoing monitoring of ELL students.	7. Fredy was transitioned into regular classes after three years and is being monitored to ensure that he makes ongoing progress.

Summary

ELLs are the fastest-growing student population in U.S. schools, and this growth is projected to continue through the foreseeable future. ELLs are diverse in language, culture, homes of origin, educational levels, and socioeconomic status. Prior to 1974, school systems routinely provided ELLs with *sink-or-swim* instruction (English-only instruction without adjustments and modifications that would make content and language more accessible). Sink-or-swim practices condemned many ELLs to academic failure. During the first part of the 20th century, there were positions in manufacturing that did not require a high level of English proficiency and a formal education, and this enabled ELLs to secure well-paying jobs. This is no longer the situation in the United States; today, a college education is often a requirement for even entry-level positions.

To become academically successful, ELLs must make annual progress that vastly surpasses that of their English-speaking peers; remedial instruction alone is insufficient.

ELLS IN MAINSTREAM CLASSROOMS

Regardless of the types of programs that districts provide for ELLs, it is likely that many ELLs will receive content-area instruction from a mainstream teacher prior to fully developing academic-language proficiency in English, and it appears that ELLs are now placed in mainstream classrooms more quickly than before. Between 1992 and 2002, the number of ELLs who received all instruction in English increased from 33.7% to 47.9%, and a recent study found that 43% of U.S. teachers provide instruction to ELLs (Zehler et al., 2003). As the Math Class vignette illustrated, the placement of ELLs with intermediate, or higher, levels of language proficiency in classes taught by content-area teachers, who are *also* well prepared to teach ELLs, may hold promise for these students.

ELLs profit from high-quality instruction that is challenging and engaging. As Collier and Thomas (1999b) explain, ELLs benefit when

> they get to work on the "cool stuff"—using computers and solving real-world problems. They teach each other, and their language repertoire expands dramatically with rich language use, both oral and written . . . [S]tudents of all levels of socioeconomic status and ethnolinguistic backgrounds and with varied levels of proficiency in the two languages of instruction are able to flourish in these classes. (para. 4)

The success of ELLs in high-level mainstream classrooms with content-area experts suggests two necessary factors—sufficient language proficiency on the part of the ELL and sufficient preparation on the part of the content-area teacher. We begin with a discussion of the first.

Proficiency Levels of ELLs in Mainstream Classrooms

The darkly shaded sections in Table 1.1 highlight the overall linguistic proficiency of ELLs who have intermediate or higher proficiency in English. These are the students who are most likely to benefit from content-area instruction in mainstream classes *if* content-area teachers are prepared to meet their language needs. It is important to keep in mind that ELLs in these classes will also continue to benefit from the ongoing support of an ESOL teacher.

Intermediate English proficiency is used broadly within this text and in general refers to students who are able to do the following:

- Engage in basic interpersonal communication and academic conversations with friends and teachers, although frequent repetitions and visual cuing may be required to ensure comprehension. Students may or may not have accents.

- Follow along with classroom instruction when provided with visuals and time to process instruction in groups.

- Read in the native language or English at a level that allows students to access at least some of the instructional materials, which may have been modified for their use. (Substantial variations may exist between students' ability to read and write in their native language and English. Because the native-language reading abilities of ELLs are often not evaluated, it is difficult to know a student's actual reading ability.)

In reality, ELLs who are at the higher level of the early-intermediate category (lightly shaded) are also often placed in mainstream classrooms. These ELLs may be overwhelmed, distracted, or exhausted due to the high cognitive demand of content-area language and will, therefore, benefit from substantial additional assistance from an ESOL teacher and a native-language tutor. This support can take place within the classroom as well as during specially scheduled ESOL classes. ELLs with beginning proficiency are unlikely to access grade-level content from a mainstream content-area teacher who does not speak the language of the students even if the teacher has received specialized training. Beginners are sometimes, however, placed in mainstream classrooms. When this occurs, beginning students should receive substantive services from a well-trained ESOL teacher. Beginner ELLs should also be accompanied by a tutor who speaks their language and can make instruction comprehensible to them.

The importance of providing native-language instruction to ELLs cannot be overlooked; ELLs at all levels will benefit from the opportunity to access complex materials and express complex understandings in their first languages. The role of the bilingual teacher, native-language tutor, or well-trained bilingual paraprofessional is critical in these circumstances. When ELLs can read at or near grade level in their first languages, they benefit from access to materials that have been translated into their native languages. ELLs who cannot read at or near grade level will rely more heavily on the oral instruction provided by bilingual personnel. (Later chapters in this text provide suggestions and illustrations for working with native-language materials and tutors.)

Content-Area Teachers

The next factor that must be considered in the instruction of ELLs is the qualifications of the content-area teacher. Well-trained content-area teachers know the content and language of their subject areas, which is an essential qualification for providing high-level content-area instruction. In fact, the expertise of teachers is often thought to be the most important factor affecting student achievement (Darling-Hammond, 1996, 2000; Darling-Hammond, Holtzman, Gatlin, & Heilig, 2005; Menken & Antunez, 2001), and most particularly the achievement of students who have been placed at risk of academic failure (Au, 2002; Delpit, 1995; Ladson-Billings, 2000; Moll, 1994; Reyes, Scribner, & Paredes-Scribner, 1999).

According to Tovani (2004), content-area teachers have unique opportunities to improve students' content-area reading. Mathematicians know how to read math books, scientists know how to read science books, and English teachers know how to read across literary genres. Tovani prepares content-area teachers to share their reading expertise with students, thus improving student reading in the content areas.

Arguably, with sufficient preparation, content-area teachers also have opportunities to improve the content-area English language proficiency of ELLs. Every content area has unique language features (vocabulary, grammar, and modes of expression) that may present difficulties to ELLs; content-area teachers know this content-area language. They also know the concepts that students must master and the language and communication abilities that students must develop to demonstrate content-area knowledge. Content-area teachers understand the concepts behind difficult vocabulary and know multiple ways to explain vocabulary to English speaking students. Teachers can learn additional strategies for making this vocabulary comprehensible to ELLs. Content-area teachers also know different ways to demonstrate concepts and are able to identify students' misconceptions. With appropriate preparation, content-area teachers will be able to share this expertise with ELLs and will learn how to engage ELLs in concept-based conversations that broaden and enhance content-area understandings and promote content-area language development.

There is no replacement for a quality dual-language program with well-prepared content-area teachers providing instruction in two languages, and content-area teachers cannot and should not replace ESOL teachers, who have a depth of knowledge in language development. Yet when it comes to providing high-level content-area instruction to ELLs at intermediate and higher levels, it may be "easier and more efficient" to train content-area specialists in the basics of ESOL than to attempt to provide ESOL teachers with the depth of content-area knowledge necessary to teach effectively in *all* content areas (Troike, 1993–1994).

Review, Reflect, Apply

1. *Reflect:* In thinking about content-area expertise, consider teaching a subject with which you have little experience. For example, if you are, or are preparing to be, a secondary English language arts (ELA) teacher, consider teaching secondary chemistry or a similar subject. Compare and contrast your abilities to teach the content of each subject. How might your approach to teaching each subject differ?

2. *Apply:* Given your response to Question 1, why might teachers who are well prepared in their content areas provide more comprehensive and high-quality instruction?

PEDAGOGY FOR TEACHING ELLS

While content-area expertise is critical for teaching ELLs, content-area expertise alone is insufficient to ensure that mainstream teachers are adequately prepared to help ELLs make the steady academic progress necessary to enable them to catch up with their mainstream peers. Rather, mainstream teachers will need an understanding of how ELLs acquire academic English, knowledge of the strengths and needs ELLs bring to the mainstream classroom, a pedagogical model that is consistent with principles for teaching ELLs (Chamot & O'Malley, 1994; Echevarria, Vogt, & Short, 2003, 2007; Tharp, Estrada, Dalton, & Yamauchi, 2000) and principles of good teaching (Wiggins & McTighe, 1998, 2005). This text combines these principles in the Teaching English Language Learners in the Mainstream (TELLiM) model which is shown in Table 1.5.

Summary

ELLs like Fredy, Victor, Willy, and Ben need high-level content-area instruction to catch up with their mainstream English-speaking peers. ELLs with at least intermediate proficiency benefit from instruction in mainstream classrooms with well-trained content-area teachers, who can demonstrate the best ways to read content-area materials and express content-area understandings. ELLs always benefit from continued ESOL instruction that facilitates the development of academic English. ELLs with lower levels of proficiency will need a greater amount of ongoing support to access content in mainstream classrooms. The previous Review, Reflect,

TABLE 1.5	The TELLiM Model	
Step 1	**Review Frameworks to Determine Enduring Understandings**	Chapter 5
	• Review grade-level content-area frameworks • Determine the concepts that must be taught for *enduring understanding* • Determine the English language abilities ELLs must possess to access content and express content-area understanding	
Step 2	**Set Learning Outcomes**	Chapter 5
	• Establish content-area *learning outcomes* for enduring understanding • Determine what all students must learn as a result of instruction • Determine the language abilities ELLs at varying levels of proficiency must develop	
Step 3	**Establish Evidence**	Chapter 6
	• Decide what constitutes evidence of content-area mastery apart from English language proficiency (*assessment evidence*) • Determine what constitutes evidence of growth in academic English for students at various proficiency levels	
Step 4	**Contextualize Instruction**	Chapter 6

	• Develop *essential questions* to
	  o make enduring understandings student-friendly
	  o build on student knowledge and engage ELLs and other students in the broad theme of the unit	

Step 5	**Plan Assessments and Design Lessons**	Chapter 7
	• Differentiate assessments according to English language proficiency • Plan content *objectives* and *assessments* for individual lessons • Plan language *objectives* and *assessments* for individual lessons	
Step 6	**Make Instruction Comprehensible**	Chapter 8
	• Ensure that daily content-area language is comprehensible to ELLs	
Step 7	**Build Academic Language**	Chapters 9–13
	• Engage ELLs in planned, complex, academic conversations about their content area • Develop content-area understanding and language proficiency	
Step 8	**Build Higher-Order Thinking Skills**	Chapters 9–13
	• Teach complex thinking skills across content areas • Provide time for ELLs to practice these skills under meaningful circumstances	

SOURCE: Based on the work of Tharp et al. (2000), Chamot and O'Malley (1994), and Wiggins and McTighe (1998, 2005).

Apply asked that you think about teaching out of your content area. When teachers provide instruction outside their areas of expertise, they are more likely to cover materials rather than provide in-depth, rich instruction. Content-area expertise is critical to good teaching, yet teaching ELLs requires more than *just good teaching*. It requires additional expertise to recognize and build on the strengths of ELLs and to scaffold their language development, including the pedagogical principles outlined in the TELLiM model. Most teachers we talk to want to share their content-area expertise with ELLs, yet they have questions and insecurities, which are presented in the next section.

CONCERNS OF MAINSTREAM TEACHERS

The pre- and in-service teachers we have come to know in courses and workshops are often unaware of the important content-area strengths they bring to teaching. Yet even after learning to appreciate their own teaching strengths many of them still express varying levels of anxiety about teaching ELLs. We do not dismiss this anxiety—it requires preparation to develop the expertise needed to teach ELLs. It is, however, possible for content-area teachers to develop this expertise. And when teachers meet the needs of the ELLs in mainstream classes, they will likely find that the achievement of many other students improves as well.

Here, we present four concerns that are frequently expressed by pre- and in-service teachers. We encourage readers to consider where they agree or disagree with teachers' concerns and to think about their own concerns.

Concern 1: "I feel so overwhelmed—this is all so totally new." Some of the strategies presented in this text will be new to the reader. Other strategies, such as planning for enduring understanding, may be familiar but presented in a slightly different way as they apply to instructing ELLs. The strategies will provide content-area teachers with different ways to think about planning and delivering instruction to ELLs in mainstream classrooms. The strategies presented are compatible with the tenets of good teaching. An instructor of the Understanding by Design (UbD) curriculum and of secondary ELA methods at the University of Massachusetts Lowell explained,

> Using these types of strategies will provide ELLs and every other student in classes with the opportunity to learn the basic grade-level concepts. For example, in teaching *everlasting life* as a literary theme, teachers can make their instruction comprehensible by embedding it in context and using visuals. Then teachers can use a variety of leveled-readers for the purposes of discussion, application, and assessment. Their highest level readers can read parts of the *Bible,* students who struggle with the reading for whatever reason can read a novel like *Tuck Everlasting* (Babbit, 1975). I see this as working for ELLs *and* other students within the mainstream ELA classroom. (J. Walsh, personal communication, July 2007)

It is important to keep in mind that teachers will not be able to totally reframe their teaching in one semester or one year. Tomlinson, who writes about differentiation of instruction (1999, 2003), acknowledges that to attempt to adopt all new strategies immediately is a recipe for failure. Teachers will, however, begin to think differently about planning, delivering, and assessing instruction. We have worked with content-area experts across content areas to provide in-depth discussions of specific issues of concern and instructional strategies for the major content areas. Throughout this text, these content-area teachers demonstrate the ways in which they worked through each of these processes. As Atwell (1998) suggests, these content-area teachers "take off the top of [their] head[s]" (p. 332) and enable the reader to think through the planning process with them.

Concern 2: "My team and I are concerned with the issue of time! With the continuing influx of ELLs, it seems we need more time for planning." Time is certainly an issue, and it seems that teachers feel as though they are continually asked to do more and more with the same resources (Colombo, Jacobs, McMakin, & Shestok, 2007). Although an initial investment of time is required to plan lessons for ELLs, it is not necessary to plan multiple lessons (one lesson for mainstream students, another for transitioning ELLs, and a third lesson for intermediate-level ELLs). Rather, the content-area teachers in this text demonstrate that they plan differently. Readers are encouraged to refer to their state and local content and ELL frameworks as they work through this text. As Cheryl, a participant in the *Methods of Sheltering English Content* course, stated, "This planning is relevant for all my students. It helps all students to understand how concepts fit together."

Participants in the *Methods of Sheltering English Content* class also reported that planning for ELLs helped them think through the content that was *really* important to teach. Additionally, they spoke about the benefits of using state content and ELL frameworks together to plan lessons that improved instruction for many students in their classes. As Paul described his experience, "The more we went through [the frameworks] and used them to plan lessons, the more we understood about the ELLs' levels and what they needed." Ana quickly added that many students would benefit from the additional structure and support of the language objectives found in TESOL and her state ELL frameworks.

Concern 3: "How do I reach these students and get them excited about learning?" Content-area teachers' enthusiasm for their content begins the process of planning and implementing motivating and engaging instruction for ELLs. Throughout this text, teachers explain how they use their expertise to motivate students and build content-area understanding and academic achievement. These content-area teachers have the capacity to provide more than temporary motivation and access to academic content. They can inspire true enthusiasm for their subjects and a lifelong love of learning in students. Robin Williams's character Mr. Keating, in the movie *Dead Poets Society*, inspires his students through his tangible passion for literature and poetry. Keating shares his knowledge, interests, and insights with his students and helps them develop their own interests as well. Most readers will remember teachers who inspired them with their depth of knowledge and passion for the subject they taught. Inspiring students seems to be a beneficial product of the content-area expert's genuine passion for his or her field.

Many ELLs we have talked with have been able to identify teachers who inspired them with their content-area expertise and high standards.

According to Sandi, a Cambodian American high school senior,

> I really liked my history teacher the best. The class was really hard, but Ms. Louden had us read a lot of novels about history. We read about how people at the time felt, and Ms. Louden helped us understand that history is real. She knew what she was talking about—she could explain anything, and she explained it so that you understood it.

Mina, an 11th-grade student from Venezuela who had been in the same U.S. school system for five years, referred to an ELA teacher who had helped her become successful:

Oh, he was so hard. He said the first day of class, "This is going to be the hardest course you have ever taken. You are scholars though and should do hard work, and I will work with you." We wrote a lot, and we shared what we wrote with him and with other kids in the class. I learned so much.

Melcom, a 10th grader who had attend U.S. schools for four years, recently told his secondary science teacher,

I never knew the stuff that you are teaching us (before). Yet you explain it all with your stories. You can tell stories that make us understand everything that you teach. No one has ever taught me science this way. I really get it. I think I might want to be a scientist.

When Sam, an early-intermediate ELL from the Dominican Republic who had many gaps in his education and often struggled in class, was asked about what he liked about a robotics unit, he said,

I can make these [robots] work. I have trouble sometimes with the reading, but I can figure these out and make them work, and Mrs. P gives me the time to do that. When I'm stuck, she asks me all the right questions. Then, I can get back to it and figure it out.

Concern 4: "How important is it to know my students' cultures? How can I do that?" Our cultures determine our knowledge, beliefs, and the ways in which we make sense of our worlds. While it may be beneficial to read about the cultures of students, it is important to keep in mind that cultural descriptions may well have been written by authors who are not of that culture and therefore may be biased. Cultural descriptions also often fail to consider the socioeconomic and individual variations that exist within a "culture" and the variety of experiences that ELLs may have had. Yet teachers must concern themselves with understanding the "funds of knowledge" (the knowledge that exists within homes) (González et al., 2005) that ELLs bring to the classroom, and they must develop a sense of cultural awareness and competence to effectively teach students who may be culturally different from themselves (see, e.g., Au, 2006; Gay, 2000; Moll, Amanti, Neff, & González, 1992; Villegas & Lucas, 2002).

Our experience has shown us that among the better ways to know ELLs within our classes are meeting their families, spending time talking with the students themselves, and remaining open to multiple perspectives and knowledge. We have had the most success in reaching parents when we have visited homes or invited the family to come to school as a unit, which alleviates the issue of child care and often results in a bilingual family member accompanying the group. Culture and culturally responsive instruction are the topics of Chapter 3.

Review, Reflect, Apply

Reflect and apply: Think about a content-area teacher who inspired you to become a lifelong learner. Explain what about this teacher inspired your enthusiasm for learning and how this experience influenced your educational opportunities and choices. How does such a teacher benefit his or her students?

CHAPTER SUMMARY

This chapter discussed many topics relevant to educating ELLs in U.S. schools, including the history of education, the various programs that exist to address the needs of ELLs, and the challenges that continue to confront these students. A focal point of this picture was the role that content-area teachers play in the education of ELLs. Teachers' depth of content-area understanding and insight are necessary for native-English speakers *and* they are critical for ELLs. Content-area teachers, however, need to learn about the various strengths and needs ELLs bring to the classroom and develop strategies for effectively conveying content and scaffolding academic language. Teachers must develop a basic knowledge of second-language acquisition and skills in sheltering instruction. The assessment section at the end of this chapter provides activities to check for understanding. We recommend that readers complete these activities prior to reading Chapter 2, which discusses the complexity of language acquisition, provides a layman's view of English linguistics, and introduces models of second-language acquisition.

Assessment Evidence Activities

AE-1   Review the language proficiency chart (Table 1.1) and the profiles of the ten ELLs found in the Appendix. Describe aspects of the courses you teach that ELLs at each level will be able to access as well as areas that you think will be difficult.

AE-2   Refer to Table 1.3, Programs for ELLs in U.S. Schools. List the advantages of each program for ELLs with varying levels of English language proficiency. Within your school district, interview teachers of ELLs or directors of programs for ELLs to determine what types of programs exist. Create a chart showing each program. Next to each program describe its strengths and weaknesses.

AE-3   Make a list of the challenges that you and other teachers have encountered (or may encounter) when planning and delivering instruction for ELLs. Describe your greatest concerns.

AE-4   Describe a content-area teacher who inspired you to learn, including why this teacher stands out and the ways in which his or her content-area expertise translated to effective teaching. Based on what you have learned about ELLs, explain how these qualities would be beneficial to ELLs.

Resources for Further Reading

• NCLB Action Brief: Programs of English Language Learners. This brief provides an overview of the requirements of NCLB for ELLs (including a description of Title III). This page also provides excellent links to the report *Closing the Gap for English Language Learners*, as well as to organizations such as the National Association for Bilingual Education, the National Clearinghouse for English Language Acquisition, and the Northwest Regional Educational Laboratory. http://ncpie.org/nclbaction/english_language_learners.html

- The *Lau v. Nichols* decision can be found at www.nabe.org/documents/policy_leg islation/LauvNichols.pdf, and excerpts are available at http://ourworld.compuserve.com/homepages/JWCRAWFORD/lau.htm

- ÍColorín Colorado! provides an overview of policy, NCLB, and Annual Yearly Progress (AYP) as they relate to ELLs. This user-friendly site also provides a variety of research reports and materials for teachers, parents, and children. http://www.colorincolorado.org/

- U.S. Department of Education Office for Civil Rights has developed guidelines for programs for ELLs, including identification, assessment, placement, transition, monitoring, and evaluation. www.ed.gov/about/offices/list/ocr/ell/charts.html

- Public Education Network. This site provides NCLB Action Briefs, which are organized for accessibility. www.publiceducation.org/nclb_actionbriefs.asp

- Teachers of English to Speakers of Other Languages (TESOL) is an excellent reference site. Standards and some guidelines can be accessed from the home page. To access specific journal articles, you must join TESOL. www.tesol.org

- *School Effectiveness for Language Minority Students* is a summary of collaborative research about the long-term achievement of ELLs in a variety of instructional programs. This report includes recommendations for policy and specific action. Available as a PDF file. www.ncela.gwu.edu/pubs/resource/effectiveness/

- Readers who are interested in complete descriptions of programs, language maintenance, and the principles of bilingual education are encouraged to see Baker, C. (2006). *Foundations of bilingual education and bilingualism.* Clevedon, UK: Multilingual Matters.

2

Second-Language Acquisition

What Mainstream Teachers Need to Know

Enduring understanding: An understanding of second-language acquisition underlies effective instruction for English Language Learners.

CHAPTER 1 FOCUSED ON THE HISTORY OF EDUCATING ELLS, THE VARIOUS PROGRAMS THAT EXIST FOR THIS PURPOSE, and the important role of mainstream content-area teachers in educating ELLs who have at least intermediate English proficiency. While teaching ELLs *is* good teaching, it is more than *just good teaching* and requires knowledge of English linguistics and language acquisition models. Chapter 1 introduced the TELLiM model for teaching ELLs. To effectively implement this model, teachers must understand the basics of second-language acquisition, culture, and second-language literacy. Chapter 2 provides a basic understanding of second-language acquisition and a theoretical foundation for the teaching strategies presented in later chapters. Chapter 2 begins with Chatting in the Hallway, a vignette of three ELLs and their mainstream teacher, which illustrates the complexity of English Language Development (ELD). The chapter continues with a synopsis of first-language acquisition, including a layman's overview of linguistics. Chapter 2 then provides a discussion of second-language development, commonly accepted theories of second-language acquisition, and the applicability of these theories to instruction of ELLs in mainstream content-area classrooms.

LEARNING OUTCOMES

The following learning outcomes (LOs) serve as a guide to Chapter 2. At the end of the chapter are assessment activities that are aligned with each LO to enable readers to check their understanding.

TERMS THAT MAY BE NEW

Common underlying proficiency: The hypothesis that academic knowledge and skills (to the extent the learner has mastered these in the first language) are available to the learner in additional languages

Fossilization: The development of permanent error patterns that are difficult to unlearn

Interlanguage: The language (a mix of first and target languages) that develops as the ELL is acquiring English

Language acquisition device: The neurological structure in the human brain that enables the development of language

Morphology: The internal structure of words

Motherese: Speech used by caretakers when talking with infants

Phonology: The organization of the sounds of a language

Pragmatics: The often subtle ways in which language meaning is influenced by context to convey more than is explicitly stated; politeness

Semantics: The meaning of language (word connotations, collocations, polysemy, expressions, and level of formality (Díaz-Rico & Weed, 2002)

Syntax: Rules that govern the structure of phrases, clauses, and sentences

Universal grammar: The structure and rules that underlie all languages

CHATTING IN THE HALLWAY

Katy, Matthew, Cha, and Magaly, all ninth-grade students, congregate around their lockers. Matthew is a native-English speaker, and Katy, Cha, and Magaly are ELLs. "What's for lunch?" asked Matthew. "I think hamburgers, but I'm not sure," Katy replied. "I hate the school lunch. *Is* gross," complained Magaly. "Yeah, it is," added Cha. Ms. Allen, their mainstream homeroom teacher, supervises the students from the doorway. On overhearing the conversation, she turns to the assistant who is assigned to help in her classroom. "See, the students can and do speak English. I don't understand why Ms. Sands, the ESL teacher, thinks they need extra support. They don't really even have accents."

The conversation at the lockers is illustrative of conversational language, which was originally referred to as Basic Interpersonal Communications Skills (BICS) (Cummins, 1984b, 2000).

Within a year or two, most ELLs develop sufficient proficiency in conversational language to enable them to converse with friends and teachers on familiar social topics. While proficiency in conversational language allows students to negotiate basic social relationships, it does not provide access to academic content. Often, however, when mainstream content-area teachers, like Ms. Allen, overhear ELLs sharing stories with friends in hallways or at their lockers, they logically (albeit falsely) conclude that these students have mastered English. This inaccurate observation leads mainstream teachers to believe that ELLs will do well in regular classrooms with little or no additional support.

In reality, ELLs who have only developed conversational language will need ongoing, focused, and well-planned instruction in listening, speaking, reading, and writing in English to continue to proceed along the continuum of ELD from beginning levels to near-native abilities. The distinction between conversational and academic language is illustrated and discussed further later in this chapter.

In the process of developing English, ELLs must learn English syntax, phonology, morphology, pragmatics, and semantics. They must be able to understand spoken academic language, express themselves in class discussions, read content-specific texts, and write well enough to complete assignments across the content areas. Even after ELLs have developed an understanding of the requirements of academic reading and writing, they may make frequent errors in grammar and syntax, have difficulty with idioms, and require ongoing instructional support to ensure that their English language abilities continue to grow.

DEVELOPING A FIRST LANGUAGE

As native speakers of a language, we do not often think about the complex, developmental nature of language acquisition. To the contrary, unless we have personal knowledge of a child or an adult whose language has been delayed (or perhaps have learned additional languages ourselves), the process of language development appears almost seamless. It is, therefore, important to develop at least a basic understanding of the complexity of first-language development in order to understand the challenges that confront ELLs in content-area classrooms.

Until the 1950s, linguists believed that children were explicitly taught language by more capable speakers—that the brain was a blank slate awaiting the programming of specific bits of linguistic knowledge. Then, the linguist Noam Chomsky revolutionized the way we think about language development. Chomsky (1965, 1972) theorized that the development of language is a genetically programmed, uniquely human phenomenon; just as humans are programmed to develop arms, they are programmed to develop language.

This uniquely human capacity for language is apparent in the contrast between language development in humans and language development in primates. When children are exposed to language in natural environments, they develop and use that language creatively and purposefully to communicate with parents, siblings, peers, and others around them. Children do not simply imitate caregivers but rather generalize the rules of their language to formulate original sentences. As Pinker (2007) describes, children are *naturally born* chatterboxes. In contrast, although expert trainers may dedicate hundreds of hours to the explicit teaching of language to primates, their primate students develop only very rudimentary linguistic abilities. Unlike children, it appears that even a very well-trained ape can only imitate, not create, language (Pinker, 2007).

According to Chomsky (1965, 1992) and Pinker (2007), the human ability to acquire language at a very early age can be explained by the neurological structure within the human brain that Chomsky refers to as the language acquisition device (LAD). Within the LAD is an overall (universal) system of grammar and subsystems of language-specific (generative) grammar for each of the thousands of languages that exist throughout the world (Hayes, Ornstein, & Gage, 1995). *Universal grammar* is the system of principles and rules that underlie all languages— all languages express meaning (semantics) using combinations of sounds (phonemes) to create vocabularies of thousands of words, which can be sorted into nouns and verbs, combined into phrases (syntax), and used in a variety of contexts (pragmatics). Words can be modified and new words created by inflections (such as adding *s, ing,* or *ed* in English) and derivations (such as the prefixes *pre, a, anti,* and the suffixes *al, est, ion* in English).

Universal grammar settings are available to all infants. Once an infant is exposed to the language(s) in her environment, however, the grammar settings in the infant's LAD are then *set* to learn the principles and rules of the specific language(s) within his or her environment. Richard-Amato (2003) likens this *setting* to switching a computer to select a particular program. For example, she explains that children in Chinese, English, or Spanish language environments will *set* their LAD to subject-verb-object (SVO) constructions, whereas children in Arabic language environments will select VSO, and children in Korean environments will select SOV.

LANGUAGE DEVELOPMENT

Regardless of the language group into which they are born, newborns have the ability to distinguish speech sounds (unmarked grammar) from other sounds in their environments. By the age of two or three months, normally developing infants recognize the sounds (phonemes) of their own language and actually have been shown to prefer these language sounds to the sounds of other languages (Pinker, 2007). As babies learn the phonemes of their own language(s), they gradually lose the ability to discriminate between sounds that are not relevant to their language(s).

Generally, prior to their first birthday, children begin to understand words, and by their first birthday, they are able to communicate verbally to make their needs known and engage in social interaction, naming objects and describing actions with isolated words. Most children, by the age of two, have developed the ability to put two words together. Pinker (2007) claims that growth in vocabulary continues to increase at such a rate that children learn a new word for every two hours they are awake, and that this growth persists through adolescence.

Pinker (2007) also maintains that across language groups and cultures, children learn similar two-word combinations to express the appearance or disappearance of objects (ball allgone), describe the owner of an object (David ball), or describe the object's properties (ball red). Children's two-word combinations reflect the word order of the specific language they are acquiring.

While there is much variation in the rate at which normally developing children acquire language, by age three, children without unusual language delays have the ability to express themselves in grammatical conversation. While many three-year-olds may not always speak with grammatical correctness, they have developed intuitions about what sounds are right and what words go together and a feeling for the parts of speech of a language (Hayes et al., 1995). Regardless of the language or dialect to which children are exposed, children acquire and know the complex *structure* of their own language. They demonstrate their knowledge of structure (rather than imitation of others) when they generalize language rules in ways that they would not hear their parents use language. For example, Juliana (age three) demonstrates the generalization of adding "ed" to form the past tense:

We goed to the zoo.

We seed the animals.

He weared a hat.

While Juliana incorrectly forms the simple past tense, it is clear that she has generalized the "add *ed*" rule.

By age five, most children know between 3,000 and 5,000 words and understand commonly used idioms and figures of speech. They can follow multistep instructions and understand abstract verbal accounts of events and actions *if* they have had similar experiences. As vocabulary in English increases, it can be measured in terms of *word families*, which consist of the actual word and derivatives formed by adding affixes (prefixes and suffixes) such as *un, pre, ly, ness*, and so on. For example, *dress, dressed, dressing, dressy, dressier, dressiest, undressed, address, addressed, preaddressed, redress, redressed, dresser* are considered a word family. During each year after the age of five, average English speakers acquire an additional 1,000 word families. The educated native-English speaker has internalized the phonology, morphology, and syntax of English and has a vocabulary of approximately 20,000 word families excluding proper nouns and compound words (Nation, 2001). (Vocabulary estimates vary greatly because of the different ways of counting words. For example, some researchers count all words within word families as separate words, and some may count each meaning of multiple-meaning words as a separate word. We have elected to use Nation's methodology of counting word families because of his expertise in second-language vocabulary.)

Many researchers and theorists hypothesize that a *critical period* exists for the development of a first language (Johnson & Newport, 1989; Lenneberg, 1967; Pinker, 2007). Pinker (2007) explains that when they are exposed to language, until the age of six children are "guaranteed" normal language development, from age 6 until puberty this development is diminished, and after puberty normal language development rarely occurs. Lenneberg (1967) relates this critical theory to brain plasticity or flexibility and lateralization (the specialization of each side of the brain). It is, however, impossible to prove or disprove the critical period for first-language acquisition. Clearly, it would be unethical to deprive children of language. Thus, much support for the critical period hypothesis comes from studies of children who had been isolated from language during the early years. (These include feral children and children who have been severely abused by caretakers.) There are few such recorded cases, and it is likely that these children might have also suffered other forms trauma. The cases that do exist support Pinker's assertion that age makes a critical difference to first language acquisition. An often used example is that of Genie, who was held in isolation under abject conditions by her father until she reached the age of 13, at which time she was rescued by social workers. Once Genie was exposed to language, she struggled with phonology, was unable to develop syntactic ability, and developed only a simplistic use of language (Curtiss, 1977).

The ability of researchers to conduct ethical studies with second-language learning has resulted in a larger body of research regarding the critical period for second-language acquisition. Researchers have found that while individual variations exist, in general, early exposure to language results in greater proficiency (Birdsong, 1999; Johnson & Newport, 1989; Krashen, 1985). Research, however, does not wholly support a definitive critical period for all aspects of language development. Bialystok and Hakuta (cited in Hakuta, 2001), for example, observed a decline in the ability to acquire language that was related to age, yet did not find evidence of a definitive critical period, and Ioup (2005) suggests the term *sensitive period*, rather than *critical period*. Ioup, who conducted a review of research regarding the ideal age for second-language development, cites studies that show differences in performance among second-language learners who acquired second languages during puberty and the teen years. Generally, age is considered negatively correlated with the development of native-like proficiency, and older second-language learners will retain first language influences.

Older language learners also differ from children in the ways in which they acquire a second language for academic purposes. They have greater opportunities to use the information and ability that they have gained in their first language to make sense of their second language (Lenneberg, 1967). Older ELLs bring greater conceptual and factual knowledge to reading (Grabe, 1991). (The theory of common underlying proficiency and transfer of abilities from first to other languages is discussed later in this chapter.)

Review, Reflect, Apply

1. *Review and apply:* How do the theories of Chomsky and Pinker explain language acquisition? What specific examples do they provide to illustrate that children do not learn language by imitating? What do you think are the implications for second-language acquisition?

2. *Apply:* What implications do the findings of Bialystok, Hakuta, and Lenneberg regarding the critical period have for adolescent ELLs?

Summary

Many theorists believe that humans are uniquely capable of learning language and that humans have a neurological structure (the LAD) that enables the development of language. At birth, an infant has access to universal grammar, which is the system of principles and rules that underlie all languages. Soon the grammar settings in the infant's LAD are *set* to learn the principles and rules of the specific language(s) of his or her environment, and the infant gradually begins to lose the ability to identify sounds irrelevant to his or her language(s).

On hearing the grammar of his or her language, the young child is able to generalize rules, such as adding /d/ to form the simple past tense and to create novel language expressions. Pinker and others maintain that beyond the age of six, first-language development is diminished, and beyond puberty, it is rare. For ethical reasons, most research has taken place with second-language learners, and it suggests that there may be a sensitive, rather than critical, period for second-language acquisition. The next section explores the components of language, including phonology, morphology, syntax, pragmatics, and semantics.

THE COMPONENTS OF LANGUAGE

Acquiring a language consists of acquiring its *phonology, morphology, syntax,* and *semantics*. From early infancy on, native speakers acquire these components of their own language naturally; ELLs must catch up. In thinking about the acquisition of English as another language, it is worthwhile to consider the complexity of each linguistic component. While each of these areas represents a branch of study in itself, this section provides a brief layman's overview that will be useful as we proceed from first- to second-language acquisition. In later chapters, we will return to these areas as we discuss the challenges that ELLs confront in learning English and strategies for teaching and learning that promote the development of academic language across the content areas. The resources section at the end of this chapter provides suggestions for further reading and study for those readers who would like to broaden their understanding of linguistics.

Phonology

Phonology refers to the systematic organization of noises into language sounds (Hayes et al., 1995). Phonemes are the smallest unit of sound and consist of both consonant and vowel sounds. Infants begin to recognize the phonemes of language at a very early age and begin to prefer the phonemes of their language soon thereafter. At approximately six months of age infants begin to lose the ability to recognize phonemes that are not part of their native language (Birch, 2006; Pinker, 2007).

English relies heavily on the discrimination of vowel sounds. For example, the vowel is the distinguishing feature in the following sets of words, which is apparent in their pronunciation: *pen, pan; sip, sop; men, man; bad, bed, bid*. English is believed to have 12 vowel sounds (Hayes et al., 1995).

Native speakers use generalizations of the phonological rules of their language rather unconsciously. One way English speakers demonstrate the intuitive application of phonological rules is in the pronunciation of plurals. For example, plurals of the words *pot* and *pan* are formed by adding *s*. Native speakers of English (or speakers who have acquired native-like fluency) pronounce the final sound in pots as /s/ and the final sound in pans as /z/. Another example of the intuitive application of phonological generalizations is illustrated by the use of the past tense, *ed*, in the following words: *worked, played, awarded, smiled, stopped*, and *plugged*. The *ed* is pronounced as /t/ in *worked* and *stopped*, as /d/ in *played, smiled*, and *plugged*, and as /ed/ in *awarded* (Hayes et al., 1995).

Whereas native speakers of English acquire and apply phonological rules without thinking about them, adolescent and adult ELLs must consciously attend to the sounds of English in both *receptive language* (listening and reading) and *productive language* (speaking and writing).

Morphology

Morphology refers to the inner structure of words—the meaningful parts of any word, such as the root (free morpheme) and the prefix and suffix (bound morphemes). Morphemes are the smallest units of meaning in a language. Affixes (prefixes and suffixes) are morphemes that linguists categorize as either inflectional or derivational. Inflectional morphemes are always suffixes and when added to a word, change neither the word's meaning nor its grammatical class. For example, consider the verb in the following sentence: The children *play*. Now add the suffixes *s, ing, ed*. While each suffix changes the tense of the verb—*plays, playing, played*, the meaning and grammatical class of the word remain constant.

Derivational morphemes are prefixes or suffixes that when added to a word, change either the word's meaning or its grammatical class. When, for example, the prefixes *re* and *dis* are added to *play*, to form *replay* and *display*, the grammatical class (verb) remains the same, but the meaning changes. The suffix *ful* (a derivational morpheme) changes the grammatical class of *play* from verb to adjective *playful*.

Native speakers make and apply morphological generalizations at a young age, as an often cited study by Berko (1958) illustrates. In the most commonly discussed example in this study, children from ages four to seven were presented with drawings of an imaginary bird (a wug) and told, "This is a wug." The children were then shown a picture of two such imaginary birds, and when prompted, "Now there is another one. There are two of them. There are two_____," the children responded with the generalization "wug/z/" (Berko, 1958, p. 154). After testing children using several such nonsense nouns, the researcher concluded that children could generalize morphological rules for the formation of the plural form. Berko also found that children generalized rules for verb number, tense, and possessive nouns and were able to inflect, derive, compound, and analyze compound words. While children's responses were not always correct, their responses were consistent, thus indicating that children between four and seven years of age have developed the ability to generalize clear morphological rules. In contrast, ELLs must learn to generalize morphological rules in English. (A link to the Berko study is found in the Resources for Further Reading.)

Syntax

Syntax is the fixed code by which speakers of a language structure and interpret sentences, clauses, and phrases. When linguists refer to syntax, they are referring to the internal structure speakers of a language possess that allows them to know the underlying rules of their language.

According to Chomsky (1965), "every speaker of a language has mastered and internalized a generative grammar that expresses his knowledge of his language" (p. 8). As Pinker (2007) explains, this is not the grammar of English class but rather the internal grammar that enables speakers of a language to know that something is right or wrong with the structure of a sentence even if they cannot explain why. Ungrammatical strings of words can convey meaning (Pinker, 2007), as the following strings illustrate:

Keep always the light on.

Eat sandwich now.

Walk, ice, slip, fall.

Meaning is conveyed with each of these sentences, but to a speaker of the language, they do not sound right—there is something wrong with them. Pinker (2007) uses Chomsky's classic quote, "Colorless green ideas sleep furiously" (p. 79), to illustrate that it is equally possible to form grammatical sentences that make no sense at all. The sentence is perfectly grammatical but nonsensical. The work of Dr. Seuss (1957) provides many examples of sentences that are nonsensical yet syntactically sound. Consider the following:

I know it is wet

And the sun is not sunny

But we can have

Lots of good fun that is funny. (p. 7)

ELLs have developed an intuitive knowledge of syntax in their first languages but will have to learn English syntax.

Semantics

Semantics is the study of the meaning of words and the arrangement of words for meaning. The study of semantics is relatively new to linguistics and only came about in the 1950s. Semantics explains that words are acquired by children intuitively and then stored in their lexicons (their mental dictionaries). A child's innate semantic ability is demonstrated by his or her ability to learn new words. Preschoolers appear to intuitively group words into classifications, knowing the difference between nouns, verbs, adjectives, and adverbs (although they cannot identify them as such). They use their knowledge of syntax to make sense of new words. One of the most commonly cited studies illustrating the use of syntax in determining meaning was conducted by Roger Brown in 1957 (see, e.g., Bloom, 2000; Kako & Wagner, 2001; Pinker, 2007). Brown showed children a picture of hands kneading pieces of squares in a bowl. He asked, "Can you see any sibbing?" The children pointed to the hands and indicated that the kneading action was "sibbing." When asked, "Can you see a sib?" they pointed to the bowl (the only singular item in the picture), and when asked, "Can you see any sibs?" they pointed to the squares in the bowl (the only set of multiple objects in the picture).

Pragmatics

Pragmatics refers to the use of language in given social contexts and requires knowledge of social status, the rules governing politeness in given situations, and the implicit as well as explicit meanings of words and language structures. It is "the study of communicative action in its sociocultural context" (Rose & Kasper, 2001, p. 2). As the American Speech-Language-Hearing Association (2008) indicates, pragmatics involves three major communication skills: "using language for different purposes, changing language in different situations, and following rules for communication" (such as turn taking, clarifying, and using nonverbal communication). Pragmatic competence is influenced by social and cultural norms as well as by language development.

A former student, José, illustrated the difficulties that ELLs may encounter with appropriateness of language. José often greeted the principal by saying "What's up my man?" in lieu of "How are you, Mr. Smith?" Fortunately, the principal understood the influence of language development on pragmatics, or José's greeting might have helped form his impression of this student as punky or rude. In this case, José's lack of understanding of the social hierarchy of student-principal and the language norms associated with that hierarchy demonstrates the role of pragmatics in full language acquisition.

KNOWING A WORD

Just as we do not think about our own language development, we seldom consider the complexity of words within our language. Knowing a word is a multifaceted process, consisting of knowing other words used with it (collocation), the word's multiple meanings (polysemy), its various connotations, and the appropriateness of the word's use (Nation, 2001). Whereas native English speakers steadily and rapidly acquire words in their natural environments, ELLs must learn an extraordinary number of words to catch up.

Collocations

As native speakers of a language, we not only rapidly acquire new vocabulary words, we also acquire a sense of the ways in which certain words fit (or collocate) with other words. Using our simple example of the word *dress*, we see that in addition to having acquired the expanded word family, we also know the word's *collocations*, including *dress up, dress down, dress rehearsal, dress shoes, dress pants*, and *dress jeans*. These collocations are unalterable; while we may roughly define the verb *dress* as "to put clothes on," we do not attend a "put clothes on rehearsal." Collocations also include the use of grammatical constructions. Native-English speakers, for example, "get on" the plane, bus, or train, but they "get in" the car.

Collocations exist across academic language and within specific content areas. For example, some of the collocations that exist across general academic content areas are *in addition to, with regard to, as a result of, given these conditions, in order to, and as a consequence, given that, apply knowledge, support with evidence, point out*, and *refer to*. As Table 2.1 illustrates, collocations exist in specific content areas as well.

Polysemy

English words also have multiple meanings (or *polysemy*). Keeping with our original sample word, we can see that *dress* as a verb has multiple meanings. We can *dress* a child (clothe), *dress* a salad (mix it with oil and vinegar), or *dress* a deer (prepare for consumption). The word *dress* and its derivatives are also commonly used as nouns: a new *dress, dressing* (stuffing) to accompany our Thanksgiving turkey, and *dressing* for a wound. In common academic language, *directions, unit*, and *state* are just a few examples of words with multiple meanings that ELLs must master. Table 2.2 illustrates words with multiple meanings that are commonly found in the four major content areas. Each word has both conversational and academic meanings. Additionally, the academic meanings of words may vary from one content area to another.

TABLE 2.1 Common Collocations in Main Content Areas

Mathematics	Science	Social Studies	English Language Arts
multiplied by, divided by, of a number, sum of, square of, square root of, the average number of, the probability that, area of, length of, identity property, place value, prime numbers, expanded form, common denominator, ordered pair, least common multiple	room temperature, exponential growth, mathematical models, triple beam balance, global warming, Doppler effects, lab report, multiple physical properties, natural resources, states of energy, protein synthesis	separation of power, political party, checks and balances, primary source	chronological order, sentence fragment, thesis statement, writing process, draw conclusions

TABLE 2.2	Polysemy in Main Content Areas		
Mathematics	**Science**	**Social Studies**	**English Language Arts**
absolute, acute, average, cardinal, complex, coordinate, difference, digit, dividend, factor, formula, function, identity, independent, inequality, improper, irrational, infinity, imaginary, law, rule, mean, major, minor, negative, prism, periodic, plane, power, product, proper, plot, point, positive, proof, problem, radical, ray, real, root, scale, second, slope, solution, table, translation, operation, unit, volume, wave	adaptation, agent, bond, beam, charge, climate, colony, community, culture, current, control, diversity, reaction, work, conductor/conduct, current, down, energy, fault, force, front, gas, host, instrument, kingdom, matter, neutral, organ, order, point, property, reliable, reaction, step, state, tissue, unit, mantle, prism, reflect, relative, revolution, scales, school, subject, solution, tension, tolerance, wave, vacuum	age, article, bank, bill, climate, culture, colony, neutral, reflect, diversity, capital, directions, key, legend, party, power, product, radical, relative, right, kingdom, revolution, root, solution, state, tolerance, yield	adaptation, argument, article, elements, legend, mechanics, plot, point, object, problem, prompt, subject, solution, structure, thread, translation, tension, tone

Connotations

In addition to multiple meanings, some words have a variety of *connotations*. A simple word such as *like* can have unintended connotations. A friend was once in the midst of writing a paper that she intended to submit to a journal. She had reworked several passages within the paper and was particularly pleased with the introductory vignette. She had written that a female student *liked* a teacher and thought he was *nice*. When she asked her husband, a high school teacher, to read through the passage, he was horrified. "You can't say this," he told her. "*Like* and *nice* used in this way convey a relationship that you do not want to portray in this situation!"

Academic vocabulary, too, is generally quite specific and requires exacting comprehension to gather the correct meaning. Earlier in this chapter, it was established that educated, native-English speakers have a vocabulary of approximately 20,000 word families. Many of these words, while technically synonyms, carry distinct meaning. Consider the following example: "The union acquiesced to the terms of the contract." Full understanding of this statement hinges on the verb *acquiesce*. To know that *acquiesce* is synonymous with *agree*, for example, only provides one layer of understanding of this statement. Although the two words are synonymous, they do not have the same connotation. To understand the statement fully, one would have to recognize that *acquiesce* is a passive, often reluctant form of agreement. An understanding of word connotations, therefore, is required for both receptive and productive mastery of English. Without full understanding of the layers of meaning that each word connotes, ELLs risk vague or imprecise understanding of content and expression.

Connotations often present problems for ELLs, who may consult either a dictionary or a thesaurus in search of a synonym to improve their writing. This consultation may yield unintentional consequences. For example, a thesaurus search for *timid*, yields *nervous, shy, fearful, coy, retiring, apprehensive, faint-hearted, lily-livered, spineless, fearful*, and *diffident*—all words with different connotations. A search for an alternative for the word *problem* yields the words *mess, dilemma, complication, quandary, dispute*, and *issue*. While the connotations of some words may make them appropriate replacements, others clearly are not.

Appropriateness

Finally, speakers learn to use words that are appropriate for given situations and audiences. Vocabulary that works well with friends in casual settings may not be appropriate for a meeting with the school principal, and some words may rarely be appropriate for social settings. For example, while we know that one meaning of *fat* is *overweight*, we also learn as fairly young children that it is inappropriate to call someone *fat*. Words that specify racial groups, describe abilities, and convey gender are regularly evolving—what may have been appropriate 10 years ago may well be inappropriate today.

Review, Reflect, Apply

1. *Review and reflect:* How do native speakers use generalizations of rules of phonology, morphology, syntax, and semantics to make sense of language?

2. *Review and reflect:* Think of one commonly used English word. Adding as many affixes as possible, make a list of all the derivatives of the word (word family). How does the word change in use and in pronunciation? Speculate as to why "knowing" a word might be difficult for ELLs.

3. *Apply:* We once participated in a workshop given by a colleague, during which he asked that participants write down and share all the collocations for the word "eye." We were amazed at some of the collocations we had not considered. Try this with a small group. How many collocations did you find? How might these collocations present difficulties for ELLs? Think across your content area. What words are consistently combined with other words?

4. *Reflect:* Look across your content area and make a list of words that have multiple meanings (polysemy). How might these confuse ELLs?

5. *Reflect and apply:* How might word connotations cause difficulties for ELLs? Consider the word *ambitious*: List the positive and negative connotations. What words in your content area (or words that students use to express their content-area understanding) have positive and negative connotations?

Summary

This section provided a brief, layman's overview of linguistics, including phonology (language sounds), morphology (inner structure of words), syntax (sentence structure), semantics (meaning), and pragmatics (hidden rules and meaning). It explained that native speakers almost automatically acquire and generalize the rules of each of these linguistic structures to make sense of language and to create new language constructions. Additionally, at an early age, native speakers use the rules of one linguistic structure to make sense of another. For example, Berko (1958) illustrated the generalizations of morphological knowledge to form verb tense, plurals, and adjectives, and Brown's study illustrated the use of syntactic knowledge to identify meanings of nonsense words (*sibbing, sib*, and *sibs)*. Without intention, very young native speakers of a language begin learning and generalizing the linguistic rules of their language. This section also discussed the complexity of vocabulary development, including learning word collocations, polysemy, connotations, and appropriateness. On completing this section, readers should have begun to consider the challenges that confront ELLs who come to academic language often without having internalized the phonological, morphological, syntactic, and semantic rules of English.

ACQUIRING A SECOND LANGUAGE

Participation in foreign-language classes makes clear the differences between acquiring a second language at school and acquiring a first language at home. Yet unless the foreign-language learner has been required to learn a language for academic purposes, it is difficult to identify with the circumstances in which ELLs find themselves.

During graduate courses and workshops we have taught, at least one pre- or in-service teacher has shared an experience similar to that of Lesley, who questioned the length of time it takes ELLs to learn English:

> I really don't understand why they [ELLs] can't learn it in a year or two. I spent a semester in Spain during my senior year. I had to work hard, but I learned to speak Spanish. The kids are living in the U.S. and hear English all day.

With regard to her language learning, Lesley was referring to the development of conversational language rather than the academic language that is necessary for academic achievement. Later, Lesley added that when she first arrived in Spain, she did not speak much. Although she had completed two years of high school Spanish prior to the trip, she said she felt "self-conscious" speaking. She had difficulty understanding when her Spanish-speaking companions spoke so *rapidly*. "I just tried to figure it all out," she explained.

While vast differences in social, economic, and psychological experiences separate a semester abroad from immersion into U.S. public schools, linguistically, Lesley's experience is somewhat analogous to that of many ELLs. When first exposed to English, ELLs often go through a *silent period*. They listen to the language, take it in, and begin to make sense of it, but they often do not try to use it immediately. The duration of this *silent period* depends on the personality of the learner; it can last one to two days or can continue for up to a year. The *silent period*, hypothesized by Krashen (1985), is a perfectly normal stage in second-language acquisition, and ELLs should not be pressured to speak English during this time. The *silent period* leads us to Krashen's hypotheses about second-language acquisition.

Krashen's Theory of Second-Language Acquisition

Krashen's theory of second-language acquisition has been both widely applied in instructional settings and sometimes critiqued by researchers. According to Krashen (1981, 1985), who grounds his work in the theories of Chomsky (1965, 1972), the process of second-language acquisition is similar to the process of first-language acquisition. Krashen's theory consists of five hypotheses (acquisition/learning, natural order, monitor, affective filter, and input). It is the last two hypotheses with which we will concern ourselves in this chapter. We present these here and then refer to them in later chapters in discussions about making grade-level content accessible to ELLs. The resources section at the end of this chapter provides links to Krashen's theories.

Cognitively Undemanding

Context Embedded——–A   C——–Context Reduced

Context Embedded——–B   D——–Context Reduced

Cognitively Demanding

SOURCE: Cummins (2000).

Cognitively undemanding tasks (Quadrants A and C) are those tasks for which ELLs have developed language skills and can apply these skills with near automaticity (without thinking). The activities and tasks within Quadrants A and C, therefore, require relatively little cognitive attention. Examples of tasks in Quadrant A include engaging in day-to-day conversation, such as exchanges between students in the hallway (e.g., the conversation of Katy, Cha, Juan, and Magaly near their lockers), or a casual exchange about a known topic between a teacher and student (such as a conversation between an ELL football player and a teacher who attends the football games). Quadrant C consists of tasks such as copying notes from the whiteboard or completing fill-in-the-blank work sheets (Cummins, 2000). Although little context is provided for these tasks, the tasks themselves do not require substantive cognitive attention on the part of ELLs.

Quadrants B and D include tasks and activities that place a high cognitive demand on ELLs. An example of tasks in Quadrant B is participating in academic conversations within the classroom—the activity is cognitively demanding, yet the responses of others in the discussion provide contextual clues. An example of a Quadrant D task is independently completing an essay about an academic topic without scaffolds, such as graphic organizers, multiple opportunities to draft and revise, and conference with peers and the teacher.

Teachers can adjust instruction to provide context for the most challenging academic tasks, such as writing an essay, writing geometry proofs, solving word problems for probability, analyzing poetry, or discussing cause and effect in history. One of the best ways teachers can begin to provide context is to plan instructional units around the *enduring understandings* and *essential questions* of the content area (the topics of Chapters 5 and 6). Through teaching for enduring understanding, teachers provide context-embedded instruction by activating student schema, building relationships between student knowledge and new concepts, and making apparent the relationships between concepts.

Other common ways in which content-area teachers provide context and comprehensible input include the following:

- *Adjusting the rate and clarity of speech:* When teachers are unaware of their rate of speech, ELLs will hear speech that is too *rapid*, and sounds will be blurred. Michaela once spent the first part of a beginner adult ESL class trying to decipher and define the word *didja* after a group of students asked its meaning. Without context for the word, she wondered, "Dijon mustard?"

then "dejá vu?" It took a while to discern that students were referring to the reduction (pronouncing a phrase very quickly) of *did you.* This simple example illustrates the problems with comprehensibility that can occur when teachers speak too rapidly. We do not suggest that teachers speak with exaggerated slowness or increase their volume, which can be equally disconcerting to ELLs. Teachers should, however, be aware of their tempo and pronunciation.

- *Words and constructions:* New words that students need to know should be introduced, written, and paraphrased often. Teachers should be aware of the vocabulary and constructions they use while introducing and explaining concepts.

- *Rhythm of the lesson:* Teachers must provide time to check for understanding and allow students to make connections. (This is beneficial for all students and critical for ELLs.)

- *Embed context into instruction:* Teachers can build schema through teaching for enduring understanding (Chapter 5); focusing instruction with essential questions (Chapter 6); and accompanying lectures with props, visuals, and video.

- Teachers should include visual cues in the form of pictures, diagrams, models, videos, and PowerPoint and provide time to process both content and language.

Review, Reflect, Apply

1. *Review:* Explain why providing ELLs with instruction based on $i + 1$ has the potential to improve content-area understanding and academic-language skills.

2. *Review:* Explain how adding context to instruction improves its comprehensibility for ELLs.

Summary

This section began with a discussion of the differences between first- and second-language acquisition. According to Krashen (1981), many second-language learners experience a silent period, a normal experience lasting from a few days to several months, in which the learner processes the language but does not attempt to use it. This section also provided an overview of two other hypotheses within Krashen's theory of second-language acquisition: the affective filter and comprehensible input ($i + 1$). The $i + 1$ hypothesis forms the basis for many instructional practices presented in later chapters of this volume, and therefore it is important to understand. Providing ELLs with $i + 1$ enables them to access challenging academic context. For example, an ELL may not be able to understand the content within a lecture that is given without visuals and prompts. Yet a lecture that is accompanied by visuals, a clear outline, and a graphic organizer will be comprehensible to the ELL. As Cummins's (2000) context-embedded versus context-reduced model illustrates, some language requirements are more cognitively demanding than others. When instruction is given in context, however, even cognitively demanding tasks, such as writing an essay, become more comprehensible to ELLs.

COMMUNICATIVE COMPETENCE

The theory of communicative competence, which is also grounded in the work of Chomsky, considers language input and output. Originally introduced in the 1970s by Hymes (1972), the theory was further developed by Canale (1983). As the name of the theory suggests, second-language proficiency develops as a result of meaningful communication in the target language, and it is through this communication that ELLs develop receptive and productive proficiency in English. Canale identifies four key components of communicative competence: grammatical, sociolinguistic, discourse, and strategic competence.

1. *Grammatical competence:* ELLs beyond beginner levels of English proficiency become increasingly concerned with grammatical accuracy in their speaking and writing. They read and listen in the target language with attention to language form as well as meaning and then try these new grammatical forms in writing and conversation with others.

2. *Sociolinguistic competence:* ELLs gradually develop the ability to communicate in a variety of circumstances and with speakers of different status and adjust their communication styles appropriately. The language ELLs use within the classroom is different from the language they use on the bus, and the language they use with the school principal differs from what they use with friends.

3. *Competence in discourse:* ELLs develop the ability to express meaningful thoughts, phrases, and sentences in purposeful communication with others, and the structure of this discourse becomes increasingly complex. As ELLs seek to express themselves, *interlanguage* (Selinker, 1991), which is a mixture of first and second languages, often occurs. Thus, an ELL may be explaining a concept in science and may use a word or a grammatical construction from the first language in place of an unknown English word. These replacements are developmental and useful as the ELL acquires academic English and struggles to express ideas and concepts. The ongoing scaffolding of academic language, which is discussed in Chapter 9, lessens the likelihood that language errors will become *fossilized*.

4. *Strategic competence:* ELLs use the English language they have developed effectively in a variety of circumstances, selecting alternate known words to replace words they have not yet learned and structuring writing to use the grammatical structures they have mastered.

The development of academic communicative competence depends on ongoing opportunities for focused and purposeful content-area interaction and communication within the classroom. ELLs will benefit from academic communication with other students who have greater English language proficiency. While the theory of communicative competence is grounded in the work of Chomsky, not Vygotsky, the zone of proximal development (ZPD), discussed in the following section, highlights the importance of ongoing opportunities for focused, interactive academic conversations and activities.

ZONE OF PROXIMAL DEVELOPMENT

The type of vocabulary and communication patterns children and adults develop are influenced by other speakers with whom they communicate. Mothers and caregivers speak to toddlers in words that are just slightly beyond the toddler's linguistic ability. Teachers in early grades do much the same. Much socialization also occurs within same-age and multi-age peer groups. Children (and adults) who consistently communicate with speakers whose speech is slightly more developed than their own are likely to grow in communicative ability. This communicative growth can be explained at least in part by the ZPD theory. Formulated in the early 20th century by the

Russian psychologist Lev Vygotsky, the ZPD theory continues to inform instruction in U.S. classrooms today. The ZPD refers to the difference between an individual's abilities when working independently and her abilities when working in collaboration with an adult or a more capable peer. According to the ZPD when learners work in collaboration with slightly more competent others, their learning is scaffolded. Well-planned small-group work, reciprocal instruction, peer tutoring, and cross-age tutoring, which match students with slightly more capable peers, are all examples of the ZPD at work in the classroom. The ZPD has powerful implications for the classroom instruction of ELLs. Working in pairs or small groups enables ELLs to use academic English with more capable peers; it provides ELLs the opportunity to practice language constructions and receive meaningful feedback.

FROM INTERPERSONAL TO ACADEMIC LANGUAGE

Once ELLs start to speak, as Lesley finally did in Spain, they tend to use conversational language that meets their survival needs (Where is the bathroom? My bus stop is at the corner of Oak and Vine Streets.). Second-language proficiency continues to develop along a linguistic continuum from survival to conversational language skills (Do you want to eat lunch together? My homework is in my locker.).

The ninth-grade students in Ms. Allen's class were using conversational language, just as Lesley might have done when speaking with a waiter or a stranger on the street in Spain. This ability to engage in social conversations may have been sufficient for Lesley and others who spend a semester in another country. Here, however, is where the linguistic analogy of ELLs and students who, like Lesley, spend a semester abroad, ends. ELLs must quickly develop grade-level communicative competence with *academic language* and continue to learn content as they acquire English.

Conversational Language Versus Academic Language

Cummins (1979, 1984a, 1984b, 2000) introduced the terms *Basic Interpersonal Communication Skills (BICS)* (now more commonly referred to as conversational language) and *Cognitive Academic Language Proficiency (CALP)* (more commonly referred to as academic language). Cummins (2000) explains that distinguishing between conversational and academic language does not constitute a theory of language development but rather should guide policy and instruction for ELLs. Although there is no clear-cut distinction between conversational and academic language, the notion of difference is foundational to teaching academic-content material to ELLs. Cummins uses the metaphor of an iceberg to illustrate the differences between conversational and academic language. See Model 2.2.

Conversational language represents only the tip of the iceberg, the informal second-language communication that language learners normally acquire in one to two years (Cummins, 1979, cited in Baker, 2006). Academic language is the enormous part of the iceberg that remains underwater. It is the language of process and concepts and deep, expansive vocabulary (collocations, polysemy, connotations, and appropriateness). ELLs may require 5 to 7 years to fully develop academic language in English (Baker, 2006; Cummins, 1979). Mr. Frank Johnson's history class illustrates the challenges that ELLs encounter when teachers do not make a clear distinction between conversational and academic language.

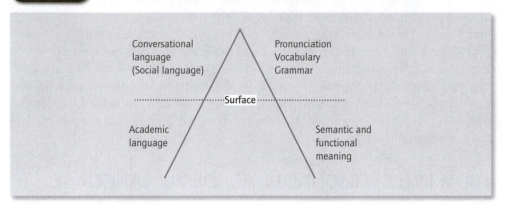

Conversational language (Social language)

Pronunciation
Vocabulary
Grammar

Surface

Academic language

Semantic and functional meaning

SOURCE: Adapted from Baker (2006).

Case of Mr. Johnson's History Class

Juan, who arrived from Ecuador the previous year, has sat at the back of Mr. Johnson's history classroom since the first day of class. Mr. Johnson generally greets students individually as they enter his classroom. He plays soccer and follows the International Soccer League, and knowing that Juan is a soccer fan, Mr. Johnson keeps tabs on how the Ecuadorian soccer team is doing. Juan and Mr. Johnson have good rapport.

Mr. Johnson, however, worries about Juan's academic progress—Juan is a good kid, but he accomplishes little in history. This day, Mr. Johnson wants his students to understand the importance of multiple perspectives in the telling of history and is focusing on propaganda in the American Revolution. Because Mr. Johnson and Juan converse without a problem, Mr. Johnson assumes that Juan understands his lectures and historical anecdotes.

The previous day, Mr. Johnson had assigned reading about propaganda and the American Revolution for homework, which he reviews in today's class. (The number of unfamiliar words in the history text has made this reading an impossible task for Juan.) Following a lecture on the use of propaganda in the American Revolution, Mr. Johnson turns on the overhead projector to display a copy of Paul Revere's drawing of the Boston Massacre. He asks students to take a few minutes and jot down the elements of propaganda they observe in the drawing. Some students pick up pens and immediately begin to write, others leaf through notebooks to find paper, and several stare at the drawing. Juan looks at the drawing for a minute and puts his head down on his desk. After a few minutes, Mr. Johnson walks down to Juan's desk and asks him why he is not working. Juan shrugs. Juan does not know how to explain that everything after the soccer discussion was a blur. He has heard Mr. Johnson use the words "proper gander" before, but he is not sure what the words mean and does not know what they have to do with the picture that is displayed. Juan thinks that the picture is something about a revolution, but he is not sure what Mr. Johnson means by revolution. He knows that Mr. Johnson is waiting. "You want me to write about the picture, right?" Mr. Johnson says, "Yes, I want you to write about elements within the drawing that could be considered propaganda." Juan nods, although he still is not sure of what he is to do. He knows the class will end soon.

Case Discussion

Juan is at an intermediate level of proficiency; his interpersonal language abilities mask the struggles he experiences with academic language. He requires more processing time than native-English speakers, and like many ELLs at this level, he is overwhelmed by the large amount of required reading. While Juan can engage in fluent conversation with Mr. Johnson about soccer (social language), he has not yet developed the academic language to access the language of history. From the exchange that occurs within the classroom, it is not possible to know whether Juan has an underlying understanding of the concepts of revolution or propaganda in Spanish, his first language.

Juan's proficiency level indicates that he is able to participate in academic conversations when he receives frequent repetitions and visual cuing. Later, when we discuss strategies for making content-area concepts comprehensible to ELLs, we will provide illustrations of similar lessons that have been redesigned so that Juan and other ELLs understand academic concepts such as revolution and propaganda and are able to complete assignments.

DOUBLE-BURDENED IN THE CLASSROOM

Unlike native English speakers who are learning academic content, ELLs must master the new language *and* academic content. Whereas Lesley had nearly completed her secondary education when she went to Spain for the second semester of her senior year, ELLs often enter U.S. schools in late-elementary, middle, or secondary grades, where content and content-area language become increasingly demanding.

Native speakers have had their first five years to acquire English naturally, have acquired an additional 1,000 word families each year, and will continue to acquire language throughout their school years. The burden on ELLs is great. An ELL who enters a U.S. school in Grade 5 must acquire 8,000 word families to be able to compete with the native speakers in his or her classes. This same student will need to acquire an additional 1,000 word families each year thereafter *and* master the fifth-grade curriculum. This fifth-grade student and other ELLs do *not* have additional years to acquire academic English. They need teachers who can help them to both understand grade-level content-area concepts and provide evidence of their understandings using academic English.

Review, Reflect, Apply

1. *Reflect:* Have you had experiences learning another language? What was this experience like for you? Were you self-conscious? If so, how? What content did you need to learn? Discuss the specific challenges you encountered. Explain the specific challenges that an ELL arriving in the United States at the age of 10 might encounter.

2. *Review:* Explain why ELLs are likely to benefit from instruction with more proficient speakers of English.

3. *Review and apply:* Discuss the benefits of group work for ELLs (with proficiency levels of early intermediate, intermediate, and transitioning), and decide which groupings might be more effective for students within each proficiency level in content-area lessons.

4. *Reflect and apply:* What has been your experience with ELLs? Have the students in your school struggled with classwork in a way that seems inconsistent with their conversational language? List several of the conversational skills that a student in your content-area class must demonstrate. Now, list several academic-language skills that are necessary to access the content in your classroom.

Summary

Whereas Krashen's theory focuses on input, the theory of communicative competence—which was first proposed by Hymes and later expanded by Canale—focuses on the interaction between input and output, and illustrates the ways in which ELLs make sense of language and develop proficiency through attention to form and production of output. Canale identifies four areas of communicative competence: grammatical, sociolinguistic, discourse, and strategic, all of which are enhanced by purposeful communication. The ZPD reinforces the importance of providing ELLs with ongoing opportunities to communicate with more capable others in academic conversations. By engaging in these academic conversations, ELLs practice language structures and receive immediate feedback, which builds academic language.

It is extremely important that teachers do not mistake conversational proficiency for academic proficiency. As Juan, the Ecuadorian student in Mr. Johnson's class illustrated, ELLs may well be able to carry on conversations about casual topics without understanding the language of the classroom. While the academic challenges that confront ELLs are great, ELLs who enter school in the upper grades also possess strengths that teachers can capitalize on. This is the topic of the next section.

ADOLESCENT SECOND-LANGUAGE LEARNERS

Middle and secondary school ELLs are not blank slates; they have proficiency in their first language(s), world knowledge, and well-developed schemata. Adolescent ELLs have a "well-developed capacity for memory, pattern recognition, induction, categorization, generalization, [and] inference" (Wong Fillmore, cited in Crawford, 2004). These capacities allow ELLs to use cognitive processes and knowledge of their first language to help them understand the linguistic structure of English and use their social interaction with native-English speakers to make sense of English (Lenneberg, 1967).

As we noted in the discussion of the sensitive period, older students and adults remain capable of developing high levels of proficiency in second languages. They will, however, often maintain their first-language influences (syntax and phonology) and may retain their first-language accents. These influences need not interfere with academic achievement, as, for example, some speakers at the United Nations; Dr. Henry Kissinger, former Secretary of State; or Arnold Schwarzenegger, Governor of California, illustrate. Their accents and first-language patterns have hardly interfered with their academic success!

Older ELLs may enter U.S. schools with well-developed schemata that facilitate the development of academic English. In the following section, we will review schema theory and then discuss the theory of common underlying proficiency, which explains the importance of helping ELLs access their schemata.

SCHEMA THEORY

Schema theory is attributed to Anderson (1977) and explains the elaborate and meaningful mental network that organizes and stores mental representations of concepts. Schemata (the plural of schema) change as learners gain more information about a concept. Simplistically, our existing schemata both shape the ways we make sense out of new knowledge and experiences and are shaped by our experiences. Consider the schemata that underlie the following everyday exchange. Mary Jones is preparing for a trip and will travel by air. She shares her plans with a close acquaintance, who tells her, "Be sure to give yourself plenty of extra time. You are leaving at rush hour; the security has increased since 9/11, and it will take you a while to get through the screening." This seems like a simple exchange—one, in fact, that could easily take place between two people passing one another in the hallway. Is it, though?

Chances are that an English-speaking student who has recently flown to a vacation spot would understand the conversation. An ELL who had recently traveled through U.S. airports might have the schemata necessary to understand the exchange but would need to learn the collocation *rush hour* and perhaps additional meanings for the words *security* and *screening*. An ELL, however, whose vacations have been mostly limited to caring for younger siblings at home is unlikely to understand the words *rush hour, security*, and *screening* or possess the schemata that underlie the conversation. He or she may not have the schemata to make sense of this exchange. We use this simplistic, everyday example to illustrate how we use the schemata we have developed to make sense of our worlds.

A variety of academic-like experiences combine to enrich our *schemata*, which are necessary to make sense of new content, vocabulary, and linguistic structures. For example, secondary students in middle and secondary grades who have regularly attended the theatre with family have likely developed schemata for standard elements in plays, such as setting, plot, and acts, as well as dramatic conventions, such as soliloquy, asides, chorus, and monologues. They may also have exposure to a variety of linguistic structures (e.g., Shakespeare's English). Students with these experiences enter the secondary ELA classroom with schemata that promote access to and understanding of the language of drama. These well-developed schemata will enable these students to actively engage in grade-appropriate discussions about plays and other dramatic productions.

The language and experiences most valued within American schools are steeped in middle-class culture, knowledge, and values. Consequently, experiences that are most valued for the development of academic schemata are upper middle class as well and may include visits to museums and art galleries, attendance at artistic performances, and travel. While other life experiences, such as learning to care for younger siblings, attending religious services, planning meals, and engaging in oral history with others in the community may be equally valid and valuable, these experiences are often undervalued in U.S. schools. To be successful in U.S. classrooms, ELLs will also need to develop academic schemata and academic standard English.

COMMON UNDERLYING PROFICIENCY

ELLs who have developed schemata and conceptual understandings in their first language(s) do not need to relearn these. The theory of a central processing system or *common underlying proficiency* (Cummins, 1981; see also Baker, 2006) illustrates one central and integrated source for thought that can be accessed by multiple languages. The schemata (mental representations of content-area concepts) that ELLs have built in their first language remain accessible. ELLs need to develop academic English for these content-area concepts stored in their schemata, but not the concepts themselves.

Common underlying proficiency (as illustrated in Model 2.3) gives emphasis to the importance of evaluating the knowledge and understandings that ELLs have in their first language(s) and then assisting them to develop English academic language to use these understandings in reading, listening, speaking, and writing in English. The theory illustrates the importance of bilingual instruction and materials for ELLs; students who learn academic concepts in their first languages can then access these concepts in English. It also helps explain the importance of evaluating ELLs' ability to read and write in their first language; ELLs who are literate in their first languages will transfer these abilities to English literacy. The dual iceberg is used to illustrate two languages; additional peaks could be added to illustrate multiple languages.

MODEL 2.3   **Dual Iceberg: Common Underlying Proficiency**

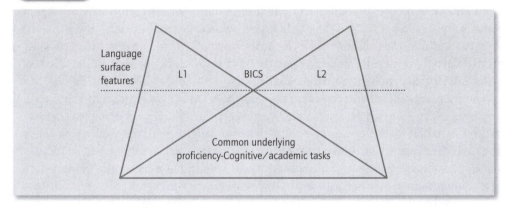

SOURCE: Cummins (2005, p. 7).

Review, Reflect, Apply

1. *Review:* How is the theory of common underlying proficiency important to the instruction of ELLs in content-area classrooms?

2. *Apply:* Why is it important to understand the schemata students bring to the content-area classroom? List and discuss at least two ways you can build schemata for your content area.

CHAPTER SUMMARY

Adolescent ELLs bring a variety of experiences to the content-area classroom, including previous experiences and first-language proficiencies. The common underlying proficiency theory stresses the importance of recognizing these strengths. ELLs do *not* have to relearn concepts; they need to learn the academic English language for these concepts. Conversely, ELLs (and other students) may not have developed the schemata necessary to access concepts. For example, it is unlikely that Fredy Solis, the ELL introduced in Chapter 1, and many other native-English speakers in an eighth-grade ELA class have well-developed schemata for the theatre. Unless Fredy has been taught U.S. history since his arrival in the United States, he is also unlikely to have schemata for topics having to do with, for example, the Civil War. It is important for teachers to determine the schemata ELLs bring to the classroom and then to build additional necessary schemata.

Planning and implementing effective instruction for ELLs with intermediate to transitioning proficiency requires an understanding of the complexity of academic-language acquisition. Content-area teachers of ELLs must understand the instructional implications of second-language acquisition theories. In addition to meeting the needs of ELLs, instruction that effectively combines content and language will improve educational outcomes for many other students in the classroom.

Planning effective instruction also requires that teachers know the students who sit in front of them in their classes. Just as this chapter began with a discussion of the complexity of first language, the next chapter challenges readers to consider the complexity of first culture, the strengths within different cultures, and the benefits of developing a culturally responsive teaching style.

Assessment Evidence Activities

AE-1 In small groups or individually, prepare a presentation for a group of colleagues explaining the principles of first- and second-language acquisition using the theories and terms in LO-1.

AE-2 In small groups, discuss the development of a sense of phonology, morphology, syntax, and semantics by native speakers of a language. Speculate as to the difficulties that might confront ELLs in each of these areas, and present your findings with clear examples to the class.

AE-3 Using content-area materials at the grade level you teach (texts or state/district curriculum frameworks), review the academic language in your particular content area (ELA, math, social studies, science, art, music, physical education, family consumer science, etc.). Discuss the schemata students need to make sense of this content-area language.

AE-4 List and discuss specific examples of social and academic language in content-area classroom communication. If you are not yet teaching, list and discuss specific examples of social and academic language that occur in communication within your college-level classes.

AE-5 Imagine that a parent asks you to explain how his daughter (an intermediate-level ELL who was recently placed in your class) will learn English. Explain English language acquisition to the parent based on what you have learned in this chapter.

Resources for Further Reading

- The Child's Learning of English Morphology by Jean Berko http://childes.psy.cmu.edu/topics/wugs/wugs.pdf

- Discussion of Krashen: Stephen Krashen's Web site contains the complete volume of second-language acquisition and second-language learning online. The site also contains a paper on academic-language proficiency presented with Clara Lee Brown. www.sdkrashen.com

- For a complete (and very accessible) discussion about linguistics and language, readers are encouraged to read Pinker (2007). *The language instinct*. New York: HarperCollins.

- For a comprehensive discussion of second language acquisition and existing programs for second language learners, readers are encourage to consult Baker (2006). *Foundations of bilingual education and bilingualism*. Clevedon, UK: Multilingual Matters.

Culture, Adolescents, and Culturally Responsive Instruction

Enduring understanding: Culture shapes the way we teach and the ways in which our students learn.

CHAPTER 2 DISCUSSED THE ACQUISITION OF A FIRST LANGUAGE, A PROCESS THAT OFTEN APPEARS SO SEAMLESS THAT it is seldom given much thought. Often, little thought is given to the acquisition of a first culture, which occurs through early immersion in cultural worlds. Yet one's cultures determine how one thinks and acts and how one learns and teaches. In the classroom, the juxtaposition of the culture of the teacher with cultures of the students either creates a positive setting for learning or causes cultural mismatches that place many ELLs at risk for educational failure. Chapter 3 focuses on the ways culture shapes teaching and learning. It begins by defining culture and cultural difference as these terms will be used in this text and then engages readers in an activity to think about their own cultures. The chapter then presents three adolescent ELLs: Fredy Solis, who was introduced in Chapter 1; Katy Boureth, a 9th-grade Cambodian American ELL; and Aadam Jasaam, a 10th-grade Iraqi-born ELL. Chapter 3 concludes with a discussion of culturally responsive teaching and guidelines for developing and implementing a culturally responsive pedagogy.

LEARNING OUTCOMES

The following learning outcomes (LOs) serve as a guide to Chapter 3. At the end of the chapter are assessment activities that are aligned with each LO.

WHAT IS CULTURE?

Regardless of how we define culture, one indisputable fact is that culture is a dynamic, ubiquitous, and uniquely human phenomenon. "Culture is man's medium; there is not one aspect of human life that is not touched and altered by culture" (Hall, 1976, p. 16). "We are, in sum, incomplete or unfinished animals who complete or finish ourselves through culture" (Geertz, 2000, p. 49). Au (2006) and Lowe (1996) use the terms *vertical* and *horizontal* to describe the general and persistent as well as the dynamic and evolving nature of culture. Vertical culture refers to traditional or historical values and orientations—for example, the traditional Cambodian loyalty and obligation to family (Chhuon, Hudley, & Macias, 2006). Horizontal culture, on the other hand, refers to the more dynamic aspects of culture, traditional values that are shaped by time, place, and other situational factors. For example, second-generation American adolescents become acculturated more quickly than their parents (Lee, 2005; Portes & Rumbaut, 2001). Adolescents who interpret for non-English-speaking parents may experience role reversal (The National Child Traumatic Stress Network [NCTSN], 2005; Portes & Rumbaut, 2001) and therefore, for example, may replace or extend the traditional cultural value of family loyalty (vertical) with loyalty to peers outside the family (horizontal). As Geertz (2000) explains, "We finish ourselves . . . not through culture in general but through highly particular forms of it: Dovuan and Javanese, Hopi and Italian, upper-class, academic and commercial" (p. 49). That is, we are continually shaped by vertical and horizontal forms of culture that influence what we think, what we do, and how we do it.

While many frameworks can be used to delimit discussions about cultural difference, we borrow from Kathryn Au (2006) and limit our discussion of difference to language, ethnicity, and socioeconomic status, factors also identified by Gay (2000), Villegas and Lucas (2002), and Nieto (1999). Table 3.1 illustrates the complex structure of culture.

TABLE 3.1 Vertical and Horizontal Nature of Culture

	Ethnicity	Language	Socioeconomic Factors
Vertical	Traditional practices; deeply held beliefs (religion, relationships, child-rearing practices); outward manifestations of culture such as traditional holidays, foods, celebrations, music	Ancestral language(s)	Historical access to education, nutrition, health care affecting deeply held beliefs and behaviors (For example, large families with many children because of high infant mortality, need for children for farming and caring for elderly parents.)
Horizontal	A mix of traditional practices with influences from the new culture—Western clothes, music, peer group influence	May be a blend of home languages and English learned in a variety of school and out-of-school settings; may result in bilingualism, or loss of the home language, and limited academic English	The mixture of historical socioeconomic status and status experienced in the United States; this can be situational or generational (Spring, 2000; Ogbu, 1990)

Ogbu (1990) and Spring (2000) explain that socioeconomic factors are determined, at least in part, by the historical and present value the mainstream culture places on the ethnicity and language of another culture. Historically in the United States, European American language and ethnicity have been valued, and the ethnicity and languages of groups such as Native Americans, Mexican Americans, African Americans, and Puerto Ricans frequently have been undervalued. Because the mainstream culture is dominant and determines what is valued, nondominant cultural groups are kept in positions without power. When a group is undervalued and considered deficient, its ethnicity, language, and/or socioeconomic backgrounds may be considered deficits to overcome.

DEFINING ONE'S CULTURE

The vertical and horizontal nature of cultures may help explain why many may have difficulty describing *their* cultures. Mainstream teachers with whom we have worked mention the ways in which they recognize and celebrate *other* cultures within their schools and classrooms. They refer primarily to traditional multicultural literature, celebrations, foods, and holidays—the vertical culture. When asked to focus on their cultures, they remain fixed on some vertical form of culture, including traditional foods and holiday celebrations. For example, Liz shares the Canadian American custom of the early-morning Christmas meal, directly following midnight Mass—a meal with poutines (meat and potato dumplings), meat pies, and then turkey with "all the fixings." Josh chimes in that his Polish traditions required sauerkraut, kielbasa, and cod to be eaten on Christmas Eve. Horizontal influences become more apparent when Maryellen, who comes from a large Italian American family, recalls boisterous and happy meals with the extended family, lots of food, and lots more talking. (The specific foods and languages shaped in part by living in the United States rather than Italy.) Kaylie reminisces about Sunday drives and dinners with aunts, uncles, and cousins at the home of her grandparents. Participants' notions of their own cultures remain centered on food and celebrations.

When asked about the culture of their childhood, participants often describe themselves as "just American" and their childhood cultural experiences as "just normal." Others lament that they "have no culture" and say that it saddens them that they have "lost" their cultures. Rogoff (2003) explains, "It is common for people to think of themselves as having no culture ("Who me? I don't have an accent") or to take for granted the circumstances of their historical period, unless they have contact with several cultural communities" (p. 11).

The vertical culture of these teachers' homelands has blended gradually and somewhat seamlessly across several generations and is reflected in new horizontal cultures, which have been and continue to be shaped by place, time, and situation. Mainstream teachers have lived in the United States (predominately in middle-class communities) for a period of time, have attended U.S. schools and colleges, and are professionally employed. By all accounts, they have successfully negotiated the U.S. school system, which represents and perpetuates the dominant U.S. culture (Guild, 2001; Cuban, 1993; Hall, 1976) and is grounded in European American traditions, experiences, and status (Gay, 2000; Howard, 2006). This culture is reflected in the textbooks students read (Gay, 2000) as well as what and how teachers teach (Au, 2006; Villegas & Lucas, 2002). The mainstream dominant culture in education has likely, at least in part, influenced all teachers who have successfully navigated the educational system from kindergarten to college graduation. As members of this dominant culture, we are like fish swimming in water. While we may not notice the water, we depend on this water—this cultural medium—for everything we know and do (Kluckhohn, 1949).

CULTURAL ORIENTATIONS

We often think of culture as something possessed by others, and at its extremes, this something is either strangely exotic, such as the noble savage to be admired, or deficient, such as savages in need of education and remediation (Rogoff, 2003). In this section, we provide an activity to encourage readers to think about their *own* culture as this culture is lived day to day. Later in this section, we will link cultural differences to the classroom. We begin, however, by discussing culture separately from education and, thus, away from the power positions of teachers and their students.

There are many different ways to consider cultural orientations (Hall, 1976). One useful model is the value orientation method, developed by Kluckhohn and Strodtbeck (1961) and widely used since that time. The model, shown in Table 3.2, proposes that cultural perspectives and behavior can be broadly understood within five major *orientations*. Within cultural groups (and again one belongs to both vertical and horizontal groups), it is thought that there are general orientations (or ingrained preferences). Great variations exist *within* cultures, however, making it more sensible to consider each *orientation* on a continuum, along which each group/culture might occupy a band or range.

Working through the value orientation model encourages us to become aware of our own orientations as well as the possible orientations of others. There is no right or wrong orientation. It is not necessary to agree with the orientations of another culture; it is however, helpful to recognize that differences within orientations exist. Orientations vary greatly within groups (vertically and horizontally) as well as from situation to situation. For example, the dominant social structure orientation for mainstream Americans is thought to be closer to *individual orientation* than to *group orientation*. Yet mainstream Americans may maintain extended family structures that are more similar to group orientation than to individual orientation. The difference between the expected and actual orientation is also evident for time. While dominant *time orientation* for mainstream Americans is widely considered to be *future*, during vacations Americans may show preferences for *present time orientation*. Orientations may also be dispositional, such as the student who does not read the course syllabus or the friend who consistently shows up at the airport at the last minute.

While reading through the cultural orientations, readers are encouraged to map their culture(s) by determining where they fit on each continuum. Are these orientations situational? Are the orientations similar across students, coworkers, family members, or other acquaintances? Readers are encouraged to challenge themselves to consider how they would negotiate day-to-day and major decisions with others who have very different orientations. When we refer to people and groups in this section, we speak in specifics and do not intend to imply that all participants from any group will act the same way.

Orientation 1: Human Nature

Our orientation toward human nature influences our perspectives on the role government should play in our lives, the ways in which we interact with neighbors and community members,

TABLE 3.2 Value Orientation Model

Value Orientation	Value Continuum
Human nature	Innately good . . . . Innately bad
Relationship with nature (and relationship with fate)	Harmony . . . . Control
Time	Past . . . . Future
Social structure	Group . . . . Individual
Activity	Being . . . . Doing

SOURCE: Based on Kluckhohn and Strodtbeck (1961).

and, perhaps most important our perspectives on the way children should be raised. If our basic *orientation for human nature* falls close to *innately bad*, we will subscribe to different child-rearing practices than if our orientation is closer to *innately good*. For example, middle-class American parents, who see children as willful and in need of correction (innately bad), explicitly teach the values of sharing and interacting "appropriately" (according to middle-class American cultural norms) with others to children as young as one year old (Rogoff, 2003). "Be a good boy, Christopher, and share your toy with Andrew," a middle-class American mother may tell her child. The mother reinforces this concept by praising the child for sharing. When Andrew is later playing with the toy and Christopher abruptly takes it from him, which makes Andrew cry, Christopher's mother may well retrieve the toy from Christopher, return it to Andrew, and explain to the now crying Christopher that it is not okay to take from others; one must be *taught* to share.

Barbara Rogoff (2003) contrasts this practice with the practices of other cultural groups and explains that within other cultures, for example, Guatemalan, Mayan, Japanese, and Inuit, toddlers may not be expected to conform to rules. In fact, it is perfectly "appropriate" (according to the norms of the Mayan populations that Rogoff observed) for the wishes of toddlers to be granted by others and for older children to acquiesce to the will of younger children. During one of Rogoff's visits to a Mayan family, a 15-month-old boy was hitting children and adults with a stick puppet. The adults and older children lifted their hands to protect themselves and the little children near them but did not attempt to stop the child. The mother later explained to Rogoff, "He couldn't have been trying to hurt anybody; he's just a baby. He wasn't being aggressive; he's too young; he doesn't understand. Babies don't do things on purpose" (p. 165). Thus, the orientation of human nature as innately good in this one Mayan community observed by Rogoff resulted in a far different pattern of child rearing than the one observed in mainstream America.

Orientation 2: Relationship With Nature and Fate

Human belief in the ability to control or to live in harmony with nature and fate also exists along a continuum. The *orientation of fate* places humans' beliefs about their relationship with fate along an orientation continuum from total *harmony* to total *control*.

Our friend Annie's trip to Costa Rica illustrates this continuum. Annie frequently traveled to Cost Rica and stayed at the home of Costa Rican friends, where David, an American businessman, and several Costa Rican students and workers rented rooms. Lack of air-conditioning often resulted in owners and tenants alike spending most of their at-home time on the expansive veranda, where David conducted much of his business. Annie soon learned that this was David's third two-month trip to Costa Rica in an attempt to finalize the purchase of a shrimp farm. David made endless phone calls to arrange for inspections and permissions, often getting his appointment book out and beginning to finalize a definite date and time only to hear the speaker on the other end of the line saying, "Sí, si Diós quiere . . . " (Yes, if God is willing). At that point, David would sigh loudly and raise his voice. Surprised, the Costa Ricans on the veranda would first glance sharply at David, then politely smile and excuse themselves. Whereas David continually sought contingencies for all foreseeable problems having to do with weather or transportation, his contacts refused to do so. They made plans to meet David, but if an issue arose, the meeting was postponed. David shared his frustration with Annie: "I just can't get anyone to commit to a firm time or place. If I hear 'Sí, si Diós quiere' one more time I'm going to scream."

David did not appear to realize that his loud voice and sighs were considered rude and made his Costa Rican hosts and co-tenants (and likely, his business associates) uncomfortable. According to Annie, David seemed nearer to finalizing the deal when she left Costa Rica, but we are not entirely sure how or if his negotiations ended.

Orientation 3: Time

Reverence for the past, the desire and ability to stay in the present, or the need to plan for the future are determined in U.S. culture, at least in part, by our socioeconomic opportunities. Mainstream Americans view time as currency that can be spent, saved, or wasted. They generally adopt a *future* time orientation (Spindler, Spindler, Trueba, & Williams, 1990), which is evident in preventative health care; investing in retirement funds; saving and preparing for college; and carefully scheduling their children's time into organized activities that will prepare them for academic, athletic, and social success, including tutoring sessions, language lessons, academic clubs, sports clinics with private coaches, and music lessons (Phelan, Davidson, & Yu, 1998).

Rogoff (2003) uses the metaphor of a racetrack to describe the importance of time in the American view of development—children are on time, behind time, or ahead of time. She attributes this understanding of time to the American model of formal schooling, which sorts children into grades depending on their ages (rather than stage of development) and then ranks them according to their accomplishments.

This relationship between milestones (being on time) and development is not common to all groups (Rogoff, 2003). In fact, Rogoff (2003) explains that when she studied at Piaget's Swiss institute, "The question of how quickly children can reach developmental 'milestones' was referred to as the 'American question'" (p. 160). Pinker (2007) and Heath (1983), too, explain that in many groups, parents do not attempt to teach their children to talk; they assume that their children will speak when they are ready. And then it will be sensible to talk with them—there is no race to development. Interestingly, Rogoff (2003) explains that in the Mayan community she studied, age is not marked by time at all but rather is relative to others within the family and community and determining who is senior to whom.

Rogoff (2003) contrasted the future orientation of middle-class Americans with the past orientation of the Mayans, with whom she worked in the 1970s. She noted that when an adult came across a child in this town, the focus was not on asking the child's name and age (as it typically is in the United States) but rather on who the child's parents were, thus focusing on the child's relationship to senior others and to the past.

Orientation 4: Social Structure

The value orientation model also places social structure on a continuum from group orientation to individual orientation. One powerful example of group orientation was provided by Hmong students in an adult ESL class. The Hmong students had attended all school events and celebrations with their families and had developed good relationships with the other students and the staff. One day, they quietly spoke of the horror of their earlier exodus to Thailand during the civil unrest and chaos.

Here is the story they told: The Hmong populations who knew the countryside well had often worked in collaboration with U.S. forces. When the U.S. forces withdrew from Vietnam and Cambodia, the Hmong had to flee as well. One evening, the members of a small Hmong village community began their long trip together. They knew that they needed to reach Thailand for survival. They traveled at night in total silence, fearing they would be ambushed by the Viet Cong. Silence was the code, as any noise could reveal their presence and result in death for the entire community. In preparation for crossing the Mekong River, the Hmong made makeshift rafts from grasses and prepared to work across the river in caravan fashion. Mothers pulled their floating babies and worked to hush their cries. Babies who could not be quieted were submerged underwater; those who died were cut loose from the caravan. The Hmong students explained that this act may have saved the entire group, including many other babies.

The Hmong account of their exodus (and the importance of protecting the group) can be contrasted with the individual orientation portrayed in the fictional rescue of Private James Ryan in the 1998 Academy Award–winning film, *Saving Private Ryan*. In the film, eight soldiers, who have experienced the unfathomable horror of the invasion at Normandy, return behind enemy lines to save *one* man, the surviving son of the Ryan family. Most of the soldiers die in this mission, but Private Ryan is saved. The contrast between the Hmong exodus and the rescue of Private Ryan is a dramatic illustration of contrasting *social structure orientations*.

Our social orientation also influences the routine decisions we make and our perspectives of the behaviors of others. Elizabeth and Yvonne have been close friends since Yvonne's immigration to the United States from Peru in the early 1990s. They share many interests and speak the same languages, and Elizabeth is the madrina (godmother) to Yvonnes's only child, which is considered a great honor. They often communicate across differences in social orientation. Yvonne has a group orientation that results in her opening her very small home to relatives and friends for extended periods of time, often months, without notice. People share bedrooms and create makeshift bedrooms when they run out of space. Elizabeth shares a larger home with her husband and has converted unused bedrooms into office space. She views her home as her sanctuary, and her position of individual orientation influences her decision not to share her home unless there is a crisis. Initially, when Yvonne and her relatives came to Elizabeth's home (generally unannounced), they commented, "This is such a *large* home for two people." Yvonne and her family viewed Elizabeth's individual orientation as American and selfish, while Elizabeth viewed Yvonne's group orientation as both generous and intrusive. Friends for many years, they have learned to interact across these different cultural orientations.

Social structure orientation also influences major decisions made within families—for example, in deciding the program of studies a secondary student will complete or whether a child should leave the family unit to attend a university located several states away or remain home to attend community college and help with family responsibilities.

Orientation 5: Activity Orientations

Doing orientations value activities that result in measurable accomplishments, whereas *being orientations* value *who* one is, one's family, position, and status. The mainstream culture of the United States is characterized by a *doing orientation*, which is related to the mainstream obsession with using time wisely. The tendency to measure accomplishments begins with the way we interact with our children even prior to birth. Expectant parents attempt to develop the intelligence of their unborn child by listening to music and talking to the baby. Once the child is born, parents invest in enrichment activities, games, and even classes. Milestones are carefully marked and measured (Rogoff, 2003). The quest to meet measurable accomplishments occurs throughout the school years. Students compete and are rewarded for their individual measurable accomplishments. Students prepare for acceptance to the best colleges, often spending considerable money on tutors and preparation for tests.

Other groups, including (but not limited to) some Native Hawaiian, American Indian, and some Latino cultures, may fall closer to the being orientation. It is not that accomplishments are unimportant; parents who ascribe to a being orientation are equally proud of their children, yet there is more value placed on less tangible accomplishments, such as being a good daughter or son, and a helpful, cooperative and productive member of the family or the community (Au, 2005).

Review, Reflect, Apply

Reflect: Where do you fall on each orientation continuum? Discuss the ways in which your cultural orientation may differ from the orientations of your students and their families.

THE MAINSTREAM CLASSROOM: MATCH OR MISMATCH?

We used the cultural orientation model as one way to consider culture and the ingrained orientations that teachers and learners bring to the classroom. Cultural orientations illustrate some of the ways our cultures influence what we consider to be appropriate forms of behavior and communication. The norms and expectations for behavior and communication in most U.S. classrooms are consistent with those of the mainstream, dominant culture. Therefore, for mainstream teachers and students, the transition between home and school is generally a smooth one. The rules and norms within the school approximate the rules and norms within the home, and the culture of the home is affirmed by the culture of the school.

This is not the situation for many ELLs. Regardless of whether they are recent arrivals or have been in the United States for many years, they come to classrooms with previous educational, personal, and background experiences that differ from those of mainstream teachers and students. When the culture of the ELL differs from the culture of the teacher and the expectations within the classroom, the ELL must navigate multiple worlds (Au, 1993, 2006; Phelan et al., 1998) and, in fact, travel from one world to another as he or she moves from home to school and back again (Au, 1993). Culture is the way we "finish" (and define) ourselves (Geertz, 2000, p. 49), and when teachers convey that a student's culture and the culture of his or her family are deficient, the implication is that the student is also deficient.

In addition to determining classroom rules and norms, the mainstream culture also determines instructional content that is either highly valued or largely ignored. Indeed, the choice of which authors' works are analyzed, whose accounts of historical events are studied, and which scientific concepts are learned is decided by the mainstream culture. History, for example, is rarely explored through the perspectives of the defeated but rather is told and perpetuated through the words of the victor. History is also told through the lenses of the dominant population. Thus, ELLs are presented with curricula that may be foreign to them—that may disregard their backgrounds and convey that their culture and history are unimportant.

The differences between home and school present difficulties for many ELLs. Additionally, ELLs may also have had experiences beyond the influence and control of the school that have caused economic, social, and emotional trauma, including difficult transitions from their homeland to the United States, especially if they or their parents have fled from countries that were made unsafe by war, civil unrest, or abject poverty. Here in the United States, many ELLs then confront prejudice and racism, which cause additional trauma.

Trauma, Uprooting, and Culture Shock

In 2005, NCTSN published findings of the condition of child refugees, which illustrate the effects of trauma on young refugees. According to the report, refugee children are often separated from parents and other primary caregivers. Even when the family unit remains intact, parents who have suffered severe trauma of violence and torture are often victims of posttraumatic stress disorder (PTSD) themselves and, therefore, less able to nurture their children. Parents who have less control over their own lives are also less able to protect their children, which fosters a lack of trust on the part of the child. NCTSN considers three stages of trauma and adjustment for refugees: preflight, flight, and settlement. These are consistent with the stages of uprooting and culture shock identified by Igoa (1995) in describing the immigrant experience.

Uprooting (Preflight)

During this stage, children of all ages are apt to experience, witness, or even participate in violence. They may or may not be separated from their parents. They often have less space in which to play and are likely to be supervised by caretakers who have little emotional energy for childlike curiosity and games. These circumstances adversely affect children's ability to attend school, which interrupts both educational and social development.

Uprooting (Flight)

While in flight, adults and children experience a sense of uncertainty. They must rely completely on outside authorities for their most basic needs. During this time, it is common for children to be separated from their parents if the family is temporarily relocated to a refugee camp, where "inhabitants are depersonalized and where people become numbers without names" (NCTSN, 2005, p. 9). The flight experience has a profound effect on adults and children of all ages and may undermine traditional cultural beliefs in children who cannot depend on their parents as authority figures during this time.

Resettlement: Culture Shock

During resettlement, children and their families are exposed to different belief systems, cultures, and languages. Often, as parents struggle to meet basic needs, their children are learning the new culture and language. Children's ability to acquire language and culture more quickly than their parents frequently results in a type of role reversal within the family structure: Parents depend on their children, which may have a negative impact on children's trust in their parents.

Conflicts also arise as children of all ages begin to develop dual cultural identities. These struggles are magnified if the adolescent refugee is discriminated against because of race, culture, or religion. All too frequently, these adolescents become increasingly susceptible to negative peer influences and become involved with drugs and gang activity (NCTSN, 2005).

The negative effects of the refugee experience may endure for generations. Parents who suffer from PTSD may be less able to provide nurturing environments to their infants, establish and patiently convey consistent rules to their toddlers, engage in creative play with their three- to five-year-olds, or help their school-age children with academics.

While only a small percentage of ELLs can be formally classified as refugees, and only a portion of individuals who experience trauma develop PTSD, many ELLs who immigrate to the United States experience difficult transitions that can be understood within the framework of preflight (uprooting), flight (uprooting) and resettlement (culture shock).

The following section introduces three ELLs: (1) Aadam Jassam Ali, a refugee from Iraq whose experience is illustrative of preflight, flight, and resettlement; (2) Fredy Solis, who experienced uprooting and culture shock when he was forced to leave his native Dominican Republic, leaving behind his mother, sister, and pet; and (3) Katy Boureth, the American-born daughter of Cambodian refugees, who experienced preflight, flight, and resettlement.

THREE ENGLISH LANGUAGE LEARNERS

Like the majority of ELLs (including those such as Maria, the speaker in the *Methods of Sheltered English Instruction* course, discussed in Chapter 1) who eventually become highly successful academically, Adaam, Fredy, and Katy struggle in school. We do not suggest that their cases represent the broad range of experiences that ELLs bring to the classroom. We do believe that Aadam, Fredy, and Katy provide three perspectives on the challenges that many ELLs experience in U.S. schools. Following the three cases, readers are asked to complete a chart of each ELL's experiences, their vertical and horizontal cultures, the differences between each ELL and mainstream teachers, and the strengths and needs that each ELL brings to the classroom.

Aadam Jassam Ali

Walking through the halls is always the worst for Aadam Jassam Ali, and he is relieved to see he is close to the classroom where, if he is quiet, he can get lost in the middle of the room—he can be invisible. Aadam turned 16 the previous August. He transferred to the West City School two months ago. This is the third school he has attended since moving to the United States two years ago. Aadam had missed much school since leaving Iraq nearly four years ago—first moving to Algeria, then to Paris, and finally to the United States, where his uncle and aunt, and their three children, have a small apartment. Aadam first attended the Central School. He, with his parents and younger brother, was living in the apartment of his uncle, Osama. After four months of working long hours at a nearby restaurant, his mother and father had saved enough money for a security deposit on a new apartment. Moving required that the children switch schools. Aadam did not mind leaving the Central School. The students made fun of the way he talked, his family, his mother's hijab; they taunted him about being a terrorist. A group of boys yelled, "Hey, Osama!" as he passed them in the halls. They could not know that Osama was in fact the name of Aadam's own uncle, an honorable name that meant "lionlike," or that Aadam and his family had nothing to do with the attack on New York City's twin towers on September 11, 2001. Aadam did not try to explain—he did not want to get into trouble. He did not want to shame his family.

Aadam was relieved when the family saved enough money for their own apartment and enrolled him in the East Side School. The family's new apartment did not work out well, however. His aunt, Ghadah, had warned his mother that it was not safe to wear her hijab, that anti-Muslim sentiment was still high in many areas of the city, although four years had passed since September 11. But Mariam, his mother, had given up much of her culture and identity since leaving Iraq nearly five years earlier. There, she was a respected pediatrician; here, she waited tables and hoped for tips that would grow into an apartment security deposit. There, she had many friends and her family; here, there were only her brother and sister-in-law, who also worked long hours to keep the apartment and buy food. The hijab was one of the few things that kept her feeling connected to the world she had left behind. Mariam was threatened as she returned to her home from work one evening: "Towel head Arab, you're in America now. We don't want any towel head terrorists here." A stone was thrown through the family's living room window. Faisal, Aadam's father, was afraid to call the police—and he knew it would not help. Aadam's family moved, and he was enrolled in the West City School.

Aadam often thinks of his school in Iraq. He was an excellent student, earned good grades, and had many friends. He thinks about his earlier math classes, in which he had excelled. Since he left Iraq, he feels sick to his stomach when he thinks about going to class. Although he has learned much English, he struggles with his work, and having learned English as an adolescent, his accent is thick.

Aadam also wonders about how he will perform the salat (prayer) as required by the Five Pillars of Islam. He turns his body to Mecca and prays in the morning before school and after sunset without a problem, but how can he possibly perform salat at noon and in the midafternoon as required? He is in class during this time. He worries about upcoming Ramadan, the holiest period in the Islamic year, and the fasting and about how he will be able to fast while at school. He must attend Eid prayer services at the end of Ramadan, and he prays that his teachers will not schedule tests or assignments during this time.

A review of Aadam's folder reveals that he is an intermediate ELL. Now in Grade 10, Aadam reads and writes in English at a level that approximates that of the sixth grade. Although he has changed schools several times, Aadam's overall grades are quite good—mostly Bs and Cs. His teachers describe him as thoughtful and bright but quiet and sometimes withdrawn. He struggles with pronunciation and is generally reluctant to speak in front of a large group. There is a note about adjustment issues, possibly due to the backlash against Muslim Americans that followed the attacks of September 11.

Fredy Solis

As an eighth-grade student at Turner High School, Fredy feels rather comfortable. He has a solid group of friends who like to play basketball and baseball after school, and though academics are not his strong suit, he is known as the silly kid who will make a crowd laugh at any moment by performing any variety of harmless pranks. Most of Fredy's friends, like Fredy himself, come from Spanish-speaking homes in his neighborhood, where everyone shares a bedroom with siblings in small, modest apartments stacked on top of one another.

Fredy likes that his friends live the same way. Once, he went over to his friend Ian's house after school—he lived across town in a beautiful new subdivision. Fredy could not believe that one family lived in that whole house, with no aunts, uncles, cousins, or grandparents! He decided that he would not ask Ian to come over and that his mom probably would not let him anyway.

At age 10, Fredy, with his father, Jorge, and his older sister, Carlota, left the Elías Piña province of the Dominican Republic to come to the United States. In Elías Piña, on the rural Dominican/Haitian border, life seemed very free to Fredy. He did not realize that his family was struggling as he did not know a different life. He spent much of his time exploring the countryside with his dog, Coco. Fredy woke up most days, walked 30 minutes to school with Coco and his little sisters in tow, and then waited for the teacher. If the teacher (whose time was mostly voluntary) did show up, Fredy stayed for classes. However, many days he waited around, and no teacher appeared. So his sisters walked home to help out his mother, Miguelina, while he and Coco went off on an adventure. Some days, when money for uniforms or books was tight, Fredy and his sisters did not bother making the trek to school. They simply stayed home and helped out on their family's small plot of land.

In Elías Piña, it is estimated that 92% of the population lives in poverty ("France Donates Money," 2006). Fredy's parents worked on a small farm, which barely supported their modest lifestyle. When the floods of May 2004 hit, life became more difficult. Large portions of their crop and much of the region's water systems were destroyed. Since then, family income, access to drinking water, and proper sanitation have been sparse in that area. Fredy's father had cousins in the United States; they lived in a small city, where local businesses operated in Spanish and there was work to be had. Fredy's parents decided to apply for family visas and move the family to a place where the work was steady and there was clean water and food to live on. They were excited that a community was in place in the United States and that their family there could help them navigate the new place.

With backlogs in the processing of family visas, however, Jorge and Miguelina were unable to make the move to the United States at the same time. It was decided that Jorge, Fredy, and his older sister would leave first. While Fredy and Carlota became established in school, Jorge would work at the factory where his cousin was in shipping. He would send money home to Miguelina and the girls and wait until their visas came through.

That was three years ago. Since then, Fredy has adjusted to American life. When he first arrived, he was in the fifth grade, and he barely understood English. He was comforted to know that the other students in his sheltered English classroom were new as well; however, he still felt out of place. He spent day after day behind the same desk, where his legs were either jumpy because they wanted to move and run or his head was nodding off because the amount of new information was so overwhelming. He had never sat in one place for so long in his life! When it came to schoolwork, Fredy was interested, but he knew from the teacher's look that she was frustrated with him. "Buh-buh-bee!" she would repeat, pointing to the first letter in the word B-O-Y. Fredy tried, but he was much more interested in the other students' projects about planets and stars he saw displayed on the hallway bulletin boards.

As the years progressed, Fredy grew frustrated with his classwork. As much as he tried, the information always seemed foggy to him. He missed his mom and wondered what his little sisters must look like now. He hoped that they were taking good care of Coco. Whenever he asked his dad when they were coming, he would reply, "Soon, soon." Maybe because he was not so good at school or perhaps in an effort to mask his sadness, Fredy began to realize that his funny faces and not so perfect English made for pretty good comic material. He was much better at making people laugh than at getting good grades.

Fredy's teachers describe him as fun and good-natured with generally low academic effort. He converses in English comfortably and speaks with only a slight accent. He reads and writes in English at a fourth-grade level; at school, he does not read or write in Spanish. He graduated from the sheltered English immersion program at the end of last year and has begun his eighth-grade year in mainstream English classes. He generally receives low Cs and Ds and an occasional F on his report cards.

Katy Boureth

Katy Boureth is one of the four Boureth children who were born in the United States. Her parents and grandparents and their parents before them had farmed the land in their small village in Cambodia. In the 1970s, members of the village fled war-ravaged Cambodia on foot, thinking that after their hazardous trek across jungles, through mountains, and across waters they would be allowed to enter the United States. Katy's parents were children at the time; her father was 10, her mother, 8. For months the members of the fleeing village lived on little food and conserved their water supply. To avoid capture, they traveled at night and slept in tall grasses and thickets during the day. The able-bodied worked to keep the elderly village members and children alive. When the group arrived in Thailand, they were sent to the refugee camps. Here, too, clean water and food were scarce. Katy's family worked in the camp—her dad, an adolescent at the time, dug trenches under the watchful eyes of the camp's Thai guards. At first, Katy's family believed that their time in the camp would be short. Yet weeks, months, and years passed. The elderly members of the community passed away, young couples married, and children were born. Katy's oldest sibling was born in the camp.

In the mid-1980s, Katy's family was allowed to immigrate to the United States and settled in a midsize city with a large Cambodian population. Here, Katy's father worked as a mechanic in a small Cambodian service station, where the owner, most of the workers, and the majority of patrons who brought their cars in for service spoke Khmer. He also attended English classes at a local church. The family grew, and Katy was the second child born to her family in the United States.

Katy's mother worked to keep the household going, preparing good food and caring for the children. At times, she worked at folding wrapping paper and packaging it in cellophane. On the days he did not attend English classes, on his way home from work, Katy's father picked up large boxes of unfolded papers and brought them to his wife. She folded these while the children napped. This job required neither English skills nor an education. While Katy's mother spoke Khmer fluently, she had never been taught to read or write in her language. She understood few words in English.

Katy's father practiced his English with his children. The children also watched their favorite cartoons on American television and frequently listened as their oldest sister and her friends, now teenagers, chatted in a mixture of English and Khmer.

When Katy entered kindergarten at the age of five, she had mastered basic interpersonal communications skills in English. Katy was placed in an English-speaking classroom in the belief that kindergarten did not require academic language and that Katy would learn English during the school year. By all accounts, Katy was a cooperative, polite, yet shy student. At the end of the school year, Katy's English had improved, but it lagged substantially behind that of the native-English-speaking students in her classroom.

Like most first-grade students, Katy learned sound-symbol relationships and began to read. She continued to make progress through Grades 2 and 3, although her teachers noted that her reading level was in the bottom quartile of the class. Katy enjoyed reading aloud. Her pronunciation was clear, and her teachers praised her. Katy, however, understood little of what she read.

Third grade became very difficult for Katy. Here, teachers assigned reading from science and social studies texts. Katy, who remained cooperative, always decoded words but often had little idea of their meaning, or understanding of what she read. By the end of the third grade, Katy had two younger siblings. Her mother continued to fold papers to bring extra money into the household, and Katy returned home after school to help her mother with the younger children. Katy and her brother sat at the kitchen table to complete their homework each night. Their parents were proud of their children's dedication to their schoolwork and were thankful for having such intelligent children. Their eldest daughter had just graduated from high school— the first in the family.

Katy's parents had no idea that she and her older brother understood little of what they read in their texts. They also had no way of knowing that their eldest child had barely squeaked through school and that her career opportunities were minimal. Community college was an option that the Boureth family did not know existed.

By Grade 5, Katy's teachers noticed that she was less cooperative, less prepared for class, and generally apathetic. Her teachers criticized her work and frequently reminded her that she was a "bright girl" but had to do her homework. She knew that they would not understand if she explained that she *had* done her homework. Katy became sullen.

Katy stopped studying at night, telling her parents that her teachers were giving her time to complete her homework at the end of classes. "I get my work done fast, and so the teachers let us do our homework there," she explained. Katy continued to go home to watch over her younger siblings, but as soon as her mother finished folding papers, Katy left to meet friends. At first, she left for an hour or two but gradually was out later and later. Her mother was concerned, but Katy assured her that this is what *all the kids* did. Her parents noticed that fewer of Katy's friends were Khmer and the Khmer friends she did have no longer acted Khmer. Some of Katy's father's coworkers complained about their children as well. Both parents worried, "Is this what it meant to become American?"

Katy is now in the ninth grade. She reads at an early fifth-grade level. She remains confused by much academic vocabulary. Her grades have slipped, and she often is off task during the day. Her teachers lament that her attitude has changed; she is quietly defiant and no longer hangs around with her former friends, all of whom were Khmer and fairly good students. Some of her new friends are Khmer, but teachers identify them as members of a bad crowd who are influenced by the local gang culture. Katy has developed an *edge*.

She still obeys her parents' wishes that she return home immediately after the school day to care for her younger siblings, but after the evening meal is over, she makes a quick excuse to head for her friends' houses. Katy and her parents have many disagreements. She no longer is the cooperative and respectful daughter she once was. Katy tells her friends,

> I do what I can in school. What good is school anyway? I'll try, but if I can't make it, I can't. Look at my sister, she graduated and is working in the supermarket. I can do that when I'm 16 without graduating.

Review, Reflect, Apply

Review and apply: Aadam, Fredy, and Katy are only three examples of the diversity among ELLs who attend U.S. schools. All three ELLs bring strengths and needs to the classroom that go beyond language. This Review, Reflect, Apply section requires you to reread each case with the following criteria in mind: What have been the experiences of each ELL (or their families) in terms of uprooting, culture shock, and vertical and horizontal cultures? What strengths and needs does each ELL bring to the classroom? Complete as much as you are able of Table 3.3 before reading on.

TABLE 3.3	Cultural Experiences, Differences, and Strengths					
ELL	**Uprooting (preflight, flight)**	**Culture shock (resettlement)**	**Vertical culture**	**Horizontal culture**	**Strengths**	**Needs**
Aadam						
Fredy						
Katy						

Summary

Aadam, Fredy, and Katy are all ELLs, yet they bring very different experiences to the mainstream classroom. The brief description of each ELL provides us with some important information that we can use to begin to understand each student.

Aadam

The experiences of Aadam Jassam Ali, shown in Table 3.4, illustrate the refugee experience as outlined by NCTSN (2005). Prior to leaving his native Iraq, Aadam's mother was a pediatrician, suggesting that the family enjoyed a middle-class lifestyle. Aadam was a good student who liked school.

Fredy

Prior to the floods of 2004, Fredy Solis lived a fairly carefree life in Elías Piña. He lived in poverty, but the family's basic needs were met, and Fredy did not have anything to compare his life with. He attended class sporadically and spent much of his time with his sisters and on adventures with his dog, Coco (see Table 3.5).

TABLE 3.4 Aadam Jassam Ali

Uprooting (preflight)	We know little about Aadam's preflight period. We do know that he and his family fled Iraq during wartime, suggesting uncertainty and trauma.
Uprooting (flight)	Since fleeing Iraq, Aadam's life has been altered dramatically. During flight, the Jassam family relocated several times within three countries, which resulted in a sense of uncertainty and long gaps in Aadam's schooling.
Resettlement and culture shock	Resettlement in the United States resulted in further economic, social, and emotional trauma. Mariam could no longer practice medicine, which meant she had to work long hours waiting on tables. The family now lives in cramped conditions and suffers the effects of prejudice. Anti-Muslim sentiment has resulted in the family being threatened and Aadam being taunted in school, which is indeed a painful place for Aadam. He is concerned about how he will perform prayers during the day, which is required by his religion.
Vertical culture	Aadam Jassam maintains much of his vertical culture. He is Muslim, and his family maintains important elements of its Muslim culture, including family honor, traditional dress, and religious practices. Aadam worries that he will shame his family if he "gets into trouble."
Horizontal culture	Aadam's living conditions make it difficult for him to maintain his traditional culture, and he feels compelled to hide aspects of his culture, including his uncle's name and his religious practices. He is embarrassed and frightened by his mother's wearing of the hijab.
Strengths	Aadam brings many strengths to the mainstream classroom; he was an excellent student in Iraq, and although he feels out of place in school, he continues to strive to do well. He is reading at the sixth-grade level in English, although he has only been in the United States for two years. Aadam's mother and father are well educated in their first language, and thus, while the culture of U.S. schools is new to them, they understand at least some of the processes of the educational system. Aadam has demonstrated resilience during his many relocations since his uprooting from Iraq.
Needs	Aadam has many unmet needs. He has found the cultural transition to school extremely difficult. Aadam needs teachers, guidance counselors, and school officials to facilitate his transition. His religion is very important to him, and he needs a way to practice this during the school day. Aadam is 16 years old and needs a peer group with whom he can identify.

Katy

Katy Boureth is a ninth-grade ELL who was born in the United States. While Katy has developed some abilities in conversational English, her academic English falls far below the level necessary for academic success. Katy's hardworking family lives in a neighborhood where Khmer is spoken. Her parents' experience is illustrative of the refugee experience described by NCTSN (2005). Katy's experience is detailed in Table 3.6.

THE NEED TO BELONG

As is illustrated by Aadam, Fredy, and Katy, ELLs in U.S. middle and high schools come from a variety of linguistic, ethnic, and socioeconomic situations. Some have experienced substantial trauma and interrupted schooling, whereas others have made a smoother transition to U.S. schools. Even under highly positive circumstances the transition to a new school with a new culture and language may present unique challenges for adolescent ELLs. In addition, at middle

TABLE 3.5 Fredy Solis

Uprooting (preflight)	The floods brought disaster to the lives of the Solis family. With their crops in ruins and scarcity of potable water, the Solis family was forced to leave their small farm.
Uprooting (flight)	The family, who had relatives in the United States, were initially excited about the new opportunities the move would provide them. Then they found that, due to lack of available visas, the family would be separated. Fredy had to leave his mother, his younger siblings, and his beloved dog, Coco.
Resettlement and culture shock	Attending school, where he was forced to sit still for long periods of time and receive instruction in a language he did not understand, was a culture shock to Fredy.
Vertical culture	Family connections appear to play an important role in Fredy's vertical culture. Prior to arriving in the United States, Fredy used to spend all his time with his family, taking his younger sisters to school and often helping out on the farm.
Horizontal culture	Fredy's horizontal culture appears to have been shaped, in part, by his time in the United States. He has many friends who, like him, speak both English and Spanish. He has replaced jaunts in the countryside with Coco with basketball and baseball with friends, and life on the farm with life in tenement housing.
Strengths	Fredy has made many friends and likes school. He has an extended support system of aunts, uncles, and cousins who live nearby. He has developed abilities in English.
Needs	Fredy has lost the ability to read and write in Spanish, his first language. He, therefore, does not have a base from which he can transfer language knowledge and skills in reading and writing. Fredy's academic English is underdeveloped; although he is in the eighth grade, he is reading on a fourth-grade level. There are indications that Fredy has begun to give up on school; he knows he can be funny but does not believe he is capable of earning good grades. He receives mostly low Cs and Ds on his report cards. While Fredy has an extended support system, he misses his mom, his sisters, and Coco.

TABLE 3.6 Katy Boureth

Uprooting (preflight)	Katy's parents experienced substantial trauma in their war-torn Cambodia.
Uprooting (flight)	Physical and emotional trauma occurred as members of Katy's parents' communities made an arduous and dangerous trek to Thailand. There, in refugee camps, the trauma continued; little clean water and food and the watchful eyes of the guards had a profound effect on Katy's family.
Resettlement and culture shock	Katy's family settled in a Khmer-speaking neighborhood. Her parents' inability to speak English limited their economic opportunities. Katy lives between two worlds as she goes from home to school.
Vertical culture	Katy's parents maintain close ties with their children and value their intelligence and dedication to schoolwork. Katy's parents maintain close ties with their language. Katy is expected to contribute to the work of the household by caring for her younger siblings.
Horizontal culture	Katy's culture has been shaped by her time in U.S. schools and communities. While her parents highly value education, Katy questions the opportunities it provides for her. Katy's father worries that she no longer "acts Khmer." She is more influenced by her peers and the culture of her neighborhood.
Strengths	Katy has some ability in both languages. Her family values education and wants Katy to complete high school. Although rebellious, Katy remains responsible for tasks required at home.
Needs	Katy has not developed academic-English skills and has fallen behind in her studies. She has stopped studying as she no longer sees education as a means to improve her life.

school and secondary levels, these students are beginning to transition toward adulthood, when the world outside the home and family becomes increasingly important.

Whereas younger children typically select friends based on common interests, middle and high school students seek friends based on common values (Phelan et al., 1998; Tatum, 2003). Adolescents seek to belong with peers who are like them socially and ethnically (Tatum, 2003). However, teachers and administrators may view students' self-grouping by ethnicity or language as undesirable. Some teachers and administrators we have known have voiced concerns about, for example, ELLs of one language group who arrive together on the school bus, sit together in the cafeteria, and seek each other's company during social time. Teachers and administrators are worried that these students will not learn the mainstream culture and language. Some middle schools may even resort to assigned seating in the cafeteria to *break up* groups and *foster* cross-cultural and linguistic interaction. Yet students, and particularly nonmainstream students, have a very real need to belong in groups of their peers. Maslow (1971) theorizes that the need for belonging is surpassed only by the needs for food, shelter, and physical safety.

If ELLs are to succeed academically, the classroom must also provide a supportive and nurturing environment that fosters belonging, one that is culturally responsive to the needs of ELLs and all students.

CULTURALLY RESPONSIVE TEACHING

In culturally responsive classrooms, cultural differences (Au, 2006; Gay, 2000; Villegas & Lucas, 2002), the strengths of ELLs, and the funds of knowledge within homes and communities are recognized and acknowledged as valid and important (Delgado-Gaitán, 2001; Delgado-Gaitán & Trueba, 1991; González & Moll, 2002; Moll, 1994). A culturally responsive classroom is characterized by respect for the abilities of all students (and their families) and the multiple ways of knowing and doing students bring to the classroom. As Gay (2000) explains, the culturally responsible teacher is characterized by a sense of genuine caring for students.

Gay (2000) maintains, "Teachers who really care about students honor their humanity, hold them in high esteem, expect high performance from them, and use strategies to fulfill their expectations" (p. 46). She contrasts this caring with *fixing*, and explains that when the culture of students collides with the culture of the middle-class classroom, teachers may devalue the culture of the student (and the student's family and community). Gay explains, "The teachers want to correct or compensate for [students'] cultural deprivations. These devaluations are accompanied by low and negative expectations about [students'] intellectual abilities, which have deleterious effects on student achievement" (p. 46).

One source of collision might be the difference between classroom discourse expectations and the discourse practices of ELLs and other students who have not been raised in middle-class American households (Delpit, 1995; Heath, 1983; Rothstein-Fisch, Greenfield, & Trumbull, 1999). The discourse pattern of many mainstream classrooms, for example, is best described as linear; the five-paragraph essay, which is common to many classroom assignments and standardized test requirements, provides an example of such linear writing. In contrast, many renowned forms of literature, such as magical realism, make use of nonlinear discourse patterns. Verbal interactions in mainstream classrooms are often categorized as initiation-response-evaluation (I-R-E) (Au, 2006; Cazden, 1988), a linear discourse pattern. In I-R-E patterns, the teacher initiates, students respond, and the teacher evaluates.

Many cultures, however, prefer nonlinear to linear discourse. Research on the discourse of Native Hawaiian students (Au, 1993, 2002, 2006) reveals the pattern of "talk-story," in which parents or older siblings begin a story or ask a question and others gradually join in. The richness of the story grows as it is created within the group. Whereas Native Hawaiian students may be less comfortable answering teachers' questions individually, they are more likely to respond when different children chime in and enrich each other's responses. In talk-story, meaning is developed through group participation. The identified student leaders are not those who can supply the correct answer but those who are able to bring others into the response (Au, 1993). Heath's (1983) ethnographic research provides an understanding of the discourse patterns that monetarily poor black children in the community of Trackton developed. "Talkin' junk" (p. 166) is a circular discourse pattern that is composed of embellished comparisons and creative narratives.

While teachers should not try to duplicate the cultures of students within the classroom, they should work to develop a type of hybrid culture—one that recognizes and values different discourse styles and strengths and at the same time enables students to learn more about the discourse expected in standard English-speaking, mainstream classrooms (Au, 2006; Delpit, 1995). In hybrid classrooms, all discourse styles and ways of knowing are valued, and high expectations are established for all students.

It may be unreasonable to expect teachers to learn about every culture, the ways a culture may have become horizontal in response to time and place, and the discourse patterns within cultures. It is reasonable, however, for teachers to learn about the funds of knowledge (Moll, 1994) that exist within ELLs' families and communities.

RECOGNIZING AND TAPPING FUNDS OF KNOWLEDGE

Students enter school with an understanding of the world based on their funds of knowledge. One way that teachers can learn more about these funds of knowledge is by talking with students and, as González et al. (2005) suggest, by involving students as researchers and producers of knowledge. For example, Aadam, Fredy, and Katy are valuable informants in helping mainstream teachers understand the funds of knowledge that exist in their communities. Aadam has a wealth of knowledge of Muslim culture, Fredy has experienced daylong adventures in the country that are foreign to most mainstream students, and Katy has perspectives of both Cambodian and American culture. (A caveat exists here. Teachers should show interest in the experiences of ELLs such as Aadam, Fredy, and Katy but should not pressure them to discuss their experiences.)

Teachers who come to know their students can capitalize on students' funds of knowledge. In her ninth-grade ecology unit, for example, Ms. Tara Goodhue encourages her students to become experts at observation of a particular natural environment. ELLs are encouraged to share their knowledge of the plant and animal life of their native countries, while native-English-speaking students share their knowledge of different regions of the United States with which they are familiar. Ms. Goodhue's classroom blends cultures by tapping into all her students as resources. Furthermore, as she provides instruction that helps her students understand the concept of adaptation, she seeks the experience of recently emigrated ELLs and other students who have moved to illustrate parallels between cultural and scientific understandings of adaptation.

Knowing students and understanding their discourse patterns also provides valuable information about students' funds of knowledge. Au's work with Native Hawaiian students (1993, 2006) and Heath's (1983) study of low-income white and African American families and communities illustrate that there are many different and valid ways to communicate. The work of Au and Heath also shows discourse differences that occur within and across groups and differences that may occur between students' discourse and the discourse used in the standard English-speaking U.S. classroom. Again, teachers cannot be expected to know about discourse patterns that exist across every culture or how these patterns differ within cultures. Teachers, can, however, vary instructional activities and assignments and monitor student discourse patterns in different settings, looking for strengths on which to capitalize. By moving from a transmission model of instruction (Villegas & Lucas, 2002) and I-R-E discourse pattern, which consists of teachers telling students what they need to know and asking them to demonstrate their knowledge of facts, to a constructivist approach (Vygotsky, 1978), teachers can promote meaningful academic discussions and activities that capitalize on student differences as strengths.

Visits to the communities and homes of ELLs also enable teachers to understand the funds of knowledge ELLs bring to the classroom (González & Moll, 2002; González, 2005). Visits to the homes of Aadam, Fredy, and Katy, for example, will reveal modest and sometimes crowded living conditions. Socioeconomic conditions dictate the neighborhoods in which families can afford to live. Visits to the Jassam, Solis, and Boureth homes will also reveal parents who care about their children and their children's education, parents who are struggling to adapt to an often inhospitable environment. Taylor (1990, 1998) and Kozol (1991, 1995, 2006) write about the inequities caused by poverty and its accompanying lack of choice in living accommodation, as well as about the resilience and strengths within many families who are often simply thought of as *poor*.

Visits to the Jassam, Solis, and Boureth families will reveal other funds of knowledge. Mariam Jassam is a pediatrician who knows much about medicine and child care from the perspective of another culture. Jorge Solis has extensive experience farming and cultivating his land without the use of chemical agents or irrigations systems. Mr. Solis is also a mechanic and has a keen sense of how machines fit together and work. The Boureths have maintained their language and cultural traditions (including the use of plants and herbs as medicines and other alternative medicine), which they could share with teachers and students alike. Additionally, Mr. Boureth is bilingual, knowing English and Khmer.

CHAPTER SUMMARY

A culturally responsive classroom creates a setting of belonging and high expectations for ELLs. González and Moll (2002) and González et al. (2005) provide suggestions for understanding the funds of knowledge that exist within the families of ELLs and other students from different backgrounds. Four ways in which teachers can tap into the funds of knowledge of ELLs and other students are (1) engaging students in conversation about their interests, (2) providing a variety of learning opportunities and observing students' discourse patterns, (3) transitioning from a transmission to a constructivist style of instruction, and (4) visiting the communities and homes of students.

In Chapters 5 and 6, we introduce planning for enduring understandings which is compatible with culturally responsive teaching. We use the TELLiM model, which provides appropriate entry to instruction for all students, regardless of academic English proficiency, and ensures that ELLs and other students are meaningfully engaged in high-level content-area instruction that recognizes multiple perspectives.

Assessment Evidence Activities

AE-1   Identify and map the vertical and horizontal natures of culture that have shaped (and continue to shape) your life. Construct a T-chart. On the left-hand side, make a list of values or beliefs that you believe are part of your culture, such as the following:

It is a sign of failure to return home after graduating from college.

If you work hard enough, you can achieve your goals.

It is important to plan for your future.

On the right-hand side, note whether you personally agree or disagree with this cultural tenet. Then, discuss your findings in small groups.

AE-2   Explain why mainstream teachers may state that ELLs "have lost their culture."

AE-3   Using the descriptions of Aadam, Fredy, and Katy, explain how they differ and are similar in the level of first-language development, country of origin, socioeconomic status (in country of origin and in the United States), trauma experienced, and prior schooling experiences.

AE-4   Referring to the descriptions of Aadam, Fredy, and Katy, list the strengths (and potential strengths) they bring to the classroom. Support your claims with evidence from the case studies.

AE-5   Reflect on a time when you felt like an outsider (awkward, intimidated, or uncomfortable). (This need not be a cultural experience.) Write a three- or four-page journal entry describing this experience. Include a discussion of the ways in which this experience may relate to experiences of ELLs. Try to be as specific as possible. Share journal entries in small groups.

AE-6   Consider a unit from your content area. Brainstorm a list of ways you could capitalize on the funds of knowledge in your classroom to further enrich that unit. Explain how these changes might benefit all students (engage more students, build on funds of knowledge, and establish high expectations).

Resources for Further Reading

- Au, K. (2006). *Multicultural issues and literacy development.* Mahwah, NJ: Lawrence Erlbaum.
- Howard, G. (2006). *We can't teach what we don't know: White teachers, multiracial schools.* New York: Teachers College Press.
- *The Classroom Mosaic: Culture and Learning.* This program discusses how culturally responsive teaching enables students to create connections, access prior knowledge and experience, and develop competence. Featured are a sixth-grade teacher and two ninth-grade teachers, with expert commentary from University of Wisconsin professor Gloria Ladson-Billings and University of Arizona professor Luis Moll. Available online at no cost at www.learner.org/resources/series172.html. Scroll to Session 6.
- *Children of War: A Video for Educators* is available online at no cost from NCTSN. http://www.nctsnet.org/nctsn_assets/pdfs/edu_materials/Children_of_War.pdf
- The United Nations defines a refugee as

  > a person who is outside his/her country of nationality or habitual residence; has a well-founded fear of persecution because of his/her race, religion, nationality, membership in a particular social group or political opinion; and is unable or unwell to avail himself/herself of the protection of that country, or to return there for fear of persecution. (NCTSN, 2005, p. 4)

  The complete document ("Mental Health Interventions for Refugee Children in Resettlement") is available online at www.nctsn.org/nctsn_assets/pdfs/promising_practices/MH_Interventions_for_Refugee_Children.pdf

- NCTSN also provides an extensive reading list for educators online at www.nctsn.org

Academic Literacy in the Content Areas

Enduring understanding: Academic literacy across content areas is essential to learning.

CHAPTER 4 EXTENDS THE TOPIC OF SECOND-LANGUAGE ACQUISITION FROM CHAPTER 2 AND PRESENTS THE FOUR domains of academic literacy: listening and speaking in academic situations, and reading and writing academic material. The top-down and bottom-up processes within each domain are presented along with an overview of instructional considerations. (Specific strategies for building academic-language abilities and literacy in mainstream classrooms are presented in Chapter 9.) The intention of Chapter 4 is to continue to provide mainstream teachers with a knowledge base they will apply to plan and implement instruction, which are the topics of Chapters 5 to 13.

LEARNING OUTCOMES

The following learning outcomes (LOs) serve as a guide to Chapter 4. At the end of the chapter are assessment evidence activities that are aligned with each LO to enable readers to check their understanding.

PROCESSES OF ACADEMIC LITERACY

To become academically successful in U.S. schools, ELLs must develop academic literacy in English; in other words, they must be able to think, listen, speak, read, and write effectively across content areas. As ELLs and other students progress through the grades, the relationship between literacy proficiency and academic achievement becomes increasingly important, and literacy requirements become increasingly complex (Biancarosa & Snow, 2006).

At its most basic level, academic-literacy development is influenced by the ongoing interaction between the students' world (top-down) knowledge and their discrete (bottom-up) knowledge, as illustrated by Model 4.1 (Birch, 2002, 2006; Flowerdew & Miller, 2005). Vocabulary requires and builds on both types of knowledge. Top-down processes supply the conceptual schemata that contribute to depth and breadth of word knowledge. Bottom-up processes contribute to recognition and retrieval of phonemes and morphemes within words, word retrieval, and retrieval of common prepositions that collocate with words (e.g., *at, of, in,* and *on*). Additionally, the relationship between academic literacy and vocabulary development is a circular one: "Having a bigger vocabulary makes you a better reader, being a better reader makes it possible for you to read more, and reading more gives you a bigger vocabulary" (Stahl & Nagy, 2006, p. 13).

As discussed in Chapter 2, the theory of common underlying proficiency (Cummins, 1981) explains top-down abilities' transfer from ELLs' native languages to English. ELLs who have conceptual knowledge in their first language will transfer this knowledge to English; they will need to learn the English words and expressions for the concepts, but will not need to relearn the concepts.

The experiences of Carlin, a college-educated, adult language learner, provide a simple example of the interrelationship between top-down and bottom-up processes. Carlin's overall

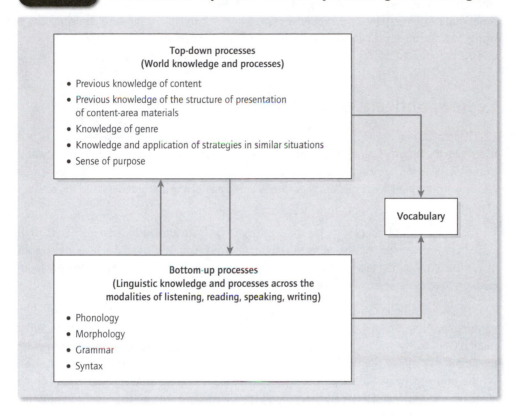

ability in Spanish was at a high-intermediate level when she enrolled in a three-week language immersion school in Mexico. Learning about the history of Mexico was included in the program of studies. As part of the history component, students read excerpts from Mexican history texts to prepare for a lecture to be given by a famous Mexican historian. The secondary- and college-level texts were quite challenging for nonnative speakers of Spanish. Carlin struggled with vocabulary, grammar, and syntax. She had, however, some knowledge of the history of Mexico and used this background knowledge to help her make sense of the text. Carlin had also read history texts in English and could therefore apply her knowledge of the overall structure of history texts to the new reading. Her linguistic abilities (phonology, grammar, vocabulary, and syntax) in Spanish were sufficiently developed that she could read some passages of the text without great difficulty. When Carlin came across unfamiliar vocabulary, she drew on her first-language reading strategies to help her identify words that she needed to know and those that she could skip over without likely interfering with the meaning. She also applied her existing schemata of vocabulary words to better understand the vocabulary in the texts. Carlin's well-developed first-language reading strategies also enabled her to self-check her understanding and return to confusing passages for further clarification.

Carlin arrived at the history lecture well prepared and with substantive background knowledge. She also had a clear purpose for attending the lecture, which she kept in mind as she listened. Having attended many lectures in the United States, Carlin brought her world knowledge of schema and scripts (the structure and pattern of a lesson) to this new situation. As Carlin listened to the speaker, she used her knowledge of phonology, syntax, and grammar (sometimes quite automatically) to make sense of his words. Although Carlin heard some unknown words and, at times, sounds blurred together, she strategically used her previous experience and background knowledge to stay focused and make sense of the lecture.

Review, Reflect, Apply

1. *Review and apply:* How did Carlin's linguistic skills help her as she read the texts and listened to the lecture? Read through Carlin's experience again; this time, identify how her world (top-down) knowledge supported her understanding. Explain the ways in which her top-down and bottom-up knowledge and abilities interacted to enable Carlin to understand the reading and the lecture.

2. *Reflect:* Think about ways in which you use top-down and bottom-up knowledge and skills in new situations (e.g., listening to a lecture in which you were unable to hear every word or reading challenging text). Explain how these types of knowledge and abilities interact to enable you to make sense of the content of lectures or readings.

The interaction of top-down and bottom-up processes is essential to academic listening, reading, speaking, and writing. For example, even the most well-developed background information (top-down) will not make a lecture comprehensible to the student who cannot access the phonology, morphology, grammar, and syntax of the language of the lecture (bottom-up); yet the student who has adequate knowledge of the phonology, vocabulary, and syntax of the language can use well-developed background knowledge to compensate for gaps in bottom-up processes, such as missed sounds and new vocabulary words.

In speaking for academic purposes, a student uses world (top-down) knowledge to construct logical arguments and then uses the conventions of standard English (bottom-up) to express his or her understanding or point of view; neither world knowledge nor the application of standard English conventions alone will suffice. A student may be able to accurately decode words (bottom-up); yet if she does not read strategically for meaning by comparing the text to self-knowledge, textual knowledge, and world knowledge and by making decisions about the text (top-down), she will likely be unable to comprehend what she has read. On the other hand, as developed as a reader's knowledge base may be, she will not be able to make sense of the reading if she does not know the language and the writing system, or cannot decode the words.

Top-down and bottom-up processes also interact in the writing process; a student who has learned to spell words and knows the rules of grammar and punctuation (bottom-up) will not be able to write cogent and compelling essays if he has not thoughtfully engaged in the process of writing (top-down). Yet, exposure to the writing process alone will likely be unproductive if the student does not know the writing system and has not also had access to models of writing or language.

Numerous factors, such as English language proficiency, literacy in their first language and in English, prior knowledge of academics, economic status, and previous experiences, are related to the ability of ELLs to develop academic literacy (Short & Fitzsimmons, 2007). These factors determine the top-down and bottom-up resources on which ELLs can draw to make sense of academic language across the content areas:

- *Language proficiency:* ELLs who have well-developed linguistic proficiency in their native language have developed the schemata necessary to more readily learn new words and language structures in English. Increased proficiency in oral English also positively influences English reading.

- *Level of overall literacy in their native language and English:* ELLs who have developed comprehension strategies in their native languages are likely to be able to transfer these to English reading.

- *Prior knowledge of academics:* ELLs who are well educated in their native language have developed content-area schemata and skills. These ELLs must learn English and keep up with their academic studies. ELLs who have a limited knowledge of academics in their native language must catch up academically and linguistically, and then continue to develop grade-level academics and academic English.

- *Economic status:* Students who live in poverty are overrepresented among those having lower reading scores. ELLs who are disproportionately economically disadvantaged are double-burdened.

- *Previous experiences:* ELLs who come from educational systems that are similar to those in U.S. schools have a better sense of school culture, discourse, and classroom literacy practices. Furthermore, ELLs whose families are formally educated are also more likely to understand the overall structure and literacy expectations of the school.

SOURCE: Short and Fitzsimmons (2007).

The different prior experiences of ELLs contribute to the discourse patterns they bring to U.S. classroom settings. We borrow from sociolinguists (Au, 1993; Farr, 1993; Heath, 1983) to expand on the notion of discourse patterns in the four domains of academic literacy. The discourse patterns that are generally valued in U.S. schools are those of the white middle class. Farr (1993) refers to this discourse style as "essayist literacy" (p. 7), which she describes as explicit, exact, and "author evacuated." Proficiency in essayist literacy is expected in classroom settings.

As Farr (1993) explains, "Those students who are relative 'newcomers' to the academic community and its discourse do not arrive as 'blank slates': They bring with them knowledge of the sociolinguistic repertoires of their home communities" (p. 6). These differences in discourse style are not limited to individual variations in English language proficiency, but rather occur in groups of ELLs and native-English speakers across the United States: Heath's (1983) seminal ethnographic study of monetarily poor whites and blacks in two communities showed non-middle-class discourse patterns in both groups. Au and Mason's (Au, 1993; Au & Mason, 1981) work with native-Hawaiian students highlighted the value of non-middle-class discourse patterns within the home and community. Farr's (1993) ethnographic study of Mexican Americans living in Chicago illustrated that the discourse valued within the community often differed substantially from that which was valued in middle-class U.S. schools.

While teachers cannot be expected to know every discourse style that students bring to the classroom, it is important that teachers be aware that ELLs (and many other students) may enter classrooms with rich discourse structures that differ from the discourse structure generally valued in U. S. classrooms. Hence, activities designed to tap into background knowledge are likely to activate different types of knowledge in different students. Farr (1993) uses an example provided by Kochman to illustrate problems that may arise when discourse styles differ markedly: At a meeting of "white academics and black community activists in Chicago," black activists argued with passion, which to them signified "commitment and honesty." The white academics were taken aback by this discourse, which they characterized as too emotional. They, instead, argued "dispassionately," which the black activists understood as "hypocritical" (p. 17). Clearly in classroom situations, where discourse styles are likely to differ, similar misinterpretations are foreseeable. In addition, teachers, who have typically adopted a middle-class discourse style, are apt to judge work that uses a similar discourse style (e.g., in oral responses and papers) more favorably than work with a different discourse style (Delpit, 1995; Hinkel, 2004).

Chapter 2 presented an overview of linguistics and the processes of second-language acquisition; the following sections of this chapter expand on Chapter 2 and discuss the language processes within each domain. While domains of academic listening, speaking, reading, and writing are interrelated, it is useful to consider the processes of each domain separately. We begin with a discussion of listening and speaking and then continue with reading and writing, which are often thought to be at the core of content-area understanding.

ACADEMIC LISTENING

Academic listening involves the use of bottom-up, top-down, and interactive processing models (Flowerdew & Miller, 2005; Rost, 2005). In the bottom-up model, a sound signal is transmitted by the speaker and then is decoded by the listener. As illustrated in Model 4.2, the listener must receive the sound signal, identify and decode the sounds, identify words, and then access the lexicon to find word meanings. When retrieving word meaning from the lexicon, the listener relies on semantic (meaning) as well as syntactic (grammatical) processes (Flowerdew & Miller, 2005; Rost, 2005; Rost & Ross, 1991). Rost (2005) explains, "Speech is recognized sequentially as words are identified through progressive elimination of alternate word candidates" (p. 208).

This process may present difficulties for the second-language learner who begins to acquire English as an adolescent or adult; as the sensitive period, which was discussed in Chapter 2, illustrates, it is often more difficult for older second-language learners to hear and discriminate between the phonemes in speech (Rost, 2005). Compounding the difficulty to discriminate between sounds is that words seemingly blend together: Listeners may not always hear the "white spaces" between words that are apparent in written text (Rost, 2005, p. 507; Rost & Ross, 1991). Chapter 1 provided an example of an adult ELL who asked about the meaning of

MODEL 2.2 **Bottom-Up Process of Listening**

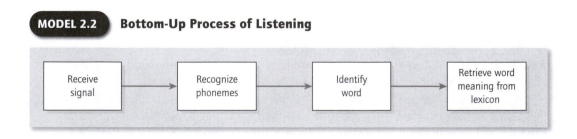

dija (did you). The ELL knew the words *did* and *you*, but the sounds blended and were reduced to *dija*, which was incomprehensible to him. As the illustration of Juan, the secondary ELL from Ecuador who attempted to listen to Mr. Johnson's lecture on *proper gander* (propaganda) suggests, academic lectures are rife with possibilities for misunderstanding. Indeed, inadequate word recognition may be the greatest barrier to academic listening (Rost, 2005). The fact that the rate of speech for an average speaker of English is between 100 and 120 words per minute (Rost, 2005) illustrates the ongoing potential challenges for ELLs in content-area classrooms.

Listening, however, like other forms of academic literacy, is more than a simple bottom-up process, which researchers uncovered when they found that listeners were unable to identify truncated words in isolation. As Flowerdew and Miller (2005) illustrate, when presented with the sound /hæ/ (made by the letters *ha*), listeners are unable to predict the sound that follows. This finding suggests that listeners rely on more than bottom-up listening skills to make sense of speech. The top-down model demonstrates that context enables listeners to identify truncated sounds. When presented with the book title *The Cat in the Hæ*, for example, listeners are able to use context to complete the truncated Hæ with /t/ to form *The Cat in the Hat*. This research finding suggests that listeners use preestablished structures (schemata) to make meaning of sounds. As described in Chapter 2, schemata are the broad-based organizational network for experiences. (In a review of the literature, Rost (2005) found that most adults have approximately 1 million schemata, which they draw on to facilitate meaning.) In a content-area classroom, for example, schemata might include the routine of a classroom lecture, such as a review of objectives, a lesson introduction, procedures for think-pair-share, procedures and rules for working in groups, and so on. According to the top-down model, schemata enable listeners to anticipate certain forms of speech (Flowerdew & Miller, 2005) and therefore make sense of speech even when some of the phonemes are not clear. The interactive model postulates that listeners use a combination of bottom-up and top-down components when listening. Both the top-down and interactive models provide teachers with a compelling rationale for providing context for listening. Adjusting the rate of speech and simplifying the syntax have also been shown to make input more comprehensible (Rost, 2005).

Research has shown that depth of vocabulary knowledge is closely linked to listening ability (Rost, 2005). Nation and Waring (1998) found that listeners must know at least 90% to 95% of vocabulary to fully access meaning, and Rost (2005) suggests that the greater the depth of knowledge of a word (polysemy, collocations, and connotations), the more able listeners are to retrieve a word from their lexicons as it is used by the speaker. Vocabulary plays such an integral role in all four modalities of listening, speaking, reading, and writing that it is discussed at length in Chapter 9, and specific recommendations for building academic vocabulary across content areas are made.

Instruction that is aligned with the TELLiM model, discussed in Chapter 1 of this text, provides ongoing opportunities for ELLs to engage in well-planned academic discussions and facilitates the development of listening abilities. Table 4.1 illustrates the listening needs of ELLs at various proficiency levels from beginner to transitioning. Like native-English-speaking students, ELLs will also require training in active listening strategies, such as connecting oral input to a schema, anticipating what will follow, forming questions, and confirming predictions. ELLs who have developed these active listening strategies in their first language will be able to transfer these to English listening.

TABLE 4.1   Listening Needs According to English Proficiency Levels

English Proficiency Levels	Instructional Considerations
Transitioning May need clarification for certain idioms, nuances, or cultural references	Be cognizant of idiom use in spoken language, check for understanding of nuances, and explain cultural references
Intermediate Frequent repetitions and visual cueing may be required to ensure comprehension	Repeat steps for transitioning level and accompany all lectures with appropriate artifacts and visuals; refer to these during lectures
Often rely on word analysis to gather meaning and therefore require more processing time than native speaker	Adjust rate of speaking and provide time for intermediate speakers to check understanding by providing frequent think-pair-share activities. Develop a system for checking understanding: A thumbs-up, thumbs-down system (Saphier & Gower, 1997) enables teachers to broadly check students' understanding across the classroom
Early intermediate Understand interpersonal conversations and academic words or phrases when spoken to in a slow, repetitious fashion	Repeat steps for intermediate level and rephrase speech as necessary (paraphrasing to simplify vocabulary and syntax)
Require breakdown, clarification, and visual cueing, especially when dense or multilayered information is presented	Use and refer to outlines, set agendas for graphic organizers, and teach ELLs how to use these to organize their thoughts while listening
May appear silent when taking time to process information	Provide wait time in instruction as well as time to think-pair-share
May also appear overwhelmed, distracted, or exhausted due to the high cognitive demand of the language	Be empathetic with the cognitive load associated with language acquisition
Beginner May range from understanding no English at all to identifying isolated and often repeated vocabulary words and phrases	Repeat steps for previous level, and provide visual cues as often as possible. Pair beginner ELLs with more proficient speakers of the same first language for think-pair-share activities, which enables ELLs to explain the instruction and confirm their understanding in their first language. Request native-language tutors to support students in the classroom, and provide the tutors with all the instructional materials prior to classes. (Chapter 8 provides guidance for working with tutors in class.) Review placement testing to determine if ELLs are literate in their first languages (testing in a first language, report cards, and anecdotal data); if no placement data are available, consult with native-language tutors regarding first-language literacy; if ELL is literate in first language, provide native-language materials when possible.
May also appear overwhelmed, distracted, or exhausted due to limited understanding and the high cognitive demand of the language	Be empathetic with the cognitive load associated with language acquisition

Aadam Jassam Ali's ELA Class

ELA is Aadam's most challenging class. Even with parts of the required novels available on audiotape, the class requires substantial amounts of reading, and students are expected to come to class prepared to discuss the reading. Classroom discussions require excellent listening abilities. Mr. Hayes has worked to make the listening component of his class more comprehensible to ELLs through attention to routine, by ensuring that continuous lecture periods are brief and accompanied by visuals and graphics, and by providing ample time for ELLs and other students to process the content and discuss their reading in pairs and small groups.

When Aadam Jassam enters Mr. Hayes's classroom, he knows that the agenda for the class period will be on the sideboard. Mr. Hayes refers to the agenda during class, enabling ELLs and others to follow the transitions from one activity to another. Aadam finds this very helpful because the sheer load of the language he must process throughout the day tires him so that, at times, he loses concentration. On this day, Mr. Hayes begins the class by explaining to students that their discussions will focus on the similarities and differences between the reactions of the characters in their novels. He relates the lesson to the unit's *essential question*, thereby presenting ELLs and others with both context and a point of reference (Rost, 2005) and activating schemata developed in previous lessons. Mr. Hayes projects an image of a Venn diagram, which he has labeled. Aadam recognizes the Venn diagram structure from an earlier class, during which Mr. Hayes modeled the use of the Venn diagram and provided students with practice. Students have used Venn diagrams several times since then, so this visual cue is useful in helping Aadam understand Mr. Hayes's lecture. Aadam knows that Mr. Hayes will not lecture for long periods of time without allowing students to check their understanding in pairs; thus he worries less about becoming confused in this class and with his affective filter lowered, he is better able to listen and process the language.

Review, Reflect, Apply

Review and apply: ELLs and other students in content-area classrooms are expected to learn through in-class instruction, much of which comes from academic listening. Review the needs of ELLs at proficiency levels from beginner to transitioning, and explain two ways that you can make your lectures, teacher-talk, and class discussions more comprehensible.

Summary

Success in content-area classes depends in part on the ability of ELLs to listen to academic content. Content-area teachers must be aware of the complex nature of listening and the cognitive load ELLs experience while listening to English. Teaching specific ELL listening strategies may be beyond the scope of the content-area teacher; however, the content-area teacher can ensure that classroom activities that require listening are comprehensible and accessible to ELLs. Content-area teachers can do the following:

- Develop and adhere to clear classroom routines
- Activate schemata prior to lessons
- Introduce new vocabulary at the beginning of a lesson
- Keep teacher talk times short and provide time for ELLs to engage in collaborative tasks with others to process content and to check their understanding
- Be aware of the rate of speech
- Paraphrase to simplify complex syntactical constructions
- Use and refer to appropriate visuals when lecturing
- Develop and adhere to a signal system so that ELLs and others can indicate understanding or confusion

- Stop to clarify confusions
- Effectively use the services of native-language tutors

ACADEMIC SPEAKING

As illustrated in Chapter 1, when teachers overhear ELLs speaking casually to one another, they often assume that these ELLs are proficient in English and will, therefore, require little support completing ordinary classroom work. ELLs generally acquire the ability to speak for basic communication purposes within a year or two. Speech for basic communication is, however, different from academic speech (Markee, 2005). Unlike speech for basic communication, academic speech, which requires mastery of language as well as academic discourse style, is often considered one of the most difficult of the academic domains for an ELL to master (Tarone, 2005). According to Markee (2005), the more distant speech is from regular, daily, casual conversation, the more institutionalized or academic it has become. The initiation-response-evaluation (IRE) discourse pattern (described in Chapter 3), which typifies much of the discussion that occurs in U.S. classrooms, is an example of academic speech.

Speech is often analyzed by form and function (Tarone, 2005). Speech forms include phonemes (language sounds), morphemes (units of meaning, including affixes), vocabulary, and syntax (the grammatical structure of language such as discourse markers), all of which are described in Chapter 2 of this text. Speakers of a second language do not often orally reproduce the form of the language as native speakers of the language do (Tarone, 2005); rather, an accent or some other influence of their first language is generally apparent in their speech. Native-like speaking proficiency, in fact, is considered to be unattainable for most second-language learners who learn an additional language after childhood. (Chapter 2 discusses the notions of a critical period and second-language acquisition after adolescence.)

Interlanguage in speaking is common (Selinker, 1991; Tarone, 2005) for ELLs and results in a blending of English language phonemes, morphemes, vocabulary, and syntax with these linguistic elements from their first languages. Many ELLs in classes we have taught and observed also maintain influences of first-language morphology, such as adding *s* to nouns with irregular plural forms (e.g., *childrens* for children), adding *s* to third-person plural verbs (e.g., they goes, plays, teaches), or confusing the use of prepositions such as *in* and *on* (e.g., *in* the plane rather than *on* the plane). ELLs may also often replace an unknown vocabulary word with one from their native language or seek to describe the word with near synonyms.

The function of academic speech is transactional (Tarone, 2005); that is, academic speech is used to convey information. The goal of academic second-language speaking, therefore, should be intelligibility and "multi-competence" (Cook, 1996, cited in Tarone, 2005) and speaking for communicative competence (Canale, 1983; Hymes, 1972), which is why it is important for teachers to define what constitutes speaking competence in the content areas they teach. The ability to hedge using adverbs such as *usually* and *often* and accurately using constructions such as *it appears* and *it seems* may, for instance, be critical to competently expressing an argument in a history course, and the use of nonliving subjects (*the results show, the experiment indicates*) are likely elements of communicative competence in science.

ELLs in content-area classrooms benefit when content-area teachers routinely engage them in well-planned and complex academic conversations that provide ongoing opportunities to practice academic speaking with peers and teacher (Tharp et al., 2000). Providing

ELLs with time to think about their responses and practice speaking with a peer in think-pair-share or small-group discussions encourages speaking by lowering their affective filter, which enables ELLs to receive feedback on the accuracy of their utterances and find out if they are able to make themselves understood. Table 4.2 shows the speaking needs of ELLs at various proficiency levels.

Fredy Solis's World History Class

Fredy Solis is an intermediate ELL with well-developed basic communication skills and low academic proficiency and literacy. Fredy compensates for his lack of academic ability with his quick wit, and, while liked by most of his peers and teachers, he is often perceived as the class clown. Ms. Paparazzo, Fredy's world history teacher, has taken the time to review Fredy's background; she knows he is from Elías Piña, Dominican Republic, and that prior to his arrival in the United States, Fredy's schooling was inconsistent. Ms. Paparazzo has conferred with the school's ESOL teacher and has reviewed Fredy's cumulative folder. She has learned that Fredy's reading level is well below grade level and that much of what Fredy is learning about history comes directly from classroom discussion. She also knows that well-planned academic discussions serve to build Fredy's academic communication abilities and allow Fredy to demonstrate his knowledge of world history. Currently, the class is studying the origins of Indian

TABLE 4.2   Speaking Needs According to English Proficiency Levels

English Proficiency Levels	Instructional Considerations
Transitional Use complex language structures when speaking; may have difficulty using idioms and nuance Some native-language influence in phonemes, morphemes, syntax, and vocabulary may be present, but these do not interfere with intelligibility	Provide ongoing opportunity for ELLs to engage in academic discussions with each other and with academically competent native speakers
Intermediate Speaking can be focused yet errors with syntax and vocabulary are common; may or may not feel comfortable speaking in front of peers	Repeat steps for transitioning level and ensure adequate time for academic discussions in pairs or small groups
Early intermediate Use basic grammar patterns in speaking and writing and often make errors when attempting more complex language combinations May be overwhelmed, distracted, or exhausted due to the high cognitive demands of the language	Repeat steps for intermediate level Understand that ELLs may experience silent periods due to processing demands: These periods are normal and should be regarded as part of the language acquisition process
Beginner May be in the silent stage and not speak in English at all, yet may communicate with others in his or her native language	Respect the silent stage as an important stage of language development. Enable the students to communicate their understanding using their first languages and gestures where appropriate

civilization in the Indus Valley. Ms. Paparazzo has posed an *essential question*: *Does the history shape the environment, or does the environment shape history?* During classes, Ms. Paparazzo provides ongoing, ample opportunities for ELLs and others to engage in focused academic conversations. She has just completed a short lecture on the achievements and characteristics of early Indian civilizations, and students are working in groups of three to create wish lists for an archeological dig based on the factual knowledge they have about early Indian civilizations. In round-robin fashion, each group member must name an artifact on his or her wish list and explain why it would be likely to be found. Fredy is actively engaged in this activity. He is comfortable trying academic vocabulary and phrases within the small group. His peers' feedback enables him to gauge the accuracy of his speech and practice academic phrases. He uses words such as *archeology, artifacts, seals,* and *amulets* and links these to descriptions of ancient life in the Indus Valley.

Review, Reflect, Apply

Review and apply: Review the needs of ELLs at proficiency levels from early-intermediate to transitioning, and explain two ways by which you can ensure that ELLs have opportunities to engage in academic speaking in a content-area unit that you teach.

Summary

ELLs must develop academic speaking abilities to engage in meaningful content-area discussions. Content-area teachers can ensure ongoing opportunities for academic speaking practice by

- planning regular, focused academic discussions;
- ensuring that ELLs have the opportunity to practice speaking in pairs and in small groups;
- engaging ELLs and others in academic discussions that enable them to use academic vocabulary and discourse patterns; and
- respecting the silent period as a normal stage in language development, and encouraging beginning students to use their native language and gestures in academic discussions.

ACADEMIC READING

Reading plays an increasingly important role in learning content and in the development of academic vocabulary in middle and upper grades. Reading not only improves students' immediate grasp of content, it also provides background knowledge that allows ELLs to listen critically to classroom lectures and instructions, participate in classroom discussions, and write more coherent essays. Unfortunately, ELLs and many other adolescent students struggle with academic reading (Biancarosa & Snow, 2006). While struggling adolescent readers can generally read the words on the page, they often have difficulty with comprehension caused by underdeveloped reading strategies (Biancarosa & Snow, 2006). A lack of fluency also interferes with comprehension (Tatum, 2005). We begin our discussion of reading with an overview of first-language reading in English. We then consider the challenges that reading in English presents for ELLs.

Learning to Read in English as a First Language

The oral language that children have acquired prepares them for reading. However, unlike oral language, which is acquired naturally, reading is a learned ability and involves the meaning-making interaction between background knowledge and all the previous experiences a reader brings to the reading, and to the text itself (Rosenblatt, 1978, 1995). The research of Harste (1994) indicates that young children see meaning in print and begin to learn to decode by focusing on the meaning of symbols. Harste found that children initially demonstrate an understanding that print has meaning when they recognize *Kellogg's* as cereal, golden arches as *McDonald's*, and *Crest* as toothpaste. Children then apply their understanding of print as meaningful to words in context found in their environment (Weaver, 2002). Although the research of Harste was conducted on middle-class children, Ferreiro (cited in Harste, 1994) studied the literacy development of Mexican preschool children and found that irrespective of their socioeconomic group and their parents' level of literacy, children "approached print with an expectation that it would be meaningful" (p. 48). As part of the literacy continuum, children then apply the understanding of print as meaningful to words in context in their environment (Ruddell & Ruddell, 1994, p. 90; Weaver, 2002; see also Richgels, 2001).

The interaction between top-down and bottom-up processes is evident in reading (Birch, 2002, 2006; Eskey, 2005). For example, consider the very simple example of an adult reader who receives a party invitation in the mail. The reader is familiar with the basic format of most invitations and knows that the text will likely include *who, what, when,* and *where* components. On a very simple level, the reader uses these top-down understandings (background knowledge, schema, comprehension strategies, and vocabulary knowledge) as she scans the invitation. While bottom-up processes assist in the process, decoding occurs with automaticity. Engagement of bottom-up processes is more apparent as the reader decodes the names of unfamiliar streets or places listed on the invitation. If, while reading the invitation, the bottom-up processor signals that invitees will be charged $1,000 for attending the party, this information probably will not fit with the reader's background knowledge (top-down) unless she has been to a lot of upscale fund-raisers. Chances are the reader will go back and carefully reread at least part of the invitation again (bottom-up) to check her comprehension of the text.

Top-Down Knowledge and Strategies

When readers have relevant background knowledge about the topic at hand, they are more likely able to comprehend what they read (Eskey, 2005). Their background knowledge enables them to make predictions about their reading and then check these predictions to confirm understanding or reread to clarify confusions. The ability to make predictions is positively associated with information gain through reading (Eskey, 2005; García & Pearson, 2000; Wildman & King, 1978–1979). ELLs who have been in U.S. schools throughout their schooling are likely to share at least some of the background knowledge considered common by mainstream teachers, and will benefit from classroom activities that serve to activate this background knowledge. ELLs from other countries, however, will enter school with different background knowledge, and they will need instruction that is focused on developing the requisite background knowledge and schemata (Short & Fitzsimmons, 2007). ELLs such as Fredy Solis and Aadam Jassam, for example, will likely experience difficulties accessing historical passages and novels that assume knowledge of U.S. historical events. Fredy, Aadam, and other recent new-comers will need to be provided with explicit background knowledge about U.S. history, a subject that spirals from 3rd to 12th grade for students in U.S. schools.

Discourse patterns and styles, discussed earlier in this chapter, are also relevant to reading in the classroom. The typical story grammar (i.e., the predictable discourse patterns found in text) encountered in U.S. classrooms tends to be linear in style and consists of an introduction, the main story, and a conclusion. Familiarity with this story grammar promotes reading comprehension in the mainstream classroom. ELLs (and other students who differ culturally from the mainstream) may, however, enter U.S. schools with different story grammars, including more circular discourse patterns, and are therefore likely to bring different sets of expectations to mainstream texts. (Readers who can remember their first experience viewing a foreign film such as *Like Water for Chocolate* [Arau, 1992]) that is replete with magical realism are likely to relate to the initial disconnect caused by a mismatch of story grammars.) When the story grammars of a text differ from the reader's story grammars, readers may even change the meaning of the text to make it more consistent with their existing schemata as is illustrated in the seminal work of Bartlett (1932/1995). This obviously interferes with reading comprehension.

Successful readers have developed (and continue to develop) top-down strategies, which they use flexibly while reading. As reading materials grow in complexity and sophistication each successive school year, so too do the reading strategies required for comprehension. When readers work through increasingly difficult (but *comprehensible*) texts, their top-down strategies become more sophisticated, which enables them to better analyze, deduce, and infer. Through the process of reading and through focused strategy instruction, proficient readers continue to develop strategies for checking understanding, questioning the text, and returning to sections to reread as necessary.

Proficient readers also establish purposes for reading and adjust the pace of their reading depending on the purpose and the difficulty of the text. Other strategies proficient readers use include summarizing the gist of the text as they read, noticing when they are confused, and returning to the text to reread strategically to clarify confusions.

ELLs who read at grade level in their native languages have developed top-down reading strategies that they can transfer to English reading (August, 2002; Cummins, 1984a, 1984b, 2000, 2005) once they have developed sufficient oral language proficiency in English. While ELLs do not need to relearn strategies, some ELLs may need explicit instruction to enable them to transfer strategies from their first language to English.

Struggling adolescent readers (ELLs and native-English readers) may not have developed their comprehension strategies well enough to use them flexibly and across content-area reading (Biancarosa & Snow, 2006). Collectively, only 4% of ELLs score at or above the proficient level in reading, and only 20% of students, who as a result of scores on English language proficiency measures have been reclassified as formerly limited English proficient, score at or above the proficient level in reading (Short & Fitzsimmons, 2007). Many U.S.-born ELLs are likely to share characteristics of other struggling readers with additional needs for vocabulary instruction.

While a need exists for substantially more research on reading practices for adolescent ELLs (Short & Fitzsimmons, 2007; Snow, 2006), some student needs that have been identified are included in Table 4.3. The table is based on the diversity of ELLs in U.S. schools, approximately 43% of whom are from other countries and territories and may enter U.S. schools with high levels of literacy or major gaps in their first-language reading abilities. Fifty-seven percent of ELLs are second, third, and subsequent generations and therefore have attended a variety of programs in U.S. schools throughout their education.

TABLE 4.3	Top-Down Instructional Reading Needs of ELLs

Characteristics of ELLs	Instructional Considerations
ELLs at all proficiency levels educated in the United States or in their country of origin	Reading is presented in context to enhance the development (and activation) of relevant schemata
	Focused vocabulary work that emphasizes depth and breadth of vocabulary (polysemy, collocations, connotations) (Nation, 2001; Stahl & Nagy, 2006)
	Ongoing, extensive reading of *comprehensible* texts (Allington, 2005; Short & Fitzsimmons, 2007)
	Ongoing opportunities to discuss the texts and build background knowledge
ELLs who read at grade level in their first language	Focused vocabulary (as above)
	Ongoing reading (as above)
	Explicit instruction on transferring strategies from their first languages to English reading (August, 2002)
ELLs who do not read at grade level in their first language or in English	Focused vocabulary (as above)
	Ongoing reading (as above)
	Explicit instruction on transferring existing strategies (as above)
	Explicit teaching of reading comprehension strategies (including modeling and practice) (Biancarosa & Snow, 2006)

Summary: Top-Down Reading

The research that is available regarding the best instructional reading strategies for adolescent ELLs, when combined with research on second-language acquisition and first-language reading, suggests that ELLs and other students from culturally different backgrounds will benefit from extensive ongoing reading of comprehensible and engaging texts and direct instruction that builds appropriate background knowledge. Additionally, ELLs, like other students, benefit from content-area instruction that includes attention to reading comprehension strategies. ELLs, who have grade-level reading levels in their first languages, do not need to relearn comprehension strategies in English; rather, these ELLs are likely to benefit from instruction that enables them to transfer these strategies to English reading. ELLs at every level will benefit from instructional activities that expand their vocabularies.

Bottom-Up Reading Strategies

While Biancarosa and Snow (2006) identify most of the problems in adolescent reading as difficulties with comprehension, Tatum (2005) found that many struggling readers lacked the reading fluency (at the word level) necessary to read for comprehension. Tatum's students (black adolescent males) could decode words, but decoded with less automaticity than proficient readers. Although Tatum's work was with native-English-speaking students, his students were not all speakers of standard academic English; his findings are consistent with those of Birch (2002, 2006).

The work of Birch (2002, 2006) focuses on the bottom-up reading abilities that ELLs must develop and the various challenges ELLs confront in developing automaticity (and thus fluency and comprehension) in English reading. Birch (2002) agrees with experts in second-language literacy, such as Snow and Biancarosa, Cummins, Krashen, Wong Fillmore, and Freeman and Freeman, that top-down literacy abilities transfer from the native language to English. While she also acknowledges the transfer of some bottom-up abilities, she explains that some bottom-up processes may not transfer at all and that other first-language bottom-up abilities may even interfere with English reading. While a full discussion of Birch's work is well beyond the scope of this chapter, some key points are summarized in the following sections. When reading the following sections, it is important to keep in mind that while interference with bottom-up transfer may exist and teachers should be aware of possible interference, the advantages of tapping into ELLs' first-language literacy remain great. First-language literacy is always advantageous.

The Writing System

To make meaning from text, readers must learn the meaning of the marks on the page (letters, punctuation, and white spaces) and be able to decode these into sounds and then words, which they then retrieve from their mental lexicon. ELLs who speak languages with nonalphabetic writing systems will need to learn the English alphabet system. It is, therefore, useful to consider the types of writing systems that ELLs may bring to the U.S. classroom. Writing systems can be classified by three major distinctions (Birch, 2002, 2006):

1. Meaning based or logographic, in which one symbol represents one word with no relationship between sound and symbol, and every new word requires a new symbol (Chinese and the language of mathematics belong in this classification)

2. Syllable based or syllabic, in which syllables (consonant-vowel, consonant-vowel-consonant) are set and cannot be broken down to separate letters (Khmer, Japanese, and Korean are examples of syllabic languages)

3. Phonemic based or alphabetic, in which letters represent sounds (English, as you know, relies on a phonemic alphabetic writing system) An advantage to the phonemic-based system is that all the words within the language can be represented by combining 26 (or some finite number of) letters or symbols. When a new word is created, there is no need to develop a new symbol for this word; rather, letters can be re-ordered to represent the new word.

To make sense of the symbols and read these writing systems, however, the reader must know the language.

ELLs enter U.S. classrooms with first languages that include different writing systems (Birch, 2002). ELLs from China, for example, have likely learned a logographic system. Like mathematic symbols, Chinese sinograms (symbols) are conceptual in nature. According to Birch (2002), many researchers liken the reading of Chinese sinograms to processing a picture. Although top-down reading abilities are likely to transfer from Chinese to English, ELLs who have learned this writing system may be less likely to make a positive transfer to decoding and encoding the writing system of English until they learn the new writing system.

Katy Boureth was born in the United States, yet the literate elders in her family learned to read Khmer, which is syllabic. The Khmer writing system also differs from English in that, while spaces are placed at the end of Khmer sentences, spaces are not used between individual words.

Arabic is an alphabetic system like English. Yet when Adaam Jasam first began to learn English, he was initially somewhat confused by reading from left to right. Like Hebrew, Aadam's native Arabic is written from right to left. English also relies heavily on vowels; consider, for example, how changing the vowel differentiates the following words (Birch, 2002, 2006): pat, pet, pit, pot, put). Arabic, on the other hand, is consonantal and vowels are often ambiguous. ELLs who are familiar with consonantal languages may be confused when presented with English, which frequently differentiates words with changes in vowels (Birch, 2002, 2006).

The phonetic structure of English also poses problems for languages that appear to be quite similar in alphabet and orientation. For example, Fredy Solis, a student from the Dominican Republic, began to learn to read in Spanish. Fredy, however, is confused by the many different vowel sounds in English and the numerous silent letters. Only 5 vowel sounds exist in Spanish compared with the 12 vowel sounds that exist in English (Birch, 2002).

Alphabetic languages also differ in their levels of transparency (Birch, 2002). A language is said to be transparent when the sound-symbol relationships remain the same. Spanish and Italian, for example, are transparent languages. Readers of these languages can be confident that the sound-symbol relationship will be consistent, that is, that the same letters will represent the same sounds. English, on the other hand, has an inconsistent sound-symbol relationship. Patterns for the pronunciation of vowels often demonstrate this inconsistency; for example, consider the sound of the vowel /a/ in the following simple words: call, callous, cat, and can. The pronunciation of consonants can be inconsistent as well, as is demonstrated in words such as knew and right, and by consonants that represent more than one sound cat, city. These inconsistencies cause English to be referred to as an opaque alphabetic system. (We recommend the work of Birch for a thorough discussion of bottom-up processing in English.)

Teachers of ELLs must become aware of the ways in which ELLs' native languages may cause possible interference, as well as positive transfer, in the acquisition of English language literacy. At times explicit instruction may be necessary. Although content-area teachers cannot be expected to teach English phonics, it is useful for teachers to be aware of the possible bottom-up differences between ELLs' first languages and English. It is also important for content-area teachers to know that when ELLs must focus attention on decoding many words within sentences, meaning will likely be lost. Providing a variety of content-area reading materials that are comprehensible to students facilitates the development of automaticity in decoding and of fluency in English reading.

Summary: Bottom-Up Reading

While top-down reading abilities generally transfer from a student's first language to English, and bottom-up abilities may well transfer (Cummins, 2005), the transfer of bottom-up abilities may vary between language systems depending on writing systems and transparency. ELLs whose first languages are more similar to English (i.e., they read from left to right and use the same alphabetic system) are more likely to independently transfer their first-language bottom-up knowledge to English reading. English, however, features combinations of same letters that make different sounds such as *now* or *own,* different letter combinations that make the same sound such as *glue* and *knew, bluff* and *rough,* and letters that are are silent such as in *knife* or *right.* An awareness of the differences in writing systems can help content-area teachers identify difficulties that ELLs may experience in content-area reading. Once difficulties are identified, teachers can consult with ESOL specialists.

Content-area teachers can ensure ongoing opportunities for improving academic reading by

- providing access to comprehensible texts (readers must be able to access 90% to 95% of the running words to understand text),
- teaching reading strategies,
- activating ELLs' first-language reading strategies and supporting ELLs as they transfer these strategies to English reading,
- dedicating instructional time to content-area vocabulary instruction,
- providing students with time to practice strategies in content-area reading,
- activating (and providing, when necessary) appropriate background knowledge,
- observing ELLs' reading patterns and asking ELLs where difficulties arise,
- becoming aware of differences in writing systems (symbols and levels of transparency), and
- conferring with the ESOL teacher regarding specific observed difficulties in ELLs' reading.

Vocabulary

Vocabulary knowledge is closely related to academic literacy (Nation, 2001; Stahl & Nagy, 2006). Extensive vocabulary knowledge serves to build conceptual understanding, background knowledge, and schemata and provides a vehicle for expressing this understanding. Vocabulary development is cumulative: The more words a reader already knows, the easier it is to learn new words (Stahl & Nagy, 2006). Considering the cumulative nature of vocabulary development, it is unsurprising that vocabulary is one of the greatest challenges confronting ELLs (Stahl & Nagy, 2006).

The relationship between vocabulary, listening comprehension (Rost, 2005), and reading comprehension (Eskey, 2005) is widely accepted. In fact, the correlation between vocabulary knowledge and reading ability is extremely high (.85 to .95) (Stahl & Nagy, 2006). As discussed in Chapter 2, the average educated native-English speaker has a vocabulary of approximately 20,000 word families (Nation, 2001), which places an extraordinary burden on ELLs, who arrive at U.S. schools in middle and secondary grades and must catch up to succeed academically.

Learning a word is generally thought to be a three-stage process. First, the learner needs to notice the word. Noticing refers to attending to the word itself rather than the word as part of the message. For example, the learner encounters a word and independently thinks, "This is a word I'm not sure about. It is used differently than I thought it would be." Noticing can also occur when a word is glossed, or when the teacher calls attention to it and defines, explains, or discusses the word, or when learners work together to elucidate the meaning of a word (Nation, 2001).

Once the word is noticed and attended to, the learner must retrieve the word. Retrieval can be either receptive (the learner encounters the word again in reading or listening), or it can be productive (the learner uses the word in speaking or writing). It is generally believed that it requires 12 intermittent retrievals of a word to learn it (Beck, Perfetti, & McKeown, 1982; Stahl & Nagy, 2006).

The third stage of the process is generative use, which is when the learner uses a word in a context that differs from the original context in which the word occurred. For example, students in Ms. Chin's class learned the word *provisions* meaning the food and equipment of troops and later used the word to discuss the provisions of a treaty.

Types of Vocabulary Words

Approximately 2,000 word families constitute 80% of academic texts. These words come from the General Service List (West, 1953). Nation (2001) explains that 165 of these are "function words, such as *a, some, two, because* and *to*" (p. 15). Words on this high-frequency list are thought to be quite stable as they appear across content-area texts; there is 80% agreement among researchers about the words on the list. According to Nation, the first 1,000 word families actually account for 77% of words found in texts. Table 4.4 illustrates the nonacademic nature of general vocabulary words. Specifically, these are the words that ELLs often encounter in social language. Beginners will need to learn high-frequency words, whereas intermediate to transitioning ELLs may need to learn the specific spellings of high-frequency general words (e.g., *there, their,* and *they're*) but they typically will not need to learn the words.

TABLE 4.4	Selected High-Frequency Words						
the	at	more	take	find	just	write	another
home	problem	line	let	report	yet	direct	care
body	measure	thus	class	death	actual	road	ago
modern	outside	island	private	English	attempt	employ	ride

SOURCE: General Service List (a list of the words of best general service to learners of English). The table includes the first high-frequency word and every 20th word on the list up to the 620th word (The resource section at the end of this chapter provides a link to the complete list of high-frequency words.)

Academic Vocabulary

It is generally accepted among researchers (Coxhead, 1998; Nation, 2001) that 570 academic words constitute approximately 9% of academic texts. These are words that ELLs (and many native-English speaking students) are unlikely to hear in everyday social language. Experts in vocabulary teaching and learning view these words as vital to the comprehension of content-area text and thus recommend teaching them (Nation, 2001). The Academic Word List (AWL) identifies these 570 academic word families. Table 4.5 illustrates the first 60 of the 570 headwords of the AWL. For example, the word family for the headword *analyze* consists of *analyzed, analyzes, analyzing, analysis, analyst, analysts, analytic, analytical,* and *analytically.*

Technical vocabulary consists of the words that are specific to each content area and includes the terms that are typically explicitly taught to all students, such as *Federalist, Loyalists,* and *Magna Carta* in U.S. history; *joule, work,* or *calorie* in science; *irrational numbers, integers,* and *prime numbers* in math; and *figurative language, irony,* and *paradox* in ELA.

Once ELLs and other students have learned the high-frequency words, AWL words, and the technical vocabulary that is generally taught as part of the unit, they will understand approximately 95% of the words in content-area text and will have an improved opportunity to learn new words during extensive reading. Dedicating instructional time to vocabulary has the potential to benefit ELLs as well as many native-English-speaking students.

TABLE 4.5   Academic Vocabulary Words

analyze	approach	area	assess	assume	authority	available	benefit
concept	consist	constitute	context	contract	create	data	define
derive	distribute	economy	environment	establish	estimate	evident	export
factor	finance	formula	function	identify	income	indicate	individual
interpret	involve	issue	labor	legal	legislate	major	method
occur	percent	period	policy	principle	proceed	process	require
research	respond	role	section	sector	significant	similar	source
specific	structure	theory	variables				

SOURCE: Massey University (http://language.massey.ac.nz/staff/awl/sublist1.shtml). The entire word list can be found at this Web site.

Reprinted with permission of the Cambridge University Press.

ACADEMIC WRITING

Academic writing, like reading, is a meaning-making activity that consists of the interaction between top-down and bottom-up processes. Early writing can be described as knowledge-telling (Graham & Perin, 2007; Hinkel, 2004). Young beginning writers write to share knowledge such as personal information and familiar stories, and gradually learn the spelling and grammar conventions of standard English. Once beginning writers enter school, they are called on to respond to writing prompts such as "What I did on my summer vacation, My favorite place to go, or My hero is . . . " (Bereiter & Scardamalia, 1987; Graham & Perin, 2007). Students' mastery of the form and mechanics of standard English writing continues to improve as they write to share familiar information. Students continue to develop vocabulary, which also enriches native-language writing.

As students progress through the grades, there is an expectation that their academic writing will become more impersonal, abstract, author evacuated, and what is referred to as *knowledge-transformational* (Bereiter & Scardamalia, 1987; Farr, 1993; Graham & Perin, 2007). Knowledge-transformational writing requires writers to synthesize information and write various types of essays, such as informational, opinion, cause and effect, compare and contrast, and analyses (Hinkel, 2004).

Unfortunately, based on National Assessment of Educational Progress (NAEP) results, fewer than one third of all students in Grades 4 through 12 write at proficient levels (Persky, Daane, & Jin, 2003) and the same statistic applies to high school students who are preparing to enter college (ACT, 2005).

While all students must develop the ability to engage in academic writing, many factors, including language proficiency, are likely to influence their writing skills. Whereas across the grades, native-English speakers have acquired the necessary language proficiency in terms of vocabulary, grammar, and syntax for both knowledge-telling and knowledge-transformation writing, ELLs are at various stages of acquiring English proficiency. ELLs also are an extremely diverse group, who differ in first- and second-language literacy, economic status, culture, and cognitive and developmental abilities. Previous experience and education influences their writing abilities and discourse style.

The National Commission on Writing (2003, 2006) recommends that more attention be given to quality writing instruction for all students. (A link to National Commission on Writing is available in the Resources for Further Reading section at the end of this chapter.) In a review of writing programs in the United States, the Commission found many examples of effective writing practices that personalize instruction and promote communities of writers, in which ELLs and other students draw on the experiences of their homes and communities and write with purpose: A native Tlingit high school student writes about Tlingit culture based on an ethnographic study she conducted with her grandmother; high school students from Mexico, whose families work at mining uranium, and students in South Carolina, whose families process uranium, collaborate to discuss the complexities of working with hazardous materials; and a multilingual Albanian immigrant high school student describes the challenges involved in communicating electronically in Spanish and English. Teachers and students in writing programs that promote this type of engaged writing are "co-inquirers and co-learners, a process that allow[s] teachers to model inquiry, study, and learning" (p. 10).

Effective programs also require students to write across genres; middle school writing programs encourage "observational, descriptive, and analytic writing" and high school programs engage students in writing "complex summaries, lab reports, book reviews, and reflective and persuasive essays" (National Commission on Writing, 2006, p. 74).

In recent efforts to identify the best instructional practices to improve adolescent writing, Graham and Perin (2007) conducted a meta-analysis of experimental and quasi-experimental studies of writing instruction. Although the study did not include smaller qualitative studies of writing practices regardless of their findings, the meta-analysis provides recommendations for writing instruction for native-English writers that are relevant to the teaching of writing to ELLs. Based on their findings, the authors recommend 11 instructional practices that should be *included* in effective writing programs; the authors of the study stress that these practices do not by themselves constitute a writing program. The left column in Table 4.6 shows the 11 recommended strategies (reprinted with permission from Carnegie Corporation of New York. For the full report, go to www.carnegie.org/literacy). The right column in Table 4.6 highlights the considerations for ELLs based upon the current research in second language literacy. When appropriate, additional recommendations are made.

Other specific recommendations for direct instruction for ELLs (Hinkel, 2004) include

1. the precise use of vocabulary (e.g., the difference between *agree* and *acquiesce*)

2. the careful and purposeful use of discourse markers (e.g., *first* and *then*)

3. attention to the impersonal and author-evacuated stance and the passive voice (as described by Bereiter & Scardamalia, 1987; Farr 1993, and Graham & Perin, 2007) and the impartial stance with the avoidance of emotive words (As described earlier in this chapter, this may depart from students' discourse styles.)

4. the use of a guarded stance avoiding absolutes (e.g., *always* and *never*) and instead using hedging adverbs (e.g., *generally* and *usually*) (Hinkel, 2004, p. 36)

Instructional practice based on the recommendations is presented in Chapter 9.

Review, Reflect, Apply

1. *Review and reflect:* What type of writing assignments does your content-area require? Review the recommendations of Graham and Perin and those specific to ELLs. Consider your classroom. Reflect on the ways in which your instruction meets their recommendations and explain ways in which your writing assignments might be improved.

2. *Apply:* Discuss ways in which you could find at least one period a week for ELLs and other students who are engaged in a content-area writing project to share their writing in small literary groups.

TABLE 4.6   Instructional Practices for ELL Writing

11 Recommendations From Carnegie Corporation Study	Considerations for ELLs
1. Writing strategies, which involve teaching students strategies for planning, revising, and editing their compositions.	Specific attention to pervasive errors that occur in second-language writing, such as "word order, verb tense, . . . word form, word choice, relative (adjective) clauses, and subject-verb agreement" (Hinkel, 2004, p. 48)
2. Summarization, which involves explicitly and systematically teaching students how to summarize texts.	Summarizing benefits ELLs who, like other students, will be required to synthesize large amounts of materials across sources to write various types of essays (Hinkel, 2004)
3. Collaborative writing, which uses instructional arrangements in which adolescents work together to plan, draft, revise, and edit their compositions.	ELLs will need specific directions, ongoing support, and direct instruction (direction and modeling) if they are to offer constructive criticism to others (Kroll, 2001). In some cultures, the high value placed on politeness will interfere with ELLs' ability to provide criticism (Carson & Nelson, 1994, 1996 in Hinkel, 2004; Hinkel, 2004). Additionally, ELLs tend to value the feedback of teachers over the feedback of their peers, and thus ongoing teacher feedback (including error correction) remains important
4. Specific product goals, which assigns students specific reachable goals for the writing they are to complete.	ELLs need specific product goals at macro and micro levels, that is, they need goals and plans for overall writing outcomes (the form and structure of academic writing) and will benefit from specific product goals and corrections at the sentence level (Hinkel, 2004)
5. Word-processing, which uses computers and word processors as instructional supports for writing assignments.	Research by Phinney (1991) and Phinney and Mathis (1990) suggests that ELLs believe that their writing improves through the use of word-processing, thus lowering their anxiety and their affective filter
6. Sentence combining, which involves teaching students to construct more complex and sophisticated sentences.	ELLs particularly benefit from support with sentence construction, including providing additional information about subordinate clauses, regularities of phrase and clause structure, and appropriate verb tense (Hinkel, 2004)
7. Prewriting, which engages students in activities designed to help them generate or organize ideas for their compositions.	ELLs will also benefit from this additional support at the discourse level
8. Inquiry activities, which engage students in analyzing immediate, concrete data to help them identify ideas and content for particular writing assignments.	This is consistent with research on second-language literacy
9. Process writing approach, which interweaves a number of writing instructional activities in a workshop environment that stresses extended writing opportunities, writing for authentic audiences, personalized instruction, and cycles of writing.	Process writing engages ELLs in writing that is authentic and teaches them what writers do when they write and thus is useful and important for ELLs (Hedgcock, 2005; Raimes, 1991). Process writing for ELLs must be accompanied by clear and direct instruction in grammar at the sentence level, by examples of clear academic writing, and by clear discourse markers (Hinkel, 2004)
10. Study of models, which provides students with opportunities to read, analyze, and emulate models of good writing.	This is consistent with research on second-language writing
11. Writing for content learning, which uses writing as a tool for learning content material.	This is consistent with research on second-language acquisition and literacy

SOURCE: Reprinted with permission from Carnegie Corporation of New York. For full report go to: www.carnegie.org/literacy

CHAPTER SUMMARY

As important as academic literacy is to achievement, high percentages of adolescent learners struggle with reading and writing across grade-level content-area subjects. Unfortunately, many students (ELLs and native-English speakers) drop out of school each year because they lack the literacy skills necessary to access the curriculum, and far too many students are unprepared for college-level writing (Achieve, 2005). Situating the challenges experienced by ELLs in the context of the greater content-area literacy problem highlights the potential benefits of providing focus and ongoing instruction in reading and writing across content areas.

Even the most proficient readers benefit from ongoing instruction in strategies that enable them to continue to grow and improve in their ability to read more challenging texts that, without focused instruction in strategies, may be beyond their reach. Tovani found that even seemingly top readers often have underdeveloped strategies when they attempt to read more difficult material.

Some ELLs may be among the top readers in native-language reading. These ELLs should be encouraged to apply first-language reading strategies to English reading. This transfer may not occur automatically; content-area teachers can, however, facilitate transfer by discussing native-language strategies with ELLs and demonstrating the use of those strategies in English.

English vocabulary and syntax are likely to present ongoing barriers to academic literacy for ELLs as they develop English language proficiency. Content-area teachers can support the academic literacy development of ELLs by providing ongoing opportunities for focused academic discussions, building academic vocabulary, teaching content-area reading strategies, supporting ELLs as they transfer native-language reading strategies to English, and supporting the development of academic writing across the content areas.

Chapter 9 focuses on specific classroom lessons and activities that build academic literacy across the content areas.

Assessment Evidence Activities

AE-1   Explain the processes involved in the four modalities of academic literacy, and describe how each of these applies to your content area.

AE-2   Identify the difficulties ELLs at intermediate and transitioning levels of proficiency might have while listening and speaking in your specific content-area classroom.

AE-3   Explain the specific strengths and needs ELLs bring to academic reading and writing considering (1) different levels of language proficiency, (2) different levels of reading and writing in English, and (3) varying reading and writing abilities in a first language. (Be sure to include top-down and bottom-up processes.)

AE-4   Prepare a brief talk illustrating the advantages that first-language academic literacy provides to ELLs.

Resources for Further Reading

- The Academic Word List: A full list of the 570 academic words compiled by Averil Coxhead of Victoria University, Wellington, New Zealand, can be found at http://language.massey.ac.nz/staff/awl/sublists.shtml
- General Service List: A full list of high-frequency words that constitute 80% of academic texts. http://jbauman.com/aboutgsl.html
- Reports from the National Commission on Writing are available at www.writingcommission.org
- Biancarosa, G., & Snow, C. E. (2006). *Reading next: A vision for action and research in middle and high school literacy—a report to the Carnegie Foundation.* Retrieved July 3, 2008, from www.all4ed.org/files/archive/publications/ReadingNext/ReadingNext.pdf
- Flowerdew, J., & Miller, L. (2005). *Second language listening: Theory and practice.* New York: Cambridge University Press.
- Graham, S., & Perin, D. (2007). *Writing next: Effective strategies to improve writing of adolescents in middle and high schools—a report to the Carnegie Foundation.* Retrieved July 3, 2008, from www.all4ed.org/files/WritingNext.pdf
- Hinkel, E. (2004). *Teaching academic ESL writing: Practical techniques in vocabulary and grammar.* New York: Lawrence Erlbaum.
- Short, D., & Fitzsimmons, S. (2006). *Double the work* (a report to the Carnegie Foundation). Retrieved from www.all4ed.org/publication_material/reports/double_work

Planning for Enduring Understanding

Enduring understanding: Instruction based on enduring understandings ensures English Language Learners access to high-level content.

Previous chapters highlighted the need to provide ELLs with culturally responsive, high-quality instruction that capitalizes on their cultural and social experiences and builds academic-language abilities. This instruction can be neither overly simplified nor transmitted to ELLs and other students as sets of discrete facts to be learned. Culturally responsive, language-rich instruction must, instead, be structured around the content-area concepts that ELLs and other students must understand well and deeply—the cornerstone concepts for which all students must develop enduring understanding. Instruction that is planned and implemented based on the enduring understandings in content areas replaces instruction that is remedial (focused on skills in isolation) and instruction by transmission (lots of information conveyed by the teacher). It is instruction that is engaging and motivating, promotes higher-level thinking, incorporates a variety of worldviews, and enables ELLs and others to demonstrate their mastery of core content through authentic, product-driven assignments. Planning for enduring understanding for ELLs is the focus of Chapter 5. In this chapter, content-area expert teachers discuss how they determine the content-area concepts that should be taught for enduring understanding and the  *enduring language abilities* necessary to master these concepts. While planning is focused on specific content areas, the planning process is relevant across content areas. Readers are encouraged to consult copies of their state or local curriculum frameworks to determine the enduring understanding in their content areas.

LEARNING OUTCOMES

The following learning outcomes (LOs) serve as a guide to Chapter 5. At the end of the chapter are assessment evidence activities that are aligned with the LOs.

THE NEED FOR HIGH-QUALITY, "JUST RIGHT" INSTRUCTION

Students who have insufficient skills in academic English are placed *at risk* for academic failure if they do not receive appropriate instruction. Years of research have shown that students *at risk* require more high-quality and relevant instruction to gain ground and catch up (Education Trust, 2005; Mid-Continent Research for Education and Learning [McRel], 1999). More often, however, they receive remedial instruction, which may water down content in pursuit of building specific skills. In *Lives on the Boundary,* for example, Mike Rose (1989) described a remedial high school English class where, for 45 minutes, students sat at their desks and completed (or did not complete) endless worksheets, filling in blanks with *then* or *than, their* or *there,* and *where* or *wear.* More recently, Tatum (2005) found examples of equally ineffective remedial reading instruction for black youths who read below grade level. Unfortunately, we have seen similar situations when ELLs have received instruction that did not prepare them to succeed in high-level academic classes.

ELLs in U.S. schools often receive instruction consisting of *way too little* or *way too much*— instruction that either focuses on specific content-area language at the expense of content-area concepts or instruction on too many concepts without the necessary context to make the concepts comprehensible. When ESOL teachers are required to provide content-area instruction outside their areas of expertise, they may provide ELLs with *way too little* content. Mr. Richard Gordon provides an example of such teaching. We recommend that while reading through Mr. Gordon's planning and lesson, readers reflect on Mr. Gordon's knowledge base and competence as well as what is missing from his instruction.

Mr. Gordon's Sheltered History Course

Granite High School established a Sheltered English Instruction program to meet the needs of its small but growing population of ELLs. The intent of the program was to provide ELLs with content-area instruction in core courses while they developed proficiency in English. The Granite School System hired Mr. Gordon to teach sheltered courses including history, science, and English. Mr. Gordon, a well-trained and accomplished ESOL teacher, had no formal training or expertise teaching history, science, or English as a subject. Mr. Gordon's sheltered U.S. history course blended history and geography. ELLs who had English proficiency levels from early-intermediate to intermediate and had not yet completed U.S. history were assigned to this course.

Mr. Gordon relied on his ESOL background to make decisions about the content of his course. He recognized that history was language heavy and that the limited vocabularies of ELLs interfered with their understanding. He was well aware that simply exposing ELLs to more English would not necessarily result in an increase in content-area vocabulary. Mr. Gordon's training in ESOL taught him that students must be able to read at least 95% of running words in a text in order to read above frustration level and they must know between 95% and 98% of the running words in the text in order to learn new vocabulary through reading. In preparation for the new school year, Mr. Gordon reviewed several textbooks used in mainstream geography and U.S. history courses to determine their academic-language difficulty. He decided (perhaps rightly) that these texts were too difficult for ELLs to read independently. He knew the ELLs placed in his class needed additional vocabulary and began to search for lessons to build this vocabulary. Finding a chapter on landforms, Mr. Gordon drew on his ESOL experience and created lessons to teach the names and definitions of landforms, necessary vocabulary terms in any geography and history course.

Mr. Gordon's second period class consisted of 14 early-intermediate to intermediate ELLs from six countries and territories. He began the class by writing "landforms" on the whiteboard and drew and labeled mountains, mesas, buttes, peninsulas, plateaus, and archipelagos. As he drew, he said each word and asked the students to repeat it. The students copied the landform drawings into their notebooks, coloring and labeling each. Once the students had completed these illustrations, Mr. Gordon provided simple definitions, which students copied from the board. While some students worked diligently, the simplicity of the instruction fostered distraction among others. Two girls at the back of the room shared a mirror to adjust their eyeliner, a boy's head rested on his desk throughout much of the class, and a girl and boy in the first row chatted for most of the 45-minute period.

While there may be value in drawing and labeling landforms or copying sentences from the whiteboard, this is hardly instruction that will prepare ELLs for academic work in high-level content-area courses. Mr. Gordon's instruction was *way too little* for his secondary ELLs.

Ms. Green's Mainstream History Course

In keeping with the Goldilocks analogy, it is illustrative to consider the instruction in Ms. Janet Green's mainstream history class. An experienced teacher with an undergraduate degree in history, Ms. Green has been teaching for six years and knows her content well. She spends much of her free time searching for supplementary materials including boxes of primary-source materials and numerous Internet resources for class reference. Ms. Green wants her students to come to love history as she does. While reading through Ms. Green's lesson, we recommend that readers reflect on her strengths, what she does well, and also what is lacking in her instruction.

There is so much that Ms. Green wants her students to learn that she moves through chapters quickly and enthusiastically. Ms. Green assumes that secondary-level students will be able to read texts without difficulty and assigns large sections of the text as independent reading. "After all," she thinks, "History *is* a reading-heavy subject." Ms. Green also requires that students analyze accompanying primary-source materials, which *do* make history come alive for many students in her class. This year, four ELLs with intermediate-to-transitioning proficiency were placed in Ms. Green's third period history class. From the first day of the new school year, she was apprehensive about the ELLs' ability to complete the assignments required in her course. By the middle of the first quarter, her apprehension had grown to frustration.

> I really don't know why they are here if they cannot do the work. I have a lot to cover in a short period of time—my students *deserve* to learn this material. And after all, I'm a history, *not* a language, teacher. I guess the ELLs will at least learn the English by reading it and hearing it. The primary-source documents are just too difficult—I just tell them to skip those. I am really working hard to help them succeed. I only grade their work for content, and even then I grade them with different standards than I have for other students. I tell them to do what they can—I don't know what else to do. Yet, quite honestly, this approach just doesn't seem fair to the other students in the class.

In reality, the four ELLs and, indeed, several English-speaking students in Ms. Green's class have little idea of how the history concepts are related. Often, they find themselves trying to learn strings of seemingly disjointed facts. Aadam Jassam Ali continues to fall further and further behind and explains that he has no idea of how all the reading "fits together." Mehmet, a Turkish speaker who has been in the United States for three years, states, "Just when I think I'm starting to get the idea of what we are doing, we go on to something else." Ms. Green's history course simply provides ELLs with *too much* content with too little context.

Review, Reflect, Apply

1. *Reflect and apply:* Does a lower level of English language proficiency indicate that the content material should be more simplistic? How might Mr. Gordon develop a broader context for understanding while maintaining a comprehensible language load?

2. *Apply:* Ms. Green has high standards for the type and amount of material she covers in class, yet ELLs and many other students in her class are lost. How might she make her instruction more accessible to the ELLs in her classes?

3. *Review:* What strengths and needs does each teacher bring to the classroom?

Summary

It is easy to see that the ELLs in Mr. Gordon's class are not getting the type of instruction that will prepare them for high-level content-area classes and the ELLs in Ms. Green's class are lost in a sea of details. A lesson on landforms *could* be appropriate if it were appropriately linked to the enduring understanding that geography has influenced human migration and culture.

Rethinking Mr. Gordon's Sheltered History Instruction

Unfortunately, however, when Mr. Gordon planned content-area instruction, he encountered the same problem as did Ms. Connolly, the middle school ESOL teacher in Chapter 1. Mr. Gordon knows about second-language acquisition, but he lacks content-area expertise in secondary-level history or geography. Working in collaboration with an expert geography teacher enabled Mr. Gordon to reconceptualize his planning and focus on the enduring understanding in this content area.

Reexamining the questions that inform his planning process has enabled Mr. Gordon to think very differently about lesson content and to plan instruction based on the strengths as well as the needs of his ELLs. As illustrated in Table 5.1, the new planning focuses on enduring understandings that ELLs must master and fosters academic conversations, critical thinking, collaboration, student engagement, and the development of academic-language abilities.

| TABLE 5.1 | Reconceptualizing Mr. Gordon's Instruction |

Mr. Gordon's Initial Planning	Planning Based on Enduring Understandings
What content can ELLs learn given their limited English skills?	What grade-level content is necessary for ELLs to know?
How can I teach ELLs the terms they need to know, such as *archipelago, mesas, buttes, peninsulas*?	How are terms important to an overall understanding of content? How do terms fit together with enduring understandings such as the relationship between landforms, human migration, and culture?
How do I keep ELLs on task while they learn the necessary English?	How do I encourage multiple perspectives, opinions, and ideas that will engage ELLs in meaningful content-area discussions, which will build enduring understanding in the content area, academic-language abilities, and communicative competence? How do I build on the cultural funds of knowledge within my group of ELLs?

Rethinking Ms. Green's History Instruction

Ms. Green and other teachers are feeling increasingly pressured to cover large amounts of material. Unfortunately, many ELLs, such as Aadam and Mehmet, as well as other native-English-speaking students, cannot provide their own context for the material—they remember disjointed facts rather than important concepts. Furthermore, students such as Mehmet sometimes infer that memorization of facts is the intention of learning.

Using primary-source materials allows students insight into an enduring understanding of history: It is told differently depending on the perspective of the historian. This is a powerful enduring understanding on which to build instruction for ELLs from different countries of origin.

Ms. Green knows her content area well, yet she has not cohesively connected the content-area standards and made them meaningful and enduring to the ELLs in her classroom. Table 5.2 illustrates how Ms. Green rethinks her planning.

As illustrated by the reconceptualization of Mr. Gordon's and Ms. Green's planning, teaching for enduring understanding begins with determining the *content* that ELLs must know and *then* determining the language abilities necessary to access this content and express content-area understanding in meaningful academic conversations, presentations, and papers.

As shown, instruction that is based on enduring understandings builds content-area knowledge and academic-language ability within the content areas. Anchoring concepts to an enduring understanding allows content-area teachers to provide grade-level instruction based on the *content* ELLs must know to become academically successful. Table 5.3 illustrates the two steps of the TELLiM model that are the focus of this chapter.

| TABLE 5.2 | Reconceptualizing Ms. Green's Instruction |

Ms. Green's Initial Planning	Planning Based on Enduring Understandings
How can I adequately cover all the standards that students (ELLs and my mainstream) need to know to understand history?	How do the standards that ELLs and other students need to know fit together to create a big picture, which represents an enduring understanding in this content area? How do I contextualize content so ELLs and other students understand how the standards fit together?
How will the ELLs in my classroom keep up with the reading?	How can I differentiate the required reading so that *all* students can access the information they need and are appropriately challenged by the reading load?
What will my ELLs read when primary documents are too difficult?	How can I make primary documents more accessible to all students and particularly to ELLs?
What do I do with the ELLs in my room while the students who are at grade level learn about concepts and multiple perspectives provided in primary-source documents?	How do I encourage multiple perspectives, opinions, and ideas that will engage ELLs in meaningful content-area discussions, which will build content-area understanding, academic-language abilities, and communicative competence? How do I build on the funds of knowledge within my group of ELLs?

| TABLE 5.3 | Steps 1 and 2 of the TELLiM Model |

Step 1. Review unit to determine enduring understandings
Review grade level content-area frameworks
Determine the concepts that must be taught for enduring understanding
Determine the English language abilities ELLs must possess to access content and express content-area understanding

Step 2. Set learning outcomes
Establish content-area learning outcomes for the enduring understanding
Determine what all students must learn as a result of instruction
Determine the language abilities ELLs at varying levels of proficiency must develop

PLANNING FOR ENDURING UNDERSTANDING

When planning the *Methods of Sheltered English Instruction* course, we begin by asking, "What is it that mainstream teachers *need* to *really understand* to effectively teach content to ELLs?" Based on our expertise, we know many concepts that would be *good* for teachers to know, yet adequately teaching all these concepts would require at least a master's degree program in ESOL, which would be impractical for the average mainstream teacher. Therefore, it is important to ask, What are the central concepts that teachers must *understand in depth* in order to teach ELLs?

Wiggins and McTighe (2005) use a diagram of three concentric circles to illustrate the concepts that should be taught for enduring understanding. The outer circle represents concepts worth being familiar with, the next circle represents concepts that are important to know, and at the core of the concentric circles are the cornerstone ideas and core tasks—the ideas that must *endure*, such as "Earth's resources are finite," "Probability is everywhere," and "History is told through the perspective of the author."

Determining Enduring Understandings and Learning Outcomes in Content-Area Classes

Many content-area teachers have shared with us their expertise in planning based on enduring understandings and then establishing learning outcomes to measure student understanding. Their combined experiences are illustrated by Mr. John Peterson, a veteran middle- and secondary-science teacher; Ms. Mia Bell, an experienced teacher and former accountant, who now teaches middle school math; Ms. Linda Chin, a fifth-year certified U.S. history teacher; and Mr. Jamie Hayes, a veteran secondary teacher of English language arts (ELA), whose desire to share his love of literature brought him to teaching. Conversations with these teachers and snapshots of their classrooms illustrate how teachers think about and plan for instruction for ELLs that is anchored by enduring understandings. Teachers begin by determining the *content* that all students must understand and then set the *learning outcomes* that ELLs and others must master as a result of this content-area instruction. They establish the same content-area *learning outcomes* for all students in their classrooms. (In Chapter 7, teachers provide examples of how they differentiate assessments to allow for differences in English language proficiency.)

The learning outcomes go beyond measuring students' factual knowledge to measure the students' understanding of how and why. The content-area teachers set *learning outcomes* with words that require a demonstration of content understanding, such as "*explain, justify, generalize, predict, support, verify, prove*, and *substantiate*" (Wiggins & McTighe, 1998, p. 47).

Mr. John Peterson, Secondary Environmental Science

Like most teachers, Mr. Peterson is required to work within the curricular constraints of his school system. He is responsible for ensuring that the academically diverse group of students in his classes, consisting of ELLs and native-English speakers, learn the topics delineated in national, state, and local standards. Mr. Peterson knows that his students must understand how all the standards fit together. He has found that planning instruction based on enduring understandings enables him to meet both the coverage requirements of his school and the developmental needs of his students. He draws on his formal science background as he reviews science standards. Mr. Peterson explains that cornerstone concepts and enduring understandings of environmental science remain the same whether he is planning for this introductory environmental science course or for more advanced courses, which he also teaches.

The cornerstone concepts he has identified include the interconnectedness of air, land, and water in the biosphere and informed stewardship. Mr. Peterson has developed each content-area unit within this environmental science course based on an enduring understanding that serves to continually build on and deepen students' knowledge and understanding of these cornerstone concepts. One of these enduring understandings is that "Planet Earth has finite resources."

Mr. Peterson identified the following learning outcomes that all students in the class will master as a result of instruction in the "Planet Earth Has Finite Resources" unit:

- Explain the environmental effects of a growing population on the earth's finite resources.

- Relate findings from individual environmental footprints to local, national, and global footprints.

- Support and justify your stance on an issue of environmental concern.

A recent observation of Mr. Peterson's class took place outside the school building. Pairs of students worked to identify, catalog, and record plant and animal species they found in 3 ft × 3 ft blocks of space they had measured and marked in environments such as a newly mowed football field, a meadow, and a wooded area. All 24 students, including 8 ELLs with proficiency levels from early-intermediate to transitioning, were engaged in this instruction. Once the students completed their inventory, they returned inside for an interactive lecture on biodiversity, where they continued to be engaged and focused.

Ms. Mia Bell, Middle School Mathematics

Ms. Mia Bell has always had an affinity for mathematics. During her first few years of teaching eighth graders, however, she struggled to understand exactly where their comprehension faltered. With the critical eye of a content-area expert, Ms. Bell reflected on an upcoming unit on probability. "Probability," she thought, "has always been an area of difficulty for ELLs and many other students. And it is a very important topic because it provides a foundation for data analysis and statistics."

When Ms. Bell began teaching, she found it comforting to follow the textbook's lesson on probability: define the term, provide the equation, model sample problems, and provide time for student practice. This approach did seem to reach many ELLs *while* they were in the classroom; they dutifully read through the problems and expressed the relationship between the number of ways a specific outcome will happen and the total number of outcomes as a simple proportion. Her ELLs were challenged by the vocabulary and linguistic structure of the word problems, which Ms. Bell handled by allowing them to work with native-English-speaking peers. Once ELLs had sorted through the language and the numbers were in place, they were able to complete the necessary arithmetic. At times, an ELL even remarked, "This is easy!" However, Ms. Bell noticed that follow-up work suffered when it was done at home and individually. The probability problems on her unit exam did not reflect something that was *easy* for her students. At the suggestion of her mentor teacher, Ms. Bell worked to establish the enduring understanding for the unit on probability. She explained that, as a visual learner, she found it helpful to write down on index cards some guiding questions for herself:

- What is most important for students to understand?
- What do I want them to remember?
- What is central to building understanding?

Reading through the pages of the unit, Ms. Bell first established what her focus had been thus far:

I began to realize that while the unit theme is probability, my focus had been on the textbook definition of probability and the formulas used to solve probability problems. This made me ask myself about the greater message about learning which I had been inadvertently giving my students. I kept glancing at my index cards, reminding myself of the questions at hand. I wondered if I had been focusing my students effectively. Were a definition and a formula the *most important* pieces for my students to understand? Is that what I want them to remember? Were they central to building understanding?

To all three questions, Ms. Bell thought, "No."

She then thought more deeply about the content and the desired learning outcomes for ELLs and other students. She explained that she had always had a clear sense that a cornerstone concept of mathematics, especially at the middle school level, is a solid "sense of number." "Instead of applying hundreds of seemingly unrelated rules, I want ELLs and others to connect concepts in a way that makes sense." Once Ms. Bell had identified the sense of number as a cornerstone concept of the mathematics curriculum, she looked specifically at the probability unit. She thought of the disconnected understanding students had regarding probability and explained,

ELLs and other students view probability as something that exists only in their math textbooks. Yet regardless of students' social and cultural experiences, probability is everywhere in their lives. ELLs from the Caribbean recently discussed their families' concerns about the *probability* of a potential hurricane. ELLs who had experienced violent hurricanes talked about probability and weather forecasting as well as other indicators they had observed, such as the change in behavior of animals— something we may not think about yet enriches classroom discussions.

Ms. Bell realized that if ELLs developed an understanding of probability as it related to their everyday lives, as well as to the study of mathematics, they would be better equipped to understand the concept. Knowing that students could always look up a formula, she wanted them to remember instead how probability affects them personally. "Central to building understanding," she explained, "is connecting concepts to something to which ELLs and other students can relate and enabling them to see the big picture."

Ms. Bell restructured her unit on probability. While she continues to use the math textbook, it is now reference material for the class instead of a daily guide. She has built a new unit on probability around the enduring understanding, "Everything we do involves probability."

The learning outcomes Ms. Bell has established for the unit on probability are as follows:

- Explain the process of solving word and arithmetic problems for probability.
- Predict the occurrence of an event based on knowledge of probability.
- Create word problems that involve probability.
- Justify responses to a case study problem that requires using probability.

Ms. Linda Chin, Secondary U.S. History

A walk by Ms. Chin's secondary history class reveals 28 students sitting at desks arranged in clusters of 4. The six ELLs with English proficiency levels ranging from intermediate to transitioning are collaborating with native-English-speaking students; two ELLs with beginning proficiency work together with the support of a native-language tutor. Today, students are working in pairs to read and discuss primary-source documents that include news stories and speeches of the time period they are studying. ELLs and other students are actively engaged in conversations about the perspectives of document authors and are completing Venn diagrams to organize their ideas.

Ms. Chin routinely uses primary-source documents to help students understand the importance of considering history through multiple perspectives. "History doesn't come alive for the students unless they can read and hear real stories about real people," she explained and continued,

> If teachers just follow the history book, some students see history as page after page of facts and truths—they miss the human story and the relative nature of history. They also miss how it connects to their lives. Using primary documents enables ELLs and other students to make this connection. I make primary documents accessible by adding explanatory notes in the margins of these documents, which really improves student understanding.

(See Chapter 8 for further discussion on adjusting documents for comprehensibility.) When Ms. Chin is asked about the enduring understandings of U.S. history, she responds,

> Students must conceptually understand history. One of the cornerstone concepts of history is that it is written through the perspective of the authors and generally portrays the viewpoint of the victors. *Who* tells the story makes a big difference in *how* the story is told. An enduring understanding is the concept of revolution. For example, we are studying the American Revolution, which is clearly an important part of U.S. history, yet students should understand that revolution is revolution regardless of where it takes place. This is powerful for ELLs from other countries and histories—it often builds on their background knowledge.

Ms. Chin has established the following learning outcomes for her instructional unit:

- Explain the different perspectives of citizens (African Americans, women, members of upper and working classes) regarding the American Revolution.
- Substantiate the positions that the American Revolution was inevitable or avoidable.

Mr. Jamie Hayes, Secondary English Language Arts

The hallway outside Mr. Jamie Hayes's secondary ELA classroom is filled with the often charged sounds of students' voices defending their opinions, challenging assumptions, and personally relating to words that were written well before their time. Mr. Hayes's class includes 24 students (including 6 ELLs who range from early-intermediate to transitioning proficiency). He has introduced the unit, which he has titled "There is More Than Meets the Lie," with an open discussion about lying.

Mr. Hayes developed the unit in response to an observation that his students, particularly ELLs and other students from culturally different backgrounds, were not very engaged in the books required for his class. While some students appeared to enjoy *The Adventures of Huckleberry Finn, Othello,* or *The Catcher in the Rye,* Mr. Hayes often fielded complaints that the books were boring, outdated, and "so unrelated to our lives." ELLs, in particular, struggled with language, reading level, and subject material. Their reactions led Mr. Hayes to think more broadly about his purpose in teaching literature to his students. Mr. Hayes explained,

I wanted students to realize that literature is meant to be contemplated beyond the pages of the book. I began working from the overarching understanding that there are universal themes across works of literature and then adopted a thematic structure to the literature we read in class.

He determined that he would no longer work through his book-driven "Huck Finn" unit, "Hamlet" unit, or "Othello" unit but would establish a unit that was unified by a theme, which allowed ELLs (and other students) a point of entry into the literature. Mr. Hayes understood that his ELLs, who often struggled to read challenging, grade-level texts in English, would benefit from context-embedded instruction. He recognized that the secondary students he knew were all trying to navigate the social system of high school as they experimented with identity, self, and how to relate to others. "The universality of themes within literature, such as truth versus lies," he thought, "is an enduring understanding that is relevant to all students."

Grounding instruction in this enduring understanding, which provided context, assisted students in the comprehension of text and thrust ELLs (and others) into a more critical style of reading and thinking. All students were put in a position where they challenged the assumptions they had asserted at the start of the unit. And all students, regardless of language proficiency or English reading level, had the opportunity to think critically about a text. When asked about his shift in approach, Hayes noted that in the past, students for whom the book was appropriate could move on to thematic analysis and more in-depth study. For ELLs and other students who, for a variety of reasons, struggled with English reading, the goal was to "get through the book." The double shame in that, he reflected, was that not only did these students miss an opportunity to develop their cognitive, analytic skills, but they were trained to find reading literature to be frustrating and without reward. By structuring instruction around enduring understandings, Mr. Hayes provides students with leveled reading options, all of which contribute to perspectives on the theme. Students who read at higher levels understand the dialogue found in *Othello* (Shakespeare), while ELLs who would struggle with such a book can read *The Catcher in the Rye* (Salinger, 1951/1982), *I Am the Cheese* (Cormier, 1977), or *Zach's Lie* (Smith, 2003). Students can relate the theme of each book to the question of truth versus lies. Students use the book they have selected (with guidance from Mr. Hayes) to discuss and deepen their understanding of the theme.

Mr. Hayes has established the following learning outcomes for this unit:

- Explain positions regarding truth and lies in one of the assigned novels.
- Justify the position regarding truth and lies.
- Support the position with specific details from the book.

Review, Reflect, Apply

1. *Reflect and apply:* Choose one unit that you teach and explain why you teach it and why it is important to student understanding. Identify the enduring understanding that anchors this unit and explain how and why it is enduring. Why do students need to *really* know this content?

2. *Apply:* Identify the learning outcomes for this unit. Content-wise, what should students be able to do as a result of this instruction?

Summary

The previous section illustrated the importance of planning based on enduring understandings (the content-area concepts that ELLs and other students must know well). As Table 5.3 illustrates, planning for content-area enduring understanding is consistent with the TELLiM model. When teachers plan for enduring understanding, they contextualize instruction so that it builds on students' prior experience. Furthermore, instruction for enduring understanding necessitates thoughtful activities that foster critical and complex thinking, collaboration, and academic content-area conversation for all students.

Teachers often agree that planning for enduring understanding makes sense to them conceptually, yet they express concern about adhering to national, state, and local frameworks. Frameworks are important; enduring understandings are determined using well-designed frameworks. Research suggests that effectively implemented standards-based instruction has the potential to improve educational outcomes for students who struggle (Darling-Hammond, 1997). A recent synthesis of research conducted on standards-based education supports the effectiveness of standards-based education; however, it also indicates that the very large number of content-area standards provided to teachers presents barriers to the effective implementation of standards-based instruction (Darling-Hammond, 2007; Marzano & Kendall, 1998). Darling-Hammond (2007) explains,

> Whereas students in most parts of the United States are typically asked simply to recognize a single fact they have memorized from a list of answers, students in high-achieving countries are asked to apply their knowledge in the ways that writers, mathematicians, historians and scientists do. (para. 9)

As Ms. Green's history course demonstrated, when teachers attempt to teach all the content-area standards without first identifying enduring understandings, they often resort to *covering* content (providing unrelated facts and details) rather than building deep and enduring understanding. ELLs, in particular, are negatively affected by this instruction; coverage alone decontextualizes material and therefore reduces comprehensibility of instruction. As content-area teachers have illustrated, it *is* possible to group important curriculum standards around an enduring understanding, thus providing a context that enables ELLs and other students to understand how all the details fit together.

Once teachers identify an enduring understanding for a unit, they then determine what students will learn as a result of the unit of instruction—the unit's *learning outcomes*. The four content-area teachers moved beyond the facts that ELLs and other students would learn within the instructional unit, and beyond teacher transmission and student response, to learning outcomes that require deep understanding of concepts. Their learning outcomes are framed in language that requires ELLs and other students to consider why and how. For example, students in these content-area classes must understand in depth

1. the concept of environmental footprints, to be able to relate from the individual to the global (environmental science);

2. how to solve for problems of probability, to be able to explain the problem-solving processes (mathematics);

3. the experiences of citizens of different races, genders, and socioeconomic groups who lived during the American Revolution, to be able to explain multiple perspectives (history); and

4. the themes in literature, to be able to take a position and then explain and justify it with examples from novels (ELA).

ENDURING ACADEMIC-LANGUAGE ABILITIES

Content and language are interrelated throughout the content areas; academic language is the vehicle for learning content and for demonstrating content-area knowledge, and content is the medium through which ELLs develop academic-language ability. If ELLs are truly to grasp new concepts, they must comprehend the *receptive* language (vocabulary, language structure, syntax, and grammar) of classroom lessons and readings.

ELLs (and other students) also need the *productive* language abilities to engage in academic conversations and convey their conceptual understandings. Although it is possible to demonstrate understanding with drawings, diagrams, and other nonverbal means (and these alternative means *should* be encouraged within the classroom), if ELLs are to become academically successful in U.S. schools, they must gradually develop the ability to speak and write in English at grade level. Planning instruction for ELLs must, therefore, include planning for language as well as content. Model 5.1 illustrates the interrelationship between content-area schemata and the development of academic-language ability.

Schemata, as discussed in Chapter 2, are the elaborate and meaningful mental networks in long-term memory where concepts and knowledge are organized. As the common underlying proficiency theory suggests, schemata developed in one language are accessible to the learner in other languages. Schemata are enriched through ongoing access to content-area concepts gained through receptive language skills and ongoing communication about concepts (using receptive and productive language skills). Increasingly enriched schemata, in turn, provide conceptual contexts that enable ELLs to make sense of new content, vocabulary, and language structures.

MODEL 5.1   **Content-Area Schemata and Academic Language**

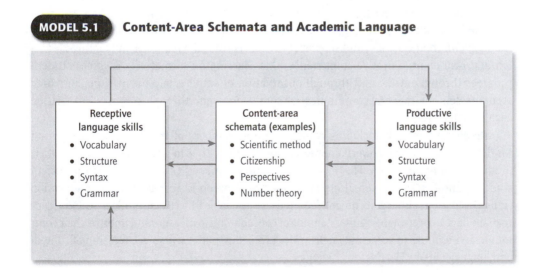

Academic-Language Learning Through Content in a Secondary Biology Classroom

Ms. Cheryl Harrington, a teacher of secondary biology, illustrates the interconnectedness of language and content in a unit based on the enduring understanding "Biotechnology impacts health care decisions." (Ms. Harrington planned the unit using the TELLiM model shown in Table 1.5, Chapter 1, this volume.) Among the concepts that ELLs and others must learn in this biology unit are the molecular aspects of genetics and the detection of genetic diseases. Twenty-four students, including eight early-intermediate to transitioning level ELLs, participate in this class.

When students enter the classroom on the first day of this instructional unit, they notice the Ms. Harrington has posted the *essential question, Genetic testing—who decides?* Ms. Harrington activates student schemata with a short film clip showing the impact of various common genetic diseases. She has developed several discussion probes, including "What are genetic diseases? Do we want to know if we are at risk for them?" and "Should everyone be tested to find out if they are at risk?" She provides these to students, who form six discussion groups, each composed of four students. (The eight ELLs work collaboratively with native-English speakers.) The academic discussion facilitates students' receptive and productive language abilities and elaborates content-area schemata.

Discussion concludes with each group briefly reporting on what they think they know about genetic disease based on the video and discussions. Ms. Harrington quickly writes student responses on a KWL (What I *know,* What I *want* to know, and what I *learned*) chart (further elaborating student schemata) and redirects students to the *essential question:* "Genetic testing—who decides?" Ms. Harrington assures students that there is no one correct response. To develop informed responses, students must learn about *genetic diseases, DNA, mRNA, protein synthesis*, and *gene codes*, and they must learn these well to participate in ongoing academic discussions. The *essential question* contextualizes instruction and allows ELLs and others to understand how all the facts fit together. Academic vocabulary and language abilities are learned in context within lessons that all relate to Ms. Harrington's essential question.

Learning outcomes for the unit require ELLs and other students to demonstrate their understandings by preparing and presenting a response to this *essential question.* As a final assessment, students create a group PowerPoint presentation, in which they take a position, *explain* their position, and *support* it with facts from the readings and lectures (written and oral communicative competence). Ms. Harrington formatively assesses student progress throughout the unit through observation of small-group discussions, in which students demonstrate oral communicative competence, and through several short written assignments.

Receiving feedback, including responses from members of the discussion group and Ms. Harrington, on their PowerPoint presentations allows ELLs to gauge the accuracy of their productive communication. The ongoing interaction between ELLs, more English-proficient students, and Ms. Harrington also serves to further develop ELLs' receptive communication skills. Discussions about government-required testing enable ELLs to use productive and receptive language to deepen their understanding of concepts and to measure and improve their communicative abilities in academic English. Model 5.2 illustrates the interrelationship of content and language in Ms. Harrington's biology class.

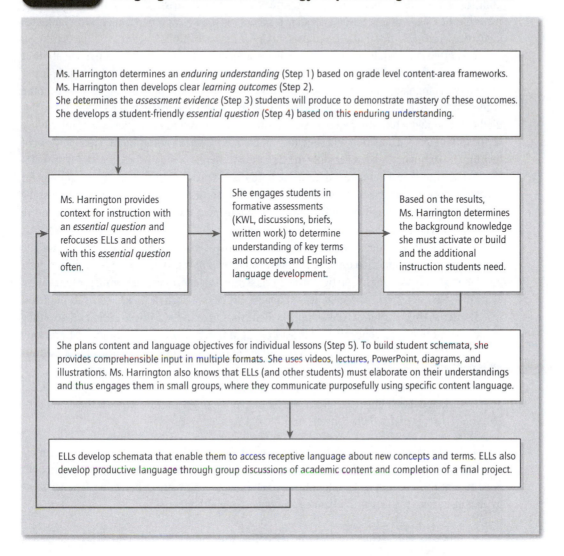

Ms. Harrington determines an *enduring understanding* (Step 1) based on grade level content-area frameworks.
Ms. Harrington then develops clear *learning outcomes* (Step 2).
She determines the *assessment evidence* (Step 3) students will produce to demonstrate mastery of these outcomes.
She develops a student-friendly *essential question* (Step 4) based on this enduring understanding.

Ms. Harrington provides context for instruction with an *essential question* and refocuses ELLs and others with this *essential question* often.

She engages students in formative assessments (KWL, discussions, briefs, written work) to determine understanding of key terms and concepts and English language development.

Based on the results, Ms. Harrington determines the background knowledge she must activate or build and the additional instruction students need.

She plans content and language objectives for individual lessons (Step 5). To build student schemata, she provides comprehensible input in multiple formats. She uses videos, lectures, PowerPoint, diagrams, and illustrations. Ms. Harrington also knows that ELLs (and other students) must elaborate on their understandings and thus engages them in small groups, where they communicate purposefully using specific content language.

ELLs develop schemata that enable them to access receptive language about new concepts and terms. ELLs also develop productive language through group discussions of academic content and completion of a final project.

CONTENT-AREA LANGUAGE

Different content areas require different receptive and productive language abilities. Listening to a poem, for example, requires different receptive skills from listening to instructions for a chemistry laboratory experiment. History texts present different reading challenges than do math texts, technical manuals, or literary works. Writing a geometry proof, a lab report, a persuasive essay, a poem, or a short story each requires different productive language abilities.

Content-area teachers face a dual challenge: They must make content accessible and measure content-area understanding apart from English language proficiency, and they must also ensure that ELLs receive instruction that promotes the development of their academic English abilities. To meet these challenges, content-area teachers must clearly identify the language abilities that ELLs eventually have to master. Teachers must also become familiar with language structures and activities that present particular difficulty for ELLs.

It is often difficult, however, for content-area teachers to tease out the language abilities necessary for their content areas. Just as native speakers are often unaware of the complexity of their own language, content-area teachers find that the language of their subjects has become second nature to them. For example, as authors of this book (and teachers ourselves), we struggled to decide which terms required substantive definitions and examples. We regularly use terms of language acquisition and therefore do not have to think about them. This question of technical vocabulary is, however, only the tip of the iceberg.

Content-area teachers must determine both the essential receptive language abilities for accessing concepts in specific content-areas and the productive language abilities necessary for demonstrating conceptual understanding. Content-area classes often, for example, require students to access concepts through different media, including a variety of types of reading, discussions, lectures, videos, and demonstrations. Content-area teachers often expect students to demonstrate content-area understanding through essays, journals, poetry, research papers, and lab reports, as well as by participating in classroom discussions and giving presentations. Teachers must determine the specific language abilities that each of these activities requires.

Earlier in this chapter, Mr. Peterson, Ms. Bell, Ms. Chin, and Mr. Hayes explained how they identified content-area concepts that must be taught for enduring understanding. Here, they share the grade-level language abilities (*enduring language abilities*) that ELLs must eventually acquire to *access* concepts (independently) and *express* content-area understanding.

All four content-area teachers shared a somewhat common understanding of the ideal academic-language abilities that all students should possess. We venture to guess that few teachers would disagree with their consensus.

- Students should read on grade level, which includes having well-developed comprehension skills such as the ability to infer. This also assumes grade-level vocabulary and knowledge of syntax. In other words, students should be able to read with sufficient proficiency so as to be able to read the text and other assignments independently.

- Students should enter courses with the prerequisite subject knowledge in the content area.

- Students should have grade-level writing skills that they can apply across content-area assignments.

- They should have well-developed listening and speaking skills so they can learn from lectures and participate in academic discussions.

The four teachers then considered the realities of their classrooms, which are that few native-English speakers meet the ideal requirements and ELLs bring a special set of challenges to mainstream content-area classrooms. The four teachers identified issues of vocabulary, syntax, reading, and writing as *enduring language abilities* within and across academic content areas. Table 5.4 illustrates the identified language abilities and specific difficulties that ELLs experience.

Well-developed vocabulary is important across the content areas and, as illustrated in the previous chapters, knowing a word is a complex process that includes knowing the word's

TABLE 5.4   Necessary Abilities and Difficulties in Academic English

Ability	Difficulty Encountered by ELLs	Supporting Research
Academic vocabulary	Understanding the vocabulary in content-area classes and in texts	Vocabulary presents one of the greatest academic challenges to ELLs. Of the running words in academic text, • 2,000 word families account for 80%, • 570 general academic vocabulary terms account for 9%, and • specific technical terms account for 6% (Nation, 2001)
	Multiple meanings of words	Academic vocabulary presents difficulties due to • polysemy (Table 2.2); • collocations (Table 2.1); and • use of words as discourse markers that indicate relationships between clauses and sentences (such as *though, if, unless, so that*, and *whereas* (Nation, 2001, p. 213)
Syntax	Extensive use of the passive voice, which occurs across academic literature Relationship between verb tense and meaning Use of markers that indicate changes in tense (*currently, 30 years ago, soon*) Use of signaling markers to indicate relationships between clauses and sentences (meaning of *though, if, unless, so that*, and *whereas* in sentence structure) and use of these in written work Use of constructions containing nonliving doers, such as *the report shows, data indicate*	Use of tense in academic writing presents difficulties for ELLs; history texts, for example, are predominately written in the past tense, whereas science texts are often written in the present tense (Hinkel, 2004). Tense markers and signaling words present difficulties to ELLs (Hinkel, 2004). The extensive use of noun clauses presents difficulties in comprehension of written texts and production of written work (Hinkel, 2004; Nation, 2001). Nonliving doer constructions are confusing too because such constructions do not exist in all languages (Hinkel, 2004)
Extent of reading	Reading large amounts of text in different genres to learn content	Difficulties with vocabulary and syntax often interfere with comprehension and fluency (Birch, 2006).
Variety of writing	Extensive writing across content areas and across genres within content areas	Writing across various genres requires ELLs to adjust for voice (active, passive), use of hedging (*it appears* rather than *it is*, *it may* rather than *it will*), and productive use of academic vocabulary (Hinkel, 2004).

multiple meanings (polysemy), collocations, connotations, and appropriateness. ELLs encounter three major types of vocabulary in the content areas: general vocabulary, academic vocabulary, and technical terms. As Mr. Richard Gordon, the ESOL specialist, explained, to develop new vocabulary through reading, ELLs must know at least 95% to 98% of the running words in the text.

PLANNING FOR ENDURING LANGUAGE ABILITIES

Mr. Peterson, Ms. Bell, Ms. Chin, and Mr. Hayes plan instruction for the *enduring language abilities* in their content-area units. They then establish learning outcomes based on the language abilities that ELLs and other students need to access content and demonstrate their mastery.

Enduring Language Abilities in Secondary Environmental Science

Mr. Peterson cites vocabulary as essential to accessing the content of environmental science:

Science is vocabulary-heavy and vocabulary knowledge is closely linked to conceptual understanding. ELLs must know vocabulary well, recognize key vocabulary terms encountered in reading, understand vocabulary in lectures, and appropriately use vocabulary in academic conversations and written assignments. In the "Finite Resources" unit, for example, students must conceptually understand the scientific meaning of terms such as *solutions* and *concentrations* or they will be unable to understand pollution levels and commonly used expressions such as *parts per million*.

Mr. Peterson has found that throughout instructional units in the sciences, ELLs encounter many words from the The Academic Word List (AWL), and the ability to comprehend and use these words in reading, writing, and academic conversations also represents an *enduring language ability*.

Mr. Peterson indicates that another *enduring language ability* is the use of strategies to self-check comprehension and to clarify confusions. As ELLs develop greater language proficiency, they will need to listen for key words and terms, know how to take notes from lectures, and learn to evaluate their own understanding so that they can ask clarifying questions when necessary.

Regarding the productive language abilities that ELLs will need to demonstrate content-area mastery, Mr. Peterson cites the ability to

- write accurate, detailed, and well-structured lab reports and orally share findings with others;

- write essays and prepare presentations to explain various points of view; and

- write persuasive essays and prepare presentations that evince understanding of informed responsible stewardship.

As they develop greater English proficiency, ELLs will need to use the language of science within the structure of standard writing conventions. Writing across scientific fields requires the use of nonliving doers as subjects, for example, *the experiment shows* and *the study suggests*, as well as the need to hedge by means of expressions such as *the data suggest* and *from the evidence provided, it appears*.

Enduring Language Abilities in Middle School Mathematics

While math is often not thought of as a reading-intensive subject, it is, in fact, very intensive, and the language (mathematical and English) is very dense. Ms. Bell explains that language in math texts is often laden with factors that confound ELLs and other students. While the language may seem straightforward, many students are confused by polysemous words, such as *operation, table, power,* and *negative.* Solving word problems is a critical ability that helps students think systematically and logically. Yet, Ms. Bell explains, "much of the language within math problems is a labyrinth of words for English Language Learners." She provides the following problem from a standardized test as an example:

Glenn bowls in a bowling league every Saturday morning. Last Saturday, the scores from Glenn's first 3 bowling games were 141, 128, and 157. . . . Each player in Glenn's bowling league is given a handicap, which allows players of different abilities to compete equally. A player's handicap is determined with the following formula. A player's handicap is equal to 80 percent of the difference between the player's average (mean) and 220. Miguel is Glenn's teammate. If Miguel's average (mean) is 130, what is his handicap? Show or explain how you got your answer. (Massachusetts Department of Elementary and Secondary Education, 2005)

Ms. Bell explains,

While a math problem like this may seem fairly straightforward, there are many layers for an ELL to peel away in order to get to the core content of the problem. There is academic (*mean, difference*) and nonacademic (*bowling league*) vocabulary to decipher. There is the passive voice (*is determined by, is given a*), which presents difficulties for ELLs. There is the word *handicap,* which holds a meaning very different from its popular significance. And there is the mathematical definition of *handicap* which, while useful information, is an additional layer to unfold. To begin to make sense of such a problem, ELLs must work through each of these outer layers first to determine the relationships between the data provided and translate these into mathematical expressions. Additionally, the language of math word problems is often couched within questions such as "What are the chances that . . . " and "What are the odds that . . . ," which have different meanings when used in everyday life and, thus, may also create comprehension issues.

Ms. Bell explains that productive *enduring language abilities* necessary to demonstrate understanding in math are, much like the receptive, quite subtle. "While students are not often asked to write lengthy essays about their experience in math, they do need to know how to communicate the processes they use to solve problems." Ms. Bell explains that ELLs, like other students, need modeling and practice in the skill of talking through their work:

Very often ELLs can write out the arithmetic, but they cannot explain their reasoning for the steps they take. When a student is stuck on a problem, I require that they talk me through exactly what is confusing them so they develop communication patterns for math.

Ms. Bell has listed the following language abilities that ELLs must access and use to complete the unit on probability:

- Use the language of probability to understand relationships between the given and unknown variables in problems.
- Access the passive voice within word problems.
- Use academic vocabulary to explain the process of solving word problems. (Ms. Bell has also determined that many words in the math text are also found in the AWL and that knowing these words represents an *enduring language ability*.)

Enduring Language Abilities in Secondary U.S. History

Ms. Chin identifies the ability to access language-heavy textbooks as well as the linguistically sophisticated primary-source materials as *enduring language abilities* necessary for understanding U.S. history. She explains,

While we can (and should) provide access to these materials for ELLs through sheltering, if ELLs are to continue to grow academically, at some point they will need to

- learn the strategies necessary to access and deconstruct difficult reading materials independently (figure out the vocabulary, use markers for tense and for change in topic/flow, and deconstruct clauses),
- develop the ability to read sentences and passages that are made dense with noun clauses and the use of passive constructions,
- effectively use discourse markers to comprehend content, and
- comprehend the meaning of hedging.

Regarding the productive *enduring language abilities*, Ms. Chin explains that eventually ELLs will need to

- write papers and make presentations using grade-level, content-area language;
- compare, contrast, and present multiple perspectives about various issues (e.g., in the case of the American Revolution, ELLs must be able to discuss the causes of this revolution in the context of the broad concept of revolution);
- use hedging to express viewpoints (rarely do clear-cut causal relationships exist; rather, ELLs and others need to use hedging [*appears, may, could*] to describe plausible relationships); and
- accurately employ tense structures to tell what happened, would have happened, or was happening during a particular historical period.

Enduring Language Abilities in Secondary English Language Arts

Mr. Hayes considers ELA to be a subject that challenges the academic-language abilities of native-English-speaking students. With that in mind, he pays special attention to the language abilities he requires of his ELLs. Receptive language abilities that stand out to Mr. Hayes include the level and quantity of language required to read the class literature. "ELLs are often overwhelmed by the amount of reading that they must do independently. I am continuously conscious of the frustration factor they confront when asked to read long passages of text that are in effect beyond their reading level." Mr. Hayes also cites the use of dialect, period-specific language, and high-level vocabulary as obstacles to understanding literature. He notes that poetry and other forms of language that rely heavily on figurative language, nuance, and often culturally specific allusions prove difficult for ELLs.

Mr. Hayes feels that the productive language abilities required in ELA include a heavy reliance on essay-based products. "ELLs must organize their thoughts with attention to tone and word choice. They are often graded on both grammar and ideas, which can be seen as a double-whammy for ELLs." Additionally, Mr. Hayes notes that participating in in-class conversations, which can be fast paced and make use of complex language structures, is a specific ability that ELLs must develop.

Review, Reflect, Apply

1. *Apply:* Think across the content area you teach; review curriculum frameworks and classroom materials. Describe the enduring language skills that ELLs must develop to independently *access* rigorous grade-level content. Then identify the enduring language skills that English language learners must develop to *express* content-area understanding.

2. *Review and reflect:* How do enduring language skills differ from content area to content area?

CHAPTER SUMMARY

Chapter 5 discussed the interrelationship of content and language and the importance of enduring understandings (content and language) in planning effective instruction for ELLs. Four content-area experts provided examples of how they determined enduring understandings, first in their content and then in language. Teachers also provided explicit examples of the receptive language abilities ELLs need to access content and the productive language abilities ELLs need to demonstrate their content-area understandings. It is recommended that readers review the processes by which content-area teachers established enduring understandings for content and language before completing the assessment evidence activities and progressing to Chapter 6. Chapter 6 demonstrates how the four content-area teachers build on the *enduring understanding* and *learning outcomes* they designed and create *essential questions* to frame their instruction.

Assessment Evidence Activities

AE-1   Explain the ways in which planning for enduring understandings is consistent with the input hypotheses (Chapter 2, p. 38) and the context-embedded context-reduced model (Model 2.3, Chapter 2, p. 48).

AE-2   List the enduring understanding(s) for a content-area unit to be implemented over a three- to five-week time period. Explain how the enduring understandings serve to contextualize the content-area standards.

AE-3   List the language abilities that ELLs must develop to *access* the content of the content-area unit. Now, list the language abilities that ELLs must develop to demonstrate content-area mastery.

AE-4   Determine the content-area learning outcomes that all students will master as a result of their participation in the unit of instruction.

Resources for Further Reading

- National Content Area Learning Standards:
  National Standards for Math, http://standards.nctm.org
  National Standards for Science, http://www.nsta.org/standards
  National Standards for History, http://nchs.ucla.edu/standards/
  National Standards for English Language Arts, http://www.ncte.org
  Teachers of English to Speakers of Other Languages (TESOL) Standards, http://tesol.org/s_tesol/seccss.asp?CID=113&DID=1583

- For a complete description of planning instruction for enduring understandings, readers are encouraged to review Wiggins, G., & McTighe, J. (2005). *Understanding by design*. Alexandria, VA: Association for Supervision and Curriculum Development.

6

Connecting With Context

Assessments and Essential Questions

Enduring understanding: Clear assessments and essential questions provide a contextual road map for instruction.

THE PREVIOUS CHAPTER DETAILED THE IMPORTANCE AND PROCESS OF PLANNING CONTENT AND LANGUAGE INSTRUCTION and establishing clear learning outcomes (LOs) based on enduring understandings. Determining assessment evidence and establishing essential questions, Steps 3 and 4 in the TELLiM model, are the focus of Chapter 6. This chapter begins by explaining the necessity of planning assessment evidence prior to planning and implementing instruction and provides examples of assessment evidence designed by content-area teachers. Next, Chapter 6 describes the creation of essential questions and illustrates the consistency between framing instruction with essential questions and the tenets of culturally responsive teaching. Then the process of converting a unit's enduring understanding to an essential question is illustrated with an example provided by Ms. Harrington, secondary biology teacher. Finally, the chapter shows content-area teachers sharing the process of developing student-friendly essential questions for content and language.

LEARNING OUTCOMES

The following LOs will serve as a guide as you read through Chapter 6. Assessment activities aligned with each LO are at the end of this chapter.

LO-1 Understand the importance of developing clear assessment evidence for LOs prior to planning instruction

LO-2 Decide what assessment evidence will demonstrate your students' mastery of the LOs you determined while working through Chapter 5.

LO-3 Understand how grounding instruction with essential questions is consistent with culturally responsive teaching

LO-4 Understand the broad instructional value of using essential questions to frame instruction for ELLs (and other students in your classes)

LO-5 Create content-area essential questions for the enduring understandings you have developed for your content-area unit

LO-6 Create essential language questions for the enduring language abilities that students should acquire through your content-area unit

---

TERMS THAT MAY BE NEW

Assessment evidence: Products or observable actions that demonstrate understanding of content and development of English language proficiency

Backward design: Beginning with what ELLs will understand at the end of an instructional unit and then planning instruction to enable them to reach this end point (Wiggins & McTighe, 1998, 2005)

Essential questions: Broad, open-ended questions that frame instruction in student-friendly language (Wiggins & McTighe, 1998, 2005)

Essential language questions: Broad questions that serve to frame academic-language development for ELLs

ASSESSMENT: BEGINNING WITH THE END IN MIND

"If you don't know where you are going, you might wind up someplace else." This advice from Yogi Berra illustrates the importance of designing and conveying appropriate assessments to ELLs and other students at the beginning of the instructional unit. Teachers who are unsure about the desired results of instruction may well end up someplace other than where they had intended. Without a clear picture of the assessment evidence that ELLs and other students must provide to demonstrate mastery of LOs, teachers cannot plan effective lessons and ELLs cannot know what is expected of them.

Readers who have planned clear LOs based on enduring understandings are now equipped to identify the assessment evidence ELLs and others should produce to demonstrate mastery of LOs. Establishing clear assessment evidence and sharing this with students at the beginning of an instructional unit provides context and purpose and enables ELLs like Aadam and Mehmet to see the big picture rather than a sea of unrelated details. Planning clear assessment evidence is the third step of the TELLiM shown in Table 6.1.

From Learning Outcomes to Assessment Evidence

This section presents examples of the conversion of LOs into assessment evidence. (Chapter 7 discusses the differentiation of assessment evidence according to English language proficiency levels.) Effective assessment evidence generally encompasses three types of knowledge:

| TABLE 6.1 | TELLiM Model: Step 3 |

Step 3	Establish Evidence
	• Decide what constitutes assessment evidence of content-area mastery apart from English language proficiency.
	• Determine what constitutes assessment evidence of growth in academic English for students at various proficiency levels.

- Declarative knowledge (the facts, generalizations, and concepts that we know) (Chamot & O'Malley, 1994; Marzano, Pickering, & McTighe, 1993; Tomlinson & McTighe, 2006)
- Procedural knowledge (the skills and strategies we use) (Chamot & O'Malley, 1994; Marzano et al., 1993; Tomlinson & McTighe, 2006)
- Dispositional knowledge (lifelong learning, habits of mind) (Marzano et al., 1993; Tomlinson & McTighe, 2006)

Ms. Elena Apostolos's secondary English Language Arts (ELA) thematic literature unit "Heroes and Villains" illustrates the process of planning assessment evidence. Using standards from the Massachusetts Curriculum Frameworks for ELA and English Language Proficiency, Ms. Apostolos prepared an instructional unit for a ninth-grade ELA class consisting of 25 students, including 8 ELLs (2 transitioning, 2 intermediate, 3 early intermediate, and 1 beginning). Ms. Apostolos began by determining the enduring understandings (TELLiM model, Step 1) and unit LOs (TELLiM model, Step 2).

Enduring understanding. Heroes and villains appear in the literature, drama, and films of every culture and must be understood through multiple perspectives.

Learning outcomes. By examining the plots, characters, and themes of heroic myths, fairy tales, plays, biographies, films, novels, and so on, students will gain the skills necessary to (1) critically evaluate the cultural concepts of heroes and villains and (2) make and explain decisions based on their criteria for heroes and villains.

Prior to planning assessment evidence options, Ms. Apostolos used a tree diagram to consider the type of knowledge that she would measure. Model 6.1 illustrates the first LO.

Ms. Apostolos then developed assessment evidence for the unit. She determined that to demonstrate mastery of these LOs, her students would participate in a mock trial lasting several days. Students (ELLs and native-English speakers) would prepare exhibits, drafts, presentations, and closing arguments, which would include factual knowledge—an evaluation of the concept of hero and villain through different perspectives. Students would develop their own criteria for identifying heroes and villains.

Assessment Evidence in the Content Areas

Mr. Peterson, Ms. Bell, Ms. Chin, and Mr. Hayes have identified LOs that all students must master by the end of instructional units and determined assessment evidence that will show mastery of these LOs. These LOs and the corresponding assessment evidence are presented in Tables 6.2, 6.3, 6.4, and 6.5.

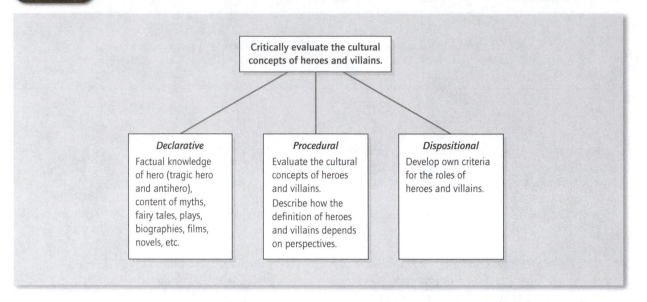

Critically evaluate the cultural concepts of heroes and villains.

Declarative
Factual knowledge of hero (tragic hero and antihero), content of myths, fairy tales, plays, biographies, films, novels, etc.

Procedural
Evaluate the cultural concepts of heroes and villains.
Describe how the definition of heroes and villains depends on perspectives.

Dispositional
Develop own criteria for the roles of heroes and villains.

TABLE 6.2 From Learning Outcomes to Assessment Evidence in Science

Learning Outcomes	Assessment Evidence
1. Explain the environmental effects of a growing population on the earth's finite resources. 2. Relate findings from individual environmental footprints to local, national, and global footprints. 3. Support and justify a stance on an issue of environmental concern.	Prepare a written, oral, and visual report for a community meeting to share facts, concepts, theories (declarative knowledge), and interpretations (procedural knowledge) regarding the effects of the growing population on Earth's resources, ending with a position statement (dispositional knowledge) that is supported by the data you have provided.

TABLE 6.3 From Learning Outcomes to Assessment Evidence in Mathematics

Learning Outcomes	Assessment Evidence
1. Explain the process of solving word and arithmetic problems involving probability. 2. Predict the occurrence of an event based on knowledge of probability. 3. Create word problems that involve probability. 4. Justify a response to a case study problem that requires using probability.	For each learning outcome, Ms. Bell provides problems that are differentiated according to level of difficulty, which enables students to demonstrate their basic level of mastery. All students are encouraged to work at the high end of their abilities. Each element of the assessment calls for evidence of declarative, procedural, and dispositional knowledge.

TABLE 6.4 From Learning Outcomes to Assessment Evidence in History

Learning Outcomes	Assessment Evidence
1. Explain the varying perspectives of different groups of people regarding the American Revolution, including Native Americans, African Americans, members of different classes, and women (across differences). 2. Substantiate the position that the American Revolution was inevitable or the position that it was avoidable.	In written, oral, and visual form, present the events leading to the Revolution (declarative knowledge) from multiple perspectives (declarative and procedural knowledge), and explain if the war was avoidable or inevitable, justifying your position (dispositional knowledge).

TABLE 6.5 From Learning Outcomes to Assessment Evidence in ELA

Learning Outcomes	Assessment Evidence
1. Explain positions regarding truth and lies in one of the assigned novels. 2. Justify a position regarding truth and lies. 3. Support your position with specific details from book.	Develop a book review presentation about a novel that you are reading, focused on the theme of truth and lies (declarative and procedural knowledge), which includes and supports a position on the theme (dispositional knowledge).

Review, Reflect, Apply

Review and apply: Review the process that content-area teachers use to convert LOs to assessment evidence. Apply this process to your LOs to determine the assessment evidence that students will provide to demonstrate mastery of these LOs.

THINKING ABOUT ESSENTIAL QUESTIONS

Once teachers have determined the assessment evidence that students will provide to demonstrate mastery of LOs, they are prepared to create the essential questions for the unit (Step 4 of the TELLiM model; see Table 6.6).

TABLE 6.6 TELLiM: Step 4

Step 4	Contextualize Instruction
	Develop essential questions to • make the enduring understanding student-friendly and • build on student knowledge and engage ELLs and other students in the broad theme of the unit.

Essential questions are broad questions that promote depth of knowledge and understanding. *What is the secret of happiness? Is honesty always the best policy? Is war ever just?* are a few examples of essential questions. These questions are posed to foster deep, critical thinking about a topic and engage students in the process of inquiry about real dilemmas. They do not have one right answer but rather encourage multiple worldviews and viewpoints. Essential questions are often repeated within content-area units, throughout courses, and at times across content-area courses, giving students opportunities to make connections in their learning and revisit topics as their content understanding (and related vocabulary) develops. Essential questions can broadly frame instruction in one content area or branch across content areas. *Who has rights to the resources?* for example, is an essential question that could frame a multidisciplinary unit or separate units in both environmental science and history.

According to Wiggins and McTighe (1998), essential questions are those questions that pique interest and help students "uncover . . . the important ideas at the heart of each subject" (p. 28). They inspire ongoing inquiry, academic conversation, and complex and critical thinking (Wiggins & McTighe, 1998), all of which are consistent with the TELLiM model. Framing instruction with essential questions contextualizes content, which increases comprehensibility (Baker, 2006; Cummins, 1984b, 2000; Tharp et al., 2000), promotes active student engagement, and fosters the development of content-area academic language for ELLs. Essential questions provide ELLs with opportunities to use academic language in meaningful ways. Essential questions foster multiple perspectives and viewpoints, resulting in a learning environment where cultural and social experiences are valued, consistent with the tenets of culturally responsive teaching (Gay, 2000; see Table 6.7).

TABLE 6.7 Essential Questions and Culturally Responsive Teaching

Essential Questions	Culturally Responsive Teaching
Essential questions get to the core of the content area.	By getting to the content-area core, essential questions help teachers provide high-level content-area instruction (rather than isolated skill builders) (Gay, 2000). Using essential questions conveys that all students can master core content, thus establishing high expectations for all students (Good & Brophy, 1994).
Essential questions are broad based and, therefore, generate critical thinking and academic conversation.	Engaging ELLs in critical thinking, academic conversations, and construction of knowledge is consistent with the tenets of culturally responsive teaching (Gay, 2000; Villegas & Lucas, 2002).
Essential questions allow for multiple interpretations and responses.	Recognizing multiple perspectives and interpretations acknowledges and capitalizes on the funds of knowledge that ELLs bring to the classroom (González et al., 2005).

FROM ENDURING UNDERSTANDINGS TO ESSENTIAL QUESTIONS

Teachers determine the content that should be taught for enduring understanding by asking the following:

- Why is this content important?
- How does it fit with the standards in my content area?
- Why is it necessary for students to understand this content?

These questions are helpful to teachers who know the content and standards and understand how the details fit together. ELLs and other students are, however, unlikely to have sufficient background knowledge to understand which concepts are important and how to make connections between the many content-area standards (Wiggins & McTighe, 1998, 2005). ELLs are even less able to identify the language abilities necessary to access content and demonstrate content-area mastery. This chapter describes how teachers can proceed from determining the content and language to be taught for enduring understanding to creating the essential questions that will engage ELLs with this content and language.

QUALITIES OF ESSENTIAL QUESTIONS

An instructor of the Understanding by Design (UbD) curriculum and secondary ELA methods stresses that it is important to keep in mind that a content-area essential question is *not* an enduring understanding in question form. Rather, essential questions must be student-friendly. He explains,

> An enduring understanding of ELA is that setting conveys theme. Rewording this enduring understanding as a question is quite ineffective, however. It is unlikely that ELLs and other students in the classroom would be engaged by "How does setting convey theme?" *Romeo and Juliet* is frequently the instructional material that teachers select when teaching about theme. "The force of love can bring happiness or destruction" is one theme from *Romeo and Juliet* that is typically relevant and appealing to high school students regardless of ethnicity, language, or socioeconomic group. Essential questions such as "How young is too young to marry?" or "Is it ever okay to defy your family?" make this theme relevant to students. These essential questions are likely to pique students' interest, foster different worldviews, and motivate ELLs and other students to engage in instruction. These essential questions will ultimately lead students to the enduring understanding, "setting conveys theme." (J. Walsh, personal communication, July 20, 2007)

This instructor's content-area expertise in secondary ELA resulted in essential questions that clarify the purpose of reading Shakespeare's *Romeo and Juliet* (Public Domain Books Classic Literature Library; available from http://william-shakespeare.classic-literature.co.uk/romeo-and-juliet) in high school. The essential questions are likely to be relevant to all high school students, including ELLs and students from different cultures. The questions also foster a challenging classroom environment in which students consider multiple perspectives and engage in academic conversations.

The essential questions suggested by the UbD instructor meet the criteria established by Wiggins and McTighe (1998, 2005), who recommend that essential questions should

- get to the enduring understandings of the content-area;
- be broad enough to have many solutions (or dilemmas without solutions);
- encourage and support a multitude of possible responses; and
- be written in engaging, student-friendly language (essential questions are not rephrased enduring understandings).

In discussing the process of creating essential questions, it is worthwhile to trace the path from standards to essential questions that Ms. Harrington followed, which is illustrated in Model 6.2.

The essential question formulated by Ms. Harrington clearly meets the criteria checklist shown in Table 6.8, which is based on the recommendations of Wiggins & McTighe (2005).

MODEL 6.2   **From Enduring Understandings to Essential Questions**

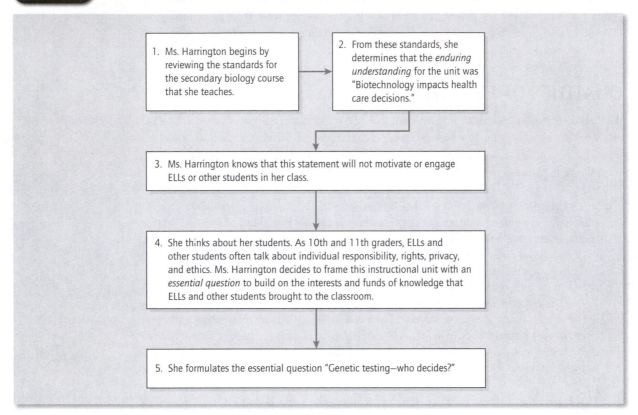

1. Ms. Harrington begins by reviewing the standards for the secondary biology course that she teaches.

2. From these standards, she determines that the *enduring understanding* for the unit was "Biotechnology impacts health care decisions."

3. Ms. Harrington knows that this statement will not motivate or engage ELLs or other students in her class.

4. She thinks about her students. As 10th and 11th graders, ELLs and other students often talk about individual responsibility, rights, privacy, and ethics. Ms. Harrington decides to frame this instructional unit with an *essential question* to build on the interests and funds of knowledge that ELLs and other students brought to the classroom.

5. She formulates the essential question "Genetic testing—who decides?"

TABLE 6.8   Criteria for Essential Questions in the Content Areas

Criteria	
Essential questions get to the enduring understandings of the content area.	√
Essential questions are broad enough to have many solutions (or to represent dilemmas without solutions) and, therefore, generate critical thinking and academic conversation.	√
Essential questions encourage multiple interpretations and responses.	√
Essential questions are student-friendly.	√

In the following sections, Mr. Peterson, Ms. Bell, Ms. Chin, and Mr. Hayes explain how they develop content-area essential questions and convey these to students. Later in this chapter, they illustrate how they design and use essential language questions.

Essential Questions in Environmental Science

Chapter 5 introduced Mr. John Peterson, an environmental science teacher, who identified the cornerstone of his secondary environmental science course as "understanding the role of informed and responsible stewardship." He explained that one unit he teaches is "Finite Resources." He had determined that the enduring understanding for this unit would be "The earth has finite resources."

Mr. Peterson explains that when he first began to draft essential questions to anchor his instruction, he simply rephrased the enduring understanding. This resulted in questions such as *How is land a finite and vulnerable resource?* He then realized that while this is what he wanted students to understand, most ELLs and other students would not relate very well to this question. The question also did not lead students to the LOs he had identified. Mr. Peterson explains, "I want students to understand the balance between finite resources, the growing population, and our life styles. The questions that I decided on are *How will we survive? How much is too much?* and *How many people are too many?*"

He explains,

> I try to build the essential questions around real environmental issues that will engage students. I decided to introduce these questions with the dilemma of chemical agents in fertilizers, herbicides, and pesticides. Regardless of which way I come to school, I pass by many homes with "XYZ Lawn Beautiful" signs on their lawns. I can't help but see them, so I assume students, regardless of where they live in the community, see the signs too. I begin the finite resources unit with introductory questions about the balance of benefits and risks in using chemical agents in our immediate environment. We may not have to use chemical agents on lawns, but given the finite amount of land available, we may need to use chemical agents to feed the earth's growing population—it becomes a balance. Once I have students engaged, I introduce the essential questions.

As suggested by Wiggins and McTighe (2005), Mr. Peterson posts the essential questions throughout his room—he asks them often during this instructional unit and encourages students to ask questions as well. Mr. Peterson has found that posting and revisiting the essential questions allows students to process the information, make connections, and generate related questions. When José asked, for example, "Why don't we make laws against using pesticides and herbicides?" Mr. Peterson used José's question to stimulate further inquiry. Mr. Peterson's students considered the benefits and risks of using pesticides and herbicides to grow affordable crops for the world's growing population. The ensuing discussion came back to the question of rights, and students engaged in a lively debate. Small- and large-group discussions, focused on these essential questions, provided ELLs with meaningful context; new vocabulary and grade-level content-area language became more comprehensible.

These discussions provide ELLs with opportunities to use content-area language for authentic purposes, which fosters the development of communicative competence. Mr. Peterson's essential questions allow ELLs and other students to use content understanding to process facts and concepts, instead of merely memorizing them. Mr. Peterson's ELLs learn content for a real-world purpose: to apply knowledge to a problem.

Essential Questions in Mathematics

Ms. Mia Bell plans her eighth-grade math unit on probability around the enduring understanding "Everything we do involves probability." She wants ELLs and other students in her math class to understand the relevance of probability to their daily lives. She hopes to use her essential questions as a mean of tapping into her students' funds of knowledge about the topic. Knowing that her students often talk about fairness in sports and games, Ms. Bell decides on the following essential question for the unit: *What are the chances that . . . ?* "I wanted students to explore probability through a subject for which they had a well-established schema." Through this essential question, Ms. Bell's students explore, discuss, and experiment with the concept of probability.

Ms. Bell and her students recently completed the probability unit, which she introduced by asking students about luck and the meaning of "being lucky." In small groups, ELLs and other students discussed the times and circumstances in which either they or others they knew had been lucky. While student responses varied from winning a school raffle to being the first 10th caller to a radio station during a quiz show in which every 10th caller was chosen to play, or beating siblings at a favorite board game, all students could relate to the universal concept of being lucky. Other responses involved getting good grades on tests, hitting a baseball, and making hoops in basketball. Ms. Bell used student responses to begin a discussion about probability. "What would you say if I told you that your chances of winning a raffle, rolling the right number on a die, or having the spinner stop on the right spot had nothing to do with luck and everything to do with chance?" she asked. Ms. Bell also explained that other activities such as grades and sports accomplishments had much to do with effort and skill, but success on these activities could also be explained, in part, by probability. She explained to students that probability played an integral role in their lives and wrote the essential question on chart paper, *What are the chances that . . . ?*

Ms. Bell asked, "What are the chances that you will come up with heads or tails when flipping a coin?" With this she paired students and handed a coin and data sheet to each pair of students. One student in each pair flipped the coin in the same manner 50 times, and the other student recorded heads or tails on the data sheet. Ms. Bell engaged each of her classes in this activity and recorded the data collected in all classes using a large data sheet she posted on the whiteboard. After the students had analyzed all the data, she explained theoretical versus actual probability and introduced mathematical expressions for probability. Wiggins and McTighe (2005) stress the importance of identifying, addressing, and correcting the misconceptions that students may bring to a unit. Ms. Bell knew from reading journal articles from the National Council for Teachers of Mathematics that "concrete probability experiments may confirm a child's faulty intuitions or even undermine concepts that he or she has already begun to acquire" (Nicolson, 2005); she therefore continued the unit by connecting the study of probability with exercises and activities to develop the students' sense of number (including exercises involving whole numbers, fractions, ratios, and proportions).

Ms. Bell's essential question gave students an opportunity to connect with the topic of probability on a personal level. She overcame a potentially overwhelming topic by demonstrating the concept as a natural extension of her students' existing schemata. Finally, by repeating *What are the chances that . . . ?* throughout her unit, Ms. Bell provided a language structure with which ELLs could discuss probability.

Essential Questions in U.S. History

Ms. Linda Chin has begun to plan instruction for her fourth period U.S. history course. It is a fairly large class, composed of 22 students, 7 of whom are ELLs with proficiency levels ranging from early intermediate to early transitioning. She has planned a unit on the American Revolution, content that is aligned with her state and district curriculum framework standards. Ms. Chin knows that if she wants students to apply their understanding of the American Revolution to later study of the revolutions in Cuba, Poland, China, and other countries, as well as to the study of other types of revolutions (such as industrial or cultural), she must teach revolution as a concept. She has planned to stress the combination of political, economic, and social factors that often, when woven together, form the basis for revolution. Ms. Chin has developed several essential questions that she believes could anchor instruction and promote critical inquiry into the concept of revolution: *What is the difference between freedom and liberty? Do citizens have the right to rebel against laws that are unfair? How does perspective affect the way history is told?* and *Was the American Revolution inevitable?* Ms. Chin explained,

> These are not exhaustive possibilities for essential questions, but any two or three of these could serve as questions to frame my instruction in such a way that students will understand the context of the American Revolution and the underlying concept of revolution. My challenge is to narrow the questions down to no more than three that will really engage all students and enable them to focus on the enduring understanding of the unit. These essential questions will contextualize instruction, thus making it more comprehensible to ELLs. Also, adolescents, who are developing cognitively, socially, and emotionally, will be *hooked* by a question that challenges them to look at revolution through different perspectives. I use multiple types of reading for this unit, including texts, excerpts from historical fiction, and primary-source documents, to help students understand the big picture and the supporting details.

Visitors in Ms. Chin's classroom have witnessed the active engagement of ELLs and other students in small-group discussions and have listened to their lively debates. Last year students engaged in a mock debate about the Revolution from the perspectives of the Loyalist and Patriot residents of a small New England town, including men and women, wealthy and poor. The debate required ELLs to understand the issues from a variety of perspectives. Ms. Chin explains,

> All my students, whether they struggle with English or not, have the cognitive capacity to apply cause-and-effect reasoning; interpret primary sources; understand the differences between propaganda, fact, and opinion; and draw reasonable conclusions. Developmentally, my ELLs need to be challenged in this way, and it is my job to give my ELLs access to this cognitively challenging material. I know that anchoring instruction upon the essential questions provides context that improves comprehensibility of instruction.

Ms. Chin is aware that ELLs and many other students in this secondary U.S. history class will benefit from questions that will prepare them to meet the advanced language requirements of U.S. history. Later in this chapter, in the discussion of essential language questions, Ms. Chin will share her thoughts about how she addresses this instructional challenge.

Essential Questions in English Language Arts

In the previous chapter, Mr. Jamie Hayes explained that he had replaced some of the book-centered units he once taught in his secondary ELA course with thematic units that were more relevant to his students. He based his unit on the enduring understanding that universal themes are found across works of literature. One theme he thought would capture the interest of his students is "Truth does not always represent right action, and lies can serve many purposes." Mr. Hayes named his instructional unit, "There's More Than Meets the Lie." He then tackled the task of crafting essential questions that would foster engaged study and inquiry. He decided on the essential questions *Is it ever better to lie than to be truthful?* and *Are there circumstances that justify a lie?* In thinking about his students, Mr. Hayes decided that these essential questions would pique their interest because regardless of students' language or culture, the dilemma of truth versus lies is universally relevant. Thinking about differing cultures, Mr. Hayes also included excerpts from works such as Amy Witting's novel *I for Isobel*, Leo Tolstoy's novel *Anna Karenina*, and Benigni and Cerami's film *Life Is Beautiful* (*La Vita è Bella*). By accumulating shared literary experiences grounded in different cultures, students from differing cultural backgrounds will be better able to connect with each other in their discussions of the theme of truth and lies.

When ELLs and other students entered his classroom on Monday morning, *Is it ever better to lie than to be truthful?* was printed in large black letters that nearly covered the whiteboard. Above the entire length of the white board was a paper banner with the same question—this banner would remain throughout the instructional unit, where it would remind ELLs and other students of the essential question. Mr. Hayes began his lesson by engaging students in a short, open, large-group discussion about truthfulness and lies. He then separated students into small groups. ELLs and native-English-speaking students worked together. Students collaborated to complete T-charts about their own experiences with lies. In the left-hand column, students identified the lies they had told to friends, teachers, parents, or others. On the right-hand side, they listed the lies they had been told by others.

As Mr. Hayes circulated, he listened to the small-group discussions. Aadam said that his parents had lied to him when they told him that he would have a better life in America. In another group, Maria explained that friends and cousins who had come to the United States before she did had lied when they told her how wonderful life was here. "There are a lot of good things about living here," she said, "but the food is different, everything is different." Maria explained that she feels different from others, and when she shops with her friends, or even her mother, other people in stores look angry when she speaks in Spanish.

Cultural differences within groups generated questions such as Maya's: "Mr. Hayes, do you mean really lying or just not being rude? When I couldn't go to my cousin's wedding, I didn't want to hurt her feelings, and so I told her I was going to go. I didn't want her to feel bad. Is that a lie?" Then Rob responded, "If you knew all along you wouldn't go, you should have told your cousin. I think saying you are going when you know for sure you are not is definitely dishonest." The conversation became lively, with several students strongly agreeing with Rob and others agreeing with Maya. Mr. Hayes stopped the group, "Is there another way to look at this situation? Let's come back to our question, *Is it ever better to lie than to be truthful?*" Cha hesitated and then added, "Sometimes, here, Americans can be rude when they think they are being truthful." Mr. Hayes continued the conversation probing with his other essential question: *Are there circumstances that justify a lie?* Later, Mr. Hayes will bring the essence of this discussion to the readings and relate to another enduring understanding in ELA, "Setting conveys theme."

Review, Reflect, Apply

1. *Review:* Review the essential questions that each teacher generated. Does each question meet the criteria for essential questions in Table 6.8?

2. *Apply:* Think about the content that you teach for enduring understanding. Formulate an essential question that will pique the interests of your students.

3. *Reflect:* Does your question have the necessary ingredients? Does it get to the core of the content area? Is it broad enough to generate critical thinking? Does it allow for multiple interpretations and responses? Is it written in student-friendly language? Discuss your question with course participants, colleagues, or friends and get feedback using the questions above. Review the criteria for essential questions listed in Table 6.8.

Summary

Thus far in this chapter, teachers have shared the ways they develop essential questions for content. Essential questions are broad based and present ELLs and other students with dilemmas that encourage critical thinking and multiple interpretations. Such questions create opportunities for ELLs to use academic language while processing content. Presenting instruction based on essential questions contextualizes standards and gives value to the funds of knowledge that ELLs and others bring to the classroom. Content-area essential questions are motivating and engaging to students when they are written in student-friendly language. Standards and facts remain important, but their contextualization represents the first step in providing comprehensible instruction to ELLs.

Teachers often struggle to decide on the best essential questions and regularly report that there is no single right question; rather, finding the best essential questions has been a process of trial and error. As the UbD instructor introduced in Chapter 1 explains, "At the heart of the challenge of developing essential questions is the balance between using student-friendly language while at the same time diving deeply into concepts." Teachers agree that engaging in this process has been well worth the effort, explaining that ELLs and other students have been more engaged in instruction and have more completely grasped the enduring understandings within units when instruction has been framed with essential questions.

THE INTERRELATIONSHIP BETWEEN ESSENTIAL CONTENT AND LANGUAGE QUESTIONS

As Mr. Peterson, Ms. Bell, Ms. Chin, and Mr. Hayes have shown, content-area instruction based on essential questions creates a classroom climate that is compatible with the tenets of culturally responsive teaching; it is context rich, engaging, and motivating—hence it creates a setting for learning that enhances educational opportunities for ELLs. Content-area essential questions also provide context for instruction, which enables ELLs and other students to understand how all the standards, concepts, and facts fit together.

To fully access content and express content-area understandings, however, ELLs require ongoing instruction in academic language. Essential language questions provide a framework for this instruction. While content-area essential questions engage ELLs in inquiry about problems or dilemmas that may not be solvable, essential language questions serve to call ELLs' attention to language and frame language instruction within content-area courses.

Ms. Laurie Caulder, a secondary ELA teacher, demonstrates how she integrates essential questions and essential language questions in her classroom. This year, Ms. Caulder's tenth-grade students (ELLs and native-English speakers) are reading *Romeo and Juliet*. Ms. Caulder has determined an enduring understanding for this unit: "Themes within literature recur across time periods." ELLs and native-English speakers in Ms. Caulder's class compare themes in *Romeo and Juliet* with themes in contemporary literature, such as Toni Morrison's *Beloved*, Ernesto Quinones' *Bodega Dreams*, and Carlos Ruiz Zafon's *The Shadow of the Wind*. Ms. Caulder explains that one theme present in all these works is "The force of love can bring happiness or destruction." She begins the instructional unit with an essential content question that she believes will motivate her secondary students: *Is love worth it?* Ms. Caulder posts these essential questions throughout the classroom and on each lesson handout and refers to them often.

Based on her teaching experience, Ms. Caulder knows that building instruction around content-area essential questions will not suffice for the ELLs and many other students in her classroom. She has observed students' struggles with reading and writing, observations confirmed by an article she had read about the large number of U.S. adolescents who experience difficulties with reading comprehension (Biancarosa & Snow, 2006) and a report from the National Commission on Writing (2006) stating that many students "cannot systematically produce writing at [the] high levels of skill, maturity, and sophistication" required in today's economy (p. 56). Indeed, both papers supported Ms. Caulder's concerns; the extensive amount of reading and writing required at the secondary level poses difficulties for ELLs and many other students. Many of Ms. Caulder's students, including all her ELLs, need instruction in reading and writing in English.

Based on the needs of her students, Ms. Caulder develops essential language questions to help students in her ELA class make connections between text and self. She explains,

> I try to frame reading with questions that keep students interacting with the text—for example, "If I were [character], what would I do?" "How is character similar to characters in other works?" and "Could this happen in my life?" These essential language questions encourage ELLs and others to make connections between their experiences and the readings as well as to check their understanding as they read.

Ms. Caulder explains that once ELLs are engaged with the characters, making text-to-self and text-to-text connections, under the umbrella of the essential questions, she poses more specific questions that draw their attention to language and help them access academic language for academic discussions, reading responses, and formal writing assignments.

Ms. Caulder, who has worked in collaboration with ESOL teachers for many years, also knows that reading and writing instruction designed for native-English speakers is not enough for ELLs, who need to develop academic language. The language needs of ELLs include the development of academic vocabulary and the understanding of English morphology and syntax. Ms. Caulder explains that she uses the same essential language questions to frame more specific questions (derived from Nation, 2001) for vocabulary development, such as the following:

- Which vocabulary words interfere with my understanding? (See McLaughlin, 1990; Nation, 2001.)
- Is this a new way of using a word I know, or is it a totally new word?
- Does the word seem as if it will be important to my understanding?

- Do I know any of the parts of the word (root or affixes)?
- Is the word (or a related word) on the word wall?

Ms. Caulder also uses specific questions to help ELLs notice and access complex grammatical constructions in their reading (Aebersold & Field, 1997) and begin to use more complex constructions in their written work (Hinkel, 2004). Ms. Caulder's collaboration with ESOL teachers has helped her understand the important relationship between noticing language constructions and developing academic language (Baddely, 1990; Hinkel, 2004; Nation, 2001). To bring ELLs' attention to the value of noticing grammatical constructions, Ms. Caulder uses questions such as *Is the whole a sum of its parts?*

As a final project for the unit, students in Ms. Caulder's class demonstrate content-area understanding by collaboratively creating a thematic reading guide, illustrating themes that are common to literary works as well as motifs and symbols from each work. (Exemplary guides will be placed in Ms. Caulder's resource box as references for students.) When Ms. Caulder introduces this assignment, she stresses writing skills and mechanics and frames this discussion with the essential language question *Who is the audience?* As Ms. Caulder guides and assists students through the writing process, she uses a variety of probing questions that focus attention on word choice and English syntax (Hinkel, 2004). Ms. Caulder explains, "Providing essential language questions and referring to them often focuses ELLs and other students on language. It highlights the importance and purpose of language learning."

FRAMING ACADEMIC-LANGUAGE INSTRUCTION WITH QUESTIONS

In developing essential language questions, teachers must consider the unit LOs and the language abilities that ELLs and other students will need to demonstrate mastery of unit LOs. Essential language questions provide students with a road map for first accessing content-area language and then using language to demonstrate their understanding of this content. Whereas essential questions in content areas generate critical thinking and academic conversation, essential language questions draw ELLs' attention to language, make language an integral part of all instruction, and frame *language* instruction. They often do not, unfortunately, lend themselves to student-friendly language. Mr. Peterson, Ms. Bell, Ms. Chin, and Mr. Hayes focus on academic-language development within their content-area classes. In the following section, they illustrate how they create essential language questions to frame this instruction.

Essential Language Questions in Environmental Science

Mr. Peterson explains that the language of science and the amount of required reading present challenges for ELLs and several other students in his class. He responds to these challenges by differentiating the type and number of reading assignments as well as the assessment evidence that ELLs need to produce to demonstrate mastery of LOs. While differentiation of materials and assessments is helpful to ELLs, Mr. Peterson also wants to ensure that ELLs continue to develop academic-language abilities in science. ELLs need to develop vocabulary that goes beyond the new terms he teaches all students. He believes that the National Science Standards' recommendation to guide students "to understand the purposes for their own learning and to formulate self-assessment strategies" applies to language as well as content. Mr. Peterson's essential question for receptive language, is *What's the point?* He explains to students that after they read each section they should be able to state the point (the main idea) of the section in their heads, using either English or their first language. They should know the gist of the section. Mr. Peterson explains,

> I spend considerable time with this essential question at the beginning of the school year. I model reading the textbook using think-alouds. I try to let students see that summarizing is not always easy but is critical to their understanding. I call attention to the structure of the textbook and the ways in which the vocabulary words are bold-faced. I also demonstrate how I use discourse markers to make sense of the text. For example, *although, because, and regardless* are fairly simple words, but they signal meaning. I frame all of this with "What's the point?" I demonstrate how I determine if a word is important to the meaning of the text, and if the word seems important I model strategies for finding the meaning of the word. When I first began doing this, I worried about my better readers, but reading *Do I Really Have to Teach Reading?* (Tovani, 2004) made me realize that good readers experience difficulty with comprehension when reading more challenging selections.

Helping ELLs and other students access the text has been so successful for Mr. Peterson that he has established a class blog (web log) with podcasts, where he models simple text-accessing strategies. Mr. Peterson also explains that his students keep lists of vocabulary that interfere with their ability to respond to "What's the point?" He has a word wall of Academic Word List (AWL) words found in the science text to which he frequently refers ELLs and other students.

Mr. Peterson discusses the LOs he established for this unit and explains that his students must produce accurate lab reports based on experiments and field experiences. They must also prepare a position paper or presentation explaining their position on an issue related to the world's growing population and finite resources. ELLs need to convey this information in standard English (as much as possible). "I know that language is developmental," he explains, "I am careful to ensure that my ELLs can demonstrate content understanding that is independent from their ability to use academic English." He continues, "On the other hand, ELLs need to continue to develop English language proficiency, and therefore it's important to keep them focused on language." According to Mr. Peterson, the essential language question that guides his students' language development in this unit is *How do scientists communicate?*

Mr. Peterson explains that he posts these essential language questions in his room. He says,

> For me, essential language questions provide a good way to draw all students' attention to the importance of clear writing. I explain that scientists must be systematic; others should be able to duplicate their work. When students write a position paper, presentation is important. I link drafting, revising, and editing to the essential language questions.

By including essential language questions in his environmental science class, Mr. Peterson keeps ELLs focused on checking their reading comprehension and helps them demonstrate understanding in purposeful and authentic ways. Teaching language doesn't soften content; in fact, it has the opposite effect. As Mr. Peterson's students learn new, complex concepts and new vocabulary words, they develop a greater linguistic toolbox for processing new concepts. From the beginning of the unit, Mr. Peterson weaves together essential questions and essential language questions, making it clear to all students that they must *not only* develop content-area understanding, they must also develop language abilities to demonstrate this understanding.

Essential Language Questions in Mathematics

Ms. Bell explains that the greatest language challenge for ELLs in her math class is the comprehension of vocabulary and syntax in math textbooks and in specific word problems. Reading the math textbook is difficult for ELLs; the language is dense, and the vocabulary is difficult. Yet being able to read the textbook is important for understanding. Students refer to the text to understand the concepts and the language of mathematics and often to understand the steps necessary to solve number and word problems. According to Ms. Bell, "Understanding word problems is often difficult for native-English-speaking students and even more challenging for ELLs, who confront new academic vocabulary and syntax." Ms. Bell has generated two essential language questions that together provide a framework for her language instruction. Borrowing from the television show *Jeopardy*, Ms. Bell asks, *"And the question is . . . ?"* She also uses the question *Does it make sense?* Ms. Bell posts these essential language questions in various parts of the room and refers to them throughout the unit. She uses these to engage ELLs in academic conversation about their work.

Under the umbrella of these questions, Ms. Bell provides ongoing instruction on using the structure of the math textbook to find necessary information to complete math assignments. She explains, "Often, understanding what the problem asks and how to begin to solve the problem necessitates returning back to the text to review concepts and examples." Like Mr. Peterson, Ms. Bell demonstrates reading the math textbook and uses a think-aloud to show the strategies she uses when she becomes confused. She explains,

> Parents of my ELLs sometimes do not have the English language ability necessary to help their children with reading the textbook. I also have many students who cannot stay after school for extra help. They may have issues with transportation, or they have responsibilities at home, such as caring for younger siblings. These students must learn to read the text themselves.

Ms. Bell also keeps a word wall of mathematic terms and AWL words found in the math text, many of which have been translated into French, Portuguese, Spanish, and Arabic. Ms. Bell knows that ELLs and other students have different language (and content-area) needs, and she continually groups and regroups students according to the questions they ask, the observations she makes while circulating during instructional time, and her ongoing review of student homework. Ms. Bell knows that solving word problems is an ability that enables students to think systematically and organize their thinking. She wants to ensure that difficult to understand features, such as passive voice, noun clauses, academic vocabulary, and the confusing mixture of academic and everyday language, which characterize the language of word problems do not disable ELLs from participating in problem solving. Ms. Bell uses her essential language question *And the question is . . . ?* to help ELLs sort through the English language within the problem and break the problem into smaller parts.

Essential Language Questions in U.S. History

When asked about how she formulates the essential language questions for the unit, Ms. Chin admits that she struggles with this task:

> It is always a balance for me. I want to keep standards high, yet I also want to grade students on their content-area understanding. While I want students to read the text and primary-source documents, I also differentiate the amount of reading to make it manageable and useful.

Ms. Chin continues,

History requires an extensive amount of reading. I have simplified some of the reading with gloss-ing, highlighting, and providing summaries [discussed in Chapter 8 of this book], yet the reading requirements remain substantial for ELLs. The textbook is very dense; one chapter may span hun-dreds of years, and feature many important events, and twice as many important historical figures. I provide outlines that help students know what is important, yet it is still very difficult for ELLs to understand the transitions between topics in the text. An essential language question I use to encour-age ELLs and many others to check their understanding is "Whose line is it anyway?"—taken, of course, from the television show with the same name. I use this to encourage ELLs to consider who is telling the history.

These essential language questions keep students focused and remind them to check their comprehension. As a question that encourages students to discover and explore multiple per-spectives, "Whose line is it?" also brings a sense of social justice to the history course, which capitalizes on students' sense of fairness. It motivates ELLs and others to read primary-source documents and historical novels. Students' understanding of the Industrial Revolution, for example, is greatly enhanced by reading accounts of the mill girls, which are available on the Internet and in the novel *Lyddie* (Patterson, 1991). Ms. Chin explains, "I stress that a critical understanding of history demands that we know who is telling the story."

Ms. Chin explains that she provides a variety of graphic organizers to ELLs and others to organize multiple historical perspectives. According to Ms. Chin, using graphic organizers not only facilitates comprehension, it also enables ELLs to organize their notes and ideas for pre-sentations and written work. She consistently tries to find ways to convey to ELLs that they must continue to develop academic language without discouraging them from submitting work that is written in academic English language that is weak or below grade level:

I differentiate the assignments that students submit to demonstrate mastery of content-area learn-ing outcomes; this differentiation enables ELLs to show their understanding in different ways. The essential language question I use for written work is 'Will your voice be heard?' I use this question to focus ELLs on the form and clarity of their writing and presentations. I take an individual approach to helping students with their written work. I do hold ELLs accountable for correct word use, spelling, and syntax if I have worked with them on these constructions.

Essential Language Questions in English Language Arts

Mr. Hayes explains that using essential language questions to frame instruction supports all students, including ELLs, in developing strategies for reading and writing:

Every student in my course is a member of a community of readers and writers. My role is to help them develop strategies to continually grow in each of these areas. One of the standards put forth by the International Reading Association and the National Council of Teachers of English is learn-ing how to learn. Skillwise my students are at many different levels. For example, some students begin the course with a real appreciation for reading—they have been successful readers. Others seem to avoid reading at all costs. They began to struggle at some point and either did not develop comprehension strategies or cannot flexibly apply these strategies. My ELLs fall into both of these groups. While all ELLs struggle with reading at grade level in English, I have had ELLs in my classes who have not missed any schooling in their journey from their native country to this school system; those students often are able to read very sophisticated works in their native language. For example, last year, Ajay, an ELL from India, was in my third-period class. According to his records, he had intermediate-level proficiency in English. Ajay was an avid reader though, and he had begun to read in English while still in India. The comprehension strategies he had developed in his first language were transferred to his English reading. Most of my ELLs, however, such as Aadam Jassam Ali, have missed much formal schooling, have been traumatized by their experiences, and have become discouraged and frustrated. Their experiences and struggles with English, and now with reading and writing in English, have placed them at risk for failure. I have been inspired by Alfred Tatum's book *Teaching Reading to Black Adolescent Males: Closing the Achievement Gap* (2005). While few of my students are black and an equal number of my students are female, like Tatum's students, many struggling students in my class have been traumatized by life circumstances and have experienced too many unsuccessful remedial programs. I tell all students when they enter my class, "We are all members of a literate community. Here, you will learn strategies to help you realize your potential." The essential language questions I pose are *What does it mean to understand?* and *What does it mean to be understood?*

Mr. Hayes refers often to these essential language questions to anchor mini lessons for reading comprehension, vocabulary building, and writing. According to Mr. Hayes, the school district's ESOL teacher has been invaluable in providing advice, support, and suggestions for resources to improve his understanding of the needs of ELLs. Depending on the needs of his students, he presents mini lessons to the whole class or to small groups of students.

Review, Reflect, Apply

Review and reflect: Review each teacher's planning process. What is effective? Explain how establishing clear essential language questions will benefit ELLs in each content area.

The previous section provided examples of the ways in which teachers in different content areas use essential language questions to bring focus and purpose to student efforts to develop academic-language skills. The section also highlighted the important role essential language questions play in content-area classrooms. Mr. Peterson, Ms. Bell, Ms. Chin, and Mr. Hayes explained how they determine and convey essential language questions that will aid the language development of ELLs and simultaneously improve the instruction for all students in their classes. Essential language questions are beneficial for all students; they are critical to ELLs, who must continue to develop academic-language proficiency across content areas.

CHAPTER SUMMARY

Chapter 6 showed that teachers who have a clear understanding of what constitutes mastery of concepts are able to convey this information to ELLs and other students at the start of a unit. Knowing the assessment evidence they will produce helps all students understand how content-area lessons fit together. Context is also provided through essential content-area questions, the broad, student-friendly questions that get to the enduring understandings of the content area and promote critical thinking and academic conversations. The focus on academic language is maintained with essential language questions. The assessment evidence activities include developing essential content-area and language questions. Chapter 7, then, demonstrates the differentiation of assessments according to English language proficiency.

Assessment Evidence Activities

AE-1   Explain the importance of designing assessment evidence prior to planning and implementing instruction.

AE-2   Create assessment evidence for the LOs you identified in Chapter 5.

AE-3   Review the essential questions that each teacher has established for content and language. Then look at Table 6.7, Essential Questions and Culturally Responsive Teaching. (You may also wish to refer to Chapter 3 to review the criteria that define culturally responsive teaching.)

Create a T-chart to illustrate the connection between each teacher's essential questions and the tenets of culturally responsive teaching.

AE-4   Refer to the case studies of Aadam Jassam, Fredy Solis, and Katy Boureth in Chapter 3. Explain the value of using essential questions (content and language) for each of these students.

AE-5:   Create 1–3 essential questions that align with content-area enduring understandings that you determined for your instructional unit. Be sure to review local, state, or national frameworks to ensure that your essential question is aligned with these.

AE-6:   Create 1–3 essential language questions that align with the enduring language understandings that you have determined for your instructional unit.

Resources for Further Reading

- Wiggins, G., & McTighe, J. (2005). *Understanding by design*. Alexandria, VA: Association for Supervision and Curriculum Development.
- The Galileo Educational Network provides guidance for developing meaningful essential questions and presents exemplars of inquiry-based projects, along with a rubric for evaluating an inquiry-based project. www.galileo.org/tips/essential_questions.html
- *Writing Essential Questions*. According to the author of this Web page, well-crafted essential questions promote inquiry in students. Tips are provided for developing essential questions. www.myprojectpages.com/support/ess_questpopup.htm

Assessing Content and Language

Enduring understanding: Effective assessment facilitates targeted instruction and evaluation of content and language.

CHAPTERS 5 AND 6 ILLUSTRATED THE PROCESS OF DETERMINING *ENDURING UNDERSTANDINGS* FOR CONTENT-AREA units, identifying long-term *learning outcomes* (LOs) that specify what ELLs and other students will know and do as a result of instruction, determining assessment evidence, and developing *essential questions* to frame classroom instruction. The focus of Chapter 7 is assessment.

Chapter 7 begins by distinguishing between the two major types of assessment that influence the education of ELLs: standardized, large-scale testing and ongoing classroom assessment. The chapter continues with a discussion of classroom assessment, framed by principles for effective assessment (Tomlinson & McTighe, 2006) as they relate to content and language instruction for ELLs in mainstream content-area classrooms. Content-area teachers share differentiated assessments that measure content mastery and language development for ELLs at various proficiency levels. The interplay between assessments and objectives is then explored and modeled using the example of a secondary English language arts (ELA) content-area unit.

© Chris Schmidt.

LEARNING OUTCOMES

The following LOs serve as a guide for Chapter 7. The assessment evidence activities aligned with each LO are at the end of this chapter.

ASSESSMENT FOR ENGLISH LANGUAGE LEARNERS

ELLs, like other students in U.S. schools, are assessed in two primary ways: large-scale standardized assessment and classroom-based assessment. As Gottlieb (2006) explains, assessments differ in both scale and purpose.

- Large-scale assessment measures student knowledge and abilities at discrete points in time (e.g., state content-area and language-proficiency exams); classroom assessment measures knowledge and abilities at various times throughout semesters.
- Large-scale assessment is unidimensional, generally consisting of objective-response questions or requiring a specific type of writing sample; classroom assessment is multidimensional, including teacher observations, written work, oral presentations, and multimedia demonstrations.
- Large-scale assessment is summative; classroom assessment consists of a combination of preinstructional, formative, and summative measures.
- Large-scale assessment reports the progress of the group; classroom assessment may reveal group progress, but largely focuses on the progress of individual students.

Standards and Large-Scale Standardized Testing

Since the 1980s, national educational organizations such as the National Council of Teachers of Mathematics, the National Council of Teachers of English, and the National Science Foundation have established content-area standards and student LOs that should be achieved as a result of instruction (Gottlieb, 2006). More recently, the federal government has required states to adopt and/or develop content-area standards and to assess the progress of students in meeting these standards (No Child Left Behind [NCLB] Act of 2001). Initially, NCLB obligated states to develop assessments in mathematics and reading/language arts; science assessments became mandatory in the 2005/2006 school year. NCLB states that content standards "specify what *all* [italics added] students are expected to know and be able to do" (U.S. Department of Education, 2007, p. 2) irrespective of English language proficiency.

Currently, under NCLB, ELLs, like their native-English-speaking peers, are assessed in content-area subjects such as reading, math, and science in Grades 3 through 8 and again in secondary school (Kunnan, 2005). Results of standardized tests have implications for schools and districts as well as for individual students. NCLB requires that schools and districts break down test results by student demographics, including economic status, race, ethnicity, inclusion in special education, and English language proficiency, so that the progress of each student subgroup can be measured. The results from these tests indicate whether or not districts and individual schools have made adequate yearly progress (AYP) in academic achievement. Schools that do not make AYP in *all* student subgroups may be subjected to improvement plans, corrective action, and, finally, restructuring (U.S. Department of Education, 2002). Individual students in many states are affected by minimum standardized test score requirements, which are a requirement for high school graduation.

Unfortunately, as measures of content-area knowledge, standardized tests do not take into account varying levels of English language proficiency. As a result of the conflation of content-area knowledge with English language proficiency, ELLs who are in the process of developing English language skills may be classified as failing or needing improvement in content areas even though their content-area knowledge has not been appropriately measured (Abedi & Dietel, 2004; Short & Fitzsimmons, 2007; Teachers of English to Speakers of Other Languages [TESOL], 2003). The level of English language proficiency required by test items has precluded ELLs from adequately demonstrating their content-area knowledge.

While general acceptance of the need for accountability in education exists, the efficacy of standardized test scores as the sole measure of accountability has been disputed by groups such as the National Association for the Advancement of Colored People (NAACP), the Mexican American Legal Defense and Educational Fund (MALDEF), and the National Association for Bilingual Education (Kunnan, 2005). In addition to the criticism that content-area standardized tests conflate language proficiency and content-area knowledge, such tests have been criticized for cultural bias (TESOL) and for measuring content that is not taught in minority districts (Kunnan, 2005). Kunnan cites the 1997 lawsuit filed by MALDEF against the Texas Education Agency and members of the Texas State Board of Education. This suit claimed that the use of the Texas Assessment of Academic Skills (TAAS) as a requirement for high school graduation discriminated against Mexican American and African American students because they did not receive instruction that equally prepared them for this test. According to the lawsuit, this high-stakes test lacks validity because it is "not appropriately related to what is actually taught or made available to many minority high school students" (*GI FORUM v. Texas Education Agency*, 2000).

In addition to the misuse of high-stakes standardized testing as a graduation requirement, overreliance on standardized content-area assessments for programmatic decisions, including the placement of ELLs in lower-tracked, remedial, and test preparation classes, has also received criticism (Collier & Thomas, 1999b; Menken, 2008).

More recently, NCLB has extended the standards and assessment mandates to include the measurement of English language proficiency apart from content. NCLB now requires states to adopt and implement English language proficiency standards and annually assess the progress of ELLs based on these standards; thus, ELLs are required to participate in two major types of testing. Standards from TESOL were first implemented in 1997, and a new version, which more closely aligns language with the four content areas, has recently been released (TESOL, 2006).

As described in Chapter 1 of this text, ELLs are first assessed for proficiency in English for initial placement purposes and then assessed across the domains of listening, speaking, reading, and writing each year thereafter. (ELLs in kindergarten through Grade 2 are assessed for listening and speaking only.) While the establishment of language standards and assessments for ELLs is, in some ways, a positive development (Gottlieb, 2006), questions exist regarding the validity and reliability of language proficiency tests as the sole measure of language development (Davies & Elder, 2005). Davis and Elder question if "a single writing task can capture the highly variable language demands of [writing]" (p. 807) and whether any measure of writing ability can actually be separated from content. Researchers have also questioned the effectiveness of large-scale, discrete point, standardized testing in measuring aspects of language proficiency, such as communicative competence and discourse competence (Chalhoub-Deville & Deville, 2005).

While large-scale standardized language proficiency tests may be imperfect measures of student progress, they serve as one tool for measuring the language development progress of ELLs. When test results are used appropriately, they can be useful in two broad ways: (1) individual results provide a snapshot of the ELL's language development and proficiency, and (2) group results provide one piece of valuable information to the administrators and program directors who are responsible for program development and evaluation.

Effective Classroom Assessment

Appropriately designed classroom assessments provide ongoing evidence of ELLs' progress in developing content-area understanding and academic English. Classroom assessments also serve as important diagnostic tools for teachers as they plan instruction. As illustrated in Table 7.1, classroom assessments are an important step in the Teaching English Language Learners in the Mainstream (TELLiM) model. When well-designed assessments are conveyed to ELLs and other students at the beginning of instructional units, they provide a clear picture of what students must learn and do as a result of instruction; effective assessments then provide a road map for the journey through the instructional unit.

Well-designed assessments allow for sufficient differentiation to accommodate the different learning styles and academic-language proficiency levels of ELLs and other students in the classroom. Effective classroom assessments provide evidence in two broad areas: (1) they enable ELLs to demonstrate content-area understanding apart from academic-language proficiency, and (2) they require ELLs to provide evidence of academic-language development. As indicated by Model 7.1, content-area understanding and academic-language ability develop along a continuum (Gottlieb, 2006; Tomlinson & McTighe, 2006). Effective assessment must simultaneously measure growth in each of these areas. It is important to remember that ELLs can be at very different points on each continuum; an ELL with beginning

TABLE 7.1	TELLiM Model: Step 5

Plan Assessments and Design Lessons

- Differentiate assessments according to English language proficiency levels
- Plan content *objectives* and *assessments* for individual lessons
- Plan language *objectives* and *assessments* for individual lessons

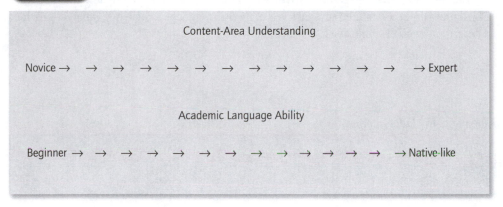

English language proficiency, for example, may have a near-expert understanding of complex chemistry concepts. Effective assessments allow ELLs to demonstrate their understanding/proficiency on each continuum.

The next sections of this chapter present principles of effective assessment in content areas, based on the work of Wiggins and McTighe (1998) and Tomlinson and McTighe (2006), and in language, based on the work of Gottlieb (2006). Effective assessments (a) measure a depth of understanding and performance in content and language, (b) are well matched to the LOs that they measure, and (c) include multiple measures (Tomlinson & McTighe, 2006). Content and language are of equal importance; the order of presentation in this chapter is simply for organizational purposes.

ASSESSMENT PRINCIPLE 1: MEASURE DEEP UNDERSTANDING AND PERFORMANCE IN CONTENT AND LANGUAGE

The first principle for effective assessment is that it must measure a student's understanding rather than his or her ability to restate factual knowledge that has been transmitted by the teacher. Quizzes and tests often provide snapshots of students' mastery of discrete facts. While facts are important for students to learn, assessments must also measure progress toward mastery of the unit's *enduring understandings*. Mr. Peterson, for example, regularly uses quick quizzes and end-of-class "tickets to leave," a brief, informal (written or oral) assessment of student understanding to ensure that his students grasp the factual knowledge within an instructional unit. Other assessments that he implements, however, require students to use facts from class readings and discussions to develop understandings about the finite nature of resources, which calls for conceptual understanding of the interrelationship of finite resources, population growth, and sustainability. These assessments require more than knowledge of facts; students must use the facts to demonstrate a depth of conceptual understanding.

Wiggins and McTighe (1998, 2005) identify six elements of understanding that assist teachers in planning high-level content-area instruction and assessment for ELLs and other students. While understanding cannot always be so neatly categorized, keeping these elements in mind when planning assessments increases the likelihood that the assessments and the accompanying instruction are of a high level and based on what ELLs need to understand rather than on what ELLs can easily access at their present levels of English language proficiency. Table 7.2 provides a description and example of each element.

TABLE 7.2   Six Elements of Understanding

Element	Examples of Implementation in Content-Area Classrooms
Explanation	Explanation goes beyond recall of specific facts and ideas and requires the ability to explain the content to others in unique conversations or demonstrations. Students in Mr. Jamie Hayes's *There's More Than Meets the Lie* instructional unit, for example, are reading one of four literary works depending on their English reading levels: *Othello, The Catcher in the Rye* (chosen partly because of its availability in multiple languages), *I Am the Cheese,* and *Zach's Lie.* ELLs and other students work together throughout the instructional unit in same and mixed-book groups to discuss the novels and the ways the author of each novel conveys the theme. ELLs have the opportunity to engage in academic conversations based on literary conventions such as plot, theme, setting, and character development. Explanation, therefore, requires that ELLs not only explain what has happened but also be able to explain how and why.
Interpretation	The summative assessment for the *There's More Than Meets the Lie* instructional unit requires students to go beyond explaining novels' themes and requires the type of interpretation usually expressed by literary critics. Students demonstrate their ability to make interpretations by creating a book jacket, poster, book review, or PowerPoint presentation about the novel that they are reading. This interpretation requires that students have developed a deep understanding of theme.
Application	The application of knowledge to new situations provides evidence of understanding. In the summative assessment for the *Finite Resources* instructional unit, Mr. Peterson's students apply the knowledge and understandings that they have developed to the *Ecological Footprint Case Study* assignment in which they collect data regarding their use of resources over a period of 2 weeks, calculate their footprint, and discuss the implications of their footprints on global sustainability.
Perspective	Learners demonstrate deep understanding when they can consider the various perspectives that surround an issue of study and make decisions about which perspectives may be similar, or which may be greater in validity and importance than others (Tomlinson & McTighe, 2006). Often in Mr. Peterson's environmental science course, students must consider multiple perspectives around issues such as location of a landfill, taking land for public domain use, and protection of natural resources.
Empathy	Another facet of understanding is empathy or the ability to thoughtfully place oneself in the position of another. Ms. Linda Chin's *American Revolution* instruction unit focuses on the perspectives of members of various groups during revolutionary times. Historical fiction and primary source documents enable students to learn about and empathize with members of various groups and understand how they experienced the Revolution. Ms. Chin's summative assessment requires that students discuss key historical events of that time period through the perspectives of men, women, and children from different socioeconomic groups and political affiliations.
Self-knowledge	Self-knowledge requires students to self-assess their progress and evaluate what they know, what they do not know, areas in which they have improved, as well as areas in need of improvement. Portfolio assessment requiring students to select their best pieces of work and provide reasons for their selection is one way to assess self-reflection. Assessments that require students to explain what they do not know about specific topics that they have studied (e.g., the American Revolution, conveying a theme in literature, analyzing data as part of a probability unit, or understanding finite resources) requires students to demonstrate self-knowledge.

SOURCE: Wiggins and McTighe (1998, 2005).

Review, Reflect, Apply

Review and apply: Review the six elements of understanding and explain how the assessments you will use to measure mastery of LOs are consistent with one or more types of understanding.

Planning With English Language Proficiency Levels in Mind

To effectively assess ELLs, teachers must be aware of each ELL's English language proficiency level. Here, both standardized tests and classroom assessments are useful. Because language proficiency is assessed at school registration and annually thereafter, the cumulative folder provides one resource for determining an ELL's level of proficiency. Classroom assessments, including writing samples and focused observations of an ELL's language in small- and large-group settings, provide additional resources for learning about the ELL's language proficiency. Understanding the proficiency levels of ELLs serves a double purpose: (1) it enables teachers to differentiate assessment evidence (not LOs) so that ELLs can demonstrate content-area mastery apart from language proficiency and, equally important, (2) it provides a measure of growth in academic-language proficiency, thereby enabling teachers to plan instruction that continually scaffolds ELLs' language proficiency. Appropriately differentiated assessment enables ELLs to aim for challenging, yet attainable, levels of competency in academic English. Table 7.3 provides a broad overview of language proficiency levels and examples of assessments that are appropriate at each level.

Content-area teachers must first consider the proficiency levels of ELLs in their classes and then make appropriate adjustments to the assessments to ensure that the assessments allow for differences in academic language, yet continue to measure the same LOs. Mr. Peterson, for example, has identified three LOs that all students must master as a result of the *Finite Resources* instructional unit. Although all students must master the same LOs, Mr. Peterson provides options in assessments to allow for differences in student strengths and interests. He then further individually differentiates assessment rubrics depending on student academic English language proficiency. Students must choose from the following assessment options, illustrated in Table 7.4: a written report, a presentation, or a poster.

ELLs at several different levels of English language proficiency have been placed in Mr. Peterson's third period environmental science class. Table 7.5 illustrates how Mr. Peterson differentiates the assessments for the first LO, "Explain the environmental effects of a growing population on the earth's finite resources," for beginner and intermediate ELLs.

Each option requires ELLs to demonstrate mastery of the LO. Mr. Peterson encourages beginner ELLs to select the poster option because it provides a way for them to show their understanding apart from their English language proficiency. Mr. Peterson is also cognizant of the need to develop content-area academic language, and thus, the poster must include the title and labeling of each environmental effect. He will grade students' work based on the assessment requirements (content and language). Once the graded work of beginner ELLs indicates that they can successfully complete this assessment, Mr. Peterson adds *slightly* to the required linguistic complexity. An advanced beginner, for example, may have to include a sentence describing each environmental effect, and as illustrated in Table 7.5, an intermediate ELL will write a paragraph about each effect. ELLs are continually required to demonstrate language

Suggested Assessments

Beginner ELLs

Listening	May rely entirely on visuals and graphic cues.	1. Identify objects, illustrations, symbols, or words by pointing or naming
Speaking	May use gestures to communicate, speak isolated words or use basic phrases, and may need time to process information prior to speaking.	2. Match and label pictures and words 3. Follow one-step directions
Reading	May need simplified/sheltered materials, with substantial support.	4. Sort objects or illustrations with words into groups 5. Illustrate and label words in graphic organizers
Writing	May be able to match vocabulary words with concept pictures and write short sentences with support.	6. Make collages or photo journals about stories or topics

Advanced-beginner ELLs

Listening	May understand social exchanges when spoken to slowly and isolated academic words and terms when provided context. May use previous knowledge (when available) to make sense of concepts, when these are accompanied by visuals and other cues.	1. Name and describe objects, people, or events with phrases 2. Plot timelines, number lines, or schedules 3. Define and categorize objects, people, or events with visual or graphic support
Speaking	May use gestures to facilitate communication, use basic phrases, and need time to process information prior to speaking.	4. Analyze and extract information in charts and graphs 5. Sequence pictures with phrases
Reading	May be able to access simplified/sheltered materials with support.	
Writing	May be able to match vocabulary words with concept pictures, write brief sentences, lists, and simple paragraphs with support.	

Early-intermediate ELLs

Listening	May need visual and graphic cues, paraphrasing, and frequent repetition.	1. Compare and contrast objects, people, events with sentences
Speaking	May use basic grammar patterns in speaking, but often make errors when attempting more complex language combinations. May appear silent when processing information.	2. Outline speech and text using graphic organizers 3. Use information from charts, graphs, or tables 4. Follow multiple-step directions[a] 5. Make predictions, hypotheses based on illustrated stories, events, or inquiry
Reading	Can access simplified/sheltered materials that provide grade-level content.	6. Take notes
Writing	May write in sentences or short paragraphs and create longer work with support.	7. Produce short stories, poetry, or structured reports with support

Intermediate/high-intermediate ELLs

Listening	May need visual and graphic cues and paraphrasing.	1. Explain processes or procedures with extended discourse or paragraphs
Speaking	Can participate in academic conversations in meaningful ways. May be self-conscious speaking in front of a large group and more comfortable in pairs or small groups. Errors in syntax are common.	2. Produce original models, demonstrations, or exhibitions 3. Summarize and draw conclusions from speech and text

		Suggested Assessments		
Reading	May rely on word analysis and decoding and therefore read more slowly than native speakers. May benefit from sheltered materials.	4. Construct charts, graphs, and tables 5. Discuss pros and cons of issues 6. Use multiple learning strategies		
Writing	Can write paragraphs with supporting details. Grammatical, mechanical, and spelling errors are common. May need focused instruction to self-edit.			

Transitioning ELLs

Listening	Can understand most content from discussions and lectures. May require clarification of cultural references, nuance, and some idioms.	1. Justify and defend positions through speeches, multimedia reports, or essays 2. Research and investigate academic topics using multiple resources		
Speaking	Can use complex sentence structures. First-language influence may be present in syntax, phonology, and morphology.	3. Explain relationships, consequences, or cause and effect 4. Debate issues		
Reading	Can read on levels similar to those of native-speaking peers (depending on actual reading level, which varies among all students).	5. React and reflect on articles, short stories, or essays of multiple genres from grade-level materials 6. Author poetry, fiction, nonfiction for varied audiences		
Writing	Can produce complex writing. Some first-language influence may be present in the formation of complex sentences (passive structures, complex clauses)			

SOURCE: Suggested assessments are reprinted with permission from Gottlieb (2006, p. 30).
a. Classified as beginner's level by Gottlieb.

TABLE 7.4   Choice in Assessment: Science

Learning Outcomes	Evidence: Choose One Assessment for Each Learning Outcome		
	Written Report	Presentation: Group or Individual	Poster Session
1. Explain the environmental effects of a growing population on the earth's finite resources.			
2. Discuss the local, national, and global implications of findings on the impact of individual environmental footprints.			
3. Support and justify your stance on an issue of environmental concern.			

Poster session: Beginner
On a 20 × 30 poster, create a collage illustrating at least two of the environmental effects of a growing population on the earth's finite resources.
Title the poster.
Label each photo/graphic in the collage.

Poster session: Intermediate
Complete requirements 1 to 3
Include a paragraph to explain each environmental effect illustrated in the collage.

Written paper: Intermediate
Submit a written report (3–4 double-spaced pages, including visuals) discussing at least two effects of a growing population on the earth's finite resources.
Use charts, graphs, tables, or illustrations to demonstrate each effect.

development; goals are attainable yet challenging. Once ELLs successfully reach the language bar that Mr. Peterson has set, he raises the bar slightly.

Review, Reflect, Apply

Review and apply: Choose a content-area assessment that you have created. Review the assessment to ensure that it measures mastery of a unit LO. Then, using Table 7.4, differentiate the assessment for ELLs at beginner, intermediate, and transitioning levels. Ensure that the LO remains the same.

ASSESSMENT PRINCIPLE 2: MULTIPLE MEASURES

Another principle of effective assessment is that ELLs and other students should be assessed at multiple times using multiple measures (Short & Fitzsimmons, 2007; TESOL, 2000; Tomlinson & McTighe, 2006), and these measures should allow for differences in academic-language proficiency (Gottlieb, 2006). Tomlinson and McTighe (2006) explain that assessment should look like a "photo album" rather than a "snapshot" (p. 60). This text uses the analogy of a travel album. The first snapshot of each instructional unit represents pre-instructional assessment, which is then followed by pages of formative assessment snapshots as ELLs and others journey toward the established learning objectives. Finally, the photo album includes a summative assessment, which is a type of collage, summing up the journey and showing mastery of LOs. Table 7.6 illustrates each type of assessment and its purpose.

Multiple Forms of Assessment

Varying the form of assessments increases the likelihood of compatibility between assessment and students' learning styles, preferences, and academic English proficiency levels. Some students (ELLs and native-English speakers), for example, may have difficulty expressing understanding in

TABLE 7.6	Multiple Assessment Types

Assessment Type	Time	Purpose
Pre-instructional assessment: The starting position	Prior to instruction	Evaluates the knowledge and language abilities of ELLs prior to instruction. Enables teachers to build on strengths and address learning needs, identify confusions, and plan appropriate instruction. Pre-assessment may be formal or informal and should not be graded (Tomlinson & McTighe, 2006)
Formative assessment: The signposts along the way to mastery	Throughout the instructional unit	Evaluates progress toward the learning outcomes. Enables teachers to measure the progress of all students and to adjust instruction to meet the identified needs. Formative assessments provide ongoing feedback to students regarding their progress. Formative assessment may be formal (quizzes, brief writing assignments, tickets to leave, self-assessments) and informal (observations). Formative assessments may be graded and ungraded. When graded, more weight should be given to assessments toward the end of the unit—students should not be penalized for taking longer to meet learning outcomes (Tomlinson & McTighe, 2006)
Summative assessment: Measuring the overall success of the journey	Long-term assignment to be completed at the end of the unit	Enables students to demonstrate their mastery of the learning outcomes. Summative assessments are graded by teachers (and may also be self-evaluated and/or peer evaluated). The forms of student assessment should allow for multiple ways to demonstrate mastery (written, visual, and oral)

short writing assignments, but they can effectively convey their understanding in panel presentations or discussions. Other students are excellent test takers but have difficulty with oral presentations. Offering a variety of assessment options enables students to choose the way they will provide evidence of their understanding. Varying the form of assessments also provides ELLs with opportunities to demonstrate content-area mastery apart from academic language proficiency (Short & Fitzsimmons, 2007) and for teachers to measure the progress of ELLs in each of these areas. In a comprehensive review and discussion of assessments for ELLs, Gottlieb (2006) suggests that combinations of assessments are most effective when they consider self-assessment, the ability to work with and contribute to a team, motivation, and effort along with performance measures.

Multiple assessments throughout a unit of instruction provide a series of snapshots that measure student progress along the developmental continua of content and language. Students' travel albums might include the following assessments, which have been recommended by Tomlinson and McTighe (2006) and experts in the field of second-language assessment (such as Garcia & Pearson, 1994; Gottlieb, 2006; Huerta-Macías, 1995; Leung, 2005; Rea-Dickins, 2001):

- A variety of quizzes and tests (Tomlinson & McTighe, 2006)
- Written products such as journals (Huerta-Macías, 1995; Huerta-Macías, 1995, cited in Leung, 2005), essay papers, and lab reports (Tomlinson & McTighe, 2006)
- Visual products (Gottlieb, 2006; Tomlinson & McTighe, 2006), including posters, diagrams, and concept mapping
- Oral presentations (Gottlieb, 2006; Tomlinson & McTighe, 2006) such as speeches, debates, and panel reviews

- Multiple-measure products: for example, a PowerPoint presentation or a presentation with visuals
- Summative assessments that include a variety of products and performances (Tomlinson & McTighe, 2006)
- Portfolio assessment (García & Pearson, 1994, cited in Leung, 2005; Tomlinson & McTighe, 2006)
- Informal and formal observations and checklists (García & Pearson, 1994, cited in Leung, 2005; Huerta-Macías, 1995, cited in Leung, 2005; Tomlinson & McTighe, 2006)
- Student self-assessments (Huerta-Macías, 1995, cited in Leung, 2005; Tomlinson & McTighe, 2006)

Mr. Jamie Hayes demonstrates multiple assessments in his ELA classroom. He begins the "There's More Than Meets the Lie" unit with informal pre-assessment of content-area knowledge by engaging students in small- and large-group discussions about theme and setting. He also reviews students' writing samples and portfolios to assess their level of academic English writing proficiency prior to beginning the unit. These pre-assessments enable Mr. Hayes to gauge student understanding and preparedness and engage in instructional planning to meet the needs of all students. This year, for example, Emerson Beya, a beginner ELL, was placed in Mr. Hayes's class. By reviewing placement scores and the home language survey in Emerson's cumulative folder, Mr. Hayes was able to ascertain that Emerson read at a fifth-grade level in French. Mr. Hayes ordered copies of *The Catcher in the Rye*, one of the unit reading choices, in French; he also requested a French tutor to work with Emerson. He ensured that the tutor and the ESOL teacher both received copies of *The Catcher in the Rye* in both languages.

Throughout the unit, Mr. Hayes formatively assesses the progress of the students. He observes discussion groups to informally assess student content-area understanding and academic-language development. ELLs and others also submit quick-write summaries of their discussions as tickets to leave; these assessments require students to explain one key point or question that resulted from their readings or academic discussions. (Mr. Hayes informs students that these are content-based assessments; he does not grade the quality of the writing.) Both these formative assessments provide snapshots of student understanding and enable Mr. Hayes to make adjustments to lesson objectives, if needed. Mr. Hayes, for example, may adjust a lesson objective to reteach how authors use rhetorical devices for aesthetic purposes based on evidence of student misunderstanding gained from formative assessments. Mr. Hayes also consults with the ESOL teacher and the French tutor at various times through the unit to ensure that Emerson is making progress in content and language. Additional information related to working with ELLs at the beginning level of English proficiency appears in Chapter 8.

Mr. Hayes regularly gauges academic-language development through short-response writings to questions that he poses in class. ELLs and other students begin these as in-class writings and complete them for homework, which provides ELLs with additional time to compose, revise, and edit their written responses. Mr. Hayes differentiates the requirements for these writing assessments. Aadam, an ELL with intermediate proficiency, for example, responds to prompts in lists of sentences, whereas ELLs with greater proficiency and native-English speakers typically respond in paragraphs. Mr. Hayes encourages Emerson to use interlanguage; that is, Emerson routinely writes his responses in French and includes English vocabulary words and phrases as he learns them. Mr. Hayes uses student assessment results to provide feedback to individual students and to plan and implement relevant content and language mini-lessons with small and large groups of students.

Throughout the instructional unit, Mr. Hayes's students work on long-term writing assignments in which they draw connections between the novels that they are reading and their personal lives. Students write both in and out of class and engage in academic discussions during the planning, writing, and revising stages. Students keep all stages of their work in writing portfolios. Mr. Hayes frequently shares his own writing (at various stages of completion) with students. He conferences with groups and with individual students throughout the semester, using the differentiating assessment guide (Table 7.3) as one tool that informs his conversations with the ELLs. Mr. Hayes requests that the French-speaking tutor be present during conferences with Emerson. The tutor's presence enables Mr. Hayes to work more productively with Emerson, and it enables the tutor to learn techniques for future conferences with Emerson.

Review, Reflect, Apply

1. *Apply:* The first principle of effective assessment stresses the importance of multiple assessments. List at least three different types of assessment that you will use in your instructional unit that will enable ELLs to demonstrate content-area knowledge or misconceptions that need to be retaught.

2. *Review:* Explain the importance of pre-instructional, formative, and summative assessments.

ASSESSMENT PRINCIPLE 3: MATCH ASSESSMENTS WITH LEARNING OUTCOMES

The third principle of effective assessment is that the assessment should match the desired LO (Tomlinson & McTighe, 2006) and should enable students to demonstrate content-area understanding independent of academic-language proficiency. Collecting multiple forms of evidence throughout instructional units also makes it possible for teachers to choose an assessment that measures each type of knowledge: declarative, procedural, and dispositional. Knowledge of facts (declarative), for example, can be measured by objective items in quizzes and tests; the ability to interpret (procedural) might be measured more effectively with an open-ended writing assignment or teacher observation of student discussions; and application in unique circumstances (procedural and dispositional) might be best measured by performance of some type. Dispositional knowledge might also be measured with student portfolios, displays of effort and perseverance toward completing assignments, and the ability to self-select and self-critique work.

Assessments from Mr. Peterson's science unit, shown in Table 7.7, summarize how various forms of assessment can be used to measure different types of knowledge and the mastery of content and academic language.

Review, Reflect, Apply

1. *Apply:* Return to the LOs that you developed in Chapter 5. Identify at least two forms of pre-instructional assessment that will enable you to better plan instruction and at least two forms of formative assessment and summative assessment that will provide evidence of student mastery of LOs.

2. *Review:* Explain what type of knowledge (declarative, procedural, dispositional) each assessment serves to measure.

TABLE 7.7 Assessments: Different Types of Knowledge

Type of Assessment	Type of Knowledge
Pre-assessment: Content	
Oral: Student discussion/observation	Declarative: Facts, generalizations, and concepts about the
Written: Quick write explaining the interrelationship of land, air, and water based on demonstration	interrelatedness of land, air, water in the biosphere
Pre-assessment: Language	
Oral: Communicative ability (ELLs and others understand lecture when made comprehensible with visuals and props.)	Declarative: Vocabulary Procedural: Communicative ability and communicative strategies
Formative: Content	
Structured observations within discussion groups	Declarative, dispositional (inquiry, effort)
Student lab reports	Procedural, dispositional (inquiry, effort)
Student quick writes, oral reports	Declarative and procedural
Quizzes	Declarative
Formative: Language	
Same as above	Procedural: Communicative oral language, written language abilities
Summative: Content and language	
Essays, article reviews, and position paper	Declarative, procedural, dispositional
Tests	Declarative, procedural

Summary

In planning effective assessment for ELLs and other students, teachers must ensure that the form of the assessment is aligned with the knowledge that they want to measure. Knowledge of facts and some procedures, such as number operations, can be measured by items in tests and quizzes, whereas elements of understanding are more accurately measured by performance assessments, such as lab reports, essays, and presentations. Content should be assessed apart from language proficiency; the guidelines for content-area assessments for ELLs at varying levels of English language proficiency (Table 7.3) are useful for planning effective instruction.

Planning effective assessments, which allow ELLs and others to demonstrate mastery of LOs, requires attention to the various elements of understanding: explanation, interpretation, application, perspective, empathy, and self-knowledge (Wiggins & McTighe, 2005). While each unit may not involve all six elements of understanding, varying the form of assessments based on different facets ensures that assessments measure deep understanding, rather than recall. Teaching and assessing self-evaluation of academic-language skills and difficulties is particularly important to the continued development of academic-language proficiency. According to Tomlinson and McTighe (2006), three broad principles that teachers should keep in mind when planning and implementing assessments are as follows:

1. Assessments must go beyond measuring knowledge (recall and regurgitation) and measure understanding (explanation, interpretation, application, perspectives, empathy, and self-knowledge).

2. Assessments should be both comprehensive and varied, consisting of a photo album rather than snapshots. Assessments should provide ELLs and other students with multiple ways to demonstrate understanding that are compatible with their learning styles and should not conflate language and content.

3. Assessment should match the desired LO. With a finite amount of instructional time, appropriate assessments provide the most expedient route to measure progress toward LOs. For example, a quick quiz will reveal factual knowledge as effectively as a PowerPoint presentation and will require only a fraction of the time.

FROM OUTCOMES TO OBJECTIVES: "HEROES AND VILLAINS"

Teachers with a clear understanding of the LOs for instructional units are equipped to plan summative assessment options that enable ELLs and others to demonstrate mastery of the LOs. With the LOs in mind, teachers then work backward (Wiggins & McTighe, 1998) to determine the lesson objectives and assessments to guide students toward mastery of these LOs. Ms. Elena Apostolos's secondary ELA thematic literature unit "Heroes and Villains" illustrates the process of dissecting LOs to plan summative assessments and the backward process of planning lesson objectives and accompanying assessments.

Ms. Apostolos has developed the following LOs for the "Heroes and Villains" unit described in Chapter 6 (p. 206):

- *LO-1:* Students will gain factual knowledge of (a) the concepts of hero, tragic hero, and antihero and (b) the content of myths, fairy tales, dramas, biographies, and fiction.
- *LO-2:* Students will (a) evaluate the differing cultural concepts of heroes and villains and (b) describe how the designation of heroes and villains depends on perspectives.
- *LO-3:* Students will develop their own criteria for the roles of hero and villain.

She has developed the following assessments for the same unit:

- *Summative assessment:* Students will develop their own criteria for heroes and villains. They will use these criteria to present their perspectives during a mock trial lasting several days. Students (ELLs and native-English speakers) will demonstrate content-area mastery by preparing at least one of the following: an exhibit, a court draft, a presentation, or a closing argument, each of which will include factual knowledge and an evaluation of the concepts of hero and villain through different perspectives.
- *Pre-instructional assessment:* Students will identify heroes and villains from American pop culture and other cultures and explain why they are heroes or villains.
- *Formative assessments:* Students will be assessed individually (via quick writes, tickets to leave, journals) and in small groups (via observation of discussions and group discussion forums and review of completed graphic organizers and highlighted notes.). Formative assessments are retained in student portfolios.

After determining that the assessments she designed would accurately measure her LOs, Ms. Apostolos reviewed the elements of understanding to ensure that the instructional unit and accompanying assessments measured understanding at various levels. Table 7.8 shows her checklist.

TABLE 7.8	Six Elements of Understanding Assessed in the "Heroes and Villains" Unit
Explanation	In discussions and written tickets to leave, students explain the concepts of hero and villain.
Interpretation	In preparation for a mock trial, students use their analyses and interpretations of heroes and villains to support or attack author William Golding's accusation that humanity is essentially villainous.
Application	Throughout the unit, students apply their knowledge of heroes and villains to new situations.
Perspectives	The mock trial requires students to consider two perspectives regarding humanity. Considering heroes and villains from multiple perspectives is the focus of the Lesson 3 text excerpt from *To Kill a Mockingbird*. Real-life heroes, such as Martin Luther King, Jr., and Che Guevara, are also discussed through dual perspectives. Lesson 3 requires students to name a person who could be viewed as both a hero and a villain.
Empathy	The mock trial requires students to demonstrate empathy for various heroes, antiheroes, and villains.
Self-knowledge	Throughout the unit, students are challenged to draw on their background knowledge and experiences, as well as their reading and class discussions, to create their own definitions of villain and hero. Each lesson of the unit also requires students to assess their content-area learning and their use of language strategies.

Ms. Apostolos also reviewed the English language proficiency levels of her ELLs: two transitioning, two intermediate, three early intermediate, and one beginner. Using the guidelines provided in Table 7.3, Ms. Apostolos differentiated assessments according to the language levels of her ELLs. Table 7.9 illustrates summative assessment, which is differentiated for ELLs with proficiency levels ranging from beginner to transitioning.

FROM LEARNING OUTCOMES TO LESSON OBJECTIVES AND ASSESSMENTS

Ms. Apostolos has identified three major LOs that frame and provide context for instruction. She has determined that each LO requires three types of knowledge (declarative,

TABLE 7.9	Differentiated Summative Assessment by Level of Language Proficiency
Beginner	Identify three qualities of heroes and three qualities of villains. Using the Internet and other traditional sources, find visual representations of these qualities. Prepare an exhibit for the court: Using a 20 × 30 poster, illustrate the qualities of heroes and the qualities of villains. Label each section of your poster. (You may use a Venn diagram format to show differences and similarities between heroes and villains.)
Early-Intermediate	Prepare a poster as described above with a two paragraph brief detailing the qualities of heroes and villains.
Intermediate	Prepare a court draft or presentation to the court:
	Using the definitions of heroes and villains that you have determined, support or refute William Golding's accusation that humanity is essentially villainous. You may do this in a 5-minute presentation using PowerPoint or in a 2-page double-spaced paper.
Transitioning	Prepare a closing argument for the court in the form of a 2- to 3-page paper or a PowerPoint presentation.

procedural, and dispositional) and includes various elements of understanding, as shown in Table 7.8. From these LOs, Ms. Apostolos develops content and language objectives for individual lessons and then aligns lesson assessments with these objectives. Each lesson spans one to five instructional periods depending on the complexity of its objectives and on the assessment evidence. Ms. Apostolos uses the assessment data to guide instruction: When assessment evidence indicates that ELLs and others have not mastered the lesson objective(s), Ms. Apostolos either reteaches the entire group or provides small-group-focused instruction and practice to those students. The cyclical and spiraling nature of assessments and objectives is shown in Model 7.2.

Table 7.10 illustrates content and language lesson and assessment objectives for the "Heroes and Villains" unit as they align with each LO.

Review, Reflect, Apply

Apply: Revisit your LOs. Establish lesson objectives (both content and language) that will enable ELLs and other students to achieve mastery of these LOs.

MODEL 7.2   **From Objectives to Assessment to Objectives**

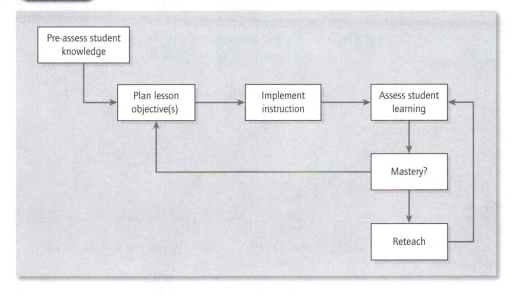

TABLE 7.10 Lessons: Objectives and Assessments

Lesson 1
Learning outcome: Factual knowledge of (a) heroes (tragic hero and antihero) and (b) the content of myths, fairy tales, drama, biographies, films, and fiction

Content objectives	*Assessments:*
1. Students will demonstrate prior knowledge of the concepts of heroes and villains.	1. Teacher observation of small-group discussions, report-out by one student in each group
2. Students will deepen their understanding of the concepts of heroes and villains by reading or listening to different fairy tales and comparing and contrasting characters.	2. Teacher observation of small-group discussions and ticket to leave paragraph or list of characteristics of heroes and villains

Language objectives	*Assessments*
1. Students will be able to discuss the topics of heroes and villains effectively in small groups.	1. Teacher observation (teacher sits in on each small group)
2. Using graphic organizers, students will group the characteristics of their fairy tales' heroes and villains.	2. Review of students' graphic organizers

Lesson 2
Learning outcomes: (a) Use declarative knowledge of heroes and the content of the readings to evaluate the cultural concepts of hero and villain and (b) describe how the definitions of hero and villain depend on perspectives.

Content objectives	*Assessments*
1. Students will be able to explain why Oedipus is a tragic hero.	1. Observation of groups, ticket to leave quick-write
2. Students will be able to provide other examples of characters from literature, movies, and popular culture that fit the criteria for tragic heroes.	2. Observation of groups, ticket to leave, students list at least one additional tragic hero

Language objectives	*Assessments*
1. Students will learn strategies (using highlighters and Post-its) for dealing with difficult text and apply those strategies to reading an excerpt from *Oedipus Rex*.[a]	1. Observation of students' use of highlighters and Post-its to demonstrate strategies; group work conversion of selected sentences into modern English vernacular
2. Students will be able to identify when they do not comprehend what they are reading and be able to ask for additional help from various resources.	2. Review of student highlighting of *Oedipus Rex* excerpts and student notes

Lesson 3
Learning outcome: Same as previous

Content objective	*Assessments*
1. Students will critically evaluate the role of perspective in determining whether characters are perceived as heroes or villains.	1. In small groups, students list why some people considered Atticus Finch a hero and others did not. After discussion of controversial historical figures who are perceived as heroes or villains, students identify someone famous, or someone in their lives, who could be considered either a hero or a villain, depending on perspective. Students write a paragraph explaining their viewpoint. (Intermediate and early-intermediate ELLS have the option of creating a list)

Language objectives	*Assessments*
1. Students will be able to discuss the role of perspective in determining who they believe is a hero or a villain.	1. Observation of groups
2. Students will be able to write a paragraph explaining their views on the subject. (Modify to a list for early-intermediate and intermediate ELLs.)	2. Review of student paragraphs/lists

Lesson 4
Learning outcomes: (a) Demonstrate factual knowledge of (i) the concept of an antihero and (ii) the content of drama, biographies, films, and fiction and (b) describe how the definition of *antihero* depends on perspectives.

Content objectives	*Assessments*
1. Students will identify antiheroes based on their characteristics and actions.	1. In pairs, students report-out their decision about the antihero in Act III of *A Raisin in the Sun*[b]
2. Using textual evidence from *A Raisin in the Sun*, students will be able to identify the antihero.	2. Provided with a photocopy of Act III, students highlight and make notes to identify the antihero. These are submitted and reviewed

Language objectives	*Assessments*
1. Students will be able to discuss the concept of an antihero and identify several examples from literature, movies, and popular culture.	1. Observation of paired discussions
2. Using graphic organizers, students will be able to list specific characteristics of antiheroes.	2. Review of graphic organizers
3. After analyzing an excerpt from *A Raisin in the Sun*, students will be able to discuss which characteristics and actions make Walter an antihero.	3. Observation of paired discussion

Lesson 5
Learning outcome: Develop personal criteria for the concepts of hero and villain.
(This lesson represents the summative activity/assessment for the unit. After studying different types of heroes and villains in several fairy tales, *A Raisin in the Sun*, *To Kill a Mockingbird*, and *Lord of the Flies*, students will engage in a mock trial and debate the nature of humanity. This activity draws on students' abilities to locate evidence from all texts in this unit [as well as outside sources], students' analyses and interpretations of their evidence, and students' abilities to synthesize information into coherent arguments that either support or attack an indictment that accuses humanity of being essentially villainous. This activity is estimated to take anywhere from 2 to 5 days to complete.)

Content objectives	*Assessments*
1. Students will find evidence both to support and to refute the following statement: Without the socializing effects of government and rules, most humans would display the characteristics of villains.	1. Student evidence forms to be submitted (differentiated according to proficiency level)
2. Students will synthesize information from several sources to form their arguments.	2. Completed projects (drafts and final copy). For the mock trial, the prosecution's job is to argue that William Golding is wrong to say that humans are naturally villainous; the defense's job is to argue that he is right to say that humans are naturally villainous

Language objective	*Assessments*
1. Through researching their positions, conferencing with peers, and giving oral arguments, students will develop and strengthen their written language and oral expression skills.	1. Mock trial: Written/performance assessment is differentiated according to language development as is illustrated in Table 7.9, p. 156. Oral assessment: Beginner, early intermediate, and intermediate level students should not be assigned the roles that require the most public speaking (i.e., the lawyers). These students develop their oral expression skills while conferring with their peers, but they will not be expected to be the primary spokesperson for their groups.

NOTE: Assessments for Lesson 1 are graded on content only. Errors in mechanics do not affect assessment results. In Lesson 2, it is anticipated that early-intermediate ELLs will have difficulty reading *Oedipus Rex*, which presents difficulties for many English-speaking students. The excerpt chosen is relatively short and will be reread aloud in modern vernacular to facilitate understanding, and the teacher will guide the reading by explaining and paraphrasing as necessary. ELLs will work collaboratively with native speakers.

a. This strategy is explained in Chapter 9.

b. Beginner and intermediate ELLs will be provided with an adapted text and audiotapes of the reading.

CHAPTER SUMMARY

As Ms. Apostolos's instructional unit illustrates, established LOs encompass the important knowledge and understandings that all students must master as a result of the instruction. Content and language objectives and assessments for individual lessons flow from these larger LOs. Each lesson assessment is aligned with a clear objective, which enables teachers to make informed instructional decisions such as whether to move forward or to reteach/reinforce instruction. Assessments are differentiated for language proficiency levels. Clearly established lesson objectives for content and language, as well as assessments to measure student mastery of these objectives, enable ELLs to move closer to mastery of the unit's overall LOs.

Like Ms. Apostolos, by conveying assessments to ELLs at the beginning of the instructional unit, teachers provide context for the instruction and for the ongoing assessment; they provide ELLs and others with a clear road map toward the LO, with numerous signposts along the way that serve to indicate that the students are on the right track or to identify and deal with misconceptions.

This chapter focused on planning and implementing effective assessments and lesson objectives for ELLs in mainstream content-area classrooms. Chapter 8 provides suggestions and recommendations for making lesson content comprehensible to ELLs.

Assessment Evidence Activities

AE-1   Draft a letter to parents to describe the purposes of and differences between standardized testing and classroom assessments.

AE-2   Explain the types of knowledge (declarative, procedural, dispositional) and demonstrate how your instructional unit is aligned with each type of knowledge.

AE-3   Design assessments that meet each part of the LO. Using Table 7.6, explain how each assessment will be adjusted to allow for ELLs with beginner, early intermediate, intermediate, and transitioning proficiency.

AE-4   Explain the six facets of understanding and how each is used in your LOs, assessments, and lesson objectives.

AE-5   Create summative assessment for each identified LO that will ensure student choice and allow for students with differing strengths and abilities to produce evidence that demonstrates their knowledge/understanding.

AE-6   Prepare a presentation for preservice teachers explaining the importance of planning differentiated assessments prior to planning instruction and of conveying these assessments to ELLs.

Resources for Further Reading

• For a comprehensive and excellent resource on the assessment of ELLs, see Gottlieb, M. (2006). *Assessing English language learners: Bridges from language proficiency to academic achievement*. Thousand Oaks, CA: Corwin Press.

- For a comprehensive discussion of differentiating assessments, see Tomlinson, C. A. (2001). *How to differentiate instruction in mixed-ability classrooms* (2nd ed.). Alexandria, VA: Association for Supervision and Curriculum Development.

- Tomlinson, C. A., & McTighe, J. (2006). *Integrating differentiated instruction and understanding by design.* Alexandria, VA: Association for Supervision and Curriculum Development.

8

Making Content Comprehensible

Enduring understanding: Grade-level content can be made comprehensible.

THE PREVIOUS CHAPTER DESCRIBED THE IMPORTANCE OF EFFECTIVE CONTENT-AREA AND LANGUAGE ASSESSMENTS. Content-area teachers demonstrated how they develop summative assessments that enable students to demonstrate mastery of learning outcomes (LOs). The assessments featured multiple options, such as written papers, posters, and presentations, to accommodate learners' strengths; they also provided options that differentiated the final product to accommodate English language proficiency levels. With clear summative assessments as a goal for teaching and learning, teachers were able to plan pre-instructional assessments that would measure the understandings students brought to the unit and formative assessments that would serve as instructional guideposts throughout the unit. Building clear objectives into each lesson enabled teachers to evaluate student understanding and reteach as necessary. This thoughtful and thorough planning set the stage for well-implemented instruction intended to result in student learning. Even the best planned instruction is ineffective for ELLs, however, if they do not understand the language of instruction.

Making content comprehensible is the focus of Chapter 8. This chapter shows how content-area teachers contextualize instruction and make instructional materials, presentations, and lesson activities comprehensible to ELLs. It begins by presenting current research on the benefits of sheltered instruction. Next, the role of context and its relationship to comprehensibility are discussed; the importance of the first five steps of the Teaching English Language Learners in the Mainstream (TELLiM) model is highlighted in terms of contextualizing instruction. The relevance of culture and background knowledge is discussed as they relate to context. While this book is intentionally focused on ELLs with proficiency levels of early-intermediate and above, it is a reality that newcomers are sometimes placed in mainstream classrooms before developing even rudimentary skills in English. To address this reality, we have included recommendations for mainstream teachers working with beginner ELLs. We then introduce and illustrate methods for building the comprehensibility of materials and presentations across content areas. The chapter concludes with an activity that challenges readers to apply the strategies they have learned throughout the chapter and to plan comprehensible instruction for ELLs at beginner, early-intermediate, intermediate, and transitioning proficiency.

LEARNING OUTCOMES

The following LOs serve as a guide for Chapter 8. At the end of the chapter are assessment activities that are aligned with each LO to enable readers to check their understanding.

LO-1   Explain the benefits of making content-area instruction comprehensible to ELLs at various levels of English language proficiency

LO-2   Demonstrate the ability to make content-area materials comprehensible to ELLs with varying levels of English language proficiency

LO-3   Prepare a presentation in your content area that is comprehensible to ELLs at various levels of proficiency

TERMS THAT MAY BE NEW

Comprehensible: Understandable

Easification: The process of simplifying text (Bhatia, 1983; Nation, 2001)

Glossing: Making boldface or highlighting a word to draw attention to it, then defining the word as it is used in the passage, and writing this definition in the margins next to the word

Scaffolding: Teacher or peer support that enables a learner to understand or do what he or she cannot yet do independently

COMPREHENSIBLE INSTRUCTION

The nature of the process of English language development suggests that ELLs at different stages along the language continuum (from beginner to transitioning) will confront varying degrees of difficulty with grade-level content-area language. Depending on their levels of English proficiency, ELLs may find that some or much of the academic language of content-area instruction is incomprehensible. ELLs, therefore, will benefit from instruction that makes the complex structure of content-area language more comprehensible.

Sheltered instruction is one approach to making grade-level curriculum comprehensible to ELLs. In sheltered instruction, teachers adjust the rate and type of speech, use realia and visuals, develop ELLs' academic vocabulary, provide opportunities for interaction between students (and between teacher and students), adapt materials, and provide supplemental materials (Echevarria, Short, & Powers, 2006; Genessee, 1999; Snow, 2004). One commonly used model of sheltered instruction is the Sheltered Instruction Observation Protocol (SIOP) developed by

Echevarria et al. (2003). In the SIOP model, teachers plan instruction around clear content and language objectives, prepare sheltered materials, provide comprehensible input, allow time for ELLs to practice new strategies, and assess the learning of ELLs. Sheltered instruction has been found to improve the academic writing of ELLs, as measured by the Illinois Measurement of Annual Growth in English (IMAGE) test, which measures language production, including focus on the main idea, use of supporting details, organization, and mechanics (Echevarria et al., 2006). The effectiveness of sheltered English instruction depends on both making complex content comprehensible and developing academic-language abilities.

While there is widespread agreement that immersion in academic settings that consistently provide $i + 1$ input (i.e., input that is comprehensible and always just beyond the current ability of the ELL; Krashen, 1981, 1985; see Chapter 2, this volume) coupled with ample opportunities for academic communication promotes language acquisition and communicative competence (Canale, 1983; Canale & Swain, 1980), there is concern that, particularly in middle and secondary classrooms, the instructional focus often remains on content at the expense of language (Short, cited in Snow, 2004; Short, 2002; Snow, 2004; Swain, 1988). Research suggests that attention to language can and should be systematically integrated into classroom instruction (Snow, 2004); making content comprehensible and building academic language are necessary components of instruction for ELLs.

A single instructional practice may at times result in making content comprehensible as well as building academic language, and therefore separating these components may seem a bit artificial. Yet, for the purpose of discussion and illustration, separating comprehensible content instruction from building academic language provides a clearer picture of the intent, benefits, and potential outcomes of each. With this clear picture in mind, teachers can ensure that they plan lessons that make content comprehensible and at the same time build language. Chapter 8 focuses on making content comprehensible; Chapter 9 focuses on purposefully and intentionally building academic language across content areas.

An overarching concern of many mainstream teachers regarding comprehensible instruction was voiced by Karen, a graduate student in the Methods of Sheltered Instruction course, who in a recent class asked, "How can I make the short stories of Poe comprehensible without oversimplifying them and watering down the content?" Effective, comprehensible instruction does not refer to giving ELLs less or different content. Nor does it mean presenting high-level content to ELLs, hoping that they will "get at least some of it," and then arbitrarily modifying expectations, assignments, and assessments to allow for language differences between ELLs and other students. Comprehensible instruction, rather, is "just right" instruction for ELLs. Comprehensible content-area instruction occurs when content-area experts identify enduring understandings and then, applying their knowledge of principles of second-language acquisition, of relevant areas of English linguistics, and of routes to academic literacy, skillfully adjust and adapt both materials and style of presentation. Content-area instruction that is made comprehensible in this way maintains its academic integrity, yet it is accessible to ELLs and other students who may, for whatever reason, struggle with language. Table 8.1 illustrates how sheltering instruction fits into the TELLiM model.

The following sections first describe how the first five steps of the TELLiM model create classroom environments that contextualize instruction. The chapter then focuses on Step 6 of the model, "Ensure that daily content-area instruction is comprehensible to ELLs," and explains the strategies that content-area teachers can use in their mainstream classrooms to make daily lessons within instructional units comprehensible.

Step	Description	Result for ELLs	Chapter
1	Review unit to determine enduring understandings.	Content is grounded in standards, and context is provided.	5
2	Set LOs, and determine what all students must learn as a result of instruction.	Content-area LOs for ELLs are rigorous; instruction has context.	5
3	Establish appropriate AE (content and language).	AE does not depend on language proficiency—assessments are accessible.	6
4	Contextualize instruction with essential questions.	Instruction is thematic, has context, is engaging, and builds on knowledge of ELLs and other students.	6
5	Differentiate assessment to measure content and language LOs. Plan content and language objectives and assessments for individual lessons.	Content-area and language assessments are both accessible and challenging.	7
6	Ensure that daily content-area language is comprehensible to ELLs.	ELLs have access to grade-level content.	8

TABLE 8.1 Building Comprehensibility: TELLiM Model

The Appendix provides profiles of 10 ELLs who study and learn with native-English speakers in content-area classes. These students, along with the ELLs introduced in earlier chapters, help illustrate sheltered instruction in content-area classrooms. The profiles are used in the Review, Reflect, Apply sections, which encourage readers to consider the specific needs of ELLs when planning lessons.

WORKING WITH BEGINNERS

In the mainstream content-area classroom, ELLs at the early-intermediate level (minimally) and above require specialized instruction that embeds context, provides comprehensibility, and builds language. Beginning-level ELLs do not yet have the language skills to benefit from such instruction. However, beginners are often placed in mainstream classrooms. Students with little or no English require support that differs from the support needed by ELLs with greater levels of English proficiency. While some beginner ELLs have strong native-language-literacy skills, this is not always the case. It is imperative that mainstream teachers work with ESOL teachers and bilingual tutors, where available, to appropriately assess and plan for the beginner ELL.

ESOL teachers can serve as a primary reference when planning instruction for ELLs, and beginner students in particular. When a beginning-level ELL is enrolled in a mainstream classroom, the mainstream teacher should consult immediately with the ESOL teacher to review placement testing results and school records (if available) in order to gain a preliminary understanding of the student's linguistic and academic background. After the initial consultation, regular, ongoing meetings with the ESOL teacher are useful. During these meetings, teachers can discuss the intersection of content and language and identify goals for each of these learning areas. ESOL teachers may be able to provide resources such as bilingual dictionaries, picture dictionaries with content-related vocabulary, glossaries, and visual tools to complement the classroom materials. In addition, ESOL teachers with access to professional organizations and specialty catalogs will be able to help acquire specific resources.

The placement of a beginner ELL in a mainstream content-area classroom can generate anxiety on the part of both student (Baker, 2006) and teacher (Sánchez, 2007). Teachers, naturally, may feel helpless about their inability to instruct beginners. The result of this can be frustration with oneself or the student, as well as a feeling of sympathy for the student's situation. Teachers who feel ill-prepared to properly instruct the student may not interact with the student. Beginners may be left to "absorb" what they can, taking courses in an auditing fashion. Beginner students experience a similar run of emotions. To be placed in an all-English classroom with little or no understanding of the language can be frightening, frustrating, and overwhelming (Baker, 2006; Skutnabb-Kangas, 2000). Students' affective filters are generally highly activated in such a situation. They may become more quiet, distracted, tired, or saddened. Many beginners fear being noticed for their differences and therefore make attempts to become "invisible" within the classroom.

Beginner ELLs should be introduced to a student mentor (referred to as a "student buddy" for younger students), who, whenever possible, speaks the same first language (Peregoy & Boyle, 2004). The services of a certified bilingual teacher, a bilingual tutor, or a paraprofessional inside the mainstream classroom are also invaluable for beginner ELLs. Tutors can help lower the affective filter of newcomers and make content comprehensible to them. Not only are beginner ELLs immersed in a foreign language, but the entire schooling system and its norms may be unfamiliar to them. Tutors and student mentors can ease the transition for beginner ELLs by explaining general school/classroom expectations and routines.

The following list (based on the recommendations of the American Institutes for Research [2005]) provides some suggestions for working with tutors in the classroom. A link to the online document is available in the Resources for Further Reading section of this chapter:

- Introduce the tutor to the entire class, to make him or her a regular part of the classroom setting.
- Meet with the tutor individually to discuss his or her role in the classroom.
- Discuss pedagogy and instructional methods and ensure that the tutor feels competent with the instructional methods.
- Share enduring understandings and LOs with the tutor.
- Show the tutor where to locate classroom resources and materials.
- Use the tutor to help you talk directly to the student.
- Share copies of classroom materials with tutors.
- Use the services of the tutor to initiate communication with the ELL's family through translated notes and/or phone calls.

While tutors should not be made responsible for classroom instruction, they assist the teacher in working directly with the ELL, either individually or during small-group work. Alternatively, tutors may monitor the mainstream students while teachers spend some time working directly with the ELLs.

MAKING CONTENT COMPREHENSIBLE THROUGH CONTEXT

Context makes content more accessible to ELLs. The instructional model of context-embedded instruction (as opposed to context-reduced instruction [Cummins, 2000]), described in Chapter 1 of this text) suggests that providing context can help ELLs complete even the most cognitively demanding tasks, such as writing academic essays and learning new, challenging content from lectures. The first step in planning comprehensible instruction is to provide context that enables ELLs and others to understand the interrelatedness of details and facts and make connections between known and new concepts and processes. The TELLiM model contains five context builders: (1) enduring understandings, (2) clear LOs, (3) clear assessments, (4) essential questions, and (5) differentiated assessment and objectives for content and language. This section explains how each of these context builders creates instructional settings that contribute to comprehensible instruction.

Context Builder 1: Enduring Understandings

Consistently connecting instruction to enduring understandings provides context for the instructional unit as a whole and for individual lessons within the unit. In Chapter 5, content-area teachers planned thematic instructional units based on enduring understandings, and thus provided context for instruction. Mr. Gordon, the ESOL teacher who planned "too little," and Ms. Green, the history teacher who planned "too much," reconceptualized their instruction based on enduring understandings in their content areas. Their new instructional units are "just right" and provide context that allows ELLs such as Aadam, Katy, and Fredy to understand how concepts and facts come together.

Context Builders 2 and 3: Determining Learning Outcomes and Providing Assessments

Establishing LOs and giving students appropriate assessments at the beginning of an instructional unit provide a contextual road map that helps ELLs (and other students) to know "where they are headed and why" (Wiggins & McTighe, 1998, p. 190). LOs spell out the content-area concepts that all students must master; clear, appropriate assessments enable ELLs and other students to choose the format in which they will demonstrate mastery. This contextual road map (with many checkpoints along the way in the form of formative assessments) helps all students to self-monitor their understanding throughout the instructional unit. This ability is critical for ELLs, who must struggle to know what is most important to learn and to measure their progress toward mastering the most important content.

A snapshot of Mr. Peterson's class illustrates how conveying LOs and assessment requirements provides a contextual road map. Mr. Peterson begins this day by explaining the LOs to the entire class. He has posted these on chart paper, and he begins class by calling students' attention to the essential question and then to each LO. Consistent with the TELLiM model, content-area LOs are the same for all students (ELLs and native-English speakers). Mr. Peterson explains to the class,

> You will all address this essential question by (1) explaining the environmental effects of a growing population on the earth's finite resources; 2) calculating your own global footprint and applying it to local, national, and global issues; and (3) supporting and justifying your stance on an issue of environmental concern.

Mr. Peterson points to each LO as he reads it and paraphrases when necessary. He anticipates Julián's confusion, acknowledges this with a nod, and makes an "in a minute" gesture with his hand to convey that he will make the assignments clear.

He explains to the larger class,

> These are challenging learning outcomes, but you can meet them. Every day for the next five weeks, you will work individually and together in groups to learn the content and skills needed to help you meet the unit LOs. We will have quizzes, and you will submit writing that helps both of us measure your progress.

At the mention of quizzes and writing, some students groan, and Katy rolls her eyes; yet, overall, the students are attentive. Mr. Peterson explains, "As usual, you will be able to choose how you prove mastery of these learning outcomes." He proceeds to show students the assessment matrix from which they will choose (see Chapter 7). Mr. Peterson's students understand what they will learn and do as a result of the instruction. Instruction is contextualized.

When Mr. Peterson posts and distributes rubrics that detail the requirements for each assessment, he meets with the students in groups. Katy, Aadam, Julián, and Natka (profiles of each student are provided in the Appendix) have alternate rubrics, which reflect their differing stages of language development. The written report option, for example, requires a three- to five-page paper, which is a valid option for many native-English-speaking students. Aadam, Katy, and Natka (intermediate-level ELLs) are provided the option of using charts, graphs, and illustrations and explaining each of these with a supporting paragraph. Julián (beginner ELL) is required to bullet main points in simple sentences and support these with charts, graphs, or illustrations. The alternate assessments measure the same content but provide comprehensible formats for demonstrating content-area mastery. Mr. Peterson conferences with students to ensure that they understand the assessment requirements; each student has a clear road map to guide her or him toward meeting LOs and demonstrating content-area mastery.

Context Builder 4: Essential Questions

Anchoring the instructional unit with essential questions (Chapter 6) also serves to contextualize instruction. The prominent display of essential questions on posters and in headers on handouts and PowerPoint presentations, and referring to these essential questions during lessons, provides context for each lesson and activity. Unlike Mehmet and Aadam, who struggled to understand how Ms. Green's early history lessons fit together, ELLs who have received instruction grounded with essential questions should be able to make connections between individual lessons and unit understandings. As Ms. Chin explains

> Framing instruction with the essential question provides context for every instructional activity. It enables all students to know where the instruction is going. And I find it really helps ELLs who are struggling with the language to understand how concepts, facts, and procedures all fit together.

The following snapshot of Ms. Chin's class illustrates how the essential question provides context.

The essential question *Was the Revolutionary War inevitable?* is displayed prominently on chart paper and as a banner above the whiteboard. Ms. Chin has created and distributed identity cards to all students. The essential question is typed on the top of each card; the body of the card contains the profile of a citizen living in the colonies during the time of the Revolution, including name, age, race, and socioeconomic status. Half the cards contain profiles of citizens who are in favor of revolution, and the other half contain profiles of citizens who are loyal to England. Ms. Chin distributes the identity cards early in the unit. Adopting the identities on their cards, students maintain diary entries for the most important events leading up to the Revolution—always connecting to the essential question *Was the Revolutionary War inevitable?* Today, in mixed-identity groups, ELLs and other students are discussing the multiple perspectives on events leading to the war that they have captured in their diaries. Soan Meng and Katy Boureth work in a group with two native-English speakers. Context, combined with adapted reading and other materials (discussed later in this chapter), has made content comprehensible to Soan and Katy, who use the terms *different perspectives* and *points of view* in their discussion about the inevitability of war. "It is not that you are wrong," Katy explains to Soan. "Your perspective is different from mine—you just see it differently than me."

Ms. Chin explains,

> Katy and Soan's diaries have many grammatical and spelling errors, and they need support with the primary-source documents—this I know is a normal part of language development. They do, however, really understand the big picture. They relate to the essential questions and engage in conversations based on concepts and multiple perspectives. Context provided by the essential questions is supporting their access to the content.

Context Builder 5: Lesson Objectives and Assessments

Daily objectives and formative assessments, which are clearly planned and conveyed to students, also provide context for instruction. Teachers such as Ms. Apostolos, the secondary ELA teacher introduced in Chapter 7, develop lesson objectives that guide ELLs and other students toward mastery of LOs. They post objectives on the whiteboard, convey objectives at the beginning of each lesson, explain the relationship of lesson objectives to essential questions and LOs, and refer to objectives throughout the lesson. Knowing the content and language objectives enables ELLs to understand the relationship of lesson content to essential questions and LOs. As one ELL explained, "I like it when teachers are organized and can tell us what we will do. I understand the lessons better then." Ms. Bell's eighth-grade classroom illustrates how clear lesson objectives provide context.

Every day, Ms. Bell posts lesson objectives (content and language) in the same space on the whiteboard. Next to each objective, she lists the assessment for the objective. Ms. Bell reviews objectives and assessments at the beginning of the lesson. Before students leave the classroom at the end of the instruction period, Ms. Bell assesses understanding and provides prompt feedback. Students leave Ms. Bell's room with assessment evidence that confirms their understanding or suggests the need for more practice; they leave knowing what they know. Contrast Ms. Bell's carefully planned lessons with the following description of another class provided by a high-achieving and highly motivated ELL:

I had a history teacher last year, and all she did was talk, talk, talk, and talk, and we just had to write down what she said, and that was how we [were supposed to] learn. She didn't write on the board at all; we had to listen to her orally; and by the second week, she would give us a test.

This ELL explained that she liked her classes but often did not understand the objectives of the lesson and felt that she had to learn on her own.

Review, Reflect, Apply

Review and reflect: Review the previous sections in which content-area teachers provided context for instruction by adhering to the steps of the TELLiM model. Review the enduring understandings, essential questions, LOs, and assessments that you have designed for your instructional unit. Explain how each of these will build context for instruction for ELLs and other students in your classes.

Summary

Overall, an instructional unit that provides context includes a clear road map from the beginning of instruction to mastery of LOs. The unit contains the steps of the TELLiM model: enduring understandings, clear LOs, differentiated assessments, essential questions, and clear lesson objectives. Developing instruction based on these steps increases comprehensibility through context.

The next section focuses on the sixth context builder, "Building on Students' Background Knowledge."

Building on Students' Background Knowledge

A sixth context builder is tapping into and building on background knowledge that ELLs and others bring to the mainstream classroom. A tenet of good teaching is that the teacher should activate the schemata and background knowledge of students prior to instruction (Saphier & Gower, 1997); good teachers know that even students with similar background experiences are likely to differ in conceptual knowledge, understanding, preconceptions, misconceptions, and vocabulary. A tenet of culturally responsive teaching is to tap into the backgrounds of students who may not share the culture of the mainstream school.

Regardless of background differences, students who have been educated in U.S. schools are likely to bring with them previously acquired academic knowledge that teachers can activate. ELLs who enter U.S. schools in middle and secondary grades bring to the classroom cultural and academic knowledge that differs from that of students who have been educated in U.S. schools. In U.S. history, for example, curricula are spiraled, which enables teachers to provide context for instruction by activating student background knowledge and connecting known concepts to new content concepts.

Aadam Jassam, Natka Jigovic, and Julián Alencastro, for example, have no background in U.S. history. Yet Aadam, Natka, and Julián do not come to school as blank slates: they (and all students) come to the classrooms with rich funds of knowledge (Au, 2006; González et al., 2005). ELLs who have been educated in other countries are likely to have limited knowledge of U.S.

history and government, but they may well know about the history and government of their country of origin. When tapped, this knowledge has the potential to benefit other students in the classroom. A colleague who taught middle school history used a three-foot-deep timeline that spanned from ceiling to whiteboard across two sides of the classroom. Several students in her class were from the Dominican Republic and several others from Puerto Rico. As this colleague plotted events from U.S. history, she also added historical events from the Dominican Republic and Puerto Rico. Although the Dominican and Puerto Rican ELLs (in this particular class) knew very little about the displacement of Native Americans during the settling of the United States, they did know about the displacement of the Taínos in the Caribbean. Our colleague tapped into this knowledge to help build an understanding of the Westward Expansion. The understanding of students who were educated in the United States was also extended by learning about historical events in the Dominican Republic and Puerto Rico.

Student progress in subjects such as mathematics, which are often thought of as language neutral, also depends on students' prior knowledge. A study of arithmetic processing showed substantial differences in brain activity between native-Chinese and native-English-speaking students (Tang et al., 2006). The authors of the study concluded that the differences were at least partially attributable to differences in language and writing systems and that children reading Chinese characters developed an ability to form mental images, which transferred to arithmetic processing. There is a growing body of research in ethnomathematics that illustrates the relationship between language, culture, previous education, and mathematics (Bush, 2003). This research highlights the need for teachers to understand the role of culture in shaping mathematical development (D'Ambrosio, 2001) and to find out about the background experiences that students who differ from the mainstream bring to the classroom.

While teachers may not be able to learn different writing systems or know the history, government, literature, and accomplishments of every country and culture, they must be cognizant that ELLs bring rich, albeit sometimes incompatible, knowledge and experiences to the classroom. This recognition serves three important purposes. First, it helps teachers to create a positive learning environment that acknowledges culturally different ways of knowing. (For example, while Jaime Escalante's impassioned classroom speech about math being in the Mayan blood of underachieving Mexican American students, alone, would have been insufficient for improving student achievement, the cultural connection established a climate that promoted learning ("Jaime Escalante Still Preparing Students for the Workplace," 1998). Second, it helps teachers to plan lessons that build on student strengths. And third, it requires teachers to reject the assumption that all students have a common core of background knowledge; ELLs may or may not come to an instructional unit with the requisite background knowledge to fully access content. Ungraded pre-instructional assessments, such as those discussed in the previous chapter, reveal the conceptions and misconceptions that ELLs and other students bring to each instructional unit and enable teachers to build necessary background knowledge.

Review, Reflect, Apply

Apply: Review the profiles of Aadam, Katy, Fredy, and the ELLs found in the Appendix. With your content-area unit in mind, anticipate (1) the knowledge each ELL may bring to instruction, (2) the background knowledge each may need to be taught, and (3) how you might teach that background knowledge.

- Mr. Vong uses antacid tablets, beakers of water, and balance scales to demonstrate the conservation of mass. The experiments he has designed enable ELLs to understand the concept of conservation of mass while they are learning the vocabulary for the concept.

- Ms. Harrington uses videos of scientists, doctors, and patients discussing genetics and the potential benefits and risks of knowing one's genetic profile. She first preteaches vocabulary to ELLs and others. During the video presentation, she stops after each segment of an interview to discuss the video contents with students to ensure that they understand what has been said. She explains that hearing about the issues from various perspectives makes the topic of genetic profiling more comprehensible to ELLs and other students.

- Mr. Gastón has found an Internet site that allows students to type in their parents' and grandparents' phenotypes in order to discover their own genotype for eye color as well as learn about the possible phenotypes for eye color for children they may have in the future. According to Mr. Gastón, this demonstration and hands-on activity is engaging and shows ELLs and others about genotypes and phenotypes. He extends the activity with lessons using Punnett Squares.

Using Realia and Visuals in Other Content Areas

- Ms. Jones, family consumer science teacher, uses sales flyers, nutrition labels, recipe books, calorie counters, and menus from restaurants to show students how to plan healthful diets. ELLs and others can see nutritional information and participate in calculating calories and percentages of minimum daily requirements. When she begins an instructional unit on toy safety, Ms. Jones brings real toys she has collected to demonstrate safety guidelines and infractions of these guidelines.

- Ms. Ruiz, a physical education teacher, uses a model and various photos to illustrate circulation in the healthy heart and respiration in healthy lungs. She also uses Internet resources such as National Geographic to illustrate health and health problems (http://www.nationalgeographic.com).

- Students in Mr. Ray's American music class see a local jazz band perform at their high school auditorium. Mr. Ray also makes videos of band performances available so that students can see the artists play. He has students access jazz online to better understand the history of American jazz, read authentic reviews, and listen to artists' discussions about topics such as improvisation.

Comprehensible Presentations: Show, Don't Tell

After Ms. Deborah Goguen accepted an invitation to appear as a guest reader in Ms. Mario's seventh-grade class, of which ELLs constituted nearly 30%, she was informed that she would be reading *The Monkey's Paw* (Jacobs, 1902). The old-fashioned language and unfamiliar setting made the story fairly difficult to follow for native-English-speaking students and even more difficult for ELLs. The topic (a horror story of three wishes), however, has been played out in more modern versions to which students were likely to relate, such as *The Tale of the Twisted Claw* (Brown & MacHale, 1992).

Summary

ELLs enter U.S. classrooms with valid background knowledge that may or may not be compatible with content-area instruction. Recognizing ELLs' knowledge enables teachers to

- establish a positive classroom climate for learning,
- draw forth the strengths that ELLs bring to the classroom,
- identify gaps in requisite background knowledge and areas of misconception, and
- build necessary background knowledge to contextualize instruction.

MAKING UNIT LESSONS COMPREHENSIBLE

Regardless of the specific lessons taught within content-area units, presentations and content-area materials must be comprehensible to students. Content-area materials fall into two basic categories: in-class materials presented by the teacher and out-of-class materials that ELLs and others must access in small groups or independently. This section begins with a discussion of materials employed by teachers to make their presentations more comprehensible, including realia (real objects or facsimiles of real objects, such as maps, globes, photos, videos, and audio recordings), diagrams, and graphic organizers.

Realia and Visuals

Several years ago, friends returned from a trip to the Grand Canyon, where, marveling, they took hundreds of photographs. While their photographic skills and camera were adequate, they were disappointed when they saw the photos. "We just couldn't capture the wonder of being there on film," they thought. Other friends who had been to the Grand Canyon agreed. Friends who had never seen the canyon firsthand, however, told them, "You've really made the Grand Canyon come alive in these photos." The message of this story, of course, is that the real thing is best and the next best thing is a representation or a model.

Teachers tend to use realia extensively in the earlier grades with show-and-tell, multiple local field trips, and a variety of hands-on activities that allow students to experience new content through multiple senses. Yet as students progress through the grades, teachers' use of realia often diminishes. Middle-grade and upper-grade teachers have so many standards to teach that they may feel they do not have time for realia. This is unfortunate, because research indicates that increasing the contexts in which concepts, strategies, and skills are presented also increases the likelihood that learners will remember and be able to retrieve information and strategies (Nation, 2001; Rhawn, 1996). ELLs who are not fully proficient in academic language especially benefit from experiencing the real thing and from multiple sensory representations of the real thing. The more context ELLs can associate with a concept, the more readily retrievable the concept is likely to be.

Using Realia and Visuals in Middle and Secondary Math Classes

- All the seventh-grade students in Ms. Perone's school district take a field trip to the historical section of a nearby city to see and experience math. They measure distances between locations, work with proportions and ratios, and identify geometric shapes in historic buildings. According to Ms. Perone, this context enables ELLs (and many other students) to understand the influences of math on the real world and to relate math formulas to their lives. Katy and her classmate Serey attended one of these field trips and were awed by the architecture. Ms. Perone extended the experience by asking students to observe geometric architectural shapes in buildings in their neighborhoods. Katy and Serey, who lived in the inner city, returned the following day with many drawings and illustrations, which were then used to illustrate math formulas.

- Mr. Colón's 10th-grade physical science class is composed of 11 ELLs and 12 native-English speakers. As part of a lab activity, students created paper airplanes, which they then let fly to see the relationship between distance, speed, and time. Mr. Colón extended this experience with other relatable distance, speed, and time examples to which students applied formulas. Thinking of Geoffrey, an intermediate ELL from South Africa, Mr. Colón had students locate South Africa on a map. He provided students with distance and speed and asked them to calculate the amount of time it would likely take to arrive at the Cape Town International Airport. Geoffrey and others were engaged throughout the problem-solving period and solved the problem correctly.

- Ms. Fornier's sixth-grade students work with balance scales to solve equations. According to Ms. Fornier, Tamara (an intermediate ELL) and Paola (a beginning ELL), who often have difficulty with math instruction, are able to write numerical expressions for equations while using the scales and can demonstrate their understanding of the concept behind numerical expressions.

- Mrs. Snow's 10th graders also work with simulated scales available from the National Library of Virtual Manipulatives to solve equations.

- Ms. Bell's eighth-grade math students use dice, coins, playing cards, and statistics from local and national sports to investigate probability. They also use the National Library of Virtual Manipulatives for probability simulations.

Using Realia and Visuals in English Language Arts Classes

- Ms. Shaw has collected a wide variety of photos that evoke different emotions. Prior to a literary reading, Ms. Shaw's ninth graders look at selected photos and discuss mood. Her observations of ELLs at all proficiency levels indicate that the photos enable students to understand *mood* better than any definition or description she provides. She extends the use of photos from her collection to help ELLs and others to understand *imagery* and also, most recently, *setting* in pastoral literature.

- Mr. Kim uses videos of plays that illustrate dramatic devices such as *aside*, *soliloquy*, *dialogue*, and *narration*. He also uses movies and videos to preview classroom reading selections. As he explains, "For ELLs like Fredy and other students who have never been to a play, showing, rather than telling, makes literary devices clear. Students still need to learn the vocabulary, but they understand the concepts."

- Mr. Webster has saved a collection of poems he has written as well as samples of each step of his personal writing process and each successive draft of the poems. With these, he shows and models the writing process. According to Mr. Webster, ELLs and others need to see the process, and they are more willing to try their hand at poetry once they have seen his drafts.

- Mrs. Patel borrows maps from the geography teacher and uses these to show students story setting. She also uses timelines and historical facts to illustrate and build understandings about setting. ELLs listen to her discussion of setting, and they read and discuss setting in pairs and small groups, but "seeing the setting" makes it comprehensible to them.

- Ms. Welch uses the Internet to find photos and student-friendly images that she copies into PowerPoint. She routinely uses these images to introduce setting and mood in her secondary ELA class.

Using Realia and Visuals in History

- Mr. Billings has collected political cartoons that he uses to introduce new topics, such as relating the past to the present. Mr. Billings often refers students to the cartoons, which he has enlarged and posted around the room. He acknowledges that it is necessary to dedicate instructional time to teach ELLs and others how to interpret and use political cartoons, which he accomplishes by introducing simple cartoons. According to Mr. Billings, several ELLs have drawn political cartoons as assessments of unit mastery: "When they can convey conceptual knowledge with a political cartoon that they explain, I know they really understand."

- Mr. Michaels uses the primary sources available from the Library of Congress and other online resources to ensure that all students see the original records. He shelters these documents (a process that is discussed later in this chapter) to make them comprehensible to all students.

- Mr. Marx has several globes and numerous maps in his room. He refers to these often and consistently makes them available to students. The National Geographic Web site offers a variety of current maps.

- Ms. Patrón uses a variety of photos to illustrate various time periods and events. Some of these she has collected on trips to historical museums; others she found in picture books on historical fiction.

- Ms. Yu uses Web quests to direct students to sites that show history; students can listen to the music of the times, look through newspapers, and understand what students their age were doing when historical events occurred. She is careful to include sites that show, as well as talk about, the times. According to Ms. Yu, seeing the events makes them more comprehensible to ELLs.

Using Realia and Visuals in Science

- Mr. Peterson uses the world population clock (Princeton University; http://opr.princeton .edu/popclock/) to show students population growth. His three sections of environmental science are composed of native-English speakers and ELLs. Mr. Peterson claims that the clock illustrates population growth in a powerful way for all students and transcends language barriers.

- He also uses the environment around his school site to illustrate ecosystems and climates. Tia, Pedro, and José, all intermediate-level ELLs, were able to complete site maps of ecosystems, discuss these within small groups, and then write interpretive paragraphs about differences in findings.

If Deborah were to simply read the story aloud, ELLs and many other students would likely comprehend little. A simple introduction seemed insufficient. Deborah decided to find multiple ways to make the presentation comprehensible to ELLs. Using the Internet, she found images depicting life in 19th-century England. She also found photos of various talismans and images that conveyed an ominous mood. She arranged these in a PowerPoint presentation.

She began the reading session by assessing the students' background knowledge about horror stories and movies. She built on student knowledge with a discussion of setting in stories of horror and suspense. She then showed them images depicting life in England at the end of the19th century—a time before video games, television, and computers. Two ELLs were beginners, and to ensure that they understood the introduction, Deborah encouraged them to collaborate with more proficient ELLs who spoke the same first language.

Deborah then read *The Monkey's Paw* in a clear voice but without exaggerated slowness. She conveyed mood and *foreshadowed* story events by varying the pace, volume, and rhythm of her voice. She paused a few times to ask students to predict what might happen next. The students, including the ELLs (even the beginners), sat focused throughout the story. The discussion that followed the story reading showed that the ELLs both enjoyed the story and understood its most salient components.

Ms. Shaw's "Edgar Allan Poe" unit provides another snapshot example of ways to make a presentation (and challenging reading) comprehensible. Ms. Shaw began planning the unit by reviewing state ELA frameworks and conducting online research that led her to many helpful sites. (The site she found particularly helpful in planning her Poe lesson is included in the Resources for Further Reading section at the end of this chapter.) Ms. Shaw introduced her first lesson on *The Raven* (Poe, 1845) by establishing the mood of the poem. She circulated photographs and asked ELLs and other students to discuss them. She then introduced the word *melancholy*, and ELLs and English-speaking students, in pairs, discussed the personal events that had caused them to experience melancholy. Ms. Shaw guided students to understand that the action of the poem takes place in the evening after dark while the narrator is alone in his home, reading. Next, she played a recording of James Earl Jones's reading of *The Raven* to enable ELLs and others to develop a sense of the poem's rhythm. Ms. Shaw then showed an episode from the television show *The Simpsons*, which features a comic version of *The Raven* (Poe, Simon, & Silverman, 1990), to further increase the poem's comprehensibility. Next, students read the poem in groups of three (ELLs working in groups with native-English speakers). Marí, an ELL in the class, later explained that she enjoyed listening to James Earl Jones—she liked "the sounds of the language." Yet, she explained, she did not really understand the story until she watched the *Simpsons* version. Watching the *Simpsons* version and listening to the audio reading enabled Mari to successfully read the poem herself, understand its gist, and appreciate the sound and rhythm of the language.

Review, Reflect, Apply

1. *Reflect:* Using the profiles of the 10 ELLs in the Appendix, anticipate some of the challenges these students may experience in your classroom and with the content-area materials that you generally use (or intend to use). Be as specific as possible.

2. *Apply:* List three instructional changes you might make to improve the comprehensibility of instruction for each ELL *without* changing the complexity of the content you will teach.

Summary

In the early grades, teachers routinely use realia and images to make content comprehensible and engaging for ELLs and native-English speakers. Often, however, in the middle and secondary grades, as content grows in scope and difficulty, teachers tend to abandon realia and visuals. This is unfortunate, because research indicates that exposure to learning through a variety of contexts is likely to promote retrieval of knowledge. ELLs who struggle to comprehend grade-level language benefit from instruction that illustrates vocabulary and concepts with realia and visuals. The Internet provides excellent resources for content-area teachers who are searching for realia. Several useful resources are found in the Resources for Further Reading section at the end of this chapter.

Diagrams and Graphic Organizers

Diagrams, teacher-drawn illustrations, and graphic organizers can also be used effectively to make content comprehensible. Each of the content-area teachers featured in this text routinely uses diagrams to teach concepts.

- Ms. Bell uses a number line when teaching math to ELLs and other students. She has a number line permanently displayed in the room, and all students are required to have number lines in their math notebooks; she wants students to see the process of number operations. She also frequently uses tree diagrams in the unit on probability, as she believes that these visual aids enable ELLs to see probability in an orderly format. Ms. Bell routinely uses drawings and diagrams as she thinks aloud through word problems; and she requires ELLs and others to draw or diagram their thought processes as they begin to solve word problems.

- Ms. Bell makes use of the Frayer model and graphic organizer to build vocabulary in her math classes. (Use of the Frayer model is illustrated in Chapter 11.)

- Ms. Chin uses large-scale timelines to provide students with a sense of historical time. She also uses overheads of T-charts (shown in Table 8.2) as she explains the U.S. and British perspectives on events leading to the American Revolution. Ms. Chin compares and contrasts perspectives using overheads of Venn diagrams.

- Mr. Peterson routinely illustrates important points with diagrams. For example, he draws the water cycle, ocean currents, food chains, nitrogen cycles, and so on, as he explains them to students. He uses flowcharts and T-charts as he guides students through a decision-making model.

- In teaching academic language, Mr. Peterson uses the Cornell note taker (http://ccc.byu.edu/learning/note-tak.php, accessed July 9, 2008) as one graphic organizer for note taking and concept maps for vocabulary building.

- Mr. Hayes graphs the elements of *plot* (*exposition, rising action, climax, falling action,* and *resolution*) as he explains these to ELLs and others. He also uses T-charts and Venn diagrams to highlight similarities and differences in *theme,* setting, and *character* between novels read as part of the thematic unit.

In addition to using graphic organizers to make presentations comprehensible, content-area teachers also teach ELLs and other students how to use graphic organizers independently.

To accomplish this, teachers select one graphic organizer, explain its use and benefit, teach students how to use it properly, allow practice time, and assess students' ability to use it.

Table 8.2 illustrates some effective uses for the most commonly used graphic organizers.

Review, Reflect, Apply

Reflect and apply: Consider the content material for the unit you are developing. What graphic organizer might be helpful to the ELLs you have met in this and in previous chapters? Explain why this graphic organizer is effective, how you might use it to illustrate concepts and lessons, and how you will teach ELLs and other students to use it.

Summary

Diagrams, teacher drawings and illustrations, and graphic organizers can be powerful tools to make complex content more comprehensible to ELLs. To promote the efficient and effective use of graphic organizers, teachers must model its use, provide student practice, and assess student competence. Teachers should introduce one graphic organizer at a time and should provide ample opportunities for students to practice using this graphic organizer.

MAKING CONTENT COMPREHENSIBLE THROUGH INTERACTION

Purposeful academic discussions make content more comprehensible by providing ELLs and other students with ongoing opportunities to check and clarify their understanding with other students. In a synthesis of research on instructional grouping, Ward (1987) found that when students worked in small groups that provided immediate feedback, they learned content with greater understanding and more quickly than they did while completing seatwork independently. Teachers can use a variety of grouping strategies to ensure that ELLs have opportunities

TABLE 8.2	Graphic Organizers
Graphic Organizer	**Uses**
Cause-effect diagram	Used to show the relationship between cause and effect
Concept map	Shows multiple traits related to a concept or a word
Cycle diagram	Illustrates how events are related to one another cyclically
Flow chart	Shows events with possible multiple outcomes at various decision points
KWL chart	Know/want to know/learn (KWL)—used to activate background knowledge, stimulate inquiry, and record and measure learning
T-chart	Used to identify two facets of a topic, such as fact and opinion, pros and cons, advantages and disadvantages
Venn diagram	Used to compare and contrast and also illustrate similarities and differences (double Venn diagram for two topics, triple for three)

for academic conversations. Four easy to implement grouping strategies for content-area classrooms featured in this text are Think-Pair-Share (Lyman, 1981), the Three-Minute Pause (McTighe, cited in Jones, 2006), Numbered-Heads (Kagan, 1994), and Jigsaw (Aronson, Blaney, Stephin, Sikes, & Snapp, 1978).

- Think-Pair-Share enables ELLs to process input, check their understanding through purposeful communication with a partner, and then speak to the larger group. During Think-Pair-Share, the teacher asks a question or provides a prompt, gives students a minute to think about the question independently and another few minutes to talk with a partner, and then selects students to report to the larger group.

- The Three-Minute Pause can be used with Think-Pair-Share or with groups of as many as four to summarize and extend concepts and pose clarifying questions. In the Three-Minute Pause, students summarize the key concepts introduced in the lesson, discuss how these concepts connect to prior knowledge, and then ask clarifying questions or predict where the lesson is going.

- In Numbered-Heads, students work in small groups (usually of four or five) to solve a problem, respond to a teacher prompt, or summarize a concept. Each student in each group is assigned a number (accomplished by having each group count off or by distributing numbered cards early in the lesson). The goal of the group is that each member must understand how to solve the problem or summarize the concept. After the allotted period of time, the teacher calls one number. The student with that number in each group is called on to respond.

- In Jigsaw, students work in groups of five or six. The day's lesson is divided into five or six sections. Ms. Chin's class, for example, is learning about the factors that led to the Revolutionary War. She has formed four groups of six students each. Within each group, she provides handouts on (1) the Stamp Act, (2) the Townshend Act, (3) the Sugar Act, (4) the Boston Massacre, (5) the Intolerable Acts, and (6) the Boston Tea Party. Each student in each group is assigned to learn one section and does not have access to the other sections. Students are provided with time to read their sections twice. Students then form expert groups by working with other students who have read the same section. They discuss their section, clarify the main points, and practice presentations that they will make when they return to their groups. The experts then return to their original groups and explain the section allotted to them.

As with any other classroom activity, teachers should begin by using one type of cooperative-learning activity and teach students the purpose and procedure of this activity. Students should then be provided with sufficient practice so that the activity may foster learning. Cooperative-learning activities that are implemented with heterogeneous groups have been shown to improve cross-cultural interactions and relations between students of different socioeconomic and ability levels and to increase academic achievement, while long-term ability grouping has been shown to have the opposite effects on student achievement (Ward, 1987).

MAKING READING MATERIALS COMPREHENSIBLE

Regardless of the effectiveness of realia and other visuals in making instruction comprehensible, at some point ELLs will (and should) use texts and other reading materials to access content. ELLs, in the process of developing academic vocabulary and familiarity with the structure of written English, typically read substantially below the level of English-speaking students. While it is critically important for teachers to develop the reading skills of ELLs so that they become more proficient readers, the focus of this chapter is rather on ways of making written materials more comprehensible to ELLs. It should be noted, however, that many of the activities that make reading more comprehensible also serve to scaffold reading abilities and academic language (topics that will be discussed in detail in Chapter 9).

Making Text Comprehensible

One obvious way to shelter texts is to offer them on tape. The International Reading Association supports the use of texts on tape for read-along activities, which help develop the reading abilities of ELLs. Some texts on tape are commercially available, and chapters or excerpts from other texts can be recorded by teachers, paraprofessionals, or students. Librivox.org (www.librivox.org) offers free audio recordings of public domain documents. ELLs can listen to an audio recording as they follow along in the text, stopping and starting the audiotape when necessary and returning to passages they did not initially understand. Over a period of time, content-area teachers can develop a resource box of tapes that can be made available to ELLs.

Mr. Hayes often uses an assessment option that allows students to record their favorite passages from a novel or short story and then analyze those passages. Dramatizing the passages requires that students read beyond the words and demonstrate understanding of tone, mood, and theme. This activity improves student comprehension and provides Mr. Hayes with another tool for his sheltered resource collection, which he makes available to all students.

It is also possible to create a specialized set of comprehensible texts that ELLs and other struggling readers can use year after year. One of the easiest ways to build comprehensibility into content-area texts is to highlight the most salient passages. Ms. Chin explains that the structure of some individual sentences, the use of the passive voice or noun clauses, and very long sentences often present great difficulties for ELLs. A short (and seemingly simple) excerpt from *American Athenas: Women in the Revolution* (Nguyen, n.d.; found on a Web site that Ms. Chin's students accessed to investigate multiple perspectives and sociocultural conditions during Revolutionary times) illustrates some of the difficulties that ELLs may confront:

> Despite their low positions in society, women did participate. On the home front, they sewed uniforms and knitted stockings for the soldiers. With their husbands away fighting, some women had to take over as weavers, carpenters, blacksmiths, or shipbuilders.

This relatively simple and readable passage has introductory phrases and clauses that may decrease comprehensibility for ELLs. Their position at the beginning of each sentence may confuse ELLs who are learning vocabulary and grammar, who may anticipate that the subject (a noun) will be found early in the sentence (Clair, 2001). The words *despite*, *low positions*, and *home front* are also likely to confound some ELLs, who may not yet know the high-utility word *despite*, may not understand the way *low* is used in collocation with *positions*, and may be completely confused by *home front* (which may conjure images of the front of the women's houses). These confusing notions may well come together to make this short passage virtually unreadable. Teachers can unpack sentences (separate and call attention to their parts) to make them more comprehensible. Although introductory phrases or clauses, for example, provide important information that should not be overlooked, the passage is made more readable when it is unpacked by highlighting the independent clauses:

Despite their low positions in society, *women did participate*. On the home front, *they sewed uniforms and knitted stockings for the soldiers*. With their husbands away fighting, *some women had to take over as weavers, carpenters, blacksmiths, or shipbuilders* (Nguyen, n.d.).

Highlighting of parts of sentences calls attention to sentence structure. The act of noticing structures within English sentences increases the likelihood that ELLs will be able to attend to the structures (Hinkel, 2004).

A second type of highlighting draws ELLs' attention to the most important passages in a text. In this process, the teacher previews text that ELLs will read, identifies passages that are critical to content-area understanding, and highlights these passages. The teacher then reads through the highlighted text to identify words and text structure that may present difficulty for ELLs. The teacher underlines these words and structures and in the margins of the text, writes specific word meanings *as they are used in this passage*. Glossing words in this way serves to make content-area text more comprehensible and draws ELLs' attention to new words, a necessary step in vocabulary instruction (which will be discussed in Chapter 9). Once the vocabulary words and expressions are defined, the teacher then unpacks the text structure to improve its comprehensibility. For example, a sentence such as "Researchers estimate there are six major adjustments U.S. residents can make to address global warming ..." can be unpacked by underlining "six major adjustments" and then placing a numeral (1–6) next to each of the six adjustments listed. Particularly difficult grammatical structures in the highlighted sections can also be unpacked by rewriting them in the margins using brief sentences and clear language. Bhatia (1983) refers to this process as "easification."

Some content-area teachers highlight within textbooks; others highlight photocopies of text, which they then store in resource boxes for ELLs and other students who may struggle with reading. Unless teachers have support staff who can be taken away from their work with students to highlight and easify texts, the process may be too time-consuming for regular use. The teachers with whom we have worked select one unit per year and make the accompanying materials comprehensible. Each year, they adapt additional text passages.

One effective and time-saving way in which teachers have made articles and resources comprehensible is by assigning highlighting and easifying as a class assessment option. Mr. Peterson's students, for example, collect articles that are relevant to the instructional unit, highlight key points, and make legible notes in the margins summarizing these key points. This purposeful assignment forces the students who are doing the highlighting to focus on the most important parts of the reading, and it also adds to Mr. Peterson's collection of comprehensible reading materials. As part of another assessment option, students summarize articles using 4 × 6 Post-its, which they attach to the original articles. Mr. Peterson reviews these and keeps the most clearly written summaries along with their accompanying articles in the unit resource box. These summaries allow all students to get the gist of articles prior to reading them. Mr. Peterson also includes copies of exemplary papers written by former students in the resource box. According to him, students are motivated to write papers that will be used for authentic purposes, and well-written student papers are often more comprehensible than either the course text or related articles. Allowing students to contribute articles in multiple languages has also served to strengthen the resource box.

Making Primary-Source Documents Comprehensible

ELLs often experience difficulty with the language in many primary-source documents; yet primary-source documents make history come alive, and ELLs should have the opportunity to work with them. Assigning excerpts from primary-source documents as readings and then unpacking (explaining) difficult language in the margins makes these important readings more accessible to ELLs. All students should have access to the language of the Declaration of Independence, the Constitution, and the Federalist Papers, for example. Yet, as Soan Meng explained, "I hate reading old documents in history class, like the Declaration of Independence and the Constitution. I don't even understand half the words they are using. They use weird and big words and I don't know why."

ELLs and English-speaking students who struggle with reading will benefit from an explanation of phrases such as "We hold these truths to be self-evident."

ELLs benefit from seeing and using primary-source documents but also often need explanatory notes to fully understand these documents. Table 8.3 presents an example of glossing and unpacking difficult language from a primary-source document.

Blogs for Building Comprehensibility

Classroom blogs (Web sites that contain text, audio, and video postings) have made it possible for teachers to shelter reading materials for ELLs and other students (Colombo & Colombo, 2007). In a classroom blog, teachers can read through excerpts of text with students and explain concepts that are particularly challenging. ELLs and other students can access class blogs at home, in the school media center, or at the public library. Students need only an iPod or Mp3 player to access podcasts and vodcasts from blogs. When the technology is available to teachers, blogs provide powerful tools for making content-area reading comprehensible.

TABLE 8.3 Making Primary-Source Documents Comprehensible

Language in original document	Comprehensible language in margin
We hold these Truths to be self-evident, that all Men are created equal, that they *are endowed by their Creator with certain unalienable Rights,* that among these are Life, Liberty and the Pursuit of Happiness.	*We believe* that all men and women are created equal, and *have rights that cannot be taken away*, such as life, liberty, and the pursuit of happiness.
That to secure these Rights, Governments are instituted among Men, deriving their just Powers from the Consent of the Governed, That *whenever any Form of Government becomes destructive of these Ends, it is the Right of the People to alter or to abolish it, and to institute new Government, laying its Foundation on* such Principles ...	*To protect these rights, men and women create governments. The power of government comes from the people.* When any form of government destroys life, liberty, and the pursuit of happiness, *it is the people's right to change it or do away with it and start a new government based on* life, liberty, and the pursuit of happiness ...

Creating a Resource Box

It is helpful to develop a resource box to organize articles and comprehensible materials. Teachers can develop such a resource box over time and make it available to ELLs and other students. Mr. Peterson has created such a box for the "Land Is Finite" unit.

Mr. Peterson's "Land Is Finite" resource box contains articles at various reading levels that have been highlighted by Mr. Peterson and previous students, article summaries, and articles in multiple languages. ELLs (and struggling readers) can also access some content-area material in video format. Mr. Peterson's wide choice of reading materials at a variety of levels makes this high-level content accessible to students.

Regardless of the content area, teachers will need to find, borrow, and adapt supplementary materials over time to make content-area materials comprehensible. In Chapters 10 to 13, four content-area teachers share specific lessons and demonstrate the methods of sheltering that have been most effective for these lessons.

Review, Reflect, Apply

1. *Review and reflect:* Review the various suggestions for sheltering content-area materials. Then think about the content-area unit you are developing. Make a list of those materials that are likely to be difficult for ELLs and indicate the ways in which you will shelter them.

2. *Apply:* Using the content-area unit you have developed and at least two student profiles from the Appendix, make a list of concepts, materials, and vocabulary words with which each student will likely experience difficulty; then explain the ways in which you will make these materials and your presentation style comprehensible. (You may adjust students' ages and grade levels so that they are appropriate for your grade level.)

CHAPTER SUMMARY

While every content area will have different concepts, there are common considerations to keep in mind when planning and implementing content-area instruction for ELLs at varying levels of English language proficiency.

- The TELLiM model (enduring understandings, clear LOs, engaging essential questions, and varied assessment) provides necessary context for lessons.
- Content should be at grade level and sheltered for comprehensibility.
- Presentations and materials should be made comprehensible.
- Realia, visual images, hands-on materials, videos, mixed-media presentations, and graphic organizers, as well as clear but unexaggerated speech, pausing for understanding, and paraphrasing should be used to make presentations comprehensible.
- Text can be made comprehensible by providing audio recordings, highlighting the most salient passages, simplifying language in text margins, and glossing vocabulary words.
- Contents of texts can also be made comprehensible with text summaries (written by the teacher or other students).
- Assessments should be aligned with ELLs' proficiency levels and differentiated according to proficiency-level guidelines (Chapter 7).

Assessment Evidence Activities

AE-1   Using the profiles of ELLs in the Appendix, explain the problems that ELLs will experience in the mainstream content area that you teach and the ways in which they are likely to benefit from sheltered instruction.

AE-2   List the sheltering strategies that you can use to make each lesson within your content-area unit comprehensible.

AE-3   Prepare a sheltered content-area presentation in your content area.

1. Make a list of materials you would need to shelter one content-area unit.

2. Using photocopies of a grade-level text, use highlighting and glossing to shelter one section.

3. Use margin notes to make one piece of literature, primary history source, or text more comprehensible.

Resources for Further Reading

- *Working Together: Teacher-Paraeducator Collaboration*, Guidelines for effective collaboration and planning tools compiled by the American Institutes for Research. www.k8accesscenter.org/training_resources/documents/Tchr-ParaCollaboration.pdf

- National Library of Virtual Manipulatives. http://nlvm.usu.edu/en/nav/category_g_4_t_2.html

- Political cartoons: www.history.org/history/teaching/enewsletter/volume3/october04/teachstrategy.cfm

- Electronic history field trips are available at www.history.org/history/teaching/eft.cfm

- Read Write Think has links to a wealth of other Web resources that it has reviewed. www.readwritethink.org

- Lesson Plan ideas for teaching Poe www.lessonplanspage.com/LATheRaven AtmosphereSymbolismIn-Halloween612.htm

- Primary sources for history: www.indiana.edu/~jah/teaching/installments.shtml, www.historyplace.com/unitedstates/revolution/revwar-75.htm, www.theamerican revolution.org/hevents.asp

- Online resources index: www.academicinfo.net/histusteach.html, http://www.ala .org/ala/rusa/rusaourassoc/rusasections/historysection/histsect/histcomm/instructionres/ usingprimarysources.cfm

- Finding your genotype: http://museum.thetech.org/ugenetics/eyeCalc/ eyecalculator.html

- Graphic organizers:

  www.graphic.org/goindex.html

  Free printable graphic organizers:

  http://edhelper.com/teachers/graphic_organizers.htm

  Freeology: www.freeology.com/graphicorgs/page8.php

- The Cornell Note Taking System. http://ccc.byu.edu/learning/note-tak.php

9

Building Academic Language

Enduring understanding: Academic language must be specifically addressed in content-area classrooms.

THE STRATEGIES PRESENTED IN CHAPTER 8 MAY SERVE TO BUILD ACADEMIC LANGUAGE, YET THEIR PRIMARY INSTRUCtional intent was to make high-level content comprehensible. The development of academic language was largely incidental, which is often true of, and a source of criticism of, content-based instruction. ELLs in middle and secondary grades need focused instruction to develop academic language and literacy across content areas. Building academic language (vocabulary, reading, speaking, and writing) is the focus of Chapter 9. This chapter begins with a discussion of content-area teachers' concerns about the academic literacy levels of both ELLs and native-English-speaking students alike. Next, strategies for vocabulary development, reading, and writing are presented, discussed, and illustrated by content-area teachers.

Although steps 7 and 8 of the Teaching English Language Learners in the Mainstream (TELLiM) model (Table 9.1) focus on the improvement of academic content-area literacy and understanding for ELLs, these steps are also useful for improving academic literacy for many English-speaking students in the mainstream classroom.

LEARNING OUTCOMES

LO-1 Understand the importance of building content-area academic language

LO-2 Apply instructional strategies to develop ELLs' academic vocabulary

LO-3 Apply instructional strategies to develop ELLs' academic reading

LO-4 Apply instructional strategies to develop ELLs' academic writing

CONTENT-AREA TEACHERS' CONCERNS ABOUT ACADEMIC LITERACY LEVELS

For many years, Mr. Peterson has worried about the amount of reading ELLs and other students in his class do once they leave the classroom at the end of each day. He explains, "Many of my students listen in class and get as much as they can from lectures and activities, but they do not read the text at home." Ms. Greene is often confounded when confronted with the writing of ELLs and many other students in her classes: "I have so many papers to correct—I am sometimes overwhelmed by the lack of quality in students' writing. I wonder if I am supposed to sift through the paragraphs for evidence of understanding. If so, then how does their writing improve?" Ms. Chin voices concern about the limited vocabulary that ELLs use, illustrating her point with a student writing sample in which the word *people* appears seven times in one paragraph.

Students who struggle with academic literacy sometimes concur with their teachers. Katy Boureth, for example, regarding reading at home, says, "I read the book sometimes. I just don't always understand it. My teachers explain it all in class the next day, so it doesn't really matter."

Yet it does matter—ELLs and native-English-speaking students who cannot read grade-level content are at a clear academic disadvantage. When students are unable to complete readings, classroom lessons and instruction are less comprehensible. Students with low reading scores are more likely to drop out of high school (Achieve, 2005; Biancarosa & Snow, 2006). Nearly 30% of the English-speaking students in U.S. classrooms may be completing the assigned reading without understanding it and without knowing what they don't understand, and the percentage of ELLs who fail to understand what they have read is much higher (Biancarosa & Snow, 2006).

TABLE 9.1	Teaching ELLs in the Mainstream (TELLiM): Steps 7 and 8	
Step 7	**Build Academic Language**	**Chapters 9–13**
	• Engage ELLs in planned, complex, academic conversations about their content area • Develop content-area understanding and language proficiency	
Step 8	**Build Higher-Order Thinking Skills**	**Chapters 9–13**
	• Teach complex thinking skills across content areas • Provide time for ELLs to practice these skills in meaningful circumstances	

Some students in Mr. Peterson's science classes may actually go through the ritual of reading their science assignment only to complete the reading with no understanding of what they read (Tovani, 2000). They arrive at science class the following day unprepared to answer the questions posed by Mr. Peterson and unable to participate fully in classroom discussions that are based on the assigned reading. Other students may not even have attempted to read the text. They may have simply given up and, like Katy, wait for Mr. Peterson to explain the reading. Because students have been unable to complete the assigned reading, Mr. Peterson often must dedicate extra time to review, rather than elaborate on the concepts introduced in the text.

The high percentage of students who struggle with content-area reading and writing suggests the need for literacy instruction across content areas, including lessons that build vocabulary, strengthen reading strategies, and scaffold writing. An extensive and well-developed vocabulary is important across all domains of academic literacy (Carkin, 2005) and thus appears to be a predictor of academic success. It contributes to listening abilities (Rost, 2005), is closely correlated with reading achievement (Nagy & Scott, 2000; Stahl & Nagy, 2006), and enhances the ability of ELLs to write academically (Hinkel, 2004). Vocabulary development is cumulative; the more words ELLs have learned, the more they are able to learn (Hinkel, 2004; Nation, 2001; Stahl & Nagy, 2006).

As described in Chapter 2, learning a word is a complex and complicated task, and ELLs must quickly learn a large number of academic words in a short period of time (Nation, 2001; Stahl & Nagy, 2006). Indeed, academic vocabulary presents quite a challenge to ELLs and their teachers.

This chapter presents three broad instructional approaches that may assist ELLs with the development of academic vocabulary: (1) providing comprehensible input in a language-rich setting, (2) rich word instruction, and (3) specific vocabulary-building strategies.

COMPREHENSIBLE INSTRUCTION IN A LANGUAGE-RICH SETTING

Chapter 8 provided numerous examples of teaching strategies through which experienced teachers have succeeded in building comprehensibility. This section explains how ongoing exposure to comprehensible input in a language-rich setting, which expert teachers provide to their students, also serves to build academic vocabulary. The following strategies for building comprehensibility also serve to develop academic vocabulary.

Glossing and Attention to Words

The importance of noticing words in text is a first step in vocabulary development (Gass, 1997; Schmidt, 2001) Effective glossing of targeted words directs ELLs' attention to these words as they occur in the text, thereby increasing the likelihood that the students will notice these targeted words. The repeated retrieval of new words is also an important process in vocabulary development (Gass, 1997; Nation, 2001). Word retrieval is fostered through glossing words and then calling ELLs' attention to these words. It takes approximately 12 intermittent retrievals to learn a word (Stahl & Nagy, 2006).

In a review of studies on the effectiveness of glossing, Nation (2001) found that most studies reported positive effects on vocabulary development, and some reported that glossing new vocabulary was more effective than preteaching it. The glosses that were found to be most effective were those that were written in the margins of the text in clear and accessible language.

Contextualized Instruction

Contextualized instruction promotes the repetition and retrieval of key words. For example, Ms. Chin teaches the words *inevitable* and *perspective*, which are critical to students' understanding in the "Revolutionary War" unit. She has included these words as part of the unit's essential question, which is displayed on the wall throughout the unit, and she and her students use the words regularly throughout the unit lessons. As a result, Julián Alencastro, an ELL with early-intermediate proficiency, learns the words *inevitable* and *perspective* and begins to use them in academic discourse.

With so many new words to learn, the guessing strategies that first-language learners use to acquire vocabulary may also be used effectively by ELLs when sufficient context is provided (Dycus, 1997) and ELLs have developed sufficient English proficiency. For example, although Katy does not know the meaning of the word *revenue*, she is able to correctly guess at the meaning while listening to Ms. Chin preview the text selection that students will be assigned for homework. Ms. Chin begins by activating students' knowledge of the French and Indian War, strategically using and paraphrasing the word *revenue*. She reminds students about the duration and great *costs* of the war. She explains that the British needed additional revenue to help pay off their war debt. She purposefully connects to students' awareness of current events and the *cost* of the war in Iraq and talks about collecting money and raising revenue. Katy's knowledge of context enables her to guess that revenue means income, which is later confirmed when Ms. Chin, herself, uses the word *income* to paraphrase the word *revenue*.

Easification

It is accepted that extensive reading is an effective way to continually develop vocabulary (Pigada & Schmitt, 2006). Readers, however, must be familiar with 95% to 98% of the running words to comprehend the text and learn new vocabulary from it (Nation, 2001). Easification of text reduces the number of unknown words that ELLs must read and may, therefore, increase the likelihood that new vocabulary will be learned through reading. When the goal of reading is to increase academic content-area vocabulary, ELLs should be repeatedly exposed to a variety of reading passages that include the targeted academic vocabulary (Kinsella, 2005). Mr. Peterson's students, for example, read their texts, selected passages from the Internet, and student writing for any content-area unit they are studying. As a result, they encounter (and retrieve) the same key vocabulary words multiple times.

RICH WORD INSTRUCTION

While incidental vocabulary learning is valuable, some vocabulary words are too important not to be taught directly (Beck, McKeown, & Kucan, 2002; Kinsella, 2005; Nation, 2001; Stahl & Nagy, 2006). Because vocabulary instruction is very time-consuming, content-area teachers must ensure that ELLs and other students receive maximum benefits from this instruction. First, teachers need to carefully select the words that are worth this time investment (Beck et al., 2002; Kinsella, 2005; Nation, 2001; Stahl & Nagy, 2006). Table 9.2 illustrates how teachers decide which words should be explicitly taught.

TABLE 9.2	Identifying Words for Instruction	
Content-specific terms	Academic language that is specific to a particular content area and at times to a specific unit within the content.	Explicitly taught through rich instruction; normally glossed by publisher of texts
Academic content-area words	Academic language: words that are unlikely to be heard outside of academic conversations; words that are found across one or more content areas (AWL[a] vocabulary)	Explicitly taught through rich instruction
High-utility words	Words that are used in social language and also in the classroom and that are easily explainable using illustrations and first-language translation	Learned in context and through accessible reading

a. The Academic Word List.

Stahl and Nagy (2006) use the analogy of the food pyramid to help teachers decide which words should be taught explicitly within content-area classrooms. The words at the very top of the pyramid are high-utility words that are required for understanding concepts and accessing academic text. These words are not encountered outside of academic situations and therefore must be taught for understanding. Of these, technical terms present the least instructional challenge to content-area teachers; these are often the new vocabulary terms that all students must learn to understand the content. Technical terms are often carefully introduced and glossed in the text, and content-area teachers normally spend time introducing and reviewing these terms with all students.

The 570 high-utility Academic Word List (AWL) words identified by Coxhead (2000) are not normally glossed by textbook publishers (Nation, 2001; Stahl & Nagy, 2006), yet they are critical to success in academic English (Stahl & Nagy, 2006) and provide difficulties for ELLs and many other students. Content-area teachers can help ensure that ELLs (and other students) learn AWL words by spending instructional time on AWL words that occur in their content areas. Beck et al. (2002) recommend that teachers ask themselves the following questions to determine if a word deserves rich instruction:

- How useful is the word?
- Will students encounter it in other texts?
- Will they need this word to discuss and write about content?

This section presents rich instructional activities that are appropriate for middle and secondary grades and that researchers and practitioners recommend for use with ELLs and also with the entire class. Regardless of the teaching strategy used, vocabulary instruction should be routinized and focused. It is recommended that teachers choose one strategy they believe to be most appropriate based on the specific content area and the types of words to be taught and then let students practice using this strategy before introducing another. Staying with one strategy for teaching new words builds context by allowing students to know what to expect during instruction. A well-organized, systematic presentation of vocabulary also ensures that ELLs and other students realize the importance of vocabulary instruction and its relationship to content-area instruction.

It is generally advisable to teach only a few words at one time and provide instruction for the entire word family. So, for example, when Mr. Hayes teaches the word *theme*, he will also teach *themed* and *thematic*. The vocabulary word should be presented visually, orally, and in written form; it is important that ELLs hear the correct pronunciation as they see the word (Kinsella, 2005). Because it is easier for students to remember the meaning of words that are pronounceable (Nation, 2001), it is important to have students repeat the correct pronunciation of the word (Kinsella, 2005). Following direct vocabulary instruction, ELLs and others should have the opportunity to retrieve the word in the course of meaningful activities, including focused academic conversations that require the use of the word. To facilitate these types of conversations, Kinsella (2005) recommends that students be provided with prompts to

- express opinions,
- paraphrase,
- request clarification,
- offer suggestions, and
- disagree (p. 7).

Vocabulary words should also be placed on classroom word walls, on portable word walls that students can carry from class to class, in student vocabulary journals, and on word cards. ELLs and other students should be held accountable for correctly using AWL words in their discussions and writing, so that they can practice retrieving these words.

Teaching Words: Concept-Mapping Activities

Concept-mapping activities are used for words and terms that represent important concepts in the instructional unit. For example, *chance* in Ms. Bell's mathematics unit, *biosphere* in Mr. Peterson's science unit, *revolution* in Ms. Chin's U.S. history unit, and *theme* in Mr. Hayes's ELA unit each represent an important unit concept. Concept mapping enables ELLs to illustrate the significant traits of a word. Concept map graphic organizers can be drawn by students on plain sheets of paper, or online graphic organizers can be used. The Frayer model (Frayer, Frederick, & Klausmeier, 1969) (along with its variations) is one such graphic organizer. The Frayer model activity is designed to be completed in small groups within the classroom (Labrosse, 2007). The model is appropriate for use across content areas and has been adopted by middle and secondary schools in the state of Maine for math vocabulary instruction (Labrosse, 2007). One clear language advantage of the Frayer model is the discussion and negotiation that occurs between ELLs, native-English speakers, and teachers as the model is completed. Vocabulary concepts are elaborated and deepened. Model 9.1 illustrates an adaptation of the Frayer model.

When introducing the Frayer model, teachers must instruct students in its use. Ms. Chin, for example, introduces the term *revolution* and asks students about the essential attributes of revolution. Students mention change and unrest, and Ms. Chin adds these two words in the upper-left-hand box. Because Ms. Chin wants to teach the concept of revolution in the broadest sense, she wants students to understand that a revolution can be cultural or political and not necessarily related to war; so when Soan suggests war as an essential attribute, Ms. Chin explains that revolutions may or may not involve war and places this word in the upper-right-hand box as a nonessential attribute. This engages students in an elaborate yet focused discussion about the term and its attributes. During one of these discussions, Katy remembers

The Frayer Model

Essential attributes	Nonessential attributes
Term	
Examples	Nonexamples

SOURCE: Billmeyer and Barton (1998).

studying the Industrial Revolution in environmental science. She shares this knowledge with her groupmates and affirms that change is a central attribute of revolution. Ms. Chin then guides students to complete the bottom two quadrants. The talk of war reminds Cathy of the Civil War and World Wars I and II, and she suggests that a nonexample would be these wars: "They are not revolutions." "Stability would be another nonexample," Phillip adds. Ms. Chin continues to work with students to complete the model. Once she has provided several practice sessions with the model, ELLs and other students will complete the guided practice, and finally in small heterogeneous groups without direct teacher support. Ms. Chin will, however, continue to check group models for accuracy as well as for misconceptions.

Stahl and Nagy (2006, p. 80) offer a slight variation on the Frayer model. As shown in Model 9.2, rather than requiring ELLs to identify nonessential attributes of a term, the variation requires ELLs to provide examples of what the term "is not."

MODEL 9.2 **Variation on the Frayer Model**

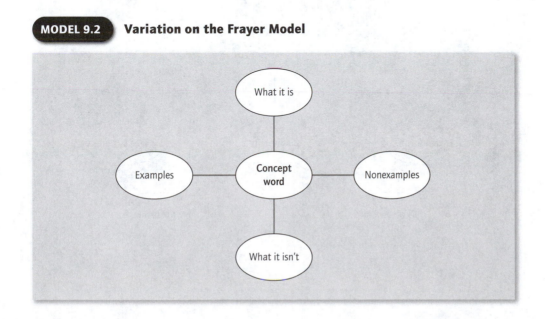

Teaching Words: Semantic Mapping

Semantic mapping encourages learners to elaborate on the meaning of a word and its connection to other known words. Semantic maps are easily made using a structure similar to that of Model 9.2 and adding spokes as needed. Model 9.3 illustrates a semantic map constructed by Aadam in environmental science.

Concept mapping and semantic mapping deepen students' understanding of important concepts and vocabulary as they help build content-area schemata.

Teaching Words: Word Guesses

Word guessing is an activity suggested by Stahl and Nagy (2006, p. 71) to provide ELLs and other students with purposeful and engaging practice that fosters exploration of content-area word meanings. We have adjusted the word guessing activity to meet the needs of intermediate ELLs. The teacher compiles a list of important academic vocabulary words from reading materials used in the instructional unit. The teacher then cuts the list into strips with one word on each strip and places word sets into a plastic bag. Students are placed in two groups of six students each. A pair of students from Team A begins by pulling one word from the bag. The pair of students collaborates in a Think-Pair-Share to create descriptions of the word without using the word itself. Members of Team A attempt to guess the word from the description. If they guess correctly, they win a point. If they do not, members of Team B may guess for a point.

MODEL 9.3   **Semantic Mapping**

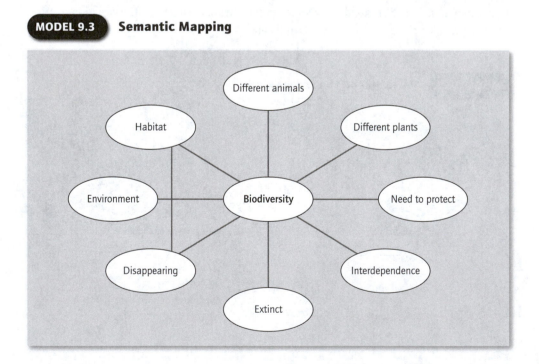

Teaching Words: Drama and Chants

A classroom that is successful in helping ELLs and others develop vocabulary is one where students pay attention to words. Drama can call attention to and prompt students to explore the meanings of vocabulary words. One activity recommended by Stahl and Nagy (2006, p. 73), which was originally developed for high school students, is Story Impressions. The teacher prepares a list of words and phrases in the order in which they occur in a reading. Using this list of words, students (individually, in pairs, or in small groups) write the story. We recommend having students work in pairs or small groups to ensure academic conversation about words and sharing of ideas. When students have completed their story, they then compare the stories they have written with the reading. Story Impressions can also be used with nonfiction, as Ms. Chin illustrates with the following list of terms:

the Road to Revolution

the French and Indian War goes on

high costs

the British win

enacted acts to raise revenue

taxation without representation

resistance, disobedience, boycotts

minutemen (militia)

Jazz Chants (Graham, 2000), an activity originally developed to build English fluency, can be used as a catchy and attention-getting way to draw ELLs' attention to words in the content areas. A variation of Jazz Chants that Ms. Mia Bell has found helpful in teaching the vocabulary of mathematics is Math Talk (Pappas, 2002), a game in which poems are read in two voices. Math Talk enables ELLs and others to dramatize and become comfortable with the language of mathematics. Ms. Bell demonstrates the use of Math Talk in Chapter 11.

Teaching Words: Word Parts

It is thought that native-English speakers learn new words in three ways: (1) through explicit instruction or focused learning, (2) by encountering new words in context, and (3) by learning word parts (Nation, 2001). Studies of ELLs suggest that learning word parts (roots and affixes) is an effective way of learning words and that teachers can help ELLs by teaching them the most common prefixes and suffixes (Nation, 2001). ELLs acquire knowledge of word families by learning word parts and practicing combining these parts to make words. For example, learning the morphemes (the smallest units of meaning in a language) in the most frequently occurring affixes (such as *a, un, anti*; *ly, er, est*; *ness*) helps develop vocabulary knowledge (Nation, 2001).

Nation (2001) and Cunningham, Hall, and Shanks (1998) recommend first teaching the most common affixes (such as the prefix *un* and the suffix *ness*) and then providing ELLs with practice in making words using the affixes and then breaking the words into parts. For example, the prefix *un* can be taught deductively by presenting students with a list of commonly used words, having them work in pairs to identify the prefix and the root, and then having them infer the meaning of the prefix from the samples they have analyzed, as shown in Table 9.3. *Unbelievable, unforgettable*, and *unreliable* could also serve to teach the suffix *able*.

Nation (2001) suggests that ELLs must be able to recognize the parts within words (e.g., un/reli/able) in order to use word parts to analyze or to build words. The words in Table 9.3 provide general examples. Seventy percent of all prefixed words in English begin with the following prefixes: *un, re, in, im, il, ir* (meaning "not"), *dis, en, em, non*, and *in/im* (meaning "in"); 80% of suffixed words end with the following suffixes: *s, es, ed, ing, ly, ion, tion, ation, ition*, and *er/or* (meaning "agent") (Stahl & Nagy, 2006, p. 166). Content-area teachers should teach the affixes that are most common in the reading in their content areas.

Cunningham et al. (1998) recommend that teachers print words in large font on long strips, cut words apart, and keep word parts in envelopes for unscrambling, thus providing ELLs and others with word-building opportunities. The authors found that working with word parts improves vocabulary, reading, and spelling. We highly recommend their book *Last Chance for Struggling Readers*, which provides many activities for teaching all students the 50 most commonly used affixes that can be added to root words to form new words. Cunningham et al. provide engaging activities that are easily implemented within the classroom and are applicable across content areas.

Teaching Students Vocabulary-Learning Strategies

An important component of any program to build academic vocabulary is teaching ELLs strategies for independent vocabulary development. One strategy that is recommended by several researchers (with slight variations) is the Vocabulary Self-Selection Strategy (VSS) (Haggard, 1986 [now Ruddell]; Ruddell & Ruddell, 1994; Ruddell & Shearer, 2002).

The Vocabulary Self-Collection Strategy

This strategy is designed to provide students with ownership of the words they select and want to learn; self-selecting words is motivating to students. The VSS can be used with common reading materials, or students can nominate words from differentiated readings. Each student nominates one new word that the class should learn. At the time of nomination, students explain where they found the word. Then they use the word in context and explain the reason for their

TABLE 9.3   Word Parts

Word	Prefix	Root word	Prefix meaning
untrue			
unhappy			
unbelievable			
undone			
unsurprising			
unforgettable			
unreliable			

selection, noting why the word is important. Once the words have been selected, students and teacher define each word and students write the words and definitions in their vocabulary note-books. The words are taught using a variety of activities for rich instruction. The VSS has shown to be effective in increasing both breadth and depth of students' vocabulary as well as increasing students' ability to independently use strategies to learn new words (Ruddell & Shearer, 2002).

Teaching Students to Notice

An easy and time-efficient way to help ELLs and other students to notice new words is to model the noticing process aloud. As teachers come across words in the text, they think aloud, "This is an interesting word. I wonder if it is important. Can I infer its meaning from the context? Should I look it up?"

Using Word Cards

ELLs should be encouraged to use word cards for important content-area words. Unlike long lists of words that must be memorized (which is very ineffective), word cards provide ongoing opportunities for word retrieval, which strengthens word knowledge. Nation (2001) noted that word cards provide several advantages: They are an efficient use of time and energy, they provide ELLs with word meanings that may be more useful than dictionary meanings, and they foster independent learning by giving ELLs complete control over the number of retrievals they make. Nation recommended that ELLs use small (2 inch × 3 inch) index cards for portability and suggested that they prepare the cards in the following way:

1. Put the word on one side and the meaning on the other to encourage recall

2. Use first language translations

3. Use pictures where possible

4. Keep cards simple

5. Suit the number of words in a pack [of word cards] to the difficulty of the words. (pp. 303–305)

Review, Reflect, Apply

1. *Review and reflect:* Review vocabulary-building strategies. Which strategies do you currently use?

2. *Apply:* What other strategies might benefit ELLs and other students in your classes?

Summary

A well-developed academic vocabulary is the foundation for academic literacy. ELLs (and other students) develop vocabulary incidentally through ongoing immersion in comprehensible instruction, through focused learning and direct instruction, and by using vocabulary-building strategies effectively. It is important to limit strategy instruction to one strategy at a time, let students practice using the strategy, and monitor the effectiveness of their strategy use. The importance of AWL words to content-area knowledge and academic literacy, and the unlikelihood that ELLs will encounter these words outside of academic settings, suggests that these words be taught directly. Concept mapping, semantic mapping, calling attention to word parts, word games, and drama are some effective instructional strategies for teaching ELLs and other students vocabulary in mainstream classrooms.

BUILDING ACADEMIC READING STRATEGIES

As explained earlier in this chapter, many ELLs and native-English-speaking students struggle with academic reading, which indicates a clear need for reading instruction throughout the content areas. Content-area literacy strategies are most likely to be effective when modeled by a content-area expert (Biancarosa & Snow, 2006; Meltzer & Okashige, 2001; Tovani, 2004) who is familiar with teaching reading and, more specifically, teaching reading to ELLs (Short & Fitzsimmons, 2007). "Reading is a different task when we read literature, science texts, historical analyses, newspapers, tax forms. This is why teaching students how to read the texts of academic disciplines is a key part of teaching them these disciplines" (Key Ideas of the Strategic Literacy Initiative [2001] cited in Meltzer & Okashige, 2001, p. 1).

Ms. Chin's extensive expertise with history texts and historical primary source documents enables her to model her thought processes for students as she makes connections between the text and her world knowledge, predicts what will happen next in the text, and then confirms or rejects these predictions. As Ms. Chin models reading in history, she illustrates the way questions arise in her mind as she reads through a document; she then poses questions to which she seeks answers; and, finally, she demonstrates how she retells what she has read so as to check her understanding. Mr. Hayes models similar processes for his ELA students, through the lens of an expert reader of literature. As a content teacher, Ms. Bell models the way mathematicians (and aspiring mathematicians) read math content.

Tovani (2004) has shown that it *is* possible for content-area teachers to enrich the academic literacy of students within the context of regular class instruction. She suggests that rather than thinking of themselves as teaching content-area reading, teachers "think of [teaching reading] as teaching students how to remember and reuse the information they ask them to read" (p. 7). And there is an additional benefit in providing instruction that facilitates content-area literacy: When students comprehend their classroom reading, they will have richer class discussions that provide teachers with more time to enrich and reinforce the content itself.

Tovani (2004) explains, "Good readers separate themselves from struggling readers when they recognize that they are confused and then do something to repair meaning. Good readers use 'fix-up' strategies, which can be taught to readers at any age" (pp. 5-6). Tovani borrows from students' discussions and cites the strategies they use (p. 6), which are consistent with the strategies outlined by the report of the National Reading Panel (National Institute of Child Health and Human Development [NICHHD], 2000) and very achievable within content-area classrooms. The following list consists of strategies recommended by Tovani, with examples provided by content-area teachers of ELLs.

Ten Easily Implemented Comprehension Strategies

1. *Make text-to-life, text-to-world, and text-to-text connections:* Mr. Hayes begins his themed unit by engaging students in discussions about truths and lies in their lives. The ensuing

small- and large-group discussions foster text-to-world connections. Mr. Hayes later relates the unit theme to the different novels that students will read. The unit's essential question, *Is it ever better to lie?* keeps ELLs and others focused on *text-to-life, text-to-world, and text-to-tex*t connections throughout their reading and discussions; this focus also encourages them to check their understanding as they read.

2. *Make predictions:* Mr. Hayes models making predictions while reading; later, students practice making predictions about their novels in mixed novel-reading discussion groups. Ms. Chin also models making predictions and then encourages a group of ELLs and other students, who are reading *Sarah Bishop*, to use this strategy, keeping in mind what they have learned about revolutionary times, to predict what will happen next in the novel.

3. *Stop and think about what you have already read:* Mr. Peterson models the strategy of summarizing sections of the science text as he reads. Using the overhead projector, he displays a section of text, reads it aloud, and then thinks aloud, sharing his summary with students.

4. *Ask yourself a question, and try to answer it:* Ms. Chin models questioning as she reads through sections of the U.S. history text. After she completes a section that links the French and Indian War to the American Revolution, she pauses to ask, "How are these two events related?" She then models her response and demonstrates how she goes back to the text to clarify any confusions.

5. *Reflect in writing about what you have already read:* Mr. Peterson engages students in summarizing sections of the text after they have read them. He explains,

> Sometimes I stop and say, "Wait a minute . . . I'm not sure how this part fits. Let's go through this again slowly." Then I work through the reading and jot down key concepts and write notes about interrelationship of concepts. I try to show students that writing is an important tool for checking understanding and identifying when they are confused.

6. *Retell what you've read:* Content-area teachers use Jigsaw and Think-Pair-Share activities in which heterogeneously grouped ELLs and other students share what they have read. Another effective strategy for retelling and writing about readings is GIST (Generating Interaction between Schemata and Text) (Rhoder, 2002). Teachers introduce the GIST strategy by explaining to students that it is a valuable tool for summarizing or "getting the gist" of a passage or story. Next, they model GIST using a high-interest reading selection projected on the whiteboard. As teachers and students work through the reading together, they identify the who, what, where, when, why, and how (5 Ws and H). Teachers then model writing a summary using the 5 Ws and H. In a follow-up strategy lesson, teachers read through the reading selection with students and then have students write summaries that they then share. Subsequent lessons provide guided and independent practice with the strategy. GIST can be used effectively across content areas.(GIST and other effective strategies are available online from *Read, Write, Think*, a publication of the International Reading Association and the National Council of Teachers of English). A link is provided in the Resources for Further Reading section of this chapter.

7. *Adjust your reading rate and slow down or speed up:* Efficient readers adjust their rate of reading according to the level of text difficulty and their purpose in reading. Ms. Bell shows students how she adjusts her reading, slowing down, speeding up, and rereading as she goes through math problems.

8. *Reading for a purpose:* Proficient readers often approach reading with a clear purpose in mind. Reading for a purpose forces students to ask, "Does this fit with what I know, want to find out, or understand?" ELLs and other students who struggle to read in English often have difficulty in setting a purpose for their reading. Even the most dedicated students, who complete the reading because the teacher tells them to do so (or to prepare for a quiz on the following day), may not have a clear purpose in mind as they read text. As Mr. Hayes's students set out to read the first chapter of their novels, he directs them to discover how the authors convey setting and to notice what they find *interesting* or *confusing* about the author's writing. The students know that the following class will bring them together in mixed groups to share and discuss the ways in which different authors convey settings. They will have opportunities to express their understandings and raise their concerns. Groups will be composed of at least one student who is reading *Othello,* another who is reading *Life Is Beautiful,* another who has chosen to read *Zach's Lie,* and perhaps one who has chosen to read *I Am the Cheese.* Students read purposefully to prepare themselves for a discussion of the setting of their novel with their peers.

9. *Self-assessing reading comprehension:* When ELLs and other students are assigned large amounts of material to read, they sometimes lose track of where they have become confused, continue reading, and at the end of the reading realize (or don't realize) that they cannot remember much of what they have read. When asked by teachers to highlight what they do not understand, they are often at a loss as to what to highlight. Tovani (2000) suggests that students work with two different colored highlighters; as they read through text, they should highlight in yellow everything they understand well enough to teach others and words or short passages that they do not understand in pink. Students can then use Post-it notes to indicate what part of a pink-highlighted passage confuses them. Mr. Peterson and Ms. Chin found that they had to invest several class periods teaching and providing scaffolded practice with this strategy; but once students had mastered the strategy, they used it regularly and came to class increasingly prepared for instruction.

10. *Choosing appropriate reading:* Research has shown that readers increase their reading fluency and improve their reading comprehension by engaging in ongoing, systematic reading of text at their instructional levels—that is, text that is neither too difficult nor too easy but just right (Allington, 2005; Fountas & Pinnell, 1996). Readers can read just-right texts with a high degree of accuracy and fluency. Students, however, may have difficulty selecting texts that are neither too easy nor too difficult. To help young readers select appropriate texts teachers provide instruction and practice using the Goldilocks rule (Ohlhausen & Jepsen, 1992), which includes asking themselves the following questions: Is the text new to me? Are there only a few words on each page that I don't know? Can someone help me if I reach a difficult spot in the text? If the reader answers yes to all three questions, the text is likely to be appropriate. Selecting and reading just-right text builds motivation, fluency, and comprehension in young readers. Researchers looking at ways of helping struggling middle school readers to develop strategies for selecting and reading appropriate texts found that adolescents with access to readable and interesting texts gained in motivation to read and in reading fluency (Broaddus & Ivey, 2002; Ivey & Broaddus, 2001). Ivey and Broaddus therefore recommend that teachers across content areas offer adolescent readers a wide variety of reading materials, including books, articles, material from the Internet, newspapers, and informational pamphlets. They also recommend that reading be made an integral component of content-area instruction and that content-area teachers

provide time during class for students to read a variety of content-area materials that coincide with their various reading levels. Providing reading time in classrooms stresses the importance of content-area reading and allows teachers to work one-on-one with ELLs and other students who may struggle to comprehend texts.

Explicit instruction in comprehension strategies that is embedded in sessions of authentic reading makes a difference in reading outcomes (NICHHD, 2000). The International Reading Association and the National Council of Teachers of English recommend limiting the number of strategies introduced at one time. Teaching one strategy until students have mastered it before moving on to the next one allows students to practice the strategy and use it appropriately in other reading situations. Strategy instruction begins with modeling by the teacher.

Review, Reflect, Apply

1. *Review and reflect:* Review the reading comprehension strategies listed above. Which strategies do you currently use?

2. *Apply:* What other strategies would benefit ELLs and other students in your classes?

Summary

All readers benefit from learning comprehension strategies. ELLs and other struggling readers need strategy instruction to access grade-level content, and proficient readers benefit from ongoing instruction in strategies that enable them to continually improve their ability to read more challenging texts that, without focused instruction in strategies, may be beyond their reach. Most strategy instruction can be implemented with the entire class. The previous section provided 10 strategies for improving reading comprehension. For strategy instruction to be effective, teachers should teach one strategy at a time and provide students with time to practice and master the strategy.

TEACHING STRATEGIES FOR ACADEMIC WRITING

Writing, like reading, is a meaning-based activity and a powerful means for communication. Any writing program for ELLs and other students must be one that creates a literate environment for all students (Bomer, 1995), empowers them to write, teaches them that they can write (Elbow, 2000), and invites them to become members of a community of writers (Bomer, 1995; Graves, 1983). In the introduction to Peter Elbow's *Everyone Can Write*, Donald Graves writes, "As teachers we can empower our students. We can help them to like to write. We can help them trust themselves, work with others, find voices, and be more forceful and articulate in using writing in their lives" (p. xv).

The report of the National Commission on Writing (2006) recommends that more attention be given to the writing of all students, including ELLs, and recommends instructional practices that

- create a classroom climate of mutual trust and respect;
- "encourage students to bring the languages, experiences, and images of their home learning communities" to the classroom as resources (p. 10);
- allow teachers to model the process of inquiry and the writing process;

- provide in- and out-of-class time for purposeful and authentic writing that includes multiple revisions; and
- provide time for students to work in small writing groups, thus creating communities of writers.

Although the Commission found many exemplars of effective writing programs, most of these were focused on native-English writers. Simply applying first-language writing research to second-language writing has been quite ineffective (Hedgcock, 2005; Hinkel, 2004). While ELLs benefit from a meaning-based approach to writing, each ELL faces a special set of challenges (depending in part on his or her level of first-language literacy) when attempting to complete academic writing tasks. ELLs who have well-developed writing abilities in their first language will transfer these abilities at the macro level (organization and structure) yet will need focused instruction at the micro level (sentence structure and word choice) as they continue to develop English language proficiency.

ELLs who have not learned to write well in their first language resemble struggling native-English-speaking writers and experience challenges on the macro level as well as at the micro level. These students must not only learn how to write; they must learn to write in a language with unfamiliar vocabulary, phonology, morphology, and syntax.

Teaching strategies identified by the National Commission on Writing (2006) and by the Carnegie Foundation (Graham & Perin, 2007) may be used with ELL writers with appropriate considerations and accommodations (Hedgcock, 2005; Hinkel, 2004). The following list consists of strategies recommended by the National Commission on Writing (2006) and by the Carnegie Foundation (Graham & Perrin, 2007) with examples for using these strategies with ELLs and other students.

Eleven Easily Implemented Strategies for Improving Student Writing in Content-Area Classes

Strategy 1: Connect Inquiry Activities to Writing

The content-area setting provides many opportunities for inquiry:

- *Science:* Students collect and analyze data and discuss the implications of findings.
- *Mathematics:* Students work in small groups to analyze and solve challenging problems.
- *History:* Students analyze primary-source documents to uncover multiple perspectives on historical events and issues.
- *ELA:* Students meet in mixed-reading groups to discuss and analyze relevant themes found in the novels they read.

Inquiry-based activities generate meaningful topics for academic writing and provide opportunities for ELLs to learn the academic language necessary for writing. Students can be asked to engage in ticket-to-enter writing, in which they formulate questions or predictions, as well as ticket-to-leave writing, in which they report what they have learned or pose questions that remain unanswered. Projects based on long-term inquiry, such as Mr. Peterson's class's investigations of biospheres, require students to generate lab reports and position papers that contribute to summative assessments.

Strategy 2: Writing for Content-Area Learning

Writing in the content areas is correlated with improved understanding of content-area materials. Writing for learning can be defined as low-stakes writing; examples include ticket-to-leave and ticket-to-enter writing, journal entries, responses to class activities and lessons, and reactions to what the students have been learning. Because writing skills, like vocabulary and reading ability, develop cumulatively, ELLs and other students improve their writing by writing. Studies of biology classes (Graham & Perrin, 2007) and math classes (Russek, 1998) suggest that writing for learning improves content-area understanding.

- Science: Mr. Peterson provides direct instruction in summarization and then guides his students through the process using text and other readings.
- Mathematics: Students keep a math journal where they record their understandings and questions (I learned . . ., Now I understand . . . I still do not understand . . .)
- ELA and history: Students in Mr. Hayes's and Ms. Chin's classes regularly complete quick writes about their reading and their connections to the reading as ticket-to-leave assignments.

Strategy 3: Provide Content-Area Models

Quality writing instruction enables ELLs and other students to write to learn as well as to share their ideas with others. ELLs and native-English speakers alike benefit from exemplars and from models that help them organize and structure their writing according to purpose and audience. Well-done assignments completed by previous students at various levels of English language proficiency provide ELLs with exemplars. (Leveled exemplars provide ELLs with $i + 1$ input—i.e., input that is comprehensible and always just beyond the current ability of the ELL.)

- Mr. Peterson's resource box of student-written summaries of articles illustrates one way in which content-area teachers can provide exemplars.
- Mr. Hayes also keeps the written work of former students on display and available to ELLs as models of exemplary writing.

Using an overhead to review exemplars with students helps them identify exemplary qualities in writing. ELLs and other students will need time to read and discuss the exemplars.

Strategy 4: Planning

Content-area teachers, such as Mr. Hayes provide models of the planning and writing processes when they share their own writing with students. These processes might include maintaining a notebook of possible writing topics, jotting down ideas about a chosen or assigned topic, and using graphic organizers to generate and organize ideas. Teachers must explain to students that in this brainstorming phase, any idea is appropriate. Prewriting activities, which are designed to help students generate and organize ideas, provide ELLs with additional opportunities to use language and thus provide support at the discourse level.

Strategy 5: Revising

During the revision stage, teachers first model how they revise their writing at the macro level. Using the overhead, they work through the text and think aloud to decide if the overall organization makes sense and to consider what else they might add or what should be deleted (and perhaps saved for another writing). Teachers provide ongoing teacher- and peer-supported practice to help students learn to effectively revise their writing. (All students, and particularly ELLs, will need guidance and practice to provide and use peer reviews.)

Strategy 6: Editing

Content-area teachers provide ELLs with ongoing support with editing. Teachers pay specific attention to the errors that are pervasive in second language writing and have been shown to be judged most harshly by instructors.

- Ms. Chin, Mr. Hayes, and Mr. Peterson assist ELLs with word choice, including finding more precise language to express their ideas (acquiesced rather than agreed).
- They know that ELLs often have difficulty with the correct use of relative (adjective) clauses (Hinkel, 2004, p. 48; e.g., "the women who lived during revolutionary times" or "the shot that was heard around the world"). They provide additional modeling when helping ELLs to edit.
- Ms. Chin, Mr. Hayes, Ms. Bell, and Mr. Peterson know that ELLs have particular difficulty with subject-verb agreement with indefinite pronouns (i.e., everyone, everybody, some) or when they use modifiers between the subject and the verb (Holden together with his friends).

As content-area teachers review ELLs' writing, they note the errors and the corrections that should be made. The teachers generally focus on only one type of error at a time, beginning with the errors that interfere with meaning. Ms. Chin, Ms. Bell, and Mr. Peterson also share ELLs' written work with ESOL and ELA teachers, who can explain specific rules of grammar to ELLs.

Strategy 7: Summarizing

Mr. Peterson, Ms. Chin, Mr. Hayes, and Ms. Bell understand that summarizing is an important tool for helping ELLs and other students to write to learn and to succinctly convey their understanding of concepts, ideas, findings, and results. The teachers explain the importance of summarizing to their students, show students how to summarize through modeling and mini lessons, and provide ongoing practice and feedback. (Mr. Peterson's mini lesson is on p. 230 of this text.) The teachers have found that summarizing activities also provide opportunities for additional instruction on word choice and grammatical constructions.

Strategy 8: Collaborative Writing

The four teachers model collaborative writing practices with their classes. Mr. Hayes, for example, places his writing and writings of (anonymous) former students on the overhead and models the process of critiquing and offering useful suggestions. The teachers provide class time for ELLs and other students to write and then discuss their writing in collaborative groups.

Strategy 9: Specific Product Goals That Assign Students Specific Reachable Goals for the Writing They Are to Complete

The four content-area teachers create assessments that provide specific and reachable goals for their students. As illustrated in Chapter 7 of this text, each teacher differentiates assignments according to students' English language proficiency levels. When provided with these appropriate assessments, ELLs know the goals and plans for overall writing outcomes (the form and structure of their academic writing) and goals for correctness at sentence and word levels (i.e., AWL words and word wall words must be spelled correctly).

Strategy 10: Word Processing, Which Uses Computers and Word Processors as Instructional Supports for Writing Assignments

Providing ELLs with instruction in word processing, time to practice, and word-processing assignments is likely to result in lowered levels of anxiety and more relaxed affective filters among the students. Additionally, ELLs are likely to benefit from the ability to revise and edit their work that word processing provides. Most of the content-area teachers featured in this text take advantage of classroom computers or campus computer labs and encourage their students to use word-processing facilities at their local libraries.

Strategy 11: Using Sentence Combining to Construct Complex and Sophisticated Sentences

The four content-area teachers recognize that many ELLs use the sentence structures with which they are most familiar (Hinkel, 2004). Ms. Chin, Mr. Peterson, and Mr. Hayes provide multiple examples of exemplary content-area writing and as part of their essential language questions call students' attention to the varied sentence structures within the writing. They also model how to combine sentences in mini lessons, during chapter reviews, and as a follow-up to writing assignments.

Review, Reflect, Apply

1. *Review:* Identify the benefits of providing content-area writing instruction to ELLs and other students.

2. *Reflect:* Which strategies do you currently use?

3. *Apply:* What additional strategies could be implemented in your classroom?

Summary

Research has shown that ELLs and many other students struggle with academic writing in the middle, secondary, and college grades. Fortunately, research also suggests that appropriate instruction from content-area teachers will improve students' content-area writing. Content-area teachers can begin by developing a community of writers within the classroom. Within this nurturing setting teachers can provide instruction for and meaningful practice with specific writing strategies, including prewriting, revising, and editing.

CHAPTER SUMMARY

Chapter 9 began with a discussion of students' difficulties with academic literacy, and then focused on strategies that foster the development of academic language and literacy across content areas. Academic language cannot be left to chance; content-area teachers must provide ongoing and targeted instruction to develop students' academic vocabulary and their mastery of effective strategies for reading and writing. Chapter 9 illustrated research-based teaching strategies, and stressed that academic literacy begins in classrooms where all students are considered members of a community of learners and are engaged in focused, meaningful, and appropriately challenging activities. Part II of this text illustrates how content-area teachers build learning communities within their classrooms and engage ELLs in instruction that scaffolds their academic language. It is recommended that readers complete each of the assessment evidence activities before proceeding to Part II.

Assessment Evidence Activities

AE-1   Create a training presentation for content-area teachers in your field to help them understand the need for and benefits of building the academic language of ELLs in this content area. Include a description of how building content-area academic language will enable ELLs to participate more fully in the content-area curriculum.

AE-2   Choose one or more instructional units that you teach and create at least two lessons to build the academic content-area vocabulary of ELLs in this content area.

AE-3   Create a content-area reading lesson for ELLs that you can implement in one of your classes. Implement the lesson with the class, or demonstrate the lesson to peers. Assess the lesson's effectiveness, and describe elements that were effective and elements that need improvement.

AE-4   Create a content-area academic writing lesson for ELLs that you can implement in one of your classes. As in AE-3, implement the lesson (or demonstrate it to peers), and then assess the lesson's effect, with particular attention to elements that were effective and those that need improvement.

Resources for Further Reading

- Nation, I. S. P. (2001). *Learning vocabulary in another language*. Cambridge, UK: Cambridge University Press.
- *Read, Write, Think* (International Reading Association and the National Council of Teachers of English). Retrieved July 10, 2008, http://www.readwritethink.org/
- Russek, B. (1998). Writing to learn mathematics. *Writing Across the Curriculum.* Retrieved March 30, 2008, from http://wac.colostate.edu/journal/vol9/russek.pdf (This online article demonstrates the effectiveness of teaching writing and content in a college-level mathematics course; the suggestions are applicable across grade levels)
- Stahl, S. A., & Nagy, W. E. (2006). *Teaching word meanings.* Mahwah, NJ: Lawrence Erlbaum.

PART II

Putting It Together in Content-Area Classrooms

Enduring understanding: The TELLiM model integrates content and language instruction for all content areas.

PART I OF THIS TEXT REVIEWED THE STEPS FOR PLANNING AND IMPLEMENTING INSTRUCTION FOR ELLs IN MAIN-stream classrooms, beginning with the introduction of the TELLiM model in Chapter 1. The first four chapters provided the background knowledge necessary for instructing ELLs, including the principles of second-language acquisition and tenets of culturally responsive pedagogy, as well as strategies for building academic literacy across content areas. Chapters 5 through 9 built on this background knowledge and focused on methods of planning and teaching for enduring understanding. Four content-area teachers illustrated how they planned and implemented instruction using the TELLiM model.

In Part II of this text, the four composite content-area teachers, Mr. Peterson, Ms. Bell, Ms. Chin, and Mr. Hayes, invite readers into their classrooms and demonstrate how they use their knowledge of content and language to provide instruction that builds on the strengths of ELLs and other students in their classrooms. A single set of enduring understandings, essential questions, and learning outcomes frames Chapters 10 through 13 and is included in this Introduction. An Assessment Evidence section is included at the end of each chapter to ensure that readers have the opportunity to self-check their understanding.

This Introduction to Part II provides an overview of key points, along with suggestions for teachers who are beginning to plan and differentiate instruction for ELLs in their mainstream classrooms, including a lesson-planning checklist, based on the steps of the TELLiM model, and a checklist of standards for effective classroom settings and lesson implementation based on Steps 4 through 8 of the TELLiM model (Steps 1 through 3 were illustrated in Chapters 5–7). Readers are encouraged to make copies of the TELLiM checklist to use as a tool to complete the Review, Reflect, Apply activities in Chapters 10 through 13.

PATHS TO PLANNING DIFFERENTLY

Mr. Peterson, Ms. Bell, Ms. Chin, and Mr. Hayes have planned their instruction based on the TELLiM model. They have developed the teaching abilities, strategies, and skills required by the model over a period of several years. They are dedicated to continually improving the instructional strategies they use within the classroom through ongoing assessment of ELLs' learning, self-reflections regarding the effectiveness of the instructional strategies they use, and regular discussions about instruction with colleagues. The four teachers cite three overarching strengths that have enabled them to foster and sustain high expectations for ELLs:

- Depth of knowledge in their content areas
- Knowledge of the principles of second-language acquisition, of linguistic theory, and of methods of improving student literacy
- An understanding of, and the ability to implement, the tenets of culturally responsive pedagogy

Mr. Peterson, Ms. Bell, Ms. Chin, and Mr. Hayes contend that it is possible even for beginning content-area teachers to develop an understanding of the principles of second-language acquisition. This understanding enables new teachers to recognize the challenges ELLs face in content-area classrooms and to begin to provide instruction that is comprehensible. Mr. Peterson, Ms. Bell, Ms. Chin, and Mr. Hayes also recognize the advantages of bilingualism and other strengths that ELLs bring to the classroom. They indicate that it is possible for veteran and novice teachers alike to develop knowledge about culturally responsive pedagogy and to begin to implement this knowledge as they get to know their ELLs and the rich and varied backgrounds that have helped shape individual ELLs' ways of knowing, thinking, and doing.

Each of the four teachers believes strongly in each student's right to learn and has created an atmosphere of respect in her or his classroom. Each asserts that, with appropriate instruction, ELLs are capable of mastering the enduring understandings in content areas. The four teachers agree that presenting concepts in a variety of ways is critical to the success of ELLs and helpful to the majority of other students in their classrooms. They suggest that focusing on academic language within content areas enables ELLs to become fully proficient in English and, at the same time, strengthens the academic language of other students.

Mr. Peterson, Ms. Bell, Ms. Chin, and Mr. Hayes state that it is possible for all teachers (including novice teachers) to contextualize their lessons by building instruction on enduring understandings, framing lessons with essential questions, and using visuals and graphic organizers whenever possible. They stress, however, that creating student-friendly essential questions is often a process of trial, reflection, and revision. All agree that their units and their individual lessons have evolved and improved over time.

All four teachers indicate that differentiating assessments is very important to measure student progress. As Mr. Hayes explains, "If the purpose of an assessment is to measure content-area understanding, lack of academic-language proficiency should not obscure this understanding." Although these teachers agree that their assessments have improved over time, all four of them advocate that even novice teachers *begin* to differentiate assessment outcomes according to English language proficiency levels.

Mr. Peterson, Ms. Bell, Ms. Chin, and Mr. Hayes emphasize that it has taken considerable time to differentiate the materials they use and to develop collections of comprehensible materials for many of the units they teach. The units they present in the following chapters are model units; the teachers say that they have not yet developed all instructional units as thoroughly as they have developed these models. They continue to collect and create new materials for additional instructional units and to add to existing unit resource boxes; they believe that it is important for all teachers to *begin* to collect and create comprehensible materials before they enter the classroom. The four teachers strongly recommend, however, that new teachers focus on differentiating one type of instructional materials at a time, or materials for one unit at a time. Ms. Chin, for example, began by collecting primary documents to make history come alive for ELLs, and Mr. Peterson began by collecting electronic images and other visuals to illustrate concepts in environmental science. These teachers have built their collections of materials over time, adding to unit resource boxes as they found or created new materials.

In planning their units and implementing instruction, the four teachers follow each step of the TELLiM model, as illustrated in Table II.1.

Each chapter in Part II begins with an overview of the teacher's schedule and descriptions of his or her students. Each chapter continues with a tour of the teacher's classroom. Readers will see how content-area teachers can use space to manage grouping, regrouping, and differentiating activities. Next, each chapter describes the differentiated materials that the teacher uses to ensure comprehensibility and shows the teacher reflecting on the challenges of teaching ELLs and native-English speakers of varying abilities. Each chapter then provides a detailed account of several content-area lessons. Snapshots of ELLs and other students working together demonstrate the integration of content-area and language objectives and assessments. Review, Reflect, and Apply activities enable readers to check their understanding as they work through the teacher's lessons.

TABLE II.1   TELLiM Model Checklist

Step	Description	√
1	**Review frameworks to determine enduring understandings**	
1a	Instruction is based on frameworks.	
1b	Instruction is based on enduring understandings.	
1c	English language abilities necessary to access content are included.	
2	**Set learning outcomes**	
2a	Content-area learning outcomes are based on enduring understandings.	
2c	Language-area learning outcomes are based on enduring understandings.	
3	**Establish evidence**	
3a	Content-area mastery is assessed apart from English proficiency.	
3b	Academic-English development is assessed.	
4	**Contextualize instruction**	
4a	Instruction is contextualized with essential questions.	
4b	Instruction builds on ELLs' knowledge.	
4c	Instruction engages ELLs in the broad theme of the unit.	
5	**Assessments and lessons**	
5a	Assessments are differentiated according to English language proficiency.	
5b	There are content-area objectives and assessments for individual lessons.	
5c	There are language objectives and assessments for individual lessons.	
6	**Make instruction comprehensible**	
6a	Content-area materials are comprehensible.	
6b	Presentations are comprehensible.	
7	**Build academic language**	
7a	ELLs and the teacher collaborate in the content area.	
7b	ELLs and the students collaborate in the content area.	
7c	ELLs are engaged in planned, complex academic conversations about the content area.	
7d	Content-area English language proficiency is supported.	
8	**Build higher-order thinking skills**	
8a	Complex thinking skills are taught.	
8b	ELLs are provided time to practice skills in meaningful situations.	

LEARNING OUTCOMES FOR CHAPTERS 10 TO 13

The following learning outcomes (LOs) serve as a guide for Chapters 10 through 13. Assessment activities aligned with each LO provide opportunities for readers to self-check their understanding at the end of each chapter.

LO-1   Understand how each content-area teacher acknowledges and builds on students' funds of knowledge within their lessons

LO-2   Recognize the ways in which the lessons are consistent with the TELLiM model

LO-3   Recognize the ways in which instruction is consistent with the steps of the TELLiM model

LO-4   Understand how the lessons build ELLs' content-area knowledge and academic language

LO-5   Identify differentiation strategies in each chapter that are doable right away, doable within the first year, and doable in future years

LO-6   Explain how the teacher develops instruction based on assessment and then assesses based on that instruction

LO-7   Use the teachers' models and the lesson-planning checklist to plan a content-area unit that you are developing

10

Putting It Together
in the Science Classroom

THE INTRODUCTION TO PART II PROVIDED AN OVERVIEW OF THE WAYS THAT CONTENT-AREA TEACHERS WHO PRO-vide effective settings for learning and instruction for ELLs have learned to plan and deliver instruction differently. Teachers explained that they developed their instructional strategies and materials over several teaching years and continue to refine these through self-reflection, observations, and ongoing conversations with colleagues about pedagogy. Chapter 10 shows how Mr. John Peterson plans and implements effective instruction for ELLs in environmental science and includes a tour of his classroom, descriptions of the materials he uses, his reflections on his teaching, and several content-area and language lessons.

Mr. Peterson follows the steps of the Teaching ELLs in the Mainstream (TELLiM) model when planning his instructional units. Table 10.1 is derived from the model to illustrate classroom-specific standards for meeting the needs of ELLs. The numbers of each standard (e.g., S4-a, b; S5; S6-a) are embedded in the descriptions of his classroom and lessons to illustrate how he plans for and implements pedagogy that is consistent with the model and meets the needs of ELLs.

Mr. Peterson teaches three sections of environmental science. The average class size is 24 students; approximately one third of students are ELLs with early-intermediate to transitioning proficiency. The class described in this section consists of 16 native-English speakers and 8 ELLs. The profiles of several students from this class, Aadam Jassam Ali, Julián Alencastro, Ghia Campos, Natka Jigovic, and Soan Meng, all appear in the Appendix of this text. Also present are Iris Acevedo (high-intermediate proficiency), Betsy Ruiz (early-intermediate proficiency), and Pilar Rámirez (transitioning proficiency). A tour of Mr. Peterson's room illustrates how, with organized and well-planned routines, he creates an instructional setting that meets the needs of ELLs and other students.

TABLE 10.1 TELLiM Lesson Implementation Checklist

Standard	Description (and Evidence) of Standard				√
S4-a	Instruction is contextualized.				
S4-b	Instruction builds on ELLs' previous knowledge.				
S5-a	Learning is assessed appropriately.				
S5-b	Content-area objectives and assessments for individual lessons.				
S5-c	Language objectives and assessments for individual lessons.				
S6-a	Materials are comprehensible to ELLs. (Check each strategy used.)				
	Appropriate reading level	Glossed words	Outlines	Highlighted text	Explanations in margins
	Books on tape	Clear organization	Other	Native language	Attention to vocabulary
S6-b	Presentational style is comprehensible to ELLs. (Check each device that is used within the lesson to increase comprehensibility.)				
	Realia	Other visuals	Graphic organizers	Think-Pair-Share	Other comprehension checks
	Simplified language	Clear routines	Other	Native language	Attention to vocabulary
S7-a	ELLs/teachers are engaged in academic collaboration.				
S7-b	ELLs/students are engaged in academic collaboration.				
S7-c	ELLs are engaged in planned, complex, academic conversations about their content area.				
S7-d	The development of content-area English language proficiency is supported.				
S8-a	Complex content-area thinking skills are taught.				
S8-b	Time for ELLs to practice these skills in meaningful circumstances is provided.				

A TOUR OF MR. PETERSON'S ROOM

Visitors to Mr. Peterson's classroom notice that the room is small and somewhat crowded. (Mr. Peterson explains that he would prefer to teach in a laboratory but has been assigned to an ordinary classroom.) Before the students arrive, 25 student desks are arranged in four neat rows that nearly fill the room. Students have assigned seats. He reserves a front row center desk for himself; this gives him the option of turning the chair around to sit with the students to discuss concepts (S7-a). He says that proximity is one way he builds rapport with ELLs and other students. Throughout the day, the configuration of the room changes depending on the lesson and the task at hand. Students sometimes turn their desks toward one another for Think-Pair-Share activities (S7-b, c); at other times, they work in various focused small-group formations to discuss and apply concepts (S7-b, c). He has established and adheres to clear routines for student grouping, which facilitates smooth transitions between large-group, small-group, paired, and individual activities and ensures that instructional time is not wasted.

Posters of scientists from Galileo to Rachel Carson, artwork from the Sierra Club, and a Gonzalez print titled *La Maestra de Ciencia* (The [Woman] Science Teacher) are displayed on a side wall. Mr. Peter explains that the Spanish poster was a gift from a colleague; so far he has been unable to find similar science posters in Arabic or Portuguese, the other languages spoken by his students this year. At the far end of this wall are several world maps. The front of the room features a large whiteboard. Each side of the board is filled with assignments (in black), content objectives (in red) (S5-b; S6-b), and language objectives (in blue) (S5-c; S6-b). A daily agenda is written next to the lesson objectives so that students have a road map of the class activities. It provides context for ELLs and other students (S4-a), who are able to quickly determine what they will do in the class from the beginning. Again, adherence to routine facilitates a smooth and time-efficient start to each class.

Mr. Peterson uses the whiteboard as a projection screen for PowerPoint, Internet, and video clips. Keeping objectives at the sides of the board enables him to refer to these as the projector is being used to illustrate key points (S6-b). Above the whiteboard is a long poster showing the progression of life in geologic time. The unit's essential questions—*How much is too much? How many people are too many people? How will we survive?*—are written in large letters on strips of chart paper and prominently displayed in various locations throughout the room (S4-a). Displaying essential questions throughout the room is yet another routine that he uses to provide ELLs and others with context for instruction.

The back wall of the room features a word wall. Directly above the word wall are Mr. Peterson's *essential language questions*: *What's the point?* and *How do scientists communicate?* He uses the word wall for unit terms and for Academic Word List (AWL) words that students will encounter in their textbooks and other assigned readings. AWL words are not usually glossed in texts. He explains, "I was amazed when I started working with AWL lists and found 19 of the first 60 AWL words in the first chapter (26 pages) of the environmental science text, and these words are repeated throughout the text." He prints the AWL words on oak tag, and as they appear in the text, he conducts mini vocabulary lessons. He then tacks words on the board in alphabetical order. The following words appeared in the first chapter: *analyze, area, available, benefit, data, define, distribute, economy, environment, evident, factor, identify, individual, interpret, percent, policy, research, section, significant,* and *variables.* Mr. Peterson explains, "Using the word wall brings all students' attention to words and their uses. I no longer have students using *data* as a singular noun!" (S7-d). Mr. Peterson distributes handouts of AWL words to all students, who are then responsible for using the ones that he has taught correctly in classroom discussions and in writing assignments.

Generally, one day a week, the computer lab serves as Mr. Peterson's classroom. He has found that ELLs and other students benefit when they are given the opportunity to word process lab reports and other written assignments (S7-d; S8-b). He has also established clear routines for working in the computer lab.

APPROPRIATE INSTRUCTIONAL MATERIALS

To the right of Mr. Peterson's word wall is a bookcase on which he keeps materials for instructional units. Several copies of various texts that are no longer in use in the district are on one shelf. Opening these texts, one discovers that sections of chapters have been highlighted. In the margins are glossed words and notes that make passages comprehensible to ELLs. (Although he began to collect these materials for the ELLs in his classroom, Mr. Peterson has also found them to be useful in supporting other students who have difficulty reading at grade level). Several other research books and copies of magazines that he has collected are nearby. Some of these are also highlighted (S6-a).

Below the shelf of textbooks are several plastic boxes with unit names such as "Resources Are Finite," "Water, Water, Everywhere," and "Will Biodiversity Last?" A look within these boxes reveals manila folders of resource materials, which Mr. Peterson has collected over the years, including articles at various reading levels, and articles and environmental cases that have been glossed and highlighted by him and by his former students (S6-a, b).

On the opposite end of the room, behind Mr. Peterson's desk, is a shelf with videos, many of which are his personal materials. Just beside his desk is what he refers to as the key resource within his classroom, the technology center, which consists of his laptop and a projector. He uses the Internet as a resource for reading materials to supplement his text. The text, he explains, is very good, but provides survey rather than in-depth information about any one topic. At any time, when visiting the room, the visitor will notice that he is using the technology center for PowerPoint presentations, streaming video, or Internet reference sites (S6-a, b).

REFLECTIONS FROM MR. PETERSON

According to Mr. Peterson, he has been planning instruction based on *enduring understandings* in environmental science for many years: "It has always made sense to me to plan this way. Otherwise ELLs and native-English speakers learn disconnected bits and pieces and often are unable to make connections to the big picture." Motivating students with essential questions is a newer strategy for him. He explains that he has always shared the unit's enduring understanding with students and now finds that essential questions provide a hook that engages ELLs and others in the instruction (S4-a).

Mr. Peterson explains that he has highlighted selected sections of two older editions of the science text for ELLs who struggle to keep up with the amount of reading:

> I have written summary statements next to selected key paragraphs. For example, a section on sustainability contains three paragraphs that are language heavy for ELLs like Soan, who struggles with multiparagraph and academic-literacy devices. I have highlighted the topic sentences in each paragraph and next to the paragraph I have written a brief summary. (S6-a)

He finds that by highlighting and summarizing key paragraphs, he is able to differentiate according to language-proficiency levels and yet ensure that students have access to identical content (S6-a). Highlighting and glossing also brings new words to ELLs' attention, which has been shown to be effective in increasing vocabulary (Nation, 2001; Stahl & Nagy, 2006) (S7-d).

Mr. Peterson explains that he has developed a strong language focus because he wants students to be able to access the content material of his class:

> Several years ago, I realized that if I want to spend my class time on rich content-area instruction that extends the text, I needed to ensure that ELLs and others could access content within the text (S6-a). I have worked collaboratively with an ESOL teacher since that time. In reflecting upon my instruction, I have always worked to provide context and make instruction comprehensible, yet I continue to learn more. It is now a conscious process, which ensures that it happens regularly. Collaborating with the ESOL teacher has helped me to focus on academic language that goes beyond

the science terms and restructure lessons to include a focus on language (S7-d). I also spend more class time with study skills such as finding key points, self-checking for understanding, summarizing, and outlining so that ELLs and other students learn strategies necessary to access the text (S7-d). When I began to prepare materials for study skills instruction, I started highlighting passages and writing key points in the margins. I have developed a collection of these highlighted materials for this unit, and I make these available to ELLs (S6-a). Ghia is transitioning and often uses the same materials as other mainstream students. Soan and Adaam, however, frequently choose materials that have been highlighted and glossed. Julián uses all materials that have been easified in some way; he could not access the content otherwise. It just makes sense to allow ELLs (and other students) to use these materials if they find them helpful. Differentiating materials in this way is helpful to students who need the scaffolding, yet the highlighting does not distract students who are able to use the standard classroom materials. (S6-a, S7-d)

Mr. Peterson says that an important part of his work is to know, as best as he can, the students in his classes. He has accessed the cumulative folder for each student and therefore knows the proficiency levels of his ELLs. He also works collaboratively with the school's ESOL teacher, who often provides him with more in-depth information. He explains, "I can provide materials that meet each ELL's needs if I know what those needs are." He shares that this year a guidance counselor and the ESOL teacher spoke with him about some of the adjustment issues that Aadam is having in the United States. He describes how he has worked to build rapport with Aadam in these first few weeks of school:

I always stand at the door and greet students when they enter the room. I think it means a lot to them that I know something about them—that I want to know them. I try to make an extra effort with Aadam without singling him out. The class features a lot of team work, which I believe builds conceptual knowledge as well as language. I have always assigned seats, which makes it easier to support a student like Aadam. He sits next to Josh, a native-English speaker and a really nice, supportive kid. It's Josh that he turns to for the numerous Think-Pair-Share activities. Lately, I have noticed them chatting more spontaneously prior to and after class. Ghia, who speaks Portuguese as a first language, sits in front of Aadam. She is very mature, and again a very supportive person. Aadam is very quiet in the large group, but shares when working with Josh and Ghia.

The six other ELLs in this class are at varying levels of English proficiency and speak two additional first languages: Khmer and Serbo-Croatian. At times, Mr. Peterson has ELLs work together, and at other times, they collaborate with native-English speakers. The exception is Betsy, whose English proficiency is just barely intermediate:

I pair Betsy with Iris, who is a solid student with high-intermediate proficiency. This allows Iris to scaffold Betsy's English and to explain concepts in Spanish when necessary (S7-b, c, d). The other students around Iris are all native-English speakers so that her English language is also scaffolded (S7-d). I was advised by the ESOL teacher to ensure that Iris had the opportunity to engage in academic conversations with native speakers.

Review, Reflect, Apply

1. *Apply:* How does the setting in Mr. Peterson's room foster educational opportunities for ELLs?

2. *Review and reflect:* Mr. Peterson is a veteran teacher who has collected materials and lessons over a long period of time. Review Mr. Peterson's classroom setting, materials, and reflections, and reflect on what components a new teacher could implement immediately, which could be implemented during the first year, during the second year, and during the fifth year.

IMPLEMENTING THE "FINITE RESOURCES" UNIT

This section begins with an overview of the key unit concepts that are necessary for meeting the *learning outcomes,* and then provides the *assessment* Mr. Peterson has designed and the differentiated assessment rubrics that measure mastery of one learning outcome. Three content-area lesson narratives are then presented. Standard numbers (S4-a, b; S6-a, etc.) are embedded in the Lesson 1 narrative and Part 1 of the Lesson 2 narrative to illustrate how elements of his instruction align with the TELLiM standards. Lesson 2, Part 2 does not show standard numbers within the narrative. The Review, Reflect, Apply section encourages readers to identify specific standards present in Part 2 of this lesson. A summary follows this activity to enable readers to self-assess their understanding. Next, a lesson that has been designed to accommodate differentiated reading materials is presented. The subsequent Review, Reflect, Apply encourages readers to consider the advantages that differentiated lessons provide to ELLs and other students and the planning and classroom management that are integral to differentiated instruction. The section concludes with three language mini lessons.

Key Concepts and Essential Questions

Mr. Peterson has identified key concepts for the "Finite Resources" unit:

- The interrelatedness of Earth's systems (focusing on habitable land and potable water)
- The fact that relatively little of the earth is habitable and even less is available for agricultural purposes
- The earth's growing population, which results in an increasing demand for available resources and increasing pollution
- The effect of increasing demand for resources, increasing pollution, and loss of biodiversity

Mr. Peterson contextualizes each lesson with the essential questions, which enables ELLs and other students to understand how concepts come together. He begins by calling his students' attention to the questions and explains, "Throughout this unit, I will ask you to think about the following questions: *How will we survive? How much is too much? How many people are too many?*" (TELLiM model, Step 3). (At various times during the unit, he also asks ELLs if resource use in their countries of origin differs from resource use in the United States [S4-b].)

Assessment Options

Within the first two days of the unit, Mr. Peterson explains the learning outcomes. The final assessment options, some of which were described in Chapter 7, are written on chart paper and displayed in the front of the room to the right of the whiteboard. Table 10.2 illustrates the assessment choices for Learning Outcome 2.

TABLE 10.2

Learning Outcome 2	Assessment Evidence: Choose One		
Discuss local, national, and global implications of findings from individual environmental footprints	Written report	Presentation: Group or individual	Poster session

Mr. Peterson provides students with copies of the summative assessment options, which they keep in their science binders. (All science teachers at his school insist that students maintain a three-ring science binder, and all handouts have been punched to facilitate the use of the binder. This is yet another way that routines are reinforced within this science classroom [S6-b].)

Providing students with differentiated assessments at the beginning of the instructional unit enables ELLs and others to know how their understandings will be assessed (S4-a) and to self-monitor their learning as they proceed through the unit (S5-a). Based on his review of the English language proficiency level of each ELL in this class, Mr. Peterson creates assessments to enable ELLs to demonstrate content-area knowledge apart from language proficiency and at the same time measure growth in academic-language ability. Table 10.3 shows the basic rubric that he uses for the written report assessment option; Tables 10.4 and 10.5 illustrate how he differentiates assessments according to English language proficiency.

Differentiating Assessment for ELLs

Mr. Peterson differentiates this assessment for the ELLs in this class. For example, Ghia is a very strong student whose English proficiency is at the transitioning level. He knows from her test results, notes from the ESOL teacher, and a review of the writing samples in her portfolio that she has strong organizational skills in writing. Mr. Peterson has also noted that Ghia

TABLE 10.3   Overview of Basic Rubric: Written Report

Requirement	Points (/100)
Report is 4–5 pages in length (double spaced and word processed).	10
Global footprint data are reported accurately. (Lab reports showing original data are attached.)	30
Report clearly discusses implications of footprint data from local, national, and global perspectives using citations from textbook, Internet site explored in class, class handouts, notes, and other sources approved by Mr. Peterson.	40
Report is well organized and logical.[a]	10
Grammar and spelling are correct.[a]	10

a. Mr. Peterson understands that language and writing are developmental. He modifies this rubric as needed according to students' writing ability as evidenced by students' past work.

struggles at times with consistency in verb tense and in editing for sentence structure (specifically, she often misses sentence fragments and long run-on sentences). The rubric that he provides to Ghia is very similar to that for native-English speakers. The criteria for spelling and grammar are slightly different, however: "Word-wall words and vocabulary terms are spelled correctly. Grammatical errors that have been corrected in the first draft do not appear in the final paper." By making this adjustment to the rubric, he holds Ghia accountable for rules of grammar and spelling that she has been specifically taught, yet does not penalize her for structures that may be new to her (S5-a).

Table 10.4 illustrates differentiation of the written report assessment based on the language proficiency levels of Aadam, Soan, and Natka, all intermediate-level ELLs. From reviewing the previous work of the three ELLs, Mr. Peterson knows that they will likely experience the following difficulties with academic writing:

- Aadam: Use of academic vocabulary, writing academic paragraphs without support, subject-verb order
- Natka: Use of transitions between ideas, difficulty using multiple verb tenses, varying sentence structure
- Soan: Overall organization of writing, using transitions, correct spelling and mechanics, proofreading own errors, varying sentence structure

Based on the guidelines for differentiating assessments according to proficiency levels (Chapter 7, Table 7.3), Mr. Peterson constructs a rubric for these ELLs.

Mr. Peterson knows that Julián, an ELL with early-intermediate proficiency, can write simple paragraphs using a graphic organizer yet has difficulty with multiple-paragraph compositions, variations in sentence structure, and complex grammatical constructions. Table 10.5 illustrates the adjustments he makes to the rubric assignment for Julián.

Mr. Peterson explains, "Each of the assessment options requires ELLs and other students to master the same learning outcomes. The assessments are differentiated to account for differences in English language proficiency." Once he has reviewed the rubrics and provided students with exemplars, he begins the lessons of this instructional unit.

TABLE 10.4 Assessment Differentiated for Intermediate-Level Proficiency

Requirement	Points
Report is an outline 3–5 pages in length (double spaced and word processed), including charts, graphs, and visuals.	10
Global footprint data are reported accurately. (Lab reports showing original data are attached.)	30
The outline illustrates the implications of footprint data from local, national, and global perspectives. Under each heading of the outline (food, travel, housing, etc.) is a paragraph that includes a topic sentence and three to five supporting sentences.	40
Each section of the report is well organized (e.g., all travel statements are in the travel section). Each paragraph is logically organized with a topic sentence and supporting details.	10
Vocabulary words and other word wall words are spelled correctly. Sentences are complete. Punctuation is used.	10

Requirement	Points
Report is an outline 3–5 pages in length (double spaced and word processed), including charts, graphs, and visuals that support your statements.	10
Global footprint data are reported accurately. (Lab reports showing original data are attached.)	30
Each major section (e.g., travel, food, housing) includes a title, a topic sentence, and a list of supporting statements. Each section includes at least one citation from textbook, Internet site explored in class, class handouts, notes, or other sources approved by Mr. Peterson. Photos, drawings, graphs, and other visuals may be used in each section to help explain statements.	40
Each section of the report is organized.	10
Word wall and vocabulary words are spelled correctly. Each sentence begins with a capital letter and ends with a punctuation mark.	10

Review, Reflect, Apply

1. *Review:* Review the differentiated assessments that Mr. Peterson has provided for ELLs and the profiles of ELLs in the Appendix.

2. *Apply:* How do the assessments meet their needs?

ALIGNING LESSONS WITH TELLiM STANDARDS

The standards embedded in the narratives of Lesson 1 and in Part 1 of Lesson 2 illustrate how Mr. Peterson's lessons are aligned with the TELLiM standards shown in the checklist (Table 10.1). Readers are encouraged to try to identify the standards in Lesson 2, Part 2.

Lesson 1: Land Boundaries?

(90 minutes)

In keeping with established routines, Mr. Peterson begins by calling students' attention to the content and language objectives that he has written on the side of the whiteboard. As always, content objectives are written in red and language objectives in blue (S4-a; S6-b). He has underlined key words in the objectives (S7-d).

Content Objectives

1. Identify <u>chemical agents</u> in common lawn care products.

2. Explain the process of <u>non–point-source pollution</u> when provided with a model and diagrams.

3. Explain some of the environmental issues associated with <u>chemical agents</u>.

4. Support your position on the use of <u>chemical agents</u>.

Language Objectives

1. Use diagram in text for understanding.

2. Use academic language (from vocabulary lesson and on word wall) to discuss ingredients found in labels and diagrams of <u>non–point-source</u> pollution (Think-Pair-Share) (S4-a; S7-c, d).

3. Write and submit your position on the use of chemical agents. Support this position with facts using vocabulary from class presentation, discussions, and materials (S8-b). (S5-c)

Mr. Peterson begins this introductory lesson by reviewing the lesson objectives and explaining that these objectives will help students investigate the essential questions that are displayed around the room. He has underlined the new terms, and he points to each of these terms as he says it in the lesson. He then reviews the lesson agenda, which remains posted throughout the lesson and provides a contextual road map for ELLs and other students (S4-a): (1) The XYZ Lawn Beautiful dilemma, (2) What's in lawn products? (Think-Pair-Share), (3) Are there land boundaries? (demonstration, Think-Pair-Share, diagrams), (4) Restrictions (film clip), (5) The growing population, and (6) Get off the fence! (group work, written assignment).

Mr. Peterson tells students that he thinks they already know quite a bit about chemical agents and non–point-source pollution. He then connects to students' life experiences by projecting an image of the *XYZ Lawn Beautiful* sign, which is seen throughout the community (S4-b). Through a show of hands, students indicate that they have seen these signs (S4-b). Using the overhead projector, he shows side-by-side photos of two lawns, one treated with chemical agents and the other left natural, and asks which lawn is more likely to have the *XYZ Lawn Beautiful* sign (S6-b). Students raise their hands and indicate that the green and lush lawn is more likely to have an *XYZ Lawn Beautiful* sign. He asks for a student volunteer to explain this response (S7-c). Pilar (a transitioning ELL) offers, "The company fertilizes the lawns and that makes them green." He nods and probes, "What do you mean *fertilize*? What chemical agents does the XYZ Lawn Beautiful company use?" (S7-c). Several students volunteer that the company uses fertilizers and "weed killers" to enhance the appearance of lawns. He writes *fertilizer, weed killer (herbicides)*, and *pesticides* on the board and draws a line from each of these to the words *chemical agents* (S6-a, b, S7-d). As he points to each word, he asks students to display a thumbs-up to show that they understood and a thumbs-down to indicate that they do not understand (S5-a). Aadam Jassam gives neither sign but appears confused. Iris gives a thumbs-down for *herbicides*. Mr. Peterson points to each of the words as he explains it (S6-b). Again, he scans the room for signs of comprehension and confusion (S5-a). Once he has checked for understanding, he moves on.

Using the overhead projector, Mr. Peterson displays labels found on bags and bottles of lawn care products, which again serve to connect his lesson to something with which students are familiar—labels (S4-b). He distributes copies of labels to pairs of students and, using a brief Think-Pair-Share, has students identify and discuss known information on the labels (chemicals; other words such as *inert*, *active*, and *ingredients*; and symbols such as %). He then discusses the purposes of some of the commonly found ingredients listed on the labels and found in many lawn care products. Pointing to the photos of the two lawns (S6-b), he explains that these chemical agents are spread over lawns to make them green, weed free, and attractive.

After engaging students in brief conversation to check for understanding regarding chemical agents used for lawn care, Mr. Peterson draws a diagram on the whiteboard illustrating two houses with a clear property boundary line (S4-a, S6-b). He indicates that one house is serviced by XYZ Lawn Beautiful and the other is not. He uses a model to demonstrate that lawn products do not recognize man-made land boundaries. He demonstrates the migration of chemical agents by pouring colored water into sand, rock, and soil that cover the bottom of a large clear container (S6-b). He engages students in a two-minute Think-Pair-Share to explain what happened during the demonstration and its implications for the migration of chemical agents (S7-c; S8-a, b). He briefly circulates and informally assesses understanding. He explains to students that this is an example of non–point-source pollution and it is a somewhat simplified model. He then directs their attention to a diagram illustrating non–point-source pollution in their textbooks.

Using the Textbook

Mr. Peterson's experience teaching science has convinced him that many students (not only the ELLs in his class) often do not effectively use text illustrations. He knows that using illustrations is likely to improve student understanding and has decided to use the non–point-source diagram to help students understand content and how to better use the textbook. Using a transparency showing a page in their text, he calls students' attention to the sentence in the text that refers to the diagram; using a think-aloud, he demonstrates reading the text: "As shown in Diagram 1.6 on page 19." He thinks aloud, "Okay, I know that Diagram 1.6 shows the migration of chemical agents. I'm going to stop here and look at this diagram." (S6-b). He directs ELLs and other students to work together in pairs to discuss the processes illustrated by the diagram (S7-c; S8-a, b). He circulates to assess student understanding (S5-a); students are on task, and most appear to understand the processes illustrated by the diagram. He notices that Betsy, Iris, and a pair of native-English-speaking students appear to be confused. He projects another diagram of point-source pollution on the overhead and tells the class that once they have had an opportunity to discuss this diagram, he will ask for a volunteer to explain it (S8-b). He uses this time to work with Betsy and Iris and invites the two native-English-speaking students to join them. He walks them through the diagram on the overhead and checks for understanding while the remaining students in the class are engaged in the Think-Pair-Share activity (S7-c), which provides ELLs and other students with meaningful opportunities to practice academic language (S8-b).

When the pairs come together in a large group, Mr. Peterson asks for volunteers to explain the processes illustrated in the diagram. He is pleased to see that Adaam is one of the students who volunteers, albeit somewhat hesitantly. Having had time to practice language with Ghia during two brief Think-Pair-Share activities has enabled Adaam to become more confident in responding (S8-b). Adaam explains that the chemical agents have migrated from the lawn of the city hall building to the streets and then to the stream that flows nearby. Mr. Peterson acknowledges and reinforces Aadam's response, explaining that there are consequences for the ways we use Earth's finite resources. The Think-Pair-Share has given Mr. Peterson the opportunity to assess and build on Adaam's understanding of the content. Bringing the lesson back to the whole class, he reminds students of the essential question, asking, "How much is too much?" (S4-a)

Using Visuals

Mr. Peterson shows a film clip that provides a synopsis of Rachel Carson's *Silent Spring* and projects a short and poignant excerpt from the book on the whiteboard. He reads through this with the students (S6-b). He explains that some of the current restrictions on the use of chemical agents are a result, in part, of Carson's work.

Mr. Peterson then returns to the essential question with which he began the lesson: *How much is too much?* He tells students, "You saw that chemical agents don't know boundaries." He continues, "What if every house used chemical agents on their land?" He then goes to the whiteboard where the original diagram of the two houses remains and adds X's to illustrate more houses. "As there are more people, we need more houses," he explains, and he directs students' attention to the diagram (S6-b).

Using charts and diagrams, Mr. Peterson shows that the world population has increased dramatically since 1964. He connects this concept to students' knowledge by showing two aerial views, taken 20 years apart, of the area around the school (S4-b, S6-a). Illustrating and checking for understanding as he speaks, he guides ELLs and other students to understand that the increase in population has increased the quantity of chemical agents that are spread on land (which then migrate into water). Once he has checked for understanding, he places students in groups of four; their task is to come to a preliminary decision about whether or not chemical agents (including fertilizers, pesticides, and herbicides) should be regulated. They are directed to use the vocabulary they have been taught in previous lessons in their conversations (S7-c, d). Groups need not reach consensus but must engage in academic discussion using class materials and their texts (S7-b, c).

As a ticket-to-leave, each student must "get off the fence" and explain in writing if he or she thinks that current chemical agents used on lawns should be banned or allowed to continue, or if they are not sure. Based on their own knowledge and what they have learned in the class, students must defend their position. Mr. Peterson explains that the assignment will be graded as participation (1 point for collaborative group discussion, 1 point for submission of the assignment, and 1 point for their reasoning based on the day's lesson). "There is not one correct answer," he explains. "The purpose of this assignment is to engage in academic conversation using the vocabulary of the lesson, process the information from class today, convey your position, and support it with facts" (S5-a, b; S7-C; S8-a, b).

Although Mr. Peterson has assessed understanding throughout the lesson, this short ticket-to-leave assignment provides a more accurate picture of what ELLs and other students have learned and enables him to adjust his lesson plans for the following class meeting. It also serves as a self-assessment for ELLs and other students (S5-a). He reads the students' papers, looking for evidence of conceptual understanding and attempts to use the academic language of the unit, not grammatical structure (S5-a). Not surprisingly, nearly all his students write that chemical agents should be banned (S5-a). They have supported their responses with the understanding they gained in the lesson. In Lesson 2, Mr. Peterson uses their responses as a springboard to explain the danger of making decisions based on partial data.

Lesson 2: Growing Populations, Growing Footprints (Part 1)

(60 minutes)

Content Objectives

1. Explain how population growth and lifestyles have changed during the past 1,000 years, supporting your explanation with supporting details from the text.

2. Explain the environmental impact of these changes (support with details).

3. Predict some of the impacts of continued growth. (S5-b)

Language Objectives

1. Define and explain three new AWL words that appear in the reading (S7-d).

2. Read historical sections in the textbook, and use academic language to summarize key points in group discussions. (S5-c)

Mr. Peterson begins this lesson by summarizing what the students wrote as their ticket-to-leave in the previous class and relating their responses to the essential questions in the unit. He praises them for their attention to detail and explains that they were correct based on the facts they were given—that the previous day's lesson had presented only one facet of the use of chemical agents. Presenting only one side of an issue, he explains, sometimes occurs in reports that they will read about environmental issues. He explains that the following day's lesson will focus on evaluating the validity of sources and to do this they will need important background knowledge—the class has some reading to do. He then reviews each of the content and language lesson objectives and the lesson agenda (S4-a; S5-b, c).

Mr. Peterson explains that although students see many *XYZ Lawn Beautiful* signs, more "run-off" actually comes from farms that grow food, from oil that leaks from cars, and from salt and chemicals used to treat roads to prevent accidents. Using a Think-Pair-Share, he engages ELLs and others about the potential risks and benefits of these products (S7-b, c; S8-a, b).

Mr. Peterson explains to students that throughout the course they will read articles and ask questions necessary to become informed decision makers. He tells them that they will begin with a brief history of environmental issues. "Students often think that environmental problems are new," he explains. "Yet environmental problems have been with us for a very long time. The pace of growth and technology has exacerbated the problems." He tells students that they will work together and, using information from their textbooks, create a quick timeline depicting environmental issues (S7-c). He divides his class into groups of three; ELLs work with native-English speakers.

He tells the students that prior to reading the text, he would like to introduce three new words that are important to the chapter, but are not glossed, highlighted, or bold-faced. He explains that they will encounter these words throughout their reading of the environmental science text and in other classes. These are words that they will use in academic writing. He presents the words *analyze, benefit,* and *environment,* which he has printed on oak tag (S7-d).

He uses this time to preteach and post these three AWL words, which appear within the first few pages of reading. (Mr. Peterson knows that he should limit vocabulary instruction to no more than five words at a time [Nation, 2001].) He explains to the students,

> I know that most of you recognize these words as you read, yet, I am less confident that you use them comfortably in your own work. These are words that are used across the content areas and throughout our textbook, so it makes sense to spend some time with them. We are going to work with these words for 10 minutes today.

Mr. Peterson provides the students with handouts of sentences in which each of the words has been used. Students work together to define each word and then to generate as many members of the word family as possible. He brings students together as a large group to share their definitions and the related family words they generated. The words are placed on the word wall at the back of the room. Throughout the unit he calls students' attention to these words and other AWL words that he has taught (S7-d). (He also refers to the AWL words in filler activities [Saphier & Gower, 1997], which are discussed later in this chapter.)

Lesson 2: Growing Populations, Growing Footprints (Part 2)

(Standard numbers are not embedded in this part of the lesson.)

Once ELLs and other students have completed the vocabulary mini lesson, Mr. Peterson explains that they will use their texts to develop an understanding of the history of environmental issues and construct timelines to illustrate the progression of these issues. Mr. Peterson calls attention to the geologic timeline at the front of the room and checks to ensure that students understand the meaning of *timelines*. Using the overhead, he shows students a blank timeline that he has created for this lesson and explains that they will complete timelines during this class. He has decided to use a jigsaw activity for this assignment. (Chapter 8 explains the purpose and procedures of the jigsaw.) He has the class count off by 3s (resulting in eight teams with three students each). He then pairs three-person teams, which results in four teams of six students each (two 1s, two 2s, and two 3s). He instructs like-number students within each team (1s with 1s, 2s with 2s, 3s with 3s) to sit together. He explains that each pair of like-number students in the six-person group is responsible for explaining the environmental impacts of one of the following periods: hunter-gatherer, agricultural revolution, or industrial revolution.

In pairs, students read the appropriate sections of their text; each section consists of several paragraphs. Students read their sections aloud to ensure that each student understands the text. After they read, each student explains the section to his or her partner. In approximately five minutes, students have completed their pair work, and Mr. Peterson checks for understanding. The next task is for each pair of students to explain the section they read to others in their six-person group (1s explain hunter-gatherer period, 2s explain the agricultural revolution, and 3s explain the industrial revolution.) Students use group information to construct timelines. He assesses student understanding by circulating, listening to their conversations, and reviewing their timelines.

Mr. Peterson uses one of the group's timelines to illustrate the increase of population growth and engages students in an interactive lecture about the possible effects of this rapid increase. He explains that there are three major types of environmental issues that they will study during the course and writes each of these on the board as he pronounces them: (1) resource depletion, (2) pollution, and (3) loss of biodiversity (Arms, 2004). He connects the issues to the unit's essential questions.

During the last five minutes of the lesson, students collaborate with their Think-Pair-Share partners to make predictions about future environmental issues of concern based on current trends. Several students volunteer to share their pair's predictions. Mr. Peterson uses their predictions to introduce and provide purpose for the homework reading assignment, which he writes on the whiteboard. Each student is expected to read the same eight pages of the science textbook. ELLs (and other students) are also encouraged to choose at least one of three Internet articles of which he has made copies. He explains that the articles provided can be used in the final assessment project, which motivates students to complete this additional reading. He has arranged the articles by reading levels and assists students in the selection of appropriate articles; copies of two articles have been highlighted, words have been glossed, and explanatory notes are in the margins. (Aadam, Julián, and Soan, who are able to keep up with issues during class, often have difficulty reading the text and each borrows one of the highlighted texts that are available to the class.) Students are required to generate one question or one key point of interest from their combined readings and bring this question/key point to class in writing.

Review, Reflect, Apply

1. Review Lesson 1 and Part 1 of Lesson 2, and reflect on how Mr. Peterson aligns his instruction with the standards. Then, apply your knowledge to match the standards (Table 10.1) with the strategies used in Lesson 2, Part 2.

2. Explain the strategies that Mr. Peterson has used to make instruction comprehensible.

3. Explain the strategies that he has used to build academic language.

Summary: Self-Assessment

Table 10.6 shows how we have aligned the Lesson 2, Part 2 narrative with the standards. As one can see, some elements of the lesson are consistent with several standards.

Lesson 3: Informed Decision Making

A Lesson Differentiated by Reading Materials

(60 minutes)

As always, Mr. Peterson begins this lesson by reviewing the content and language objectives and the lesson agenda. In this lesson, students will (1) explain one key point/question from the reading, (2) support key points/questions with specific examples from the reading, (3) explain points of view in articles, and (4) substantiate their position with article statements. Once he has introduced the lesson and checked students' understanding about lesson activities, he forms discussion groups of three to five students, based on the articles students were assigned for homework. (All students were assigned to read the same pages in the textbook.)

Reading Option 1

Four students who, with Mr. Peterson's guidance, have selected the most complex article have the opportunity to expand their understanding of key concepts. Ghia is the only ELL in this group; she struggles slightly with the reading level yet grasps underlying concepts at a level beyond the majority of students in the class. On his recommendation, Ghia has read the article introduction and conclusion.

Reading Option 2

Twelve other students have read one of the articles that were written at grade level. Several native-English-speaking students and the five ELLs in this group selected a highlighted

TABLE 10.6   Aligning Mr. Peterson's Lesson 2, Part 2

S4-a. Instruction is contextualized

Mr. Peterson writes key words on the board as he pronounces them.

He explains the purpose of the reading assignment.

S5-a. Learning is assessed appropriately

During the lesson, Mr. Peterson assesses student understanding by circulating, listening to their conversation, and reviewing their timelines.

S5-b,c. Content-area and language objectives and assessments are present in lessons

Mr. Peterson posted content-area and language objectives, using a separate color for each. He reviewed them with students and referred to them during the lesson. He assessed language and content objectives informally by circulating through the room and checking understanding and reviewing students' timelines.

S6-a. Materials are comprehensible to ELLs

Students read aloud to ensure that each student understands the text.

Articles are arranged by reading levels. Copies of two articles feature highlighting, glossing, and explanatory notes. Easified textbooks are available to students. (This is also consistent with S7-d.)

S6-b. Presentational style is comprehensible to ELLs

Mr. Peterson calls students' attention to the geologic timeline and checks to ensure that students understand the meaning of timelines.

He also shows students a blank timeline that he has created for this lesson.

S7-a. Academic collaboration between ELLs and teacher is fostered

Mr. Peterson engages students in an interactive lecture about the possible effects of this rapid increase using one of the group's timelines.

S7-b. Academic collaboration between ELLs and other students is fostered

Mr. Peterson has students form groups of six, then divide into pairs. Each pair of students explains the section they read to others in their groups. (This also is consistent with standards S4-a, b; S7-c, d; S8-b.)

S7-c. ELLs are engaged in planned, complex, academic conversations about their content area

Students share and discuss their reading to create timelines.

S7-d. Content-area English language proficiency is supported

The academic conversations in which students explained sections of their text to others fosters the development of content-area English language proficiency.

S8-a. Complex content-area thinking skills are taught

Students read and discuss the text with the intention of teaching it to others. Mr. Peterson uses the geologic timeline to help students understand environmental trends.

S8-b. Time for ELLs to practice these skills in meaningful circumstances is provided

Students create timelines together based on their readings. Students make predictions about future environmental issues of concern based on current trends.

version of this article. According to Mr. Peterson, this article expands the concepts of the text but is only three pages in length and is conceptually less sophisticated than the most challenging article. He divides the 12 students into four teams of 3 students each. He directs the four teams to work at one side of the room so that he will be able to pull them together and work with all 12 students at the same time.

Reading Option 3

Six students have read the third article, which also expands the text but in less than two pages using a bulleted format. These students form two groups of three students and work at the opposite side of the room. There are no ELLs in this group.

Betsy and Julián have read only the textbook, and they work together at the front of the room. Mr. Peterson begins his work with them. He first reviews their key points and questions and asks them to share their understandings. He helps with words that they do not understand and clarifies any conceptual misunderstanding they have.

On this day, Mr. Peterson dedicates approximately eight minutes to meet with Betsy and Julián. He then checks in briefly with the team of four students who are discussing Reading Option 1 and the team of six students who are discussing Reading Option 3. He spends nearly 10 minutes with the team of 12 students who have selected Reading Option 2. On other days, more advanced or beginning readers may receive more of his time. Following an established routine, he makes announcements that 5 and 2 minutes are remaining before the collaborative team time elapses; he then brings the students together. Using the overhead projector, he explains that all the readings focused on four key concepts: (1) finite resources, (2) the growth in population, (3) increasing pollution, and (4) decreasing biodiversity. Students share key points from their team discussions.

Mr. Peterson then returns to the importance of considering all perspectives in any issue and illustrates specific examples from the readings where data are manipulated to support certain points of view. He explains the often political nature of environmental science reporting and the importance of informed decision making. He then asks students to refer to understandings gained in their reading to determine the plausible veracity of examples he provides, which include graphs, short statements from articles, and a video clip. He guides students through several examples. He then has the students work in heterogeneous groups of four to determine which examples appear to present a balanced account and which appear to skew data. He explains that there is no correct answer but students must explain, justify, and support their small-group decisions when they present these to the class at the end of the period.

LANGUAGE MINI LESSONS

Mr. Peterson regularly implements 10-minute vocabulary lessons similar to the one described in Lesson 2. He also regularly uses think-alouds to assist ELLs and others in using the structure of the textbook for comprehension, determining the meanings of unknown words from context, and deciding if unknown words in text are important to understanding. Additionally, he engages ELLs and other students in several language mini lessons to build comprehensibility of instruction and to deconstruct text. He frames mini lessons with his essential language questions *What's the point?* and *How do scientists communicate?*

setting like this, I can draw upon the ESOL strategies I have learned and my knowledge of teaching math, and ELLs make progress.

She adds that the first-language support remains very helpful.

Review, Reflect, Apply

1. *Review and reflect:* How does the setting in Ms. Bell's room foster educational opportunities for ELLs?

2. *Review and reflect:* Review Ms. Bell's classroom setting, materials, and reflections; reflect on the components a new teacher could implement immediately and which could be implemented during the first year, second year, and fifth year.

3. *Reflect:* Why has Ms. Bell struggled to teach beginner ELLs in her math class?

4. *Review:* What are some of the factors that influence Ms. Bell's effectiveness with beginner ELLs?

5. *Reflect and apply:* What factors would you consider if you were establishing a program for beginner ELLs? What resources would you need?

IMPLEMENTING THE PROBABILITY AND STATISTICS UNIT

This section begins with an overview of the key concepts that Ms. Bell has identified as necessary for meeting the learning outcomes and assessments she has outlined for this unit, and it illustrates the differentiated assessments rubrics that Ms. Bell has designed. Three content-area lesson narratives are then presented. Standard numbers (S4-a, S4-b, S6-a, etc.) are embedded within the first lesson narrative to illustrate how elements of Ms. Bell's instruction align with standards. Lesson 2 does not show standard numbers within the lesson narrative; the *Review, Reflect, Apply* that follows encourages readers to identify specific standards present within the lesson. A summary follows this activity to enable readers to self-assess their understanding. Next, a lesson that is differentiated for levels of language proficiency and conceptual understanding in mathematics is illustrated. The subsequent *Review, Reflect, Apply* encourages the reader to consider the advantages that differentiated lessons provide to ELLs and other students, as well as the planning and classroom management that are involved in such lessons. The section concludes with two language mini lessons.

Key Concepts and Essential Questions

The key concepts that Ms. Bell has identified for the "Probability and Statistics" unit are

- solve and explain the process of solving word problems for probability,
- predict the occurrence of an event based on knowledge of probability,
- create word problems that involve probability, and
- justify responses to a case study problem that requires using probability.

Ms. Bell created the unit on probability and statistics around the enduring understanding that *probability and statistics are everywhere.* Throughout this unit, she capitalizes on the diverse background experiences that ELLs and other students bring to the classroom. She strives to facilitate real-world connections between content-area concepts in ways that are meaningful to ELLs (S4-b) by contextualizing instruction (S4-a) and building on existing student schemata (S4-b).

Ms. Bell introduces this unit with the essential question, *What are the chances . . . ?* She refers to this essential question throughout the unit, and thus provides context, which improves content-area understanding and opportunities to talk math (S4-a, S7-d). Ms. Bell explains, "At the beginning of the unit, ELLs and other students relate to the question personally (S4-b); as the unit progresses they transition to relating to the question mathematically."

Building Self-Assessment Into Instruction

In the heading of each unit handout is the question, *What are the chances . . . ?* At the beginning of each unit, Ms. Bell gives students a checklist, which serves as an overview of the topics, learning outcomes, and assessments for that unit. As students progress through the unit, they are required to check off the sections they complete with a rating system: 3 = confident, 2 = somewhat confident, and 1 = not confident (S5-a). She ensures that beginner and early-intermediate ELLs understand the meaning of the rating system indicators by providing translated copies. (Each time a tutor with a new first language works in Ms. Bell's room, Ms. Bell asks for a translation of the indicators and keeps this on file.) She uses these self-assessments along with quizzes, tests, and observations of student work to design review lessons and to flexibly group students (S-5a). Regular self-assessments also encourage ELLs to analyze their understanding and to be prepared to discuss content-area and language questions or misunderstandings with Ms. Bell, the tutor, and the ESOL teacher (S6-a, S7-a, S8-a).

Along with this checklist, Ms. Bell hands out colored sheets of paper that include review problems, assessment descriptions, and assessment rubrics. From the start of the year, Ms. Bell color codes handouts, a routine that is predictable for students and assists them in self-organization (S6-a): "I am handing out the lavender paper for this unit now. Li, what is on this paper?" Li responds, without hesitation, "The purple paper says the final assessment, Miss." Once routines are firmly in place, Ms. Bell proceeds to explain the unit overview and the assessment options. Students are expected to file their assessment rubric in the two-pocket folder Ms. Bell requires them to maintain for each unit.

Assessment Options

Ms. Bell knows that her students differ from one another in terms of English language proficiency, cognitive development, and background knowledge. Keeping student differences in mind, Ms. Bell has compiled a selection of word problems for probability and statistics at various levels of difficulty. Each problem allows students to demonstrate mastery of the learning outcomes, yet at different levels. In thinking about content-area understanding, Ms. Bell knows that problems that are too difficult are likely to frustrate students and decrease motivation, whereas problems that are too easy do not encourage students to develop greater mathematical proficiency. Providing problems that are differentiated for level of difficulty enables all students to demonstrate their understanding and, at the same time, encourages them to work at the high end of their abilities (S5-a). Ms. Bell has separated word problems into three levels of mathematical difficulty. The problems are printed on laminated cards.

Ms. Bell knows that the language structure and vocabulary in word problems present difficulties for ELLs as well as for some native-English-speaking students. To ensure that limited language proficiency does not interfere with their ability to demonstrate content-area mastery (S5-a, S6-a), Ms. Bell has printed the original problem on the front of each card, and a highlighted, easified, and glossed (and sometimes translated) version on the back of each card. Prior to assigning this summative assessment, Ms. Bell has reviewed each problem to ensure that it is accessible to Silva (high-intermediate proficiency), Fredy and Leyla (intermediate proficiency), Madeline and Li (early-intermediate proficiency), and Trang (beginner proficiency) (S6-a). Table 11.2 shows the rubrics Ms. Bell has developed for differentiating assessments according to conceptual ability for Learning Outcome 1, "Explain the process of solving word problems for probability."

As illustrated in Table 11.2, Ms. Bell has established a tiered-mastery system (A, B, and C levels). Students who are not able to solve the most difficult problems still have the opportunity to demonstrate basic mastery of this learning outcome. Ms. Bell has made the language of each word problem in each box (A, B, and C) comprehensible to the ELLs in her classroom (S6-a), thus ensuring that English language proficiency does not interfere with ELLs' ability to solve the most difficult problems correctly (S5-a). Assessments are challenging and accessible. Providing ELLs and other students with descriptions of assessments at the beginning of the instructional unit creates a clear road map from learning outcomes to evidence of mastery (S4-a).

Ms. Bell conferences with ELLs, especially Trang, Madeline, and Li, throughout the instructional unit (S6-a, b; S7-a). This ensures that academic-language proficiency does not adversely affect their ability to access content or to demonstrate content-area mastery (S5-a). She also continues to conference with Trang's tutor and ESOL teacher.

ALIGNING LESSONS WITH TELLiM STANDARDS

The standard numbers (S4-a, S4-b, etc.) embedded in the narrative of Lesson 1 illustrate how Ms. Bell's lessons are aligned with the TELLiM model, which is shown in the checklist (Table 11.1). Readers are encouraged to identify TELLiM standards in Lesson 2.

TABLE 11.2 Assessment Options for Learning Outcome 1

Assessment 1: Solve two word problems for probability and two word problems for statistics. Explain your answers. Choose problems from Box A (least difficult), Box B (more difficult), Box C (most difficult). Break each word problem into smaller parts and express relationships in the language of mathematics using symbols and formulas. Accurately solve each problem, show all calculations, and label each answer.

Box A (Least Difficult)	Box B (More Difficult)	Box C (Most Difficult)
Possible 21 points per problem	Possible 23 points per problem	Possible 25 points per problem
Total possible points—84	Total possible points—92	Total possible points—100

Lesson 1: Probability—Theoretical Versus Experimental

(90 minutes)

In preparation for this lesson, Ms. Bell has written key vocabulary terms on strips of oak tag that she has backed with magnetic tape. Having the vocabulary strips accessible enables Ms. Bell to use these as she teaches, and then to add word strips to the class word wall. She has also brought several coins, black and white beans, a probability number line that spans 0 to 1, and a tally sheet for *heads* and *tails* outcomes. Ms. Bell begins by asking a student to read the lesson's content and language objectives (S5-b, c), which are printed on the easel. As each objective is read, Ms. Bell repeats and paraphrases key terms (S7-d). Ms. Bell also asks the volunteer to read the lesson's key vocabulary terms, including *predict, probability, outcome, theoretical,* and *experimental.* As each term is read, Ms. Bell places the magnetic word strip on the chalkboard, thus drawing ELLs' attention (orally and visually) to the term (S6-a, S7-d).

Content Objectives

- Students will apply their sense of number to make inferences about how probability is calculated.
- Students will predict the occurrence of an event based on their knowledge of probability.
- Students will compare the outcomes of theoretical and experimental probability experiments. (S5-b)

Language Objectives

- Students will use the language of probability to communicate relationships between given and unknown variables in problems.
- Students will communicate orally and in journals using key content terms. (S5-c)

Ms. Bell explains the agenda, which lists the steps the class will take to meet the lesson's objectives:

1. Discuss *What does it mean to be lucky?*

2. Perform the coin experiment

3. Discuss theoretical versus experimental probability

4. Activity with the chance bag

5. *What are the chances . . . ?* (Total Physical Response)

6. Return to the coin experiment (Web site)

7. Use the formula

8. Journal prompt: *Are games fair?*

On this day, she provides wait time to ensure that Trang understands (S6-b).

Ms. Bell introduces the lesson with a discussion about a topic she believes is familiar to her eighth-grade students: luck (S4-b). In groups of four, students discuss two questions that

Ms. Bell has written on the chalkboard: *What does it mean to be lucky?* and *When have you been lucky?* As Ms. Bell circulates, she hears students sharing accounts of being lucky. Alec, a native-English-speaking student, shares that he was lucky when he won basketball tickets in the school raffle. Leyla, an intermediate-level ELL in Alec's group, who was quiet at first, seems to gain some confidence and contributes, "In Lebanon my family always played Tarneeb, a game of cards. I am lucky in this game." Trang's tutor explains and he nods enthusiastically but remains quiet. Ms. Bell finds that small-group discussions paired with activating questions allow ELLs and other students to bring their own experiences into the math classroom and enable ELLs to build comprehension by listening to the responses of their peers (S4-b, S7-b).

After five minutes of discussion, Ms. Bell gives the class a signal to come together. Students recognize this familiar signal and immediately finish their conversations and refocus their attention on Ms. Bell. Summarizing the responses from the small groups, Ms. Bell points out that everyone could identify with being lucky. With this, she segues into the lesson topic. She asks,

> What would you say if I told you that your chances of winning a raffle, rolling the right number on a die, or having the spinner stop on the right spot had nothing to do with luck and everything to do with chance?

As Ms. Bell speaks the word *chance*, she picks up her magnetic vocabulary strip with the word *chance* and places it on the board (S6-b, S7-d). She then introduces the unit's essential question *What are the chances . . . ?* and writes it on the blank easel to the right of the chalkboard (S4-a).

"What are the chances that you will come up with heads or tails when flipping a coin?" Ms. Bell asks the class. Noting that Li has furrowed her brow at the question, Ms. Bell shows her a coin and adds, "Remember, heads are the side with the person on it and tails are the other side." Li seems to relax; Ms. Bell has noted her confusion (S5-a) and has provided clarification using the coin (S6-b). Ms. Bell looks to Trang and his tutor to check whether he understands. One student responds, "I think you have a 50:50 chance, right?" With that, Ms. Bell writes $50\% = \frac{50}{100} = \frac{1}{2}$ on the board, and checks for understanding. Once she is certain that ELLs and other students understand, she continues. "Yes," she responds. "We can say that, in *theory* (points to the word *theoretical* on the board), you have a 1 out of 2 chance to come up with heads." As Ms. Bell speaks, she points to each part of the number expression (S6-b) and tells her students, "Now, turn to your table partner and let's see what you come up with in a short *experiment*" (points to the word *experimental* on the board) (S6-b, S7-d). Ms. Bell hands each pair of students a coin and data sheets and instructs them to flip the coin 50 times and tally count the outcome of each trial (S7-b, S8-b). Trang works with Danny, a native-English speaker; for half the activity, Trang tosses and Danny records, then they switch roles. Trang is on task and engaged in the activity. Many students are surprised at the results. "I think the tails won!" exclaims Justin, Madeline's partner. "We have way more tails than heads." Using the overhead , Ms. Bell records each team's data. "How many heads did you and Justin flip, Madeline?" Madeline responds, "Only 18." "Okay," replies Ms. Bell, "so you have 18 heads out of 50 *trials*?" She writes $\frac{18}{20}$ on the overhead and holds up her oak tag strip of the word *trials*. Madeline nods her head and repeats, "We have 18 heads out of 50 trials." Ms. Bell continues collecting class data in this way, encouraging students to report their findings with the modeled language structures (S7-c, d; S8-b,). When she comes to Trang and Danny, they confer softly (S8-b), and Danny reports out. Ms. Bell has observed Trang during the activity and his interaction with Danny indicates that he understands (S5-a). She does not require him to speak.

Next, Ms. Bell asks students to compare the theoretical probability (50% $=\frac{50}{100}=\frac{1}{2}$) with the experimental probability of their actual coin flips. Most students express disappointment that their coin didn't land on heads 25 times. (Later, Ms. Bell adds the tallies of heads and tails for each of her four classes, and guides the students to understand that the more actual flips, the closer the results are likely to be to the theoretical probability.) Building on the contrast between their experience and the theory, Ms. Bell begins a discussion of theoretical and experimental probability. In the past, Ms. Bell had always defined the two terms for students, but building from a common experience, she notes, lays the groundwork for comprehending the sophisticated terms. "Let's talk a little more about *theoretical probability*," Ms. Bell says (S4-a; S7-a, c; S8-a, b).

Ms. Bell asks the class, "If a coin has two *possible outcomes*, heads or tails, how many *possible outcomes* are there that I will draw each of the letters in the word *probability*?" She puts the words *possible* and *outcomes* on the board and then takes a strip of oak tag and cuts the letters *P-R-O-B-A-B-I-L-I-T-Y* into individual letters. She places the letters into the "chance bag," a paper bag she has colorfully labeled with question marks, fractions, percents, and words related to probability, as students count each letter (11 in total). At their desks students write the word and count the number of each letter: 1 *P*, 1 *R*, 1 *O*, 2 *B*s, 1 *A* 2 *I*s, 1 *L*, 1 *T*, 1 *Y* (S8-b).

As she continues, Ms. Bell selects her words with great care; while her choice of words may seem unplanned to her students, she has carefully examined texts, word problems, and standardized tests to determine the words and phrases with which her students must develop familiarity and understanding, and she uses those deliberately (S7-d). "What are the *chances* that I will draw the letter *P* from the chance bag?" she asks. Students confer with their partners. Each student is handed a sheet to fill in. *The chances of _____ are _____ out of _____* is repeated down the length of the sheet. Madeline, carefully reading her sheet, responds, "The chances of *drawing a P* are *1* out of *11*." (Madeline relied on the sheet to scaffold her response; she rehearsed with her native-English-speaking partner, who clarified for her the word *draw*, which she only understood by its other, artistic definition.) (S6-a; S7-a, d; S8-b)

Ms. Bell rephrases, pointing each time at the magnetic word strips she has placed on the board. "So, Madeline, what you are saying is that out of the 11 *possible outcomes* [points], there is 1 *chance* [points] that we will select the letter *P*?" "Yes, miss." Ms. Bell then writes $\frac{1}{11}$ as she says, "So that is 1 *out of* 11." Pointing to the fraction on the board, she asks, "Are these chances *good*?" "No way!" replies one student. "Well," says another, "they're the same as every other letter." Students debate this point, and Ms. Bell quickly assesses their understanding (S5-a, S7-c).

"OK, then, I have another example for you. What are the chances of drawing the letter *I*?" she asks. Ms. Bell circulates as students turn again to their partners (S7-b). She is able to see that Leyla and Madeline have finished quickly and confidently but incorrectly, writing "1 out of 11," failing to notice the two *I*s in the word *probability* (S5-a). As the other students work, she is able to kneel down next to Leyla and Madeline and ask guiding questions: "So you have one chance to draw a *P*, right?" They agree. "Good. And how many chances do you have to draw an *I*? Let's look back at the word." "Oh!" Leyla exclaims, "there are two *I*s! So does that mean that there are two *chances*?" By structuring her class as she does, Ms. Bell encourages opportunities for students to interact and discover patterns while using structured, well-supported academic language. This organization also enables Ms. Bell to continually assess student understanding and address comprehension issues as they arise (S5-a; S7-a-d).

Ms. Bell then returns the group's attention to the front board, where she repeats her summary for the letter *I*. She writes the fraction $\frac{2}{11}$ as she repeats, "There are 2 chances to draw an

I out of 11 possible outcomes." The class repeats. Ms. Bell then asks the class what they notice about these numbers $\frac{1}{11}$ and $\frac{2}{11}$. Several students respond that these are fractions. Ms. Bell reminds the class that fractions are division problems, thus reinforcing the students' sense of number, a cornerstone understanding of mathematics and an area that Ms. Bell is committed to developing with her students. "How can we read this fraction?" Ms. Bell asks. Students recall the fractions language mini lesson from earlier in the year and volunteer: "1 over 11", "1 divided by 11", "1 out of 11", and "one eleventh." Ms. Bell writes their responses on the board. She points to "1 divided by 11," and asks the students to calculate the answer. Once she verifies that students have correctly performed the calculation, she writes .09 on the board and asks, "Is .09 more or less than 0?"

"More," the class responds in unison.

"Is it more or less than 1?" Ms. Bell asks.

"Less."

"Yes," reinforces Ms. Bell. "Probability is always a number from 0 to 1. Now do you think the probability of drawing an *I*, which we know is $\frac{2}{11}$, will be greater or less than .09?"

Students confer with members of their groups to make predictions. Ms. Bell overhears Madeline say to her team, "I think greater because you have more *I*s." "Yes," responds her teammate Michael, "and we also know that $\frac{2}{11}$ is greater than $\frac{1}{11}$. They have the same denominator so we can compare them easily." The teams are then encouraged to check their assumptions with their calculators. Students in each heterogeneous group benefit from explaining their reasoning with others and hearing each other's reasoning (S7-b, c).

For the next activity, Ms. Bell distributes an annotated number line ranging from 0 to 1 (as is shown in Figure 11.1) to each student.

Ms. Bell then engages students in a Total Physical Response (TPR) activity (Asher, 1965), which can be used to assess content-area understanding apart from English language proficiency. In this TPR activity, ELLs and other students use a physical gesture (or gestures) to respond to a content question. In this case, Ms. Bell provides students with the annotated number line (Figure 11.1). Along the number line, Ms. Bell has added key vocabulary terms associated with each quantity (*impossible, chances are poor, chances are equal, chances are good,* and *certain*). Students are then given beans to place on their number lines to make predictions (S6-b, S7-d, S8-b).

Ms. Bell begins with examples that are familiar to students, asking, "What are the chances that you will do math today?" Most students put their bean directly on the number 1, noting its correspondence with the word *certain*. Ms. Bell notices that Leyla and Madeline both pause.

FIGURE 11.1 Annotated Number Line

0	.25	.50	.75	1

Impossible	Chances are poor	Chances are equal	Chances are good	Certain

She assesses that *certain* may not be a familiar term to the students and then adds, "Remember, if you are *certain* [places word strip on the board], you know for sure that it will happen (S5-a)." Both ELLs place their bean on the 1, indicating to Ms. Bell that the paraphrasing was helpful to them. Ms. Bell continues with a list of questions, all repeating the same structure: *What are the chances that . . .*

- . . . you will do math today?
- . . . there will be a fire drill?
- . . . Ms. Bell will read today's agenda? (certain)
- . . . the cafeteria will serve ice cream sundaes for lunch today? (chances are poor)
- . . . it will snow today? (the chances are poor—it is May)

Ms. Bell circulates and informally observes students' responses. She watches as Trang places beans on the line correctly (S5-a, S6-a). The TPR activity provides a useful assessment of student understanding. Using situations that are familiar to students reinforces their understanding of the numerical representation of probability and of the academic language around the concept (S4-b).

Ms. Bell next asks students to return to their coin data sheets. On each two-desk grouping are two cups, one with white beans and the other with black beans. Ms. Bell instructs students: "Working with the person next to you, place a black bean on the theoretical probability of a coin landing on heads." Ms. Bell provides time for students to place the black bean and circulates to make sure they have done so correctly. "Now," Ms. Bell continues, "put a white bean on the actual (experimental) outcome from your experiment with your partner. If it helps, you may convert your fraction to a decimal. For example, you tossed the coin 50 times, and theoretically, the coin should have landed on heads. . .?"

A group of students respond, "25 times."

Ms. Bell writes on the board as she explains, "Yes, 25 outcomes of heads of 50 possible outcomes, or $\frac{25}{50}$. We can express probability as the fraction $\frac{25}{50}$. Can we simplify this expression?" Students work in pairs to simply the fraction: $\frac{25}{50} = \frac{1}{2}$. Ms. Bell checks for understanding and then writes the equation on the board. She then asks how many students remember how to convert $\frac{1}{2}$ to a decimal. She models this process for students and then circulates to check for understanding. She continues, "First, I want you to express the number of times your coin landed on heads as a fraction: the number of outcomes over the number of possible outcomes." She guides students to understand that the number of possible outcomes is 50 and then has students refer to their tallies to determine the number of actual outcomes. In pairs, students express their outcomes as fractions, simplify the fractions, and then convert the simplified fractions to decimals, which they plot on the number line. Ms. Bell circulates throughout the room to ensure that each pair understands the processes. She then asks students to report out and shows the results on an overhead of the same number line (S5-a).

Using the classroom computer, Ms. Bell connects to the Internet and projects a virtual-coin-flip Web site (www.betweenwaters.com/probab/flip/coinmainD.html), which records the result of every coin-flip trial at its site. At the time of her class, the site had recorded 750336732/1500795971 (heads) and 750459239/1500795971 (tails). With calculators, the students convert to decimals: .50004 and .49996, respectively. Ms. Bell allows her students to make a virtual coin flip, adding to the site's data, and then probes the class for conclusions about what happens with more trials. At their tables, students discuss their observations of how experimental probability approaches theoretical probability with more trials.

Ms. Bell strongly believes in providing her students with a math experience that provides context for concepts before students begin to work with the textbook. While she understands the importance of teaching students to access information in textbooks, she has found that her students, ELLs and native-English speakers alike, benefit from contextualizing the text early in the lesson and building from the comprehensible hands-on experiences described earlier in this lesson (S4-a, S6-b). Once Ms. Bell is convinced that students are familiar with the concept of probability, she directs them to open their textbooks, where they will find the formal definition and formula. Together, the class reads through a problem involving coin tosses. Ms. Bell displays a copy of the problem on the overhead. What might have been overwhelming to Madeline is clarified as Ms. Bell reminds students of the similarity between the solution for this problem and the solutions they have already calculated. Ms. Bell models a few problems, guiding the students through the correct placement of numbers into the formula. She leaves time for independent practice and circulates to assess understanding and answer any questions that arise as students work on the word problems (S5-a). She assigns similar problems for practice at home reminding students that they have sample problems to refer to if they become confused. Students know the routine: If they don't understand or if they become stuck on a problem, they must list what they understand, what they tried, and where they became confused. This practice enables students to work through the problem-solving process and explain their thinking (S8-a).

Finally, as a summarizing activity, Ms. Bell displays various games on the front table— cards, dice, Mancala, and Cribbage (S6-a, b):

> Many of you mentioned games at the start of class when you thought about what it meant to be lucky. Leyla talked about a Lebanese card game called Tarneeb, and Ashleigh mentioned the game of Dominoes. Now, I want you *all* to think about a game you know.

With that, she prompts the students to take out their journals and write for the last five minutes about the question *Are games fair?* "Think about the words and phrases we collected today: *probability, chances, possible outcomes. . .*" Ms. Bell motions to the collection on the board. Quietly, the students begin to write. Madeline sometimes includes Spanish words in her writing. Because Ms. Bell uses journals to help students process information and understands the developmental nature of language acquisition, she encourages students to use their native languages. She had recently read an article by a math teacher in California (Winsor, 2007), who offers his students the opportunity to write in their native language. Ms. Bell offers this same opportunity to her students, but requires that key vocabulary is written in English (S7-d; S8-a,b). Ms. Bell also encourages the use of interlanguage. Madeline's journal, for example, reads,

> In my Perú *jugamos al Perudo*. Is a game of the dice. For to play you has to *predict* how many numbers in the table have. You no see the other persons dice. If you know the *probability*, you know more información, so I think no is fair. If you know the *probability* you know the *chances are*. You can to know how many *specific outcomes out of possible outcomes*. If you no know this, you no win. So it is no fair to another person.

As Madeline's journal indicates, although she has not fully developed academic-English proficiency, she demonstrates conceptual understanding and can express this understanding in a combination of English and Spanish. Using key vocabulary terms in context reinforces

Madeline's understanding of these terms and the concept of probability. After conferring with the tutor (S6-b), Trang writes his response mostly in Vietnamese with the exception of the words *probability* and *chances*, which he copies in English.

Lesson 2: Untangling Probability Word Problems

(Standard numbers are not embedded in this lesson.)
(60 minutes)

In the previous lesson, classroom-specific standards were embedded to illustrate how Ms. Bell's instruction was aligned with the TELLiM model. It is recommended that, while reading through Lesson 2, readers identify the TELLiM standards present in the lesson.

Content Objectives

- Students will distinguish between theoretical and experimental probability.
- Students will use a formula to calculate the probability of an event.
- Students will brainstorm applications of probability in their lives and in the real world.

Language Objectives

- Students will use academic vocabulary to explain the process of solving word problems.
- Students will recognize key content language to understand the relationships between the known and unknown information when solving problems.

To begin this lesson, Ms. Bell follows the established routine for communicating the objectives and agenda to students. She then reviews the journal exercise (*Are games fair?*) that concluded the previous lesson. She does this with the essential question: *What are the chances... that you have the same opinion as your partner?* ELLs and other students volunteer responses to this question. "I don't know what my partner, Amy, will say, but I know there are only two opinions," responds Amanda, a native-English-speaking student. Ms. Bell makes the students focus on the academic language by adding, "So you are saying, Amanda, that there are two possible outcomes?" Amanda nods her head.

With a quick glance around the room, Ms. Bell notices that Madeline is pointing to her probability number line, her finger near .50. Ms. Bell encourages Madeline to tell why she came up with this answer. As Madeline does so, Ms. Bell consciously affords her more wait time than she is accustomed to giving to other students. She is aware of Madeline's affective filter and gives her sufficient time to process the content and language. After a long pause, during which Ms. Bell can see that Madeline is thinking, Madeline responds, "You have two answers, fair or not fair." "Yes," replies Ms. Bell, rephrasing, "there are two possible outcomes." Madeline continues, "Fair is one outcome out of two possible outcomes." Ms. Bell is assured of Madeline's content-area comprehension, and also notes that she has appropriately used the key words for probability in her explanation. Ms. Bell then asked the students to share their journal entries with their partner. This opening exercise allowed students to review and share their feelings around the question *Are games fair?* while building in the new language of *What are the chances...?* After sharing their entries, the students tested the theoretical probability that they shared opinions.

Next, Ms. Bell engages students in a variation of a Think-Pair-Share activity. She asks students to spend one minute reviewing their journal and two minutes sharing their thoughts with the classmate at the desk across from them. "Listen to your partner carefully because I am going to ask you to summarize your partner's opinion," she explains. The students quickly get to work, following a routine with which they are clearly familiar. This Think-Pair-Share activity allows ELLs time to rehearse and practice the language of their responses with a peer. Additionally, ELLs benefit from hearing their own thoughts expressed in the words of their partner. Trang again works with Danny. He nods as Danny speaks and shows him words. He begins to explain his opinion in a combination of gestures and words yet appears very frustrated when he cannot express himself accurately. Trang searches his bilingual dictionary until he can find the word *cheat*, which he shows Danny, who pronounces the word for him and clarifies, "You mean that people can cheat easily in this game?" Trang nods and smiles.

At this point in class, Ms. Bell regroups students into same-language groups so that students can use their first languages to interpret the language of mathematics. The Spanish speaking students (Madeline, Fredy, and a former ELL named Cristina) are assigned to the Archimedes table. While Cristina has a very high level of English language proficiency, she takes advantage of opportunities to reinforce concepts in Spanish. Additionally, she is able to explain concepts to the rest of the group, which, in turn, reinforces her own understanding. Leyla and a former ELL named Dominique, speakers of Arabic and French, work together at the Fibonacci table. Trang, who is the only Vietnamese speaker in the class, sits in a group with three native-English speakers. He listens as they speak. Ms. Bell hands each student a graphic organizer: a concept map with the word *probability* in the center circle. She asks the students to brainstorm all the key words or phrases that they connect with probability. Using notes, the word wall (Ms. Bell transferred her magnetic word strips to the word wall at the end of the previous lesson), their number lines, and the textbook, ELLs and other students work together to recall key vocabulary, such as *outcome, predict, chances, fraction, percent, zero, one,* and *experimental.* Cristina borrows one of the math glossaries to clarify a term in Spanish for her group. As a whole-group activity, Ms. Bell then consolidates students' work on a graphic organizer she projects on the overhead. She adds any missing key words that she wants student to be aware of and clarifies each term. After discussing terms and clarifying confusion, Ms. Bell transitions to the next activity.

She posts a set of data, a tally chart recording the number of times a cat chose to drink water out of a red bowl, a blue bowl, or a green bowl. Reminding students of their coin toss experience, she asks them whether these data represent experimental or theoretical probability. Because they are able to make connections to the experiment, students quickly identify the data as experimental. Ms. Bell continues to review the concepts and arithmetic of theoretical and experimental probability and uses a thumbs-up/thumbs-down to check for understanding.

After this review, Ms. Bell asks students to turn to their textbooks and look at a probability word problem. She then walks the students through a think-aloud during which she models the process for solving a word problem. She begins with an essential language question: *How do I know what the problem asks?* "Hmmm," she says, "There are a *lot* of words here. The first thing I think I'll do is find the key words that I know have to do with probability." With that, Ms. Bell takes an orange highlighter to the transparency on the overhead projector and highlights the words *what are the chances, select,* and *percent.* Ms. Bell continues in this fashion, talking out each step, demonstrating how she determines the conceptual relationships between known numbers and variables. The think-aloud focuses students on the specific strategies used in solving problems of probability.

After the think-aloud, Ms. Bell gives students word problems from the collection of differentiated index card problems she has collected. Students practice each problem in small groups, selecting and highlighting key words, noting the relationship between the numbers provided and the unknown variables, and then writing the steps required to solve the problem. During this time, Ms. Bell circulates, stopping to work with each group to assess their problem solving and ask directed questions about the processes they are using. If one group requires additional explanation or a second walk-through, Ms. Bell knows that the other students are well occupied with problems that are challenging yet attainable.

With a ring of the bell that Ms. Bell uses to get students' attention, she indicates that it is time for students to return to their team tables (the heterogeneous groups that she established at the start of the unit). With the last 10 minutes of class, Ms. Bell asks students to take out their final project descriptions. Knowing that the final project has been printed on lavender paper enables students to locate the assessment quickly without wasting class time. Ms. Bell calls students attention to one assessment activity (from Chapter 7): "In your small group, create one 'real-life probability' problem. Present this problem to the class. Solve your problem and create a separate answer sheet explaining each step necessary to solve the problem correctly." Ms. Bell explains the process each group will follow to design their own word problems and reminds students that they will find examples of real-life word problems in their textbooks and review handouts. She then clarifies any questions students have about this section of the assessment. During the last few minutes of class, students work in their groups to brainstorm ideas for the word problems they will create. Students will work on these problems throughout the unit, but Ms. Bell chooses to introduce this assessment at this point to get ELLs and other students to generate ideas about probability outside the classroom. She seeks to build on students' funds of knowledge by allowing them to contribute instances of probability in different real-world scenarios. As students begin to brainstorm their real-world experiences with probability, Leyla excitedly calls out,

> Ms. Bell! I think about how much we see this all the time now. My mom always says, when we're waiting for a bus and see one coming, we have a 33% chance that this one is ours. She knows three buses stop there! Now that makes sense to me.

Ms. Bell works with ELLs and other students to enable them to develop an enduring understanding of probability and its presence in their lives. She explains,

> This way, students not only make connections to the relevance of the topic, but their existing schemata for the familiar situation (such as probability at the bus stop) deepens their understanding. Like learning new words, once you begin to make connections between words, your vocabulary grows more quickly.

Before leaving class, each group submits a slip of paper with their brainstormed ideas, which provides a means for Ms. Bell to assess understanding.

Review, Reflect, Apply

Review and apply: Review Lesson 1 and reflect on how Ms. Bell aligns her instruction with the standards. Apply your knowledge of aligning lessons with standards using Table 11.1 on Lesson 2. Then explain how Lesson 2 is aligned with the standards.

Summary

Table 11.3 shows how some key elements in the Lesson 2 narrative align with the standards. As one can see, some elements of the lesson are consistent with several standards.

TABLE 11.3 Aligning Ms. Bell's Lesson 2

S4-a. Instruction is contextualized
Ms. Bell reads through a clear agenda with students. Ms. Bell encourages students to connect concepts to real-world situations.

S4-b. Instruction builds on ELLs' previous knowledge
Ms. Bell seeks input from students' personal experiences in the *create a problem* assignment.
Ms. Bell allows students to deepen their understanding of vocabulary through their knowledge of their first languages.

S5-a. Learning is assessed
Ms. Bell assesses student understanding by asking for quick self-assessments of understanding, circulating, listening to their conversations, and reviewing their problem solving.
Ms. Bell uses a thumbs-up/ thumbs-down check during the review.
Problem cards are differentiated, enabling each student to demonstrate mastery.

S5-b, c. Content-area and language objectives for the individual lesson
Ms. Bell posts these and reviews them with students.

S6-a. Materials are comprehensible to ELLs
Practice problems are differentiated by level of language load.
Students use the number line as they work through the problems.

S6-b. Presentational style is comprehensible to ELLs
Ms. Bell carefully explains content-specific language.
Ms. Bell uses visual tools (number line, graphic organizer, highlighting) and think-aloud modeling to present new information.

S7-a, b. Academic collaboration between ELLs, teachers, and/or other students is fostered
Ms. Bell groups students in pairs (Think-Pair-Share activity), in same-language groups for the keyword activity, and in heterogeneous groups (final assessment, *create a problem* activity). Additionally, Ms. Bell is available during group work to work alongside and guide students. (This is also consistent with S4-b; S5-a; S6-b; S7-c, d; and S8-b.)

S7-c. ELLs are engaged in planned, complex academic conversations about their content area
Students share and discuss their journals, problem-solving techniques, and ideas for real-life problems.

S7-d. The development of content-area English-language proficiency is supported
The academic conversations in which students rephrased each other's journal entries, the keyword brainstorming, and the problem-solving think-aloud encourage the development of content-area English-language proficiency.

S8-a. Complex content-area thinking skills are taught
Students are encouraged to apply learning to situations in their lives.
Students talk out the steps to solving problems.

S8-b. Time for ELLs to practice these skills in meaningful circumstances is provided
Students work in groups to create personally meaningful problems.

Lesson 3: Statistics—Graphical Representations (Stations)

Content Objectives

- Students will be able to select the correct graph for a particular set of data.
- Students will be able to interpret information from a graph using knowledge of graph type and data pattern.
- Students will recognize the ubiquitous nature of graphs in the real world.
- Students will use their understanding of graphs and probability to make predictions.

Language Objectives

- Students will be able to explain their reasoning for selecting a specific graph.
- Students will read vignettes and select appropriate information.

Ms. Bell begins this lesson by reviewing the agenda and the lesson's content and language objectives. During this lesson, students, who are already familiar with graphical representations of data from previous lessons, work at stations to practice (1) creating a graph for a set purpose, (2) making inferences about a graph's purpose, and (3) making predictions based on graph data. Ms. Bell often uses learning stations to (1) differentiate instruction, (2) refine student skills around a topic, (3) expand knowledge, and (4) address the multiple learning styles in her classroom.

She begins the lesson with a warm up: a PowerPoint slideshow, set to the song "What a Wonderful World" and featuring examples of graphs that exist in our daily lives. As the slideshow plays, the students view many examples of statistical representations, such as a bar graph from Ms. Bell's own electric bill, a business presentation with a circle graph summarizing the annual budget, and a scatter plot from a basketball fan's comparison of points scored by professional players to their salaries. Students are intrigued and urge Ms. Bell to pause at the scatter plot to see if basketball players are paid what they're worth. "You will all have the opportunity to work with these graphs," Ms. Bell reassures the students.

Ms. Bell has carefully divided the students into small groups to complete their learning stations for the day. This day, ELLs and others are grouped homogeneously (based on content, not language) for targeted instruction. Based on pre-assessments of class work, previous quizzes, homework, and students' self-assessments, Ms. Bell assigns each student to one of four stations:

Station 1: Focused instruction with Ms. Bell

At this station, Ms. Bell works with students to review instructions, address questions, and provide individualized attention. Ms. Bell has determined that Madeline and Li (ELLs with intermediate language proficiency) will participate in this station along with four of their classmates.

Station 2: Matching task

Trang, Silva, Cha, and Robbie, a native-English speaker, work at the interactive whiteboard for this hands-on matching station. Their task is to match the correct graph with its data set. With the technology of the interactive whiteboard, students are informed of errors and clues appear in the margins to help guide them to the correct answer. This station allows students to independently review and internalize concepts.

Station 3: Interpretation of a graph

Students at this station must use their understanding of a graph's purpose to interpret its significance. Students answer questions about the nature of the graph, the data represented on the graph, and what it communicates.

Station 4: Predictions

This station represents a synthesis of concepts. Employing higher-order thinking skills, students must look at the trends represented in graphs and make predictions to answer questions such as *What will Ms. Bell's electric bill be next month?* Additionally, students must explain their reasoning in writing to practice the skills of breaking down their thinking and of communicating with math language in an organized fashion.

Ms. Bell's expectations for students during stations are very clear. Early in the year, she spends substantial time explaining rules and procedures, which she reviews frequently. She models the process students follow at each station prior to assigning students to these stations. Therefore, ELLs and other students understand how to do the work at the station to which they are assigned. Ms. Bell has prepared reinforcement problems for the *I'm done* box in the event some students complete their work early. Ms. Bell recalls,

> It took time to develop the routines I was looking for within this structure, and I do believe that solid classroom management must be in place before attempting stations, but in the end the ability to individualize instruction that the stations model provides is invaluable.

LANGUAGE MINI LESSONS

Ms. Bell uses language mini lessons to reinforce the English language structures found in mathematics. She models the problem-solving process and keyword selection to address her essential language question, *How do I know what the problem asks?* Ms. Bell also provides students with opportunities to use language to explain their thinking, to work with peers, and to justify their answers in response to *How do you know that your answer makes sense?* (her second essential language question).

Mini Lesson 1: Vocabulary Development With the Frayer Model

Objective: Develop multidimensional understanding of key vocabulary
(Approximate time: 20 minutes)

Recognizing that vocabulary can be a great challenge for ELLs, Ms. Bell structures time into her units to focus on the development of academic vocabulary (mathematics terms and vocabulary from the AWL). Ms. Bell's students are all adept with the Frayer model, which is illustrated in Chapter 9. Today, they use the model to gain a deeper understanding of the words *theoretical* and *probability.* Ms. Bell allows students to work in same-language pairs and to use class glossaries to define terms in both English and their native language. Glossaries also help students find illustrations to complement their definitions and deepen understanding. Once students have a conceptual understanding of a term, they work to apply that understanding by completing the model. Working in heterogeneous (based on language proficiency) groups of four, ELLs and native-English speakers begin with the first word and write *probability.* Fredy, Karen, Cathy, and Madeline created the Model 11.1 for the term *probability.*

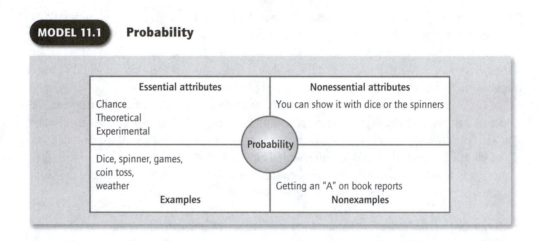

MODEL 11.1   **Probability**

Each team then presents the graphic organizer for its term to the class as a part of a vocabulary review. As teams of students discuss their model, they disagree about theoretical and experimental probability; a discussion ensues about whether both of these are essential attributes or if they should place both as nonessential attributes.

Mini Lesson 2: Math Talk

Objective: Develop recognition of math content-area language structures and collocations (Approximate time: 30 minutes, with 15-minute follow-up presentations)

Inspired by *Math Talk* (Pappas, 2002), a book that includes math poems for two voices, Ms. Bell teaches her students to consolidate key terms and phrases into spoken-word poems. She encourages students to determine common collocations to be included in the poems they create. During the probability unit, for example, students recognize that the word *chances,* for example, collocates with *are, good, bad,* and *what are the.* "I always see the word *outcomes,* with the words *different, possible,* and *how many,*" Madeline notes. Below is a poem, based on *Math Talk,* and written by Madeline and her native-English-speaking partner, Alec. Words on the same line are meant to be read together. Madeline speaks first, and then Alec responds:

Madeline's Part	Alec's Part
Probability	Probability
The words makes us think of	
Chances	Predications
Likelihood	Odds
It may be	
Theoretical	Experimental

Ms. Bell has found that academic language is emphasized and enhanced through this Math Talk activity.

CHAPTER SUMMARY

In this chapter, Ms. Bell demonstrated how she builds content-area understanding and academic-language proficiency using strategies that are consistent with the TELLiM model. Ms. Bell carefully differentiated her instructional activities, materials, and outcomes to provide meaningful and comprehensible instruction to learners at multiple levels of English language proficiency.

Assessment Evidence Activities

AE-1   Describe how Ms. Bell acknowledges and builds on students' funds of knowledge within their lessons. Provide specific examples.

AE-2   Explain the ways in which her lessons are consistent with the TELLiM model.

AE-3   Construct a T-chart illustrating the ways in which Ms. Bell's lessons are consistent with steps of the TELLiM model. The Classroom-specific Standards and the Lesson Planning Checklist are useful guides here.

AE-4   Explain how Ms. Bell's lessons build content-area knowledge and academic-language proficiency.

AE-5   Identify instances of differentiation in Ms. Bell's lessons. Explain the benefits of these instances and support your rationale with examples from the text.

AE-6   Explain how Ms. Bell assesses instruction and builds instruction based on assessment.

AE-7   Using the lesson checklist, create one new lesson for the content-area unit that you are developing.

Resource for Classroom Use

- The National Library for Virtual Manipulatives. http://nlvm.usu.edu/

Putting It Together in the History Classroom

IN CHAPTER 12, READERS ARE INVITED INTO MS. LINDA CHIN'S SECONDARY HISTORY CLASSROOM TO LEARN MORE about how she plans and implements effective instruction for ELLs. Although the snapshots are from a history class, Ms. Chin's classroom setting, the materials she uses, and the teaching strategies she employs transfer to other subjects and can be modified for use with middle and secondary school ELLs. Like previous *Putting It Together* chapters, this chapter begins with a tour of Ms. Chin's classroom, an overview of the materials she uses, and Ms. Chin's reflections on implementing the TELLiM model to provide effective instruction to ELLs (see Table 12.1). Ms. Chin then demonstrates how she differentiates a summative assessment and implements instruction for two content-area lessons and four language mini lessons.

Ms. Linda Chin is completing her fifth year teaching U.S. history. She has a bachelor's degree in history and a master's degree in education. For as long as Ms. Chin can remember, she has been fascinated with history, a fascination fostered by teachers in high school and college courses who made history come alive in their lessons. Ms. Chin decided that she wanted to be that type of teacher—one who inspires all students to approach history with a sense of curiosity and inquiry. She wants her students to understand connections between historical events and the larger social, economic, and political developments, and to consider past events through the various perspectives of those who lived them. During her masters in education degree program, Ms. Chin was fortunate to work with a faculty member who was a working historian with a passion for improving educational opportunities for students in urban school districts. This faculty member also had substantial experience working with ELLs in the classroom and preparing teachers to work effectively with this group of students. During her methods courses, Ms. Chin began to collect, create, and adapt grade-level materials that are comprehensible to ELLs at various proficiency levels.

TABLE 12.1   TELLiM Lesson Implementation Checklist

Standard	Description (and Evidence) of Standard					√
S4-a	Instruction is contextualized.					
S4-b	Instruction builds on ELLs' previous knowledge.					
S5-a	Learning is assessed appropriately.					
S5-b	Content-area objectives and assessments for individual lessons.					
S5-c	Language objectives and assessments for individual lessons.					
S6-a	Materials are comprehensible to ELLs. (Check each strategy used.)					
	Appropriate reading level	Glossed words	Outlines	Highlighted text	Explanations in margins	
	Audio Books	Clear organiztion	Other	Native language	Attention to vocabulary	
S6-b	Presentational style is comprehensible to ELLs. (Check each device that is used within the lesson to increase comprehensibility.)					
	Realia	Other visuals	Graphics organizers	Think-Pair-Share	Other comprehension checks	
	Simplified language	Clear routines	Other	Native language	Attention to vocabulary	
S7-a	ELLs/teachers are engaged in academic collaboration.					
S7-b	ELLs/students are engaged in academic collaboration.					
S7-c	ELLs are engaged in planned, complex, academic conversations about their content area.					
S7-d	The development of content-area English language proficiency is supported.					
S8-a	Complex content-area thinking skills are taught.					
S8-b	Time for ELLs to practice these skills in meaningful circumstances is provided.					

Ms. Chin currently teaches five sections of U.S. history. ELLs and native-English-speaking students have been placed in each section. The snapshots provided in this chapter are from Ms. Chin's fourth period class, which consists of 24 students: 18 native-English speakers and 6 ELLs. The ELLs have English language proficiency levels ranging from advanced-beginner to high-intermediate. Natka Jigovic, Katy Boureth, and Soan Meng are ELLs with intermediate proficiency levels whose profiles are included in the appendix of this text; Betsy Ruiz is an early-intermediate native-Spanish speaker; Mehmet Yilmaz is a native-Turkish speaker who has inter-mediate- to advanced-intermediate proficiency in English; and Tabib Aster is a native-Turkish speaker who has advanced-beginner English proficiency.

The TELLiM model standards are used to illustrate the ways in which Ms. Chin meets the needs of this diverse group of students. The numbers of the TELLiM lesson/classroom stan-dards (e.g., S4-a, b; S5-a, b, c) are embedded within the descriptions of Ms. Chin's classroom to illustrate how she plans for and implements each standard.

A TOUR OF MS. CHIN'S ROOM

The first thing that visitors to Ms. Chin's secondary history classroom are likely to notice is a row of books standing on display atop a long bookcase running the length of the windowed wall. The display is more reminiscent of a library reading area than a secondary classroom. A closer look at the titles reveals historical fiction such as *April Morning* (Fast, 1961), *The Fighting Ground* (Avi, 1984), *Johnny Tremain* (Forbes, 1943), *My Brother Sam Is Dead* (Collier & Collier, 1974), *Sarah Bishop* (O'Dell, 1980), and *Time Enough for Drums* (Rinaldi, 1986). These historical fiction selections range in reading level from early-fifth through eighth grade (S6-a). Next to each book are sign-up sheets for audio (all titles are available as unabridged audiobooks) and video versions (*April Morning* and *Johnny Tremain* are available on video) (S6-a). Providing audio and video access to quality historical fiction enables ELLs and native-English-speaking students, regardless of reading level, to access high-level content, which, in turn, stimulates thinking (S8-a) and promotes complex academic conversations with peers (S7-b, c). Five black file boxes, one for each of the five history classes that Ms. Chin teaches, sit on the end of the bookshelf closest to her desk. Within each file box is a portfolio folder, one for each student in the class, that is filled with both their completed work and work-in-progress. Each student portfolio has a cover sheet on which the student logs each assignment that she/he adds. At the top of each cover sheet are the *essential questions* that Ms. Chin has established for the U.S. history unit she is now teaching: "What is the difference between freedom and liberty?" "Is war inevitable?" "How does perspective affect the way history is told?" (S4-a).

On entering Ms. Chin's room, visitors notice the configuration of students' desks, which are arranged in groups of four. Ms. Chin moves around the room as she lectures, returning to the whiteboard at the front of the room to illustrate key points with diagrams and to call students' attention to elements in images or documents projected on the whiteboard (S6-b). "Students whose backs are facing the whiteboard simply turn their desks around for that part of the lecture," she explains. "Most of the time," she continues, "Students collaborate in small groups and I either move from group to group or call individual students to my desk to conference about their work (S7-a,b,c; S8-b)." All students benefit from academic conversations with their peers and with Ms. Chin. Tabib Aster often requires this time to confer with Mehmet, who explains concepts to him in Turkish. Furthermore, structured small-group collaboration and individual conferencing provides Tabib (and other ELLs) with time to practice their academic English (S7-a,b,c,d; S8-b).

Above the whiteboard are the essential questions that Ms. Chin has established for the American Revolution unit. She draws students' attention to these as she reviews lesson objectives and assessments at various times during each lesson (S4-a).

The wall opposite the windows is covered with (1) maps of North America during the time of the Revolution; (2) copies of documents such as the Declaration of Independence and the Bill of Rights; and (3) images of famous people such as Jefferson, Franklin, Paine, Revere, and Washington. A timeline helps students follow the progression of events leading to, through, and following the American Revolution (S4-a). A list of reliable Web sites, which provide students with images, audio files, and additional information, is posted next to the timeline (S6-a).

Three *word walls* cover the back wall of Ms. Chin's classroom. One word wall features terms specific to the current chapter that are necessary for all students to learn, such as *aristocracy, imperial, feudalism, individualism, intolerable, Parliament, representation,* and *taxation*. Another word wall holds (1) Academic Word List (AWL) words that are found in history readings, such as *advocate, amend, anticipate, arbitrary, authority, circumstance, contrary, convince, debate, establish, income, policy, principle, require, respond, strategy, sufficient, symbol,* and *unify*; (2) commonly used polysemous words that have different meanings when used in history, such as *cabinet, party, bank, branch,* and *stand*; and (3) affixes often found in history texts, such as *anti-, in-, un-, dis-, -ism, -tion, -ment, -ness, -less,* and *-al* (S7-d). The third word wall is filled with commonly misspelled words that Ms. Chin has reviewed in class and for which she holds all students accountable (S7-d).

Her American Revolution unit resource files are kept in a small file cabinet under the word walls and contain Ms. Chin's extensive collection of materials that have been made comprehensible to ELLs at various proficiency levels (and, therefore, to native-English-speaking students who have a range of reading levels). The collection includes many primary source documents which Ms. Chin views as seminal works in U.S history.

APPROPRIATE INSTRUCTIONAL MATERIALS

As mentioned, Ms. Chin has been collecting materials that are appropriate for ELLs since her master's degree program, and she continues to do so. Ms. Chin has glossed, highlighted, and easified passages in many primary source documents (S6-a). She has included these explanatory notes in the margins of seminal primary documents relevant to the U.S. history courses she teaches, such as the Declaration of Independence, the Northwest Ordinance, the U.S. Constitution, selected Federalist Papers, Lincoln's Gettysburg Address, and Lincoln's second inaugural address. Each document has a cover sheet that provides a summary in student-friendly language (S6-a).

Ms. Chin makes a large collection of historical fiction available to ELLs and other students. Studies have demonstrated the benefits of using historical fiction: They indicate that students believe historical fiction more than they do expository text, but that teachers must help students understand the context and perspectives in historical fiction (P. Fontaine, personal communication, August 1, 2007). Ms. Chin has accumulated a collection of audio- and videotapes to make historical fiction accessible to ELLs and to native-English-speaking students who struggle with reading. (S6-a, S8-a)

Ms. Chin also uses the Internet as a source of materials. She has found (1) user-friendly guidelines for using primary source documents, including how to find and evaluate primary sources, on the American Library Association Web site; (2) teacher and student-friendly worksheets to analyze primary source documents and photos on the National Archives Web site; (3) audio and video files of famous speeches on the Public Broadcasting System's Web site; and (4) the history of the American Revolution from multiple perspectives on the Web site AmericanRevolution.org (S4-a). (URLs for each of these Web sites are included in the resource section of this chapter.) Ms. Chin explains that the Internet is an excellent source for materials and activities that make history come alive and promote content-area thinking. She explains,

> When ELLs and other students can hear the words of Thomas Paine and read about the important roles that women played in the Revolution, and peruse diary excerpts and newspaper headlines from previous time periods, they are more likely to thoughtfully engage in history. (S4-a)

Ms. Chin explains that her class uses one of the school's computer labs approximately one period per week. Not all students have Internet access at home, so Ms. Chin also encourages students to use the computers in the school library after school and in the community library during the evening and on weekends. Translation software that enables ELLs to translate Web-based documents is available on the school server. While machine translations are imperfect, they provide greater access to materials for ELLs who are literate in their first languages (S6-a).

Ms. Chin has accumulated a large collection of videos produced by the History Channel. While she rarely shows an entire video, she often likes to begin class with scenes that provide context (S4-a) for the day's lesson. She also shows scenes that can enhance comprehensibility and make history come alive for ELLs and others (S6-a, b). One video series that she uses during the American Revolution unit is *The Revolution: America's Fight for Independence* (History Channel, n.d.).

Because Ms. Chin uses a variety of cooperative learning groups, she has materials that enable her to group students quickly, thereby maintaining lesson momentum and ensuring that instructional time is not lost. She uses playing cards to identify students who will be called on during Numbered Heads, and she has laminated role cards (*reporter, note taker, timekeeper,* and *moderator*) that she distributes to learning groups to facilitate participation in focused discussions (S7-c).

REFLECTIONS FROM MS. CHIN

Ms. Chin explains that she learned to plan instruction based on the enduring understandings in history during her masters in education program:

> One of the courses I completed was curriculum planning and it was based upon the principles of Understanding by Design (Wiggins & McTighe, 1998, 2005). I learned that beginning planning by identifying what all students (ELLs included) need to know, ensures the planning of high-level instruction, and framing content-area instruction with an *essential question* provides a contextual framework that motivates and benefits ELLs and other students in the class. Essential questions also make instruction relevant; questions like *Is war inevitable?* and *What should the role of government be?* are as relevant to ELLs and other students in my classes today as they were to young people during the Revolution. Many students, ELLs and native-English-speaking students alike, have family or friends who are serving in Iraq or Afghanistan, and have experienced the day-to-day changes caused by war. ELLs in our school system also come from countries that have been impacted by war. I am mindful of the possible increased sensitivity these ELLs may experience during class discussions. (S4-b)

Returning to the topic of essential questions, Ms. Chin explains that although she understands the power of essential questions to engage and motivate students, writing questions that both capture the essence of the enduring understanding and pique the interest of students is challenging. She continually rewrites and tweaks the essential questions in collaboration with colleagues in the history department until the questions get at the enduring understandings and engage students:

> I find that questions of perspective work well with this age-group. For example, *Who has rights to the land?* has been an effective question for framing instruction on Westward Expansion. This question encourages students to discuss Westward Expansion from multiple perspectives, which gets to another enduring understanding in history: the telling of history can be different depending upon the perspective of the author. All students need to understand that history is told by the victor. (S8-a)

When asked about the three word walls in her room, Ms. Chin responds that reading successfully in history depends on students' understanding of the vocabulary, which is very dense. According to Ms. Chin, she teaches terms and dedicates portions of each instructional unit to building vocabulary that will be useful to ELLs and other students throughout the history courses they will take (S7-d). The ELLs in Ms. Chin's class have ongoing exposure to all the AWL words that are found in their history text. She explains,

> My students have the opportunity to hear, see, and work with these words on a daily basis. They use them in academic conversation. They learn them. (S7-d, S8-b) Students also learn to spell commonly misspelled words such as *to*, *too*, and *two* correctly. It makes an important difference in their writing. (S7-d)

By providing ongoing time for focused student discussions, Ms. Chin reinforces one of the cornerstone enduring understandings of history: the importance of citizenship (Fontaine, personal communication, August 1, 2007).

Ms. Chin explains that she keeps "teacher talk to a minimum," and adds,

> I have arranged desks in the room in clusters to provide ELLs and other students with time to discuss concepts in class (S7-b, S8-b). I generally begin concept discussions in small groups to provide ELLs with the opportunity to practice language. (S7-b, c; S8-b)

Ms. Chin dedicates time at the beginning of each school year to discussing the value of group work and the strengths all students bring to the classroom. Ms. Chin discusses the benefits of bilingualism and biliteracy. She introduces the term *interlanguage* and describes the role it plays in language learning (S4-b). Ms. Chin explains,

> I have seen too many situations where teachers or students think that an ELL is being rude when she uses her first language. That's usually not the case. ELLs in my classroom are learning academic language and interlanguage plays a role in that process. (S4-b)

While Ms. Chin makes frequent use of student discussion groups, there are times when she does lecture. She explains that when she lectures she accompanies the lecture with visuals (S6-b), and she encourages students to use graphic organizers to help them process lecture content and organize this content for effective study (S4-a).

Ms. Chin attributes her vast collection of comprehensible materials to the influence of her history professor:

> My history methods professor had been a classroom teacher herself for many years. She helped me to understand that primary documents are very important. While these may be difficult reading for ELLs and other students, we, as teachers, must make some passages accessible. All students should see the Declaration of Independence and hear the richness of its language. In the margins or in an accompanying document, the teacher can unpack the passages that she feels are most important. (S6-a, S7-d, S8-a)

Like other teachers who work to make materials comprehensible through highlighting and glossing, Ms. Chin acknowledges that this is a time-consuming process. She focuses on making materials comprehensible for one unit each year. She explains,

If I commit to completing one instructional unit of four to six weeks for the year, the task does not seem overwhelming to me. I also collaborate with other history teachers and we share materials. As a result, after five years in the classroom, I have a fairly extensive collection of comprehensible materials. (S6-a)

IMPLEMENTING THE AMERICAN REVOLUTION UNIT

In earlier chapters, Ms. Chin has described how she determined the enduring understandings, learning outcomes, and essential questions for this unit on the American Revolution. She identifies content-area learning outcomes that remain the same for all students regardless of their English-language proficiency:

- Explain the different perspectives of citizens regarding the American Revolution.
- (While understanding that each experience is unique), discuss perspectives as they might apply to the experiences of subgroups (e.g., Native Americans, African Americans, women, members of upper and working classes) during that time period.
- Substantiate the position that the American Revolution was inevitable or that it was avoidable.

Ms. Chin next develops a variety of assessments from which students can choose to demonstrate mastery of the learning outcomes. For example, assessment options that she provides for the first learning outcome are as follows:

1. Choose at least four events leading up to the Revolutionary War and plot these on a timeline; prepare a four- to five-page essay comparing and contrasting each event from at least two perspectives.

2. Create a poster with a Venn diagram illustrating at least two perspectives on four major events leading to the Revolutionary War.

3. Adopt the role of one character (authentic or fictional) that will represent the perspectives of a particular group from revolutionary times. Prepare a PowerPoint presentation explaining your political views and the ways in which major events leading up to the war have affected your daily activities. Be sure to include a handout.

Each assessment requires students to demonstrate mastery of the first learning outcome. Option 1 requires substantial academic writing, Option 2 involves far less writing, and Option 3 requires academic speaking and bulleted writing in the form of a PowerPoint presentation and handout. Multiple options enable students to demonstrate content-area mastery apart from English proficiency and academic-language literacy (S5-a). One of Ms. Chin's goals is that all students complete her course more academically literate than when they began. For this reason, she provides students with different rubrics depending on their current academic-language abilities with the goal of building their academic-language skills.

Ms. Chin reviews the proficiency levels of each student: She accesses their cumulative folders at the beginning of the year but, as the year goes on, relies more heavily on the products within each student's portfolio. Her aim is to make summative assessments challenging, yet accessible. For example, Table 12.2 illustrates how Ms. Chin further differentiates the assessment option to "Create a poster with a Venn diagram illustrating at least two perspectives on four major events leading to the Revolutionary War" for different levels of language proficiency (S5-a, S7-d).

TABLE 12.2 Assessment Options: Poster

Proficiency	Rubric Variations	3	2	1	0	Comments
Native-English speaker at grade level	1. A paragraph describes each event					
	2. Two perspectives are provided for each event					
	3. Information is accurate and is supported by citations					
	4. Paragraph structure is logical and clear					
	5. Sentence structure is varied					
	6. Writing is without mechanical errors					
Transitioning intermediate	1–5 are same as above					
	6a. Correct use of capitalization					
	6b. Spelling of word wall words is correct					
	6c. Verb tenses are correct					
	6d. Sentence structure is correct					
Early intermediate	1. One to two sentences to describe each event					
	2. One to two sentences to describe perspectives for each event					
	3. Information is accurate					
	4. Structure of simple sentences is correct					
	5a. Correct use of capitalization					
	5b. Spelling of word wall words is correct					
	5c. Verb tenses in simple sentences are correct					
Advanced beginner[a]	1. A labeled visual image depicts each event					
	2. Two perspectives are explained with phrases					
	3. Information is accurate					
	4. Terms on word wall are spelled correctly					
Beginner[a]	1. Visual images and sentence strips are correctly positioned to label each event					
	2. Visual images are matched with sentence strips to illustrate each perspective					

NOTE: For each proficiency level, (a) the Venn diagram clearly illustrates two perspectives at four major events, (b) events are clearly labeled, (c) the Venn diagram illustrates similarities and differences for at least two perspectives for each event, and (d) perspectives are clearly labeled.

a. Assessment assumes that instruction has been made comprehensible through the services of a native-language tutor (teacher or peer) and/or ESOL support. Ms. Chin provides the ESOL teacher and native-language tutors with copies of the assessment options and the rubrics so they can support content-area learning (S7-d).

Once Ms. Chin has developed assessments, she considers the specific content-area objectives that students must master to successfully complete the assessment options. Although each assessment differs in its language requirements, all assessments require students to develop a clear understanding of the events that led to the Revolutionary War including the French and Indian War, the Sugar Act, the Stamp Act, the Townshend Acts, the Boston Massacre, the Boston

Tea Party, the Intolerable Acts, the First Continental Congress, Patrick Henry's speech, and Paine's "Common Sense." She teaches ELLs and others to consider the beliefs and political positions of various groups including Loyalists, Patriots, and Native Americans, as well as the beliefs that were influenced by geographical region, race, ethnicity, gender, and socioeconomic status (S8-a).

Ms. Chin develops the following content-area *lesson objectives*, which will lead to the mastery of unit learning outcomes:

1. Explain the political and economic factors that contributed to the Revolution.

2. Explain the development of individualism in the American Colonies.

3. Considering American individualism, interpret the reaction of colonists to Acts imposed without representation.

4. Explain the different perspectives of Native Americans, African Americans, and women.

5. Empathize with various identified perspectives.

6. Apply your understanding of the different perspectives to events leading up to the Revolution.

Ms. Chin has also established long-term English-language learning outcomes. She explains, "Making language learning outcomes visible keeps focus on academic-language goals." According to Ms. Chin, establishing grade-level language learning outcomes focuses students at various levels on the language abilities they must eventually develop. She explains how she establishes and uses language learning outcomes:

Language is developmental and ELLs will not be able to meet the established long-term language learning outcomes right away. I have students (ELLs and native-English speakers) who come to my course with reading levels that are several years behind grade level. The goal for all students is to improve throughout the year. To foster improvement, I establish overall language learning outcomes and use students' current language abilities to differentiate learning outcomes. (S5-a)

Ms. Chin identifies the following language learning outcomes for the unit:

1. Use the comprehension strategies necessary to access and deconstruct text in primary-source documents and historical novels (figure out vocabulary, use markers for tense and for change in topic/flow, and deconstruct clauses).

2. Activate the schemata and background knowledge necessary to make sense of the materials and classroom lectures.

3. Write papers and make presentations using grade-level content-area language.

4. Prepare presentations comparing and contrasting multiple perspectives regarding the American Revolution.

Ms. Chin makes the learning outcomes clear to all students and illustrates how she differentiates these language outcomes for Soan, an intermediate level ELL, from Cambodia:

1. Use comprehension strategies to analyze comprehensible primary source documents using primary source worksheets. Correctly use vocabulary terms and words that are on the word wall. (Ms. Chin will only grade Soan on words she has taught and the commonly misspelled words she has reviewed.) Correctly use the simple past tense in describing historical events (S5-a, S7-d).

2. Activate the schemata and background knowledge necessary to make sense of the materials and classroom lectures. (No changes to original learning outcome.) (S4-b).

3. Create a Venn diagram to show similarities and differences. Write topic sentences for the most important events and then list supporting details (S5-a, S8).

4. Prepare a poster presentation comparing and contrasting multiple perspectives regarding the American Revolution and explain it to your group (S7-b, c; S8-b).

Differentiating language learning outcomes that are appropriate for Soan's level of English proficiency and sharing these with him provides challenging yet attainable goals for language development in history. Unlike other classes—in which Soan is told, "Do the best you can" and is left to guess at how to do this—in Ms. Chin's class he knows exactly what he needs to do to demonstrate mastery. The learning outcomes that Ms. Chin has developed for Soan are also appropriate for Kathy, a native-English speaker who has an individualized education plan, and for Nadine, another native-English speaker who reads and writes several years below grade level. Providing students with challenging yet attainable learning outcomes serves to scaffold their academic-language development as well as their understanding of U.S. history. As students with alternate language learning outcomes improve, Ms. Chin is able to increase the language level of learning outcomes for subsequent instructional units. (S4-b, S5-a, S7-d).

Review, Reflect, Apply

1. *Review:* How does the setting in Ms. Chin's classroom foster educational opportunities for ELLs?

2. *Review and reflect*: Ms. Chin explains how she differentiates assessment evidence for content and learning outcomes for language. Review the differentiated assessments and reflect on how these improve academic opportunities for ELLs. Now review the differentiated language-learning outcomes. How do these serve to measure and scaffold language development?

3. *Apply:* Consider a summative assessment you have created for a content-area unit; decide if it sufficiently differentiates for English-proficiency levels and, if necessary, make appropriate adjustments.

ALIGNING LESSONS WITH TELLiM STANDARDS

This section presents two content-area lesson narratives. As in previous chapters, TELLiM standard numbers (S4, S5, S6, S7, S8) are embedded within the first narrative to illustrate how Ms. Chin's instruction is consistent with these standards. A *Review, Reflect, Apply* section encourages readers to identify specific standards in the second lesson. A completed chart follows this activity to enable readers to self-assess their understanding. The section concludes with four language mini lessons. (Ms. Chin has found the materials [and links] available to teachers through EDSITEment extremely valuable in teaching about the American Revolution as well as other core topics in U.S. history. A link to this source is provided in the resource section of this chapter.)

Ms. Chin's students have recently completed studying about the French and Indian War and the series of events leading to the Revolutionary War. They are also reading historical fiction selections. While some of this reading is completed at home, Ms. Chin also provides class time for independent and paired reading. During this time, students read, discuss their reading, and conference with Ms. Chin (S7-a, b, c). In conferences, Ms. Chin assesses and supports students' comprehension of the text as well as their ability to make connections between the historical fiction and their history lessons (S8-a; S5-a).

Lesson 1: The Influence of Common Sense

In Lesson 1, Ms. Chin prepares students to read *Common Sense* (Paine, 1776), which is considered a major turning point in the colonists' decision to declare independence from England. She has adapted "The Influence of Common Sense," a lesson (Barlowe, Gerwin, & Bender, 2007) that she found on the Web site, EDSITEment. As the lesson's authors recommend, Ms. Chin teaches this lesson over four 50-minute classes. Students are grouped heterogeneously (by language proficiency). ELLs work with native speakers and with other ELLs: Mehmet works in a group with Tabib and two native-English speakers; Betsy works in a group with Ana, an English-proficient student who speaks Spanish as a first language.

Content Objectives

- Identify important arguments for independence made in Paine's *Common Sense* and explain why these arguments helped persuade American colonists that independence was necessary.
- Describe the importance of *Common Sense* in the movement toward revolution.
- Define the role of Thomas Paine in the Revolution and describe the special skills that he brought to the work of the American Revolution. (S5-b)

(These three objectives are listed in the lesson by Barlowe et al., 2007.)

Language Objectives

- Engage in academic discussions about Thomas Paine's *Common Sense*.
- Use academic writing to explain why Paine's writing is important.
- Explain the meaning of key phrases in *Common Sense*. (S5-c)

Ms. Chin begins the lesson by reading through each content and language objective as she points to it on the board to ensure that ELLs and other students will know what they are to learn as a result of the lesson (S4-a). She then reads through the agenda for the day's lesson, which is posted on large chart paper: (1) Analyzing the quote—Numbered Heads, (2) Jigsaw—*Elementary Common Sense of Thomas Paine* (Wilensky, 2005) (S4-a). Ms. Chin has used both Numbered Heads and Jigsaw activities with her class many times, so students are familiar with the routines for working in these groups (S6-b). Today she explains, "Please count off in groups while I write the quote on the board." She writes, "The pen is mightier than the sword" and turns to students. "Ready?" she asks. She pauses to ensure that the students are ready to move forward. She then explains, "I want you to work in your groups to make sure that each of you understands this quote. You have three minutes to make sure that each of you is ready to explain the quote. Go" (S7-b, c).

ELLs and others engage in small-group discussions (S7-b). Some students take notes while others simply converse. Ms. Chin gives students a reminder when 30 seconds remain. She tells students when it is time to stop and randomly picks a card from the modified deck of playing cards (Ace through 4). She holds up the three of spades, indicating that the number 3 student in each group is responsible for reporting out. Jenny, a native-English speaker begins, "It means that words have the power to influence more people than violence does." Katy is next to report out and is slow to begin: "I don't know. . . " Katy pauses. Ms. Chin allows wait time for Katy to process the language (S7-d). Katy continues, "We all said it was like what we learned last year about Martin Luther King. His speeches were powerful." Ms. Chin nods and clarifies, "So he was able to influence people with written speeches?" Katy nods, "Yes." "Katy, I'm not sure if everyone heard me," Ms. Chin says. "Could you tell the others what I said?" Katy smiles and tells the larger group, "Martin Luther King had influence with his words" (S7-d). Next Minda, a native-English speaker, reports, "We agree with what others are saying. Words have great power to influence." Ms. Chin asks if any group had discussed anything different and checks for understanding before moving on (S5-a).

Ms. Chin then projects an image of Thomas Paine and tells the class,

> Today we are going to read the words of Thomas Paine. He was an immigrant to the United States and his words had great influence on the colonists. We will read his original speech together tomorrow. First, I would like you to read about his speech, which will make it more understandable. We will do this using a jigsaw.

Ms. Chin has divided Wilensky's (2005) 100-page adaptation of *Common Sense* into six fairly equal sections. The book defines key terms and illustrates key points with very engaging student-friendly drawings (S6-a).

Students read through their sections independently. Some students finish early and have time to read their historical novels. (The time Ms. Chin has spent on teaching students to work in groups ensures that students follow routines. They know what they should do if they complete their task early.) Once Ms. Chin is certain that all students have read through their sections, she brings together students who have read the same sections for discussion. Here students have the opportunity to explain, check, and refine their understanding of the selection they have read (S7-b, d). Soan is in group one. He understands much of what he has read but is unsure of some of the vocabulary. Soan knows that tomorrow he will need to explain his section to other students who have not read it, so it is important to check his understanding (S7-c, d). Discussing the section with others who have read it and listening to their interpretations makes the section clear to him (S7-b, c; S8-a, b). With five minutes remaining in the period, Ms. Chin explains,

> Tomorrow we will put Thomas Paine's speech together. You will return to your original groups and teach the section you have read to others. Right now I want you to take an index card and write the most important thing you learned about your section as a ticket-to-leave. (S5-a)

The following day students return to their original mixed groups to teach their sections to others, which serves to engage ELLs and native-English speakers in purposeful academic discussion (S7-b, c, d; S8-a, b). As students discuss the various sections of Paine's writings, Ms. Chin circulates to assess their content-area understanding and use of academic language as well as to clarify confusions (S5-a, S7-a).

Later, Ms. Chin provides students with a copy of selected excerpts from "Common Sense," which she also projects on the whiteboard. She explains to students that they will read this together in a large group much like the original might have been read in a coffee house, tavern, or meeting place in colonial times and then proceeds to read Paine's words with expression (S6-a). Following Ms. Chin's reading, students work together in heterogeneous groups to complete the question worksheet that accompanies the lesson (S7-b, c; S8-a, b). Here, they must explain the meaning of selected excerpts. Ms. Chin circulates to informally assess students' academic collaboration and conversations (S5-a) and to join in discussions as appropriate (S7-a). Student groups report their interpretations of passages to the large group (S7-b, c; S8-a, b). Ms. Chin provides students time to make adjustments to their worksheets based on the interpretations of others (S8-b).

Lesson 2: *Choosing Sides—The Native Americans' Role in the American Revolution*

(Readers are encouraged to match TELLiM standards with lesson activities as they read through this lesson; a *Review, Reflect, Apply* activity will follow.)

Multiple perspectives are an enduring understanding in Ms. Chin's unit, and she has found and adapted a lesson that is effective in helping students explore multiple perspectives, *Choosing Sides: The Native Americans' Role in the American Revolution* (Mehr & Jaffee, 2007). The learning objectives described in the lesson are consistent with Ms. Chin's content-area learning objectives; the resources provided in the lesson, including graphic organizers, maps, primary source documents, and links, make history come alive for students, and save Ms. Chin valuable time. Ms. Chin has used glossing and easification to make the most salient primary source documents accessible to ELLs and other students who need additional support with text.

Students work in heterogeneous groups throughout this lesson, and ELLs work in groups with native-English-speaking students. Ms. Chin has purposefully placed Mehmet and Tabib together in a group.

Content Objectives

- Describe the different positions and perspectives of different Native American nations during the American Revolution.
- Explain the issues involved for Native Americans in choosing the British or the American side of the conflict, such as maintaining trade or preserving homelands (Mehr & Jaffee, 2007).

Language Objectives

- Use academic language to discuss the homework reading.
- Create a T-chart or Venn diagram to demonstrate your understanding of the multiple perspectives of Native American nations.

In this lesson, ELLs and other students collaborate in heterogeneous groups to examine and analyze maps, documents, and firsthand accounts in order to identify the perspectives and positions adopted by various Native American nations (Mehr & Jaffee, 2007). To prepare for the lesson, Ms. Chin downloads the available maps, primary source documents, and primary source analysis worksheets from the EDSITEment Web site. She also bookmarks the Web site for students so they can access it from one of the two classroom computers or while in the computer lab. Ms. Chin has also used information from Native American Voices (Digital History, n.d.) to develop a PowerPoint presentation that extends the very brief discussion of the role of Native American nations in the American Revolution that is found in student textbooks.

Ms. Chin begins her class by reviewing content and language objectives, which are posted on the whiteboard. She then takes students through the agenda, which, as always, is written in large letters on chart paper: (1) Text—review, (2) PowerPoint—Native Americans in late 18th-century North America (a review), (3) Think-Pair-Share, and (4) Ticket-to-Leave.

The previous evening, students read short passages in their textbooks that included a one to two paragraph description of the roles of women, African Americans, and Native Americans in the Revolutionary War. (Ms. Chin reviewed vocabulary prior to assigning the homework. Tabib, Soan, and Betsy have texts that feature glossing of words, and easification of complex text constructions.) Ms. Chin's students know that they will be responsible for reporting their understandings of the assigned homework in groups and therefore generally read with purpose.

Ms. Chin begins the lesson by explaining that students will collaborate to review their homework and assigns a number to each of the six groups of four students. Ms. Chin begins the lesson by telling students

> After I explain directions, you will spend five minutes reviewing and discussing the reading you completed for homework. Your task will be to report out to the class about the roles of women, African Americans, and Native Americans during the time leading to the American Revolution. One person from each group will report to the class. Count off by fours within your groups.

Ms. Chin distributes task cards (timekeeper, reporter, moderator, recorder) and explains, "Ones will take notes, twos will keep track of time, threes and fours will report out. Each group will select a moderator." On the board, Ms. Chin writes, "African Americans—Groups 1, 2"; "Native Americans—Groups 3, 4"; and "Women—Groups 5, 6." She instructs students to begin.

Because students have had ongoing practice working in cooperative groups such as this, they begin their discussions immediately. Ms. Chin positions herself near Group 3 to check their progress. Rather than engaging in group discussion, Mehmet and Tabib are conversing, and Shawna and Rob are engaged in a separate discussion. Ms. Chin notices that the four students are on-task topic wise, but off-task in their group roles, and reminds them, "Make sure you are all involved in the discussion." She then asks, "Who is the moderator?" Mehmet acknowledges that he is the moderator and explains, "I'm helping Tabib." Ms. Chin has struggled with the role that Mehmet should play in situations such as this. Think-Pair-Share activities are effective in making content comprehensible to Tabib, who, when working with Mehmet, can use Turkish and interlanguage to discuss concepts and reading. Ms. Chin knows, however, that Mehmet also needs to practice language constructions with more competent speakers to continue to become more proficient in academic English. She reminds the four students of their roles and their responsibilities to the group, and reinforces that Tabib may contribute in a mixture of languages. She waits while they begin to engage in group discussion. Mehmet explains to the group, "Sorry. I was explaining about the confederation." Shawna, who is timekeeper, says, "We only have two minutes left. What should we report? What's most important?" Tabib leans in and listens attentively, but, initially, doesn't contribute. After a pause, he says, "The Iroquois was with the English." Rob adds, "I think it says just four of them [Iroquois nations], not all the Iroquois." The group discussion continues until Ms. Chin calls time. Each group reports out briefly.

Ms. Chin then calls students' attention to the essential question, which is posted above the whiteboard: "How does perspective affect the way history is told?" She tells them,

We are going to focus on this question as we discuss the roles of diverse groups, such as women, Native Americans, and African Americans. You have read the textbook version of the roles of diverse groups and you have read a lot about women in your historical novels. Today, we are going to learn more about the role of Native Americans.

Ms. Chin refers to the agenda and explains,

First I am going to present some background—a review of Native American life in the years leading up to the Revolution. As I do this, I want you to think about who Native American nations might support, the Patriots or the British, and why they might support either of these.

Prior to the presentation, Ms. Chin distributes a handout of a map showing the location of Native American nations and a numbered list of the concerns of six major Native American nations. Ms. Chin begins the PowerPoint presentation, which uses maps and photos to illustrate the concerns of various Native American nations. She speaks slowly and stops to paraphrase words when necessary. She also calls students' attention to maps that are displayed throughout the room, and students use the maps she has distributed as references. She projects the numbered list of Native Americans' concerns on the whiteboard.

Following the presentation, Ms. Chin directs students to spend five minutes in a Think-Pair-Share activity to discuss the allegiances they think each of the six Native American nations will form and to explain why they will form these allegiances. She ends the lesson by having students complete a ticket-to-leave worksheet in which they write about the positions they believe that each Native American nation will take. Ms. Chin reminds them

You are responsible for spelling all word wall words correctly. You are also responsible for beginning sentences with capital letters and ending them with a mark of punctuation. You may use texts and handouts, and you may conference within your groups.

Ms. Chin circulates as ELLs and other students work to complete this assignment, which she will review to assess understanding and identify any misconceptions.

During the following day's lesson, students will analyze primary source documents about the various positions and allegiances of Native American nations. (Ms. Chin has formatted the text of these documents to enable her to use easifications and glossing in document margins to make them comprehensible to ELLs.) Working in small groups, students will use the information gleaned from these documents to complete Venn diagrams and T-charts illustrating the positions and allegiances of the various nations.

Review, Reflect, Apply

1. *Review and Reflect:* Review Lesson 2 and reflect on how Ms. Chin aligns instruction with the TELLiM standards.

2. *Apply:* Apply your knowledge of aligning lessons with the TELLiM standards using Table 12.1. Explain how Lesson 2 is aligned with the standards.

3. *Apply:* Explain the strategies that Ms. Chin used to make instruction comprehensible.

4. *Apply:* Explain the strategies she used to build academic-language. How does she effectively use grouping to support both Mehmet and Tabib?

Summary

Table 12.3 shows how the Lesson 2 narrative is aligned with TELLiM standards. Some elements of the lesson are consistent with several standards.

TABLE 12.3 Aligning Ms. Chin's Lesson 2 With the TELLiM Standards

S4-a Instruction is contextualized
Ms. Chin provides clear content- and language-learning objectives and an agenda for the lesson.

Classwork builds on homework assignments and is linked to the essential question, "How does perspective affect the way history is told?"
Ms. Chin explains the purpose of the reading assignment.

S4-b Instruction builds on ELLs' previous knowledge
Ms. Chin reinforces the value of native languages and reminds students that Tabib may contribute in a combination of English and Turkish.

S5-a Learning is assessed appropriately
Ms. Chin informally assesses content-area understanding and group interaction skills as she circulates during the first activity. She informally assesses during Think-Pair-Share.

She assesses content-area understanding with the ticket-to-leave assignment.

S6-a Materials are comprehensible to ELLs
Texts and primary source materials are made comprehensible using glossing and easification.

S6-b Presentational style is comprehensible to ELLs
Ms. Chin uses photos and maps in the PowerPoint presentation. She also projects a numbered list that she refers to as she explains the concerns of each Native American nation. (Numbering, rather than bulleting, the list makes it easier for ELLs to follow along.)

Ms. Chin speaks clearly and paraphrases words for clarity.

S7-b Academic collaboration between ELLs and other students is fostered
Ms. Chin's students work in teams to discuss reading completed as homework. Each team member has a clear role.

Students engage in a Think-Pair-Share activity to discuss the information provided in the PowerPoint presentation.
(These also are consistent with standards S4-a, b; S5-a, S6-a, and S8-d.)

S7-c ELLs are engaged in planned, complex, academic conversations about their content-area
The two group activities provide time for planned, complex academic conversations.

S7-d The development of content-area English-language proficiency is supported
The academic conversations in which students explained sections of their text to others fosters the development of content-area English language abilities.

S8-a Complex content-area thinking skills are taught
ELLs and other students are challenged by the essential question, "How does perspective affect the way history is told?" They use knowledge of the concerns of various Native American nations to think about this question.

ELLs and other students use their knowledge of the concerns of Native Americans to predict the allegiances of Native American nations.

S8-b Time for ELLs to practice these skills in meaningful circumstances is provided
ELLs and other students engage in meaningful discussions throughout the class

They complete the written ticket-to-leave in which they write about their predictions.

LANGUAGE MINI LESSONS

Ms. Chin understands the importance of building the academic-language abilities of ELLs and other students in her history classes. She accomplishes this, in part, by making materials and presentations comprehensible and by providing ongoing opportunities for ELLs and other students to engage in purposeful academic conversations. Additionally, Ms. Chin plans and implements a series of mini lessons to promote the development of academic-language abilities. Ms. Chin plans these lessons based on the observed needs of her students. One observation, which she made early in the school year, is that ELLs and many other students struggle to comprehend text. Ms. Chin was inspired by the work of Tovani (2000, 2004), who herself taught struggling readers and provided professional development to content-area teachers. One instructional strategy used by Tovani, which Ms. Chin has found to be helpful with secondary history students, is teaching students to highlight text.

Mini Lesson 1: Highlighting Text

Ms. Chin regularly reads history selections aloud and models her thinking as she reads: paraphrasing to makes sense of the text, self-checking for comprehension, and rereading to confirm her understandings or unscramble confusions. Ms. Chin demonstrates how she slows down when reading is dense, skims text to locate specific facts or passages, and uses the structure of the textbook (headings, illustrations, boldfaced terms) to check her comprehension.

Ms. Chin has noticed that her students often do not recognize when they become confused. Following the recommendation of Tovani (2000, 2004), she asks half the students to bring yellow highlighters and the other half to bring pink highlighters. She keeps the highlighters in baskets in the classroom so they are easily accessible to students.

Ms. Chin photocopies a selection of text and provides copies to each student. She projects a copy of the text on the whiteboard and explains that she will use the highlighters to help her make sense of her reading:

> Every time I am confused by what I read, I will highlight the text in yellow. When I am very clear about what I am reading—clear enough that I could teach it to others—I highlight the text in pink.

Ms. Chin models reading the text, highlighting as she goes. She explains, "The purpose of this activity is to identify the parts of the text that you understand and those parts that you find confusing. The only wrong response is to have text that is not highlighted." After Ms. Chin models the highlighting process, she provides students with short passages of text to highlight and she circulates to assess student understanding.

Ms. Chin then calls students' attention to the text she has highlighted. She reads through the yellow sections (the sections that were confusing) and engages in a think-aloud to identify the causes of her confusion, for example, unknown vocabulary words, long complex sentences, and so on. Ms. Chin then has students return to the yellow-highlighted passages in their text to determine where they became confused. Students underline words and make notes in the margins of the text. Again, Ms. Chin circulates to assess understanding. She repeats her modeling and then students practice with the passages of text highlighted in pink. She has students teach one pink-highlighted section to a partner.

When Ms. Chin first introduces this strategy at the beginning of the year, she provides ongoing opportunities for guided and then independent practice to ensure that students can apply the strategy to their reading. She reinforces the strategy at various times during the year.

Students cannot always highlight in textbooks; for this reason, Ms. Chin asks all students to bring in 3 × 3 Post-its, which is another strategy she learned from reading Tovani (2000, 2004). She keeps Post-its in the classroom and available to students as they read. Rather than highlighting text, students use Post-its to indicate where and why they are confused by the text and to hold places in the text that are important to their understanding. As with the highlighting activity, students explain their difficulties and understandings on the Post-its.

Mini Lesson 2: Word Parts

Ms. Chin is aware of the vocabulary demands in U.S. history. ELLs must understand words they encounter in text and must also be able to retrieve and use these academic words in their writing. In brief mini lessons, Ms. Chin teaches students to use word *parts* for learning new words. Looking across history-content language, she has identified some important affixes: *a-, anti-,* and *non-* and *-ance, -ence, -ion, -ation,* and *-al.* She teaches one affix at a time, adding the new affix and words with that affix to one section of the word wall. She provides practice using word parts during lesson fillers (Saphier & Gower, 1997). In teaching the affixes *ion* and *ation,* for example, Ms. Chin provides students with a list of words found in their text and has students identify the affix and the root word, for example, *representation, taxation, cooperation, conception, rebellion, intimidation, civilization.* She guides students to understand that the affixes mean "the state or condition of being, which changes verb to noun" (IRA/NCTE, 2007). Teaching one affix at a time in focused mini lessons, Ms. Chin develops a wall of prefixes and suffixes for student practice and reference. (A teacher's guide to affixes and root words is available online at http://ReadWriteThink.org; IRA/NCTE, 2007.)

Mini Lesson 3: Collocations, Polysemy, and Idioms

Ms. Chin knows that ELLs are often challenged by language expressions that may seem quite simple. For example, in a simplified U.S. history book, students encounter the expressions: *tide of the battle, stage a showdown, win the friendship, driving force.* Ms. Chin teaches these words as *chunks* (Nation, 2001), and demonstrates to ELLs and other students their use in other historical writings. For example, in teaching *the tide of the battle,* Ms. Chin begins with the common meaning of ocean tide and illustrates the movement and force of the ocean tide. She then elicits from students the meaning of *tide* in the chunk *the tide of the battle.* She provides students with context for other expressions using *tide* that they will confront in history and current events, such as *the tide has turned* and *the turning of the tide*:

- According to the news story, the tide has turned for mine families; rescuers have located the trapped miners.
- Senator Lieberman says the tide has turned in the Iraq war.
- The mayor issued a statement that his city would reduce greenhouse emissions, indicating that the "leadership tide has turned on climate change" ("Leadership Tide Has Turned," 2007).

Mini Lesson 4: Academic Writing (Hedging in History)

Ms. Chin knows from reading (Hinkel, 2004) and from reviewing the writing of ELLs that a common error in their writing is the inability to hedge. Too often student writing is replete with overstatements, absolutes, and exaggerations. For example, in describing causes leading to the Revolutionary War, Mehmet writes,

> After the British won the French and Indian war they needed money and put taxes on the colonies. This was the first cause of the war. The British passed a lot of tax laws that made the colonists decide that it was taxation without representation. This was the next cause of the war. Some colonists did not want independence, but others did. Then Thomas Paine wrote "Common Sense." This made colonists decide to declare independence.

The spelling has been corrected, yet second-language influence remains obvious. One of the problems with the writing is that it lacks hedging, an expectation of academic writing. Consider how differently Mehmet's excerpt reads when hedging is employed (the underlining indicates hedging):

> After the British won the French and Indian war they needed money and put taxes on the colonies. The British need for money is thought to be one of the first causes of the war. The British passed several tax laws, which the colonists considered to be taxation without representation. Although some colonists did not want independence, others did. Then Thomas Paine wrote "Common Sense." This writing is often considered to have helped colonists decide to declare independence.

As the students prepare to write in U.S. history, Ms. Chin provides mini lessons to teach academic writing. To begin these lessons, Ms. Chin focuses ELLs and other students on the *essential language question,* "Will your voice be heard?" She explains to students that for their written voice to be heard, they must be able to express their ideas in academic English. She then engages them in activities that she describes as "Let's sound academic." In one mini lesson she asks students to make a list of expressions they commonly use, such as, *I always . . . ,* *I never . . . ,* and *Everybody . . .* Once students have made lists, Ms. Chin provides them with academic hedging words, such as *generally, frequently, often, ordinarily,* and *usually* to replace the more common *always.* She provides them with academic words such as *infrequently, rarely,* and *seldom* as possible replacements for *never;* and *many people, colonists, historians, writers, Native Americans,* and so on, or *some* people (etc.), a *number* of people (etc.) to replace *everybody.* Students work in pairs to convert their original sentences to academic writing. Students read their work aloud to hear the differences in their writing. Ms. Chin keeps lists of academic hedging words and also academic expressions that replace common conversational expressions, on file for student reference.

CHAPTER SUMMARY

In this chapter, Ms. Linda Chin illustrated how she has structured her classroom and lessons to promote purposeful academic-language interactions between ELLs and other students. Ms. Chin has established content-area learning outcomes that illustrate what all students must understand, and differentiated assessments that enable students to demonstrate understanding apart from English-language proficiency. Ms. Chin has differentiated language learning outcomes to allow for the English proficiency levels of her students. Ongoing assessment of student progress facilitates academic-language development.

Ms. Chin has dedicated considerable time to ensuring that materials are accessible to her students and to teaching reading, vocabulary, and writing lessons that scaffold academic-language use. Each lesson is aligned with principles of teaching ELLs and with the TELLiM standards.

Assessment Evidence Activities

AE-1   Describe how Ms. Chin acknowledges and builds on students' funds of knowledge in his lessons. Provide specific examples.

AE-2   Explain the ways in which her lessons are consistent with the TELLiM model.

AE-3   Construct a T-chart illustrating the ways in which Ms. Chin's lessons are consistent with the steps of the TELLiM model. The Classroom-Specific Standards and the Lesson Planning Checklist are useful guides here.

AE-4   Explain how Ms. Chin's lessons build content-area knowledge and academic-language proficiency.

AE-5   Identify instances of differentiation in Ms. Chin's lessons. Explain the benefits of these instances and support your rationale with examples from the text.

AE-6   Explain how Ms. Chin assesses instruction and builds instruction based on assessment.

AE-7   Using the lesson checklist, create one new lesson for the content-area unit that you are developing.

Resources for Classroom Use

- American Library Association: "What Are Primary Sources?" www.lib.washington.edu/subject/History/RUSA
- Digital History: *Native American Voices*. www.digitalhistory.uh.edu/native_voices/native_voices.cfm
- Discussion questions and lesson ideas. http://school.discoveryeducation.com/lessonplans/programs/therevolutionarywar/#sug

- EDSITEment: National Endowment for the Humanities. Contains history lessons that teachers can use or adapt for use in their classrooms. Most lessons provide reproducible worksheets and diagrams that teachers can use or adapt for use. http://edsitement.neh.gov/tab_lesson.asp?subjectArea=3
- History Channel. http://americanrevolution.org/
- Document Analysis Worksheets: These include teachers' guides for teaching with documents and student analysis worksheets for written documents, photographs, cartoons, posters, maps, artifacts, motion pictures, and sound recordings. www.archives.gov/education/lessons/worksheets
- National Archives Teaching with primary source documents. www.archives.gov/education/lessons
- National History Standards. www.sscnet.ucla.edu/nchs/standards
- National Standards for Civics Education. www.civiced.org/index.php?page=stds
- National Archives Document Analysis Worksheet. www.archives.gov/education/lessons/worksheets/document.html
- National Archives Photograph Analysis Worksheet. www.archives.gov/education/lessons/worksheets/photo.html
- National Archives Archival Research Catalogue (ARC). www.archives.gov/research/arc
- Images and audiofiles. www.pbs.org/ktca/liberty/chronicle_timeline.html
- Traill, D. www.archives.gov/education/lessons/revolution-images/activities.html

13

Putting It Together in the English Language Arts Classroom

IN THIS CHAPTER, MR. JAMIE HAYES ILLUSTRATES HOW HE USES THE TELLIM MODEL TO CREATE SETTINGS FOR learning and instructional units that meet the needs of ELLs. He teaches college-preparatory English at the secondary level, yet the understandings gained from the learning environment Mr. Hayes has established, the materials he uses, and the strategies he implements are relevant to language-based programs in the middle and secondary grades.

Consistent with the format of Chapters 10 through 12, this chapter shows how Mr. Hayes has aligned unit planning, implementation, and assessment with the TELLiM model (Table 13.1). This chapter provides a tour of his classroom, a review of the materials he uses, and reflections from Mr. Hayes, who then demonstrates how he differentiates a summative assessment and implements instruction for three content-area lesson narratives and two language lesson narratives.

Mr. Hayes teaches English language arts (ELA) to students in Grades 9 through 12 with class sizes of approximately 25 students. The class described in this chapter is a second-year college-preparatory English course. There are 24 students: 6 ELLs and 18 native-English-speaking students. The English language proficiency levels of these ELLs are beginner through transitioning: Emerson Beya (beginner proficiency), Julián Alencastro (early-intermediate proficiency), Aadam Jassam Ali and Soan Meng (intermediate proficiency), Mehmet Yilmaz (advanced-intermediate proficiency), and Maya Solis (transitioning proficiency). Profiles for Emerson, Julián, Aadam, and Soan are found in the Appendix of this text. Mr. Hayes's ELA class features leveled reading options, group work to promote academic-language development, and opportunities to develop higher-order thinking skills for ELLs at various levels of English language proficiency. This year has been very challenging for Mr. Hayes, who has had two beginner ELLs placed in his classes. Emerson is in this class; Reina Acevedo is in his third-period

TABLE 13.1   TELLiM Lesson Implementation Checklist

Standard	Description (and Evidence) of Standard				√
S4-a	Instruction is contextualized.				
S4-b	Instruction builds on ELLs' previous knowledge.				
S5-a	Learning is assessed appropriately.				
S5-b	Content-area objectives and assessments for individual lessons.				
S5-c	Language objectives and assessments for individual lessons.				
S6-a	Materials are comprehensible to ELLs. (Check each strategy used).				
	Appropriate reading level	Glossed words	Outlines	Highlighted text	Explanations in margins
	Audio books	Clear organization	Other	Native language	Attention to vocabulary
S6-b	Presentational style is comprehensible to ELLs. (Check each device that is used within the lesson to increase comprehensibility)				
	Realia	Other visuals	Graphics organizers	Think-Pair-Share	Other comprehension checks
	Simplified language	Clear routines	Other	Native language	Attention to vocabulary
S7-a	ELLs/teachers are engaged in academic collaboration.				
S7-b	ELLs/students are engaged in academic collaboration.				
S7-c	ELLs are engaged in planned, complex, academic conversations about their content area.				
S7-d	The development of content-area English language proficiency is supported.				
S8-a	Complex content-area thinking skills are taught.				
S8-b	Time for ELLs to practice these skills in meaningful circumstances is provided.				

class. ELA is intensely language heavy, and Mr. Hayes, who is normally confident of his ability to reach all students, has been challenged.

A TOUR OF MR. HAYES'S ROOM

Mr. Hayes's classroom, while small and often crowded with students, is a place where students, literature, and learning are equally revered. Mr. Hayes's connection with his students is demonstrated in the interest he shows in them and the conversations he generates and maintains with them. His love of literature is visible on his bookshelves, on his walls, and in his teaching. At the front of the classroom is a whiteboard that stretches the length of the wall. He uses the expanse of the board to capture the attention of his students, often writing *essential questions* that fill the entire space. "These are big questions," he explains, "so why not make them larger than life?" He also posts these questions on long sheets of paper above the whiteboard so that students know the questions will remain throughout the unit (S4-a). Along the side walls are posters representing a wide diversity of authors and books. Among them are posters of the original book covers of

J. D. Salinger's *The Catcher in the Rye*, Aldous Huxley's *Brave New World*, and Zora Neale Hurston's *Their Eyes Were Watching God*. Biographical posters of authors such as William Shakespeare, Amy Tan, Edgar Allan Poe, and Sandra Cisneros also make up the collection. Mr. Hayes uses this display to demonstrate to his students the great diversity that exists within the field of literature. He explains, "There are so many different expressions of literature that every person can find one to relate to. Yet as diverse as literature may be, it demonstrates the universality of the human experience."

On the sideboard, divided into three equal sections, Mr. Hayes posts his daily agenda and the content and language objectives. Students expect to see the agenda each day, written in red, to guide them through the lesson. Mr. Hayes refers to the agenda at the start of class and with each transition (S4-a). The content objectives in the middle section of the sideboard are consistently written in blue, while the language objectives are green (S4-a; S5-b, c; S6-b). Below the sideboard are shelves filled with books, many of them his personal copies. As a literature major (and enthusiast), Mr. Hayes has accumulated a collection of novels, poems, and plays, which he now shares with his students. Many of the books are weathered, with softened pages and scuffed corners, having clearly been read and reread. The students often look through the books to discover his comments and questions in the margins. He explains,

> I brought my literature collection to school to share with my students, but I didn't realize the impact it would have on my classroom. From just the presence of so many different books—books that have been read—students see what it means to love literature. As they open the books, however, they notice my notes, my connections, and my questions. They believe me now when I say that all readers have questions, and it's the good readers who seek clarification. They see, first hand, what it means to interact with a text, which is exactly what I want my students to do. (S8-a)

Baskets of books, organized and labeled by reading level and genre, continue along the same bookshelf. Mr. Hayes takes time to explain to his students the importance of reading at a challenging but not frustrating level, and he directly instructs his students on strategies for proper book selection. "My students have options, but I think that along with options they need the tools to navigate those options" (S8-a). Committed to offering a literacy-rich environment, Mr. Hayes has also included collections of *The New Yorker* magazine and *Small Spiral Notebook*, a literary magazine for emerging writers. Equally important, he says, is to include novels, texts, and magazines in languages other than English. As he reads well in French and moderately well in Spanish, he has some novels in each language in his collection.

The desks in Mr. Hayes's classroom are organized in a semicircle to facilitate classroom discussion. He frequently provides activities that encourage students to process ideas through oral discussion (S7-b, c, d). He has placed extra chairs inside the semicircle, tucked in front of every third desk or so. These chairs serve to facilitate midclass transitions into partner and group work. Students can quickly move into groups without the need to rearrange desks. Mr. Hayes also uses the extra, floating chairs to sit alongside students himself or quickly join a group discussion (S7-a). During student presentations, he blends into the group, allowing his presenters the full attention of the class (S7-b, c, d; S8-b).

Adjacent to the whiteboard is a large bulletin board that is used as a word wall. Leaning against the wall, below the word wall, is a pointer that Mr. Hayes and his students use to interact with the words on the wall. "I refer to this vocabulary actively and encourage students to do so as well." The vocabulary is drawn from the current unit, from general words that students are responsible for throughout the year, and from Academic Word List (AWL) words that he has determined to be essential for understanding and communicating in his content area. He refers to this word wall frequently, and while he does not expect perfect spelling and grammar from the ELLs in his room, he does expect them to use and spell the word wall vocabulary correctly (S6-b, S7-d). Next to the word wall is a row of closets whose doors are decorated with instructional posters created by Mr. Hayes's students accurately depicting literary terms used in his classes.

> For this unit, one language skill that I expect of my students is the ability to utilize literary terms such as *plot*, *protagonist, setting, irony, theme, figurative language,* and *tone* when discussing their novels. After a review, I post the students' work from earlier lessons, replete with examples, to encourage their recall of these terms. (S6-a, b)

APPROPRIATE INSTRUCTIONAL MATERIALS

On Mr. Hayes's desk, between two Harry Potter bookends, is a collection of teacher resources, to which he regularly refers. Included are his state's curriculum frameworks, a booklet of strategies for teaching ELLs put together by the school's ESOL teacher, a file of translated quick notes home (thus far, in Spanish, Portuguese, Vietnamese, French, and Khmer) to communicate with the parents of his ELLs, and copies of reference books such as Randy Bomer's *Time for Meaning: Crafting Literate Lives in Middle & High School* (1995). Alongside his desk are shelves with large, three-ring binders containing Mr. Hayes's collections of lessons, worksheets, graphic organizers, sample work, and rubrics. Mr. Hayes refers to these binders as his unit "kits," because they make up the tools he needs to successfully implement each unit. He updates the binders each time he teaches a unit with the latest additions, reflections, and changes:

> I see every lesson I teach as a work in progress. As I present a unit, I take notes in my notebook with reflections about what worked, what didn't work, or what I might change or add for the next time. After the fact, I go through the notes and make any adjustments to my unit. While it has taken some time to develop, I now have some very solid units that have improved with time and continuous reflection. Interestingly, they remain great references, but they continue to change depending upon the make up and levels of language proficiency within the class.

In a box alongside his binders is a collection of words written on laminated construction paper. Organized by topic, Mr. Hayes uses these words for his word wall. Each word is cut around the shape of its letters to facilitate visual recognition (S6-a, S7-d). Colorful file boxes organize more instructional materials. A red box contains folders with excerpts of plays, novels, and poetry. Copies of each excerpt are highlighted to provide support to ELLs and native-English speakers who may struggle with grade-level reading. Others are glossed and provide explanations of key terms, culturally specific references, and figurative language in the margin (S6-a, b; S7-d). A teal box to the right houses DVDs and videos of interviews with authors, movies, and television shows. Among the media collection are an interview with the author Isabel Allende on PBS (Public Broadcasting Services), an episode of *The Simpsons* (Groening, Brooks, & Moore, 1992) that satirizes *A Streetcar Named Desire*, and *Romeo and Juliet* in both modern (Martinelli & Luhrmann, 1996) and traditional (Havelock-Allan, Brabourne, & Zeffirelli, 1968) versions. Mr. Hayes uses his media collection to (1) motivate students, (2) build background knowledge, (3) preview material to be read, (4) establish an understanding of a particular setting, and (5) create opportunities to compare and contrast across media (S6-b, S8-a).

A rolling cart, now tucked away in a corner, houses much of Mr. Hayes's media equipment. An overhead projector sits atop the cart. On the second shelf is a computer, ready to be hooked up to an LCD projector. (Mr. Hayes must check the LCD projector out of his school's library as there are not enough for each teacher in the building). He frequently uses the computer and projector to display visual slideshows that he has created using PowerPoint and Photo Story 3. He explains, "I take advantage of the rich, visual library the Internet provides and enjoy creating images to enrich my students' understanding of a particular theme or setting among other concepts" (S4-a, S6-a). The bottom shelf of the cart holds a long box of cassette tapes, including books on tape and recordings of Mr. Hayes's own voice reading poems, chapters, and excerpted pieces of literature (S6-b). On the same shelf is a box containing about a dozen portable cassette players with headphones. Mr. Hayes smiles when he talks about the equipment:

> I discovered that most of my students no longer have the ability to play cassettes at home as digital audio and CDs now dominate. With my principal's permission, I sent an email to our staff soliciting donations of old portable cassette players. Many of my colleagues donated old, used players that they had sitting in their attics and basements. I received enough that I sent some home with my ELLs for the year and I have a collection for use here in class.

Mr. Hayes shares that he would eventually like to use MP3 players to bring material to students:

> I recently read articles about the use of classroom blogs and iPods as instructional tools (Colombo & Colombo, 2007; Patten & Craig, 2007). I do not have the resources to include the use of MP3 players at the moment; although many of the students already have them, not all do. I have also worked with our instructional technology teacher at the school to create podcasts of some of my language mini lessons. We have posted these on my classroom Web site so that students can watch these at home, in the school's media center, or on our classroom computers at anytime.

Hayes admits that the integration of technology in the classroom is a slow process, but he finds that incorporating one new piece each year is manageable, and the interest level of the students is improved by his use of technology.

Two computer desks, each with a classroom computer, sit in the back corner of the room. "These are great tools to differentiate instruction," Mr. Hayes explains. "Students can listen to a podcast of a mini lesson if they were absent or need a review, or they can use the computers to create their classroom presentations." He has organized the computers with student-friendly bookmarked pages, including online dictionaries, thesauruses, bilingual dictionaries, and Web sites that relate to the current unit (S6-a). Additionally, Mr. Hayes uses the computer stations for extension opportunities, including vocabulary and critical-thinking-building programs such as FableVision's Get a Clue (2005) (S8-a, b). For whole-class lessons using the computers, Mr. Hayes takes his class to one of the high school's three computer labs.

REFLECTIONS FROM MR. HAYES

Mr. Hayes entered the teaching profession because of his love of literature. He connected with the field personally because he found that he related to so many of the themes present in the literature he read. He recognizes that the connections he made naturally are not always natural for his students. "Teaching students to make those personal connections," he reflects, "was the challenge." Through the use of *enduring understandings*, however, he was able make intercurricular connections. He says,

> I work, for example, with an enduring understanding that states, *Grammar, mechanics, spelling, and punctuation facilitate communication.* Students now understand how good spelling and proper placement of an apostrophe can help their voices be heard the way they want to be heard.

Furthermore, Mr. Hayes has found that essential questions foster text-to-text, text-to-world, and text-to-self connections that, in turn, foster the personal engagement of the students with the material (S4-a, b; S8-a).

Mr. Hayes's classroom is characterized by many opportunities to develop thinking skills and language skills across the four domains of language (reading, writing, listening, and speaking) at a level that is comprehensible to his students. He explains,

> English language arts is often very frustrating to both ELLs and native-English-speaking students because there is such a high demand of reading, writing, listening, and speaking. Often, we combine these tasks with critical thinking processes, which demand a lot cognitively. I organize my class to support students' linguistic and cognitive development and try to minimize the frustration that they can so easily encounter. I have found that strong adherence to routines, flexible grouping, individually appropriate reading and writing expectations, and a balanced classroom with many opportunities for reflection and application are central to creating a constructive environment (S8-a, b).

Mr. Hayes's love of literature and the extensive classroom supports he provides have worked well for him when the ELLs placed in his classroom have had proficiency levels at or above the early-intermediate level. This year, however, Emerson Beya, a beginner ELL from the Democratic Republic of Congo, was placed in this fifth-period class.

Emerson Beya Arrives

On registration, Emerson was referred for English language assessment, where it was determined that he was a beginner ELL. Emerson, whose profile is in the Appendix, could understand basic classroom routines and engage in interpersonal greetings, such as "How are you?" and "It is a nice day." He could understand simple sentences when they were spoken slowly and clearly and generate simple questions when provided with prompts: "Where is the . . . ?" The records from Emerson's previous school were requested but did not arrive prior to his placement. Emerson and his parents explained that he could read and write French quite well. A decision was made to place Emerson in all mainstream classes with pull-out and push-in ESOL support.

Ms. Richards, the school's ESOL teacher, met with Mr. Hayes about the placement. They discussed his upcoming instructional units and his general concerns about having a beginner ELL in a secondary ELA class that focused on reading, discussing, and writing about literature. Ms. Richards assured Mr. Hayes that she could come to his fifth-period class at least three times a week. She explained that an advertisement had also been placed in the local newspaper to locate a French-speaking tutor, but even if a French-English bilingual tutor could be found, the process would likely take weeks. Together Ms. Richards and Mr. Hayes reviewed the "There's More Than Meets the Lie" unit and decided to look for French translations of the novels. They quickly located a translation of *The Catcher in the Rye*. Ms. Richards explained that with the French edition, at least Emerson would likely be able to access the reading, which would provide a base from which he could learn some academic English and participate in class activities. With a plan in place, some of Mr. Hayes's anxiety dissipated; he did not, however, feel totally confident of his ability to teach Emerson.

Review, Reflect, Apply

1. *Review:* How does the setting in Mr. Hayes's room foster educational opportunities for ELLs?

2. *Review and reflect:* Review Mr. Hayes's classroom setting, materials, and reflections, and reflect on what components a new teacher could implement immediately, which could be implemented during the first year, during the second year, and during the fifth year.

3. *Review and reflect:* What were Mr. Hayes's concerns about the placement of a beginner ELL in his ELA classroom? Does Ms. Richards and Mr. Hayes's plan make sense?

IMPLEMENTING THE UNIT "THERE IS MORE THAN MEETS THE LIE"

In earlier chapters, Mr. Hayes described how he determined the enduring understandings, learning outcomes, and essential questions for the "There Is More Than Meets the Lie" unit. He identified the following learning outcomes:

- Explain positions regarding truth and lies in one of the assigned novels.
- Justify the position regarding truth and lies.
- Support the position with specific details from book.

Mr. Hayes next developed several summative assessments, from which students can choose to demonstrate mastery of the learning outcomes. He explains to students that exemplary assessments will become part of the unit resource kit to be used by future students in this course. Regardless of the option students choose, they will present their work in a roundtable discussion.

1. Develop a thesis statement about one or more themes in the novel you are reading, and create one of the following:
   a. Prototype of a book jacket
   b. Poster advertising the book
   c. Book review
   d. PowerPoint presentation with key points from the book

   The final document must include artwork, the name of the novel, the author, publisher information, a thesis statement, and clear examples that support your thesis. Grades will be based on content, presentation, and language.

2. Write an 8- to 10-page essay about the major theme(s) and the way in which the author conveys the theme(s) in the novel you are reading. Essays will be graded for content-area accuracy, syntax, grammar, spelling, and punctuation.

3. Develop a CliffsNotes–type guide to your novel. Begin with a clear thesis statement. Write three to four topic sentences to support your thesis sentence. Under each of these sentences, create a bulleted list of passages from chapters of the novel that support the topic sentence.

While the assessment options allow for substantial variation in presentation, each summative assessment enables students to demonstrate mastery of the learning outcomes. It is important to Mr. Hayes that every student in his class become a competent writer, yet for the purposes of this assessment he does not want to conflate his students' writing ability with their understanding of setting and theme.

Mr. Hayes further differentiates each assessment according to the English language proficiency levels of the ELLs in his classroom. Table 13.2 illustrates how he has differentiated the first assessment option to make it accessible to Emerson, a beginner, and Julián, an early-intermediate ELL. Table 13.3 shows how Mr. Hayes has differentiated the second assessment option, writing the paper, to make it accessible to Mehmet Yilmaz (high-intermediate proficiency) and Maya Solis (transitioning proficiency) (S5-a).

ALIGNING LESSONS WITH TELLiM STANDARDS

Once Mr. Hayes has developed his assessments, he begins the unit by posting the essential question "Is it ever better to lie than to be truthful?" He uses this question to generate classroom discussion around the theme (S7-a, d). He shares, "Each student contributes a different perspective

TABLE 13.2	Assessment Option: Prototype of Book Jacket						
Proficiency	**Rubric Variations**		**3**	**2**	**1**	**0**	**Comments**
Native-English speaker at grade level	1.	Theme description consists of one to two paragraphs.					
	2.	Organization is logical and clear.					
	3.	Writing is of professional quality, with smooth transitions and varied sentence structure.					
	4.	Writing is *without* mechanical errors.					
Early intermediate	1.	Theme description consists of a bulleted list of simple sentences.					
	2.	Organization is logical and clear.					
	4-a.	Correct verb tense is used.					
	4-b.	Sentence structure is correct for simple sentences.					
	4-d.	Word wall words and words found within the text are spelled correctly.					
	4-e.	Punctuation is correct in all simple sentences and most complex sentences.					
Beginner	1.	Theme description consists of a bulleted list of simple sentences written with the support of an ESOL teacher.					
	2.	Word wall words are spelled correctly.					
	3.	Rules of basic capitalization and punctuation are followed.					

NOTE: For each proficiency level, (a) the prototype consists of two 8-inch × 10-inch documents, representing the front and back covers; (b) the title, author, and publisher are included and spelled correctly; (c) a visual representation of at least one major theme is included; (d) a description of at least one major theme is on the back cover; and (e) reviewer recommendations that refer to the author's development of a theme are on the back cover.

TABLE 13.3   Assessment Option: Paper

Proficiency	Rubric Variations	3	2	1	0	Comments
Native-English speaker at grade level	1. Themes are clearly identified.					
	2. Discussion of author's development of themes is clear and supported with specific examples from the novel.					
	3. Overall organization of the paper is logical and clear.					
	4. Organization at the paragraph level is logical and clear.					
	5. Writing is of professional quality, with smooth transitions and varied sentence structure.					
	6. Writing is *without* mechanical errors.					
Transitioning	(1–4) Same as above					
	5-a. Some variation in sentence structure is used.					
	5-b. Simple sentence structure is correct. Sentence structure within complex sentences with complex clauses is mostly correct.					
	5-c. Transitions between main ideas are present.					
	6-a. Grammar is accurate in most cases.					
	6-b. Spelling is correct.					
	6-c. Punctuation is correct in all simple sentences and most complex sentences.					
High Intermediate	(1–5) Same as above					
	6-a. Spelling of words from the novel and word wall is correct.					
	6-b. Grammar is accurate in simple sentences. Grammar is accurate in most complex sentences.					
	6-c. Punctuation is correct in simple sentences.					

NOTE: For each proficiency level, (a) the paper consists of 8 to 10 double-spaced typed pages and (b) a title page and reference section are included.

to this theme, just as each literary work does." Mr. Hayes has chosen this question because of its universality and its ability to draw attention to different cultural viewpoints (S4-b). He explains,

> The first time the question appears, students generally have strong viewpoints on the subject. Many feel that honesty is always the best policy, for example. Yet as they read, they see the theme of truth and lies portrayed throughout different circumstances. It is fascinating to see how their exposure to literature can impact their opinion about a very personal topic.

He presents the second essential question, "What circumstances justify a lie?" later in the unit, after students have had an opportunity to think and read about the theme. Mr. Hayes has chosen this question, with a focus on circumstance, to lead students into a discussion about setting (S8-a, b). This will be further developed in Lesson 2.

Lesson 1: Introducing the Lie

(90 minutes)

Mr. Hayes prepares for this lesson by collecting the following materials from his unit kit: T-chart graphic organizers, book summaries (exemplary work from former students), copies of each novel, literary vocabulary posters (student work), colored pictures of different settings, and unit overview and assessment handouts (S6-a).

Content Objectives

- Students will make personal connections to a theme.
- Students will discuss the connection of setting to theme.
- Students will engage in prereading activities and make predictions about a text.
- Students will teach a literary term to peers (S5-b).

Language Objectives

- Students will communicate orally, using literary vocabulary, in academic and interpersonal conversations with peers.
- Students will list personal experiences on a T-chart.
- Students will provide an oral explanation of a literary term to peers (S5-c).

As students enter the classroom, many of them begin to talk about the conspicuous essential question sprawling across the whiteboard. Mr. Hayes, while pleased with the students' enthusiasm, reminds the class of the routine: "Let's first review our agenda and objectives for today, and then we'll get to this very interesting question. I'm curious as to what you all have to say." He consciously communicates to his students the importance he places on their input to the class. He explains, "I want them to recognize their importance. My students are much more motivated when they realize that their backgrounds and experiences shape this class." Pointing to the red section of the sideboard, he reads the day's agenda: (1) To Lie or Not to Lie?—Discussion, (2) New Unit Overview, (3) Book Selection, (4) Photo Time!, (5) Prereading, and (6) Closing Time.

Mr. Hayes moves closer to where Emerson and Julián are sitting. Julián knows the class routine and, thus, is following along; Emerson looks totally confused. Mr. Hayes relies on his imperfect and rusty high school French to explain to Emerson that they are going over the agenda; he helplessly realizes that the words in the agenda do not translate easily. Cognizant that the class is waiting, he tells Emerson, "Don't worry. I will help you in just a few minutes."

Next, he moves along to the lesson's content and language objectives. Mr. Hayes reads through each item slowly, carefully rephrasing each objective to ensure that all his students are clear. "Thumbs-up if you're clear," he calls out. Noting Aadam's hesitation but trying to remain sensitive to his shyness, Mr. Hayes continues, "I see a few of you had uncertain thumbs! What are we confused about?" Noting from Mr. Hayes's comment that he was not the only confused student, Aadam raises his hand to seek clarification. (S4-a; S6-a, b)

"Now," Mr. Hayes transitions, pointing to his first agenda item, "I want you to consider this question: "Is it ever better to lie than to be truthful?" Suzie, an outspoken native-English speaker, volunteers, "No. Lying is deception. I know truth isn't always easy to hear or say, but I think it's always right." A couple of other students join the conversation, offering their opinions on the charged topic. Mr. Hayes notes that his ELLs are noticeably quiet during the whole-class discussion but feels confident that ELLs with early-intermediate proficiency and above will be comfortable enough to contribute in smaller groups (S7-b). He plans to work with Emerson briefly during the beginning of the discussion; he will again make use of his rudimentary French. Thinking about balancing the needs of the students in his class, Mr. Hayes is relieved to see Ms. Richards enter the room. He introduces her to the class and explains that she will be coteaching with him three days each week. Many of the students are familiar with Ms. Richards, and the ELLs in the room know her well.

Mr. Hayes then transitions students into small groups balanced with ELLs and native-English-speaking students. He has placed Emerson in a group with Julián and three native-English speakers. Each group is given a T-chart, and a recorder is identified.

> On the left, your group's recorder will write the lies you have told. These can be lies you've told teachers, family members, or friends. On the right, I want you to share the lies that someone has told you. Everyone must contribute at least one example for each column. You have five minutes.

Students share enthusiastically. While they come from very distinct backgrounds, Mr. Hayes notes that most seem to find an experience to share (S4-b, S6-b, S7-c). He moves to sit next to Emerson and asks Ms. Richards to visit other small groups. She is happy to hear Aadam, Maya, and Maria contributing their experiences. She notes that many of the ELLs share lies that their parents told them about what they could expect in the United States. She is pleased to hear an example from one student that two of his novel's protagonists face lies told by their parents. "That will make for a solid connection," she thinks to herself. (S4-b, S7-b, c, d).

After Mr. Hayes is certain that Emerson understands the activity (S5-a), he leaves Emerson to the small discussion group and circulates through the classroom. He notes that one small group is discussing cultural differences regarding lies. He pauses at the group and, after listening, redirects the group back to the essential question, reminding students that no one right answer exists. When he claps his hands, students end their conversations and redirect their attention to him. He says, "I'm intrigued by everyone's input to this theme." He summarizes some of the comments he heard from the groups (S6-b) as he walks over to the agenda at the sideboard. "Let's continue to our second item. We'll come back to these questions as we proceed throughout this unit, but right now I want to give you an idea of what this unit will include" (S6-b).

Mr. Hayes gives each student a handout with a description of the unit and its assessments. He carefully walks through the description, pausing occasionally to ask for questions. As he works with the large group, Ms. Richards joins Julián and Emerson to clarify and ensure that they are clear (S6-b).

Mr. Hayes is very clear and consistent about providing the big picture for his students. For ELLs, this practice contextualizes each piece of the unit and reinforces the context behind the content (S4-a). Mehmet raises his hand. Noting the long booklist, he nervously asks, "Are we going to read all of these books?" Mr. Hayes answers Mehmet's question and then asks him to rephrase the answer, "to make sure everyone heard." Mehmet responds, "We will only read one of the books, and you will help us decide which one to read." "Thank you, Mehmet," Mr. Hayes responds, confident that Mehmet has understood.

Motioning to the agenda, Mr. Hayes asks a student to read the third item. "Book selection," responds Antonio. Mr. Hayes introduces each book and describes key elements to help the students choose. "*Othello* is a great Shakespearian play. It is written in the Middle English dialect, which can be challenging; it is written in play form, and it takes place in Venice, Italy, and on the island of Cyprus." "That's near Turkey! I lived there!" Mehmet pipes up with enthusiasm. Mr. Hayes shares with Mehmet and the class that setting will be an important piece of their discussion and suggests that Mehmet may be able to share his knowledge of Cyprus with those who read *Othello* (S4-b). Mr. Hayes continues describing the key features of each book, such as the flashbacks in *I Am the Cheese*, the slang expressions in *The Catcher in the Rye*, and the more straightforward language of *Zach's Lie*.

When Mr. Hayes mentions *The Catcher in the Rye*, Ms. Richards provides Emerson with two copies of the novel, one in French and one in English (S6-a). She encourages him to join the other students and peruse all the novels even though his has been chosen. Mr. Hayes reminds students that they must choose two books and that he will make the ultimate decision as to which of the two is most appropriate. In this way, he can balance the groups and use his understanding of each student's reading level (from classwork, English proficiency levels, and standardized test scores) to guide each student's choice (S5-a). He explains, "My goal is to teach ELLs and native-English-speaking students to make appropriately challenging reading selections. They know that I will veto a choice if it is not appropriate, and they mostly select well." Uncertain, Mehmet picks up *The Catcher in the Rye* and *I Am the Cheese*. "Which do you think is better for me, Mr. Hayes?" Mehmet asks. Mr. Hayes knows that Mehmet is a strong reader who uses context clues well to infer meaning. "You might need some support to understand some of Holden's slang, but I think you'll find *The Catcher in the Rye* interesting." Mehmet agrees.

Novels chosen, Mr. Hayes asks the students to find their book groups. As they rearrange themselves, he passes out colored pictures of places to each group. The first picture is of a sandy beach with blue skies, palm trees, and crystal water. "Let's move on to our fourth agenda item, "Photo Time!" says Mr. Hayes as he points to the agenda item. "What words or feelings do you associate with these pictures?" he asks. He directs the students to discuss the feelings that the pictures arouse (S6-a, b; S7-b, d; S8-a, b). Aadam looks down at his picture and responds, "calm," "relaxed," "happy," and "serene." To a photograph of a jail cell with cinder block walls and a solitary man, several students offer, "lonely," "helpless," and "no more freedom" (S7-d). As the group discussions subside, Mr. Hayes draws the students' attention back to the front of the room. He briefly lectures about the settings in the pictures and relates the setting back to the emotional themes the groups generated. He is careful to balance his lectures with opportunities to process the information and language (S6-b). He explains to students, "During this unit, we will analyze the settings of our books. Authors choose settings deliberately—that means 'on purpose'—to send a message." Ms. Richards provides time for Emerson and Julián to process the information and to ensure that they understand (S6-b).

Next, Mr. Hayes passes out a novel and a sheet with contextual information to each student. The sheets, from his unit resource binder, are like CliffsNotes—assignments that have been created by former students as summative assessments. Today, Mr. Hayes uses a section of these Notes to provide general background information about each novel's setting (S6-a). He directs the students to read through the Notes, review the novel covers, and read the back of the book. He explains, "I teach and provide practice with prereading strategies to build context and comprehension" (S4-a, S8-a, b). He then asks students to share predictions within their group, thus encouraging higher-order thought processes. Aadam looks up from reading the back cover of *Zach's Lie*. "I think this boy will feel very alone in a new place," he shares. Mr. Hayes overhears Aadam and recognizes that he is already beginning to relate the text to his personal experience (S4-b).

Mr. Hayes ends the lesson by calling students' attention to the evening's homework assignment that is clearly written on the whiteboard. The assignment reflects the day's learning (attention to setting and the feelings associated with setting), reinforces routines (journal writing to process information), and is appropriately differentiated to meet the various reading levels in his classroom. He explains,

> Your homework is to read the first chapter of your book. Record in your journals what you find interesting or confusing about how the author portrays, describes, the setting. Record any images or examples of setting that support your opinions. You will be responsible for sharing this information with classmates from different reading groups.

Ms. Richards explains the assignment to Emerson. She encourages him to respond in French and use the bilingual dictionary to translate some key words for the next day. This, she explains, will enable him to share in his group (S6-a).

Mr. Hayes's assignment has the double intention of establishing a purpose and a focus for reading (S4-a, S7-d), and informing students of their responsibility so as to encourage reading at home. He explains,

> I know that many high school students do not complete the reading required in ELA classes. There is a lot. I believe that knowing that you can't hide behind 23 other students encourages students to come prepared to class. I have seen a difference in my classes. I also tell students to use highlighters to mark and Post-its to jot down phrases or sections of the book that are confusing to them and why these are confusing. This reinforces the importance of self-checking for comprehension (S5-a) and keeps the emphasis on learning.

Finally, Mr. Hayes leaves time to summarize the lesson and answer students' questions. He restates the day's objectives, checking them off and providing examples of how each was met (S4-a, S6-b, S7-c). "How did you make personal connections to a theme, as the first objective states?" Aadam responds, proud that he is now clear on the objective, "We talked about the theme of lies in our lives." "Yes," Mr. Hayes foreshadows, "and you will see that theme in the lives of your books' protagonists too."

Lesson 2: Making Connections

(90 minutes)

Content Objectives

- Students will use knowledge of a text setting to brainstorm themes.
- Students will make personal, text, and worldly connections to an excerpt.
- Students will react to a text's setting and compare its setting with that of a different literary work.

Language Objectives

- Students will engage in academic discussions about a reading selection.
- Students will list and voice connections to a reading excerpt.

Mr. Hayes begins today's lesson at the sideboard, on which content and language objectives are clearly written. Adhering to the routine he has established, he reviews the agenda, content, and language objectives with students. Once he has checked to ensure that students understand the objectives, he organizes them into discussion groups with a representative from each novel in each group. (Mr. Hayes assigns Emerson to work in collaboration with Jeff, a native-English-speaking student, who has read *The Catcher in the Rye* in English; together they will represent this novel.) The students' task is to discuss the theme and setting; they may refer to the notes they have made in their journal and the Post-it notes in their novels.

Mr. Hayes reviews the parameters of the discussion, which he has written on the board:

I want you to (1) describe the setting, the time, and the place of your novel; (2) tell your group what you found to be interesting or confusing about your setting; (3) draw comparisons between your findings and your group members'; and (4) please remember to use the literary terms we have discussed. They are on the word wall.

Mr. Hayes circulates among the groups, stops to listen, and sometimes comments on their discussions. In Aadam's small group, he hears Allison, who is reading *I Am the Cheese*, express her confusion about the main character's location: "I know he's in some kind of institution, but the author doesn't make it clear. I found that confusing." Mr. Hayes uses Allison's confusion as a teachable moment and asks, "Do you think the author is being unclear on purpose?" Antonio adds, "I bet there's a reason they don't tell you where he is. Maybe it's a mystery." "Well," responds Allison, "I know that the protagonist, Adam, is confused about a lot of things in his life. He doesn't remember much. Maybe the author wants us to be confused like him." "Excellent!" Hayes moderates. "Who else found their setting to be confusing or interesting?" Aadam, generally quiet in large-group situations, adds, "I think my setting is interesting and confusing. I think it is interesting because the book takes place now, in modern times. But I don't know very much about America. The main character, the protagonist, moves to Nevada." Mr. Hayes is pleased to hear Aadam and the others using the literary terms in their discussions. He also enjoys watching his students support each other as Aadam's group members chime in to contribute their impressions of rural Nevada.

Ms. Richards is not in the class today, so Mr. Hayes makes it a point to quickly move to Emerson's group. Jeff looks at the words Emerson has written and elaborates on them in English—the two boys are engaged in academic discussion about *The Catcher in the Rye*.

After the group discussions, Mr. Hayes asks students to return to their regular seats. He dims the lights and presents a slideshow to provide his students with background information about World War II and the Holocaust, the setting for the excerpt from *La Vita è Bella* (*Life Is Beautiful*; Cotone, Ferri, Braschi, & Benigni, 1997) that will be read in class today. Students watch still frames from *Schindler's List* (Spielberg, Molen, & Lustig, 1993) and History Channel documentaries, photographs of Auschwitz, and stills from *Life Is Beautiful*, the movie, as Mr. Hayes's recorded voice narrates with historical information. As the students watch and listen, he directs them to complete a note sheet with the feelings associated with the setting. Mr. Hayes quietly circulates and notes his students' responses: "scared," "unfair," "helpless," and "desperation." Emerson generates and writes the words in French and then looks for the meanings in English, which he carefully copies from the dictionary. Following the slideshow, students discuss their reactions to the setting. Mr. Hayes is careful to point out one student's response, "desperation," for later he will ask the question "Why does Guido lie to his son?" and pose the essential question "Are there circumstances that justify a lie?" The slideshow provides historical context for the reading, and the focused listening activity draws the students' attention to the power of setting to communicate theme.

Mr. Hayes reads a preselected excerpt from *Life Is Beautiful*. He reads at a moderate pace, using gestures, facial expressions, and dramatic flair to facilitate comprehension. He also stops to explain or rephrase sections of the text that might be difficult. He pauses to ask questions and assess student understanding. Students read along with highlighted, glossed, and untouched versions (their reading needs determined by pre-assessments).

After reading, Mr. Hayes distributes an organizer with three graphics to represent three types of literary connections: text-to-self, text-to-text, and text-to-world. He briefly explains these connections and models his thought process for determining a text-to-self connection: "I connect with this text because I have a son who is about Joshua's age. I have not had the same experience, but I understand the feeling Guido has, as a father, to do anything for his child." Mr. Hayes continues with examples of each type of connection and then directs the students in a Think-Pair-Share activity. Students first work individually to complete their organizers and then share their answers with a partner before discussing them with the larger group. Mr. Hayes circulates during individual work time to assess understanding and individually clarify students' confusions. Aadam shares a text-to-self connection with his partner: "My country is at war, just like in the text." Other students relate to the feeling of being protected by their parents. Jeff shares a text-to-text connection from *The Catcher in the Rye*. "Holden is running away. Isn't that what Guido wants to be able to do?" Maya includes a connection to *Zach's Lie*, explaining that Zach's father lied to protect him, just as Joshua's father had done. As students move on to text-to-world connections, many feel uncertain. Some mention the war in Iraq. Mr. Hayes scaffolds, "The Holocaust was genocide, the deliberate destruction of a race or culture. Does anyone know of any genocide happening in the world today?"

"Is that like what happened in Rwanda?" Michael asks. "I saw that movie, *Hotel Rwanda*." "Great, so is that text-to-text or text-to-world?" prompts Mr. Hayes.

"Well," responds Michael, "I guess it is both because the text [movie] was based on real-life events."

Mr. Hayes uses text connection strategies (1) to promote higher-order thinking, (2) to teach comprehension strategies, and (3) to build up to an understanding of setting as it relates to theme and then into a discussion of themes. He explains, "I have students pick out universal themes by making connections. They then can use the connections they forge as a strategy to understand theme." He writes the essential question "Are there circumstances that justify a lie?" across the whiteboard. As a whole group, the class discusses the question. Mr. Hayes times this question so that his students can use their understanding of setting as it relates to theme and their experience with the reading excerpt to inform their conversation. He will continue to revisit the essential questions as the unit progresses and as students gain insight from their texts, personal connections, and classroom conversations.

For homework, Mr. Hayes asks students to repeat the connections organizer as they read the second chapter of their book. Students are asked to come prepared to discuss the themes they uncover as they make connections to their reading. Again, Emerson is encouraged to respond in French, using key terms from the dictionary and the word wall in English.

Review, Reflect, Apply

1. *Review, reflect, and apply:* Review Lesson 2 and reflect on how Mr. Hayes aligns his instruction with the standards. Apply your knowledge of aligning lessons with standards using Table 13.1. Explain how Lesson 2 is aligned with the standards.

2. *Review:* How does Mr. Hayes make lessons comprehensible to ELLs at various proficiency levels? How does he build the academic-language abilities of ELLs at various proficiency levels?

Summary

Table 13.4 shows how Lesson 2 is aligned with the standards. As one can see, some elements of the lesson are consistent with several standards.

TABLE 13.4   Aligning Mr. Hayes's Lesson

S4-a. Instruction is contextualized
Mr. Hayes builds instruction around the essential questions. He provides background knowledge before reading the excerpt (slideshow), and he encourages students to make connections to their reading. (This is also consistent with S4-a, b.)

S4-b. Instruction builds on ELLs' previous knowledge
Mr. Hayes's students bring personal experience into the text-to-self connection exercise.

S5-a. Learning is assessed appropriately
Mr. Hayes assesses student understanding by asking for quick self-assessments of understanding, circulating, listening to their conversations, and summarizing learning.

S5-b, c. Content-area and language objectives and assessments for each lesson
He informally assesses progress towards meeting objectives during student discussions.

S6-a. Materials are comprehensible to ELLs
Students have access to journals and Post-it notes. The *Life Is Beautiful* excerpt is highlighted and glossed for ELLs (according to reading levels). Novel choices are leveled; Emerson's novel is written in French.

S6-b. Presentational style is comprehensible to ELLs
Mr. Hayes adheres to set routines. The agenda, objectives, and directions are written on the board and shared orally.

He pairs Emerson with Jeff to represent *The Catcher in the Rye* in a group discussion.

Mr. Hayes provides visual information (slideshow) and graphic organizers to provide comprehensible input.

S7-a, b. Academic collaboration between ELLs, teachers, and/or other students is fostered
Mr. Hayes's students discuss their reading in small, heterogeneous groups. Both teachers and students collaborate to make comparisons and clarify confusion. (This is also consistent with S8-b.) Students work as partners to complete the connections worksheet. (This is also consistent with S4-a; S8-a, b.)

S7-c. ELLs are engaged in planned, complex, academic conversations about their content area
Students share cross-literary connections, discuss essential questions, and journal connections between setting and theme.

S7-d. The development of content-area English language proficiency is supported
Development is supported through whole-class academic conversations (essential questions), the focused listening activity during the slideshow, the generation of words in response to photos and to *Schindler's List* and *Life Is Beautiful*, and the glossed text excerpts for ELLs.

Students are encouraged to access the literary terms from the word wall and use these in focused discussions.

S8-a. Complex content-area thinking skills are taught
Students discuss cross-literary connections from their reading and make connections to their lives and the world around them.

S8-b. Time for ELLs to practice these skills in meaningful circumstances is provided
Students practice making connections individually, with partners, in small groups, and as a whole class.

Lesson 3: The Essay

(45–90 minutes)

Content Objectives

- Students will share text connections with peers.
- Students will analyze a literary essay and highlight key features.
- Students will synthesize information to create a thesis statement.

Language Objectives

- Students will be able to explain their connections in a small-group setting.
- Students will read and critically examine an academic essay.
- Students will write thesis statements.

This class begins with routine attention to the agenda and objectives. Mr. Hayes then asks that students share their findings from the previous night's homework in their novel discussion groups. As the students share their connections, Mr. Hayes circulates, assessing his students' comprehension through their connections. Midway through the discussion, he announces,

In five minutes, I will ask you to share the themes you uncovered from your connections. If you are uncertain, perhaps your group can help. You will have the next five minutes to share these themes with your team and check your understanding.

In his group, Aadam shares that he connected Zach's relocation to his own family's move: "I am away from my family so nobody really knows me here." Aadam's classmate, Lou, adds, "So maybe one theme is identity? You know, do you change if you're in a new place or do you stay the same?" "Yes," Aadam responds, connecting with this theme, "sometimes I think I am a different Aadam here than at home. Like, in English, I can't make jokes or be funny. This place changes my identity." As Mr. Hayes overhears the conversation, he feels privileged to have a classroom with so many unique experiences and perspectives.

Next, Mr. Hayes brings the class back together. He does not lecture for long periods of time so that he does not overwhelm his students. Today, with Ms. Richards back in the classroom, he plans to workshop essay-writing skills by balancing lecture time with partner work, independent practice, and one-on-one conferencing. Both he and Ms. Richards will conference with the students.

Mr. Hayes directs students' attention to the essential language question on the whiteboard: "What does it mean to be understood?" He passes out a concept map graphic organizer to each student and says, "Turn and talk to your neighbor to brainstorm what it means to be understood when you write an essay." Students begin to brainstorm in pairs. A few minutes later, he brings the class back together and solicits input from each pair. On the overhead projector, he fills in the same graphic organizer. Students volunteer terms such as *clear, organized, neat, use the right words for your audience*, and *thesis statement*. Mr. Hayes records all the responses and highlights *thesis statement* in yellow. He asks, "Why? Juan, why is a thesis statement, or a topic sentence, important?" Juan pauses for a moment to think. Mr. Hayes waits as Juan assembles his thoughts and language. Juan responds, "It's kind of like when you start class. You tell us what to expect so we can put our minds in a focused place."

Next, Mr. Hayes distributes an essay written by a former, anonymous student, about *Life Is Beautiful*. He has redacted the thesis and conclusion statements of the essay. "Let's look at this essay. It is a former student's." He motions to the words on the overhead projector. "What elements do you notice?" He prompts his class to read through the essay individually and label any parts that demonstrate being clear, organized, and the other terms on the overhead. The students read through the essay, analyzing it for those elements they have brainstormed. Mr. Hayes circulates, checking in on students as they work.

He brings the class back together, now projecting the essay onto the screen. "I notice that this essay is organized because the writer uses transitional words such as *initially, later*, and *finally*," shares Michael. Mr. Hayes highlights these words and notices that Maya does as well and notes their significance on her copy. He restates Juan's observation about the function of the thesis statement. Then, he returns the students to their pairs and asks them to write a thesis statement for this essay. As students work together, they discuss the main idea of the essay in an attempt to distill its essence. Each pair shares its finding, and then Mr. Hayes reveals the actual thesis statement. "Any of these could work. Remember that there is no one thesis statement, but its job is always the same."

With the remaining class time, Mr. Hayes directs his students to begin brainstorming ideas for their thesis statement for the final writing assessment. He uses this time to guide students' independent practice and to conference with them individually. He explains, "Conferencing with students is both a great assessment and instructional technique. I get a strong sense of what they know and where they are confused, and I am able to address their needs individually and in that moment."

Mr. Hayes leaves the last few minutes of class to review the day's work. As a ticket-to-leave, he asks student to write down their working ideas for a thesis statement. "These are not final," he clarifies, "but I want to know what ideas you have today." He will later look through the tickets-to-leave as a means of assessing the progress of the students with whom he had an opportunity to conference and those with whom he did not.

LANGUAGE MINI LESSONS
Mini Lesson 1: Modified Jigsaw Vocabulary Review

Mr. Hayes uses this mini lesson to review the literary vocabulary that his class has already studied. He explains, "While I know we have already covered these terms, it is necessary to consistently revisit them. I expect students to use these terms when analyzing literature. If I am to expect that, then I must ensure that they have a solid understanding of the concepts behind the words." He pulls out posters that students had made in the previous semester. Each poster depicts a literary term with student- and glossary-generated definitions, images, and examples. Carefully pairing native-English-speaking students with ELLs, Mr. Hayes gives each pair of students a poster and five minutes to create an explanation of the term to present to the class. (The visuals on the poster are extremely helpful to Emerson.)

Mr. Hayes explains to the class, "Your task is to remind us what is important about the term, explain it in your own words, and provide an example. I will be around to help out." He visits each pair of students as they prepare. He helps Maria and Lee recall an example of metaphor. He also uses this review time to assess how much of this previous vocabulary lesson has endured.

After five minutes, each pair informally presents its term and displays its poster on the side wall. As they do so, Mr. Hayes asks questions of the pairs and the class, probing their comprehension and clarifying any misunderstandings. He stresses,

> I will be using these terms as we discuss our literature. I expect you to use them as well. If you do not recall the meaning of a term, or are unsure how to use it, please ask me, ask a friend, or consult the poster. Remember, you can always ask the class "experts" on each term too.

Mr. Hayes consistently makes his students aware of the resources that are available to them.

Mini Lesson 2: Dramatic Reading

Mr. Hayes developed this mini lesson to encourage the use of strategies for reading comprehension among his ELLs and other struggling readers. He uses this lesson as a response to the essential language question "What does it mean to understand?" He explains, "I have often thought of this question myself. It occurred to me that understanding is a very deep process. I use dramatic reading to encourage students to dig deeply into a text and uncover the many layers of comprehension." Initially, Mr. Hayes borrowed the book *A Dramatic Approach to Reading Comprehension* (Kelner & Flynn, 2006) from the school's resource library. He began to use dramatic readings with students as a method of developing connections with prior knowledge and building inferencing skills, visualization, oral fluency, and expression. He makes sure that ELLs and other students have manageable portions of text to study. In preparation for dramatic reading, students complete character maps; discuss setting, theme, and character motivation; and practice enunciating and using punctuation for clarity and meaning.

Mr. Hayes recently started using the free audio recording and editing software, Audacity, to help students enunciate more clearly. Students can record their voices as they practice reading a text. They are able, then, to listen and analyze their reading with attention to enunciation, pronunciation, expression, and use of punctuation. Mr. Hayes's students enjoy bringing a text to life. His work with dramatic reading provides opportunities to build reading comprehension and comprehension strategies.

CHAPTER SUMMARY

In this chapter, the secondary ELA teacher Mr. Jamie Hayes used multiple forms of group work, class discussions, and motivating inquiries to develop students' higher-order thinking skills while making personal and academic connections to content. Mr. Hayes made strong use of the unit's essential questions to activate his students' existing schemata that connect to the enduring understanding. His consistent interaction with his students in group work, whole-class discussion, and individual conferences provided many assessment opportunities. He relied on each of these assessment opportunities to inform his decisions for the unit, including students' placement in groups, need for review, and leveled reading choices. Mr. Hayes created a comprehensible environment by contextualizing his lessons through visuals and offering appropriately challenging materials and assessments. He also taught his students comprehension strategies to promote self-awareness of learning and independent practice. Each lesson aligned with the principles of teaching ELLs and with the TELLiM model.

Assessment Evidence Activities

AE-1   Describe how Mr. Hayes acknowledges and builds on students' funds of knowledge in their lessons. Provide specific examples.

AE-2   Explain the ways in which his lessons are consistent with the TELLiM model.

AE-3   Construct a T-chart illustrating the ways Mr. Hayes's lessons are consistent with the steps of the TELLiM model. The Classroom-Specific Standards and the Lesson Planning Checklist are useful guides here.

AE-4   Explain how Mr. Hayes's lessons build content-area knowledge and academic-language proficiency.

AE-5   Identify instances of differentiation in Mr. Hayes's lessons. Explain the benefits of these instances and support your rationale with examples from the text.

AE-6   Explain how Mr. Hayes assesses instruction and builds instruction based on assessment.

AE-7   Using the lesson checklist, create one new lesson for the content-area unit that you are developing.

Resources Used in Mr. Hayes's Instructional Unit

- Audacity free audio recording and editing software. http://audacity.sourceforge.net
- *Small Spiral Notebook*. smallspiralnotebook.com
- Allende, I. *Lessons for teachers*. www.pbs.org/now/classroom/allende.html
- *FableVision: Get a Clue*. www.getaclue.com

Appendix

Leyla Khalil

Grade:	8	
Age:	14	
Native language/Country of origin:	Arabic and French/Lebanon	
Native-language proficiency:	Read at Grade 6 in Arabic when entered the United States but has since regressed due to lack of use	
English language proficiency:	Intermediate	
U.S. schooling:	Sheltered English Immersion, Grades 6 and 7 Fully mainstreamed in Grade 8	Reads/writes at the 6th-grade level in English
Domain	**Assessed skills**[a]	**Assessed areas of difficulty**[a]
Listening:	Social and academic conversations, with support	Uncommon or technical vocabulary (metaphor)
	Understanding of questions about factual details and main idea	Questions that require making inferences Judging the speaker's tone or intonation to glean meaning
Speaking:	Participation in classroom discussions using simple language	Using technical vocabulary
	Expressing opinions	Rephrasing ideas of self or another
	Organizing and delivering oral presentations	Using pace and rhythm and pausing to affect meaning in speech
Reading:	Recognition of imagery in a text	Comprehension of multiparagraph text
	Understanding of text structure and significance	Comprehension of literary devices
	Comprehension of multiple verb tenses	Uncommon or technical vocabulary
Writing:	3- to 5-paragraph composition	Organization during prewriting
	Basic organization	Using transitions
	Some supporting details	Recognition of own errors
	Basic grammar with some complex structures	Independent editing
	Correct spelling and mechanics with support in editing	Varied sentence structures

a. Assessed skills and assessed levels are based on descriptors from the Massachusetts English Language Proficiency Benchmarks and Outcomes (ELPBO).

Katy Boureth

Grade:	9	
Age:	15	
Native language/Country of origin:	Khmer/United States	
Native-language proficiency:	Does not read Khmer; oral proficiency only	
English language proficiency:	High Intermediate	
U.S. schooling:	Mainstream education since kindergarten	Reads at the 5th-grade level in English

Domain	Assessed skills[a]	Assessed areas of difficulty[a]
Listening:	Interpersonal conversations Classroom discussions, with repetition	Academic vocabulary Classroom lectures Compound sentences and passive voice
Speaking:	Participation in small-group discussions Rephrasing of ideas, with assistance Expressing opinions Organizing and delivering oral presentations	Participation in whole-class discussions Using technical vocabulary Rephrasing ideas of self or another without assistance Using pace and rhythm and pausing to affect meaning in speech
Reading:	Understanding of text structure and significance Decoding Recognizes transition words to assist comprehension	Distinguishing between relevant and irrelevant information Comprehension of multiparagraph text Comprehension of literary devices Uncommon or technical vocabulary
Writing:	Use of selected academic vocabulary in writing Basic organization Some supporting details Basic grammar with some complex structures Correct spelling and mechanics with support in editing	Use of word choice to persuade Distinguishing between formal and informal language in writing Recognition of consistent spelling and punctuation errors Independent editing Use of prepositions

a. Assessed skills and assessed levels are based on descriptors from the Massachusetts English Language Proficiency Benchmarks and Outcomes (ELPBO).

Ghia Campos

Grade:	High school	
Age:	17	
Native language/Country of origin:	Portuguese/Brazil	
Native-language proficiency:	Reads at/near grade level in Portuguese	
English language proficiency:	Transitioning	
U.S. schooling:	Transitional Bilingual Education, 3 years; 2nd year in mainstream education with ESL support	Struggles slightly at writing/reading level but grasps underlying concepts
Domain	**Assessed skills**[a]	**Assessed areas of difficulty**[a]
Listening:	Interpersonal and academic conversations in small groups Understanding classroom lectures with contextual support Academic vocabulary addressed in class	Classroom lectures with little or no contextual support Comprehension of idioms Comprehension of historical or cultural references
Speaking:	Participation in small-group and whole-class discussions Rephrasing of ideas of self or another Expressing opinions Organizing and delivering oral presentations	Use of technical vocabulary Use of idioms Using pace and rhythm and pausing to affect meaning in speech
Reading:	Employing context clues to acquire new vocabulary Comprehension of words/phrases that signal cause and effect Comprehension of academic texts with text support (highlighting, glossing)	Distinguishing between relevant and irrelevant information Comprehension of academic texts and full-length articles without support Recognizing tone
Writing:	Use of selected academic vocabulary in writing Basic organization Use of supporting details Variety in sentence structure Independent editing	Editing for sentence fragments Correct usage of apostrophes Tense consistency

a. Assessed skills and assessed levels are based on descriptors from the Massachusetts English Language Proficiency Benchmarks and Outcomes (ELPBO).

Fredy Solis

Grade:	8	
Age:	14	
Native language/Country of origin:	Spanish/Dominican Republic	
Native-language proficiency:	Oral language proficiency; very basic reading and writing skills in Spanish (estimated at early 3rd grade)	
English language proficiency:	Intermediate	
U.S. schooling:	Sheltered English Immersion, Grades 5–7; Mainstream, Grade 8	Reads/writes at the 4th-grade level

Domain	Assessed skills[a]	Assessed areas of difficulty[a]
Listening:	Strong interpersonal, conversational skills	Lengthy classroom lectures
	Understanding brief classroom lectures with contextual support	Sustained academic conversations
	Peer-to-peer classroom discussions	Videos or voice recordings that lack multimodal support
Speaking:	Strong interpersonal, conversational skills	Comprehension of multistep instructions
	Participation in small-group discussions	Use of academic or specific vocabulary (often uses the word "thing" to replace a specific word)
	Asking and answering simple questions	
	Expressing opinions	
	Organizing and delivering oral presentations	Pragmatics (using appropriate phrases or levels of formality for audience)
Reading:	Recognizes rhyming words	Distinguishing between fact and opinion
	Determining the main idea of a text	Separating relevant from irrelevant information
	Understanding of visual representations of information (graphs, tables, charts, etc.)	Using context clues to develop new vocabulary
	Simple sentence structures	
Writing:	Writing brief summaries	Correct spelling of homophones
	Identifying errors in punctuation when editing	Consistent use of basic punctuation (period, comma)
	Using graphic organizers in prewriting	Irregular past tense
		Use of supporting details in writing

a. Assessed skills and assessed levels are based on descriptors from the Massachusetts English Language Proficiency Benchmarks and Outcomes (ELPBO).

Aadam Jassam Ali

Grade:	10	
Age:	16	
Native language/Country of origin:	Arabic/Iraq	
Native-language proficiency:	Reads and writes at 6th-grade level; excelled in school (attended through Grade 6)	
English language proficiency:	Intermediate	
U.S. schooling:	Mainstream with ESL	Reads/writes at the 6th-grade level
Domain	**Assessed skills[a]**	**Assessed areas of difficulty[a]**
Listening:	Understanding brief classroom lectures with contextual support Peer-to-peer classroom discussions Multistep instructions with visual reinforcement	Lengthy classroom lectures Sustained academic conversations Videos or voice recordings that lack multimodal support Multistep instructions without visual reinforcement
Speaking:	Small-group or partner discussion with adequate wait time Expressing opinions Asking for clarification Using academic vocabulary after its use has been modeled	Presenting before a group English pronunciation (influence of Arabic heard strongly in intonation and "th" and "r" sounds) Use of the auxiliary *do* ("We have homework?")
Reading:	Grade-level literature in small sections, with contextual support Academic articles with highlighted sections Classroom instructions	Lengthy texts without support Academic vocabulary Cultural or historical references Analogies in text
Writing:	Complete, simple sentences Paragraph writing on personal topics Independent prewriting using graphic organizers Paragraph writing on academic topics with support of graphic organizers Use of academic vocabulary in scaffolded sentences	Independent use of academic vocabulary in writing Paragraph writing on academic content without support Subject-verb order (often reversed)

a. Assessed skills and assessed levels are based on descriptors from the Massachusetts English Language Proficiency Benchmarks and Outcomes (ELPBO).

Julián Alencastro

Grade:	9
Age:	15
Native language/Country of origin:	Spanish/Peru
Native-language proficiency:	Reads/writes at grade level
English language proficiency:	Early Intermediate
U.S. schooling:	Mainstream with ESL

Domain	Assessed skills[a]	Assessed areas of difficulty[a]
Listening:	Classroom instructions, with repetition	Lengthy classroom lectures
	Understanding brief classroom lectures with contextual support	Casual, academic language (heads, tails, odds)
	Peer-to-peer classroom discussions	Sustained academic conversations
Speaking:	Requesting additional information/expressing confusion	Presenting before a group
Reading:	Simple sentences	Passive voice
	Short excerpts of text, with glossing and/or highlighting of key terms	*If . . . then* statements
		Distinguishing between relevant and irrelevant information
		Polysemy
Writing:	Prewriting/idea organization using graphic organizers	Multiple-paragraph compositions
	Simple paragraph with topic sentence and supporting details	Phrasal verbs (*put on, look for*)
	Correct spelling of Academic Word List vocabulary, with available word wall	Use of the pronoun it
		Variation in sentence structure
		Complex grammatical structures

a. Assessed skills and assessed levels are based on descriptors from the Massachusetts English Language Proficiency Benchmarks and Outcomes (ELPBO).

Emerson Beya

Grade:	High school
Age:	17
Native language/Country of origin:	French/Congo
Native-language proficiency:	Reads/writes at 6th-grade level
English language proficiency:	Beginner
U.S. schooling:	Mainstream with ESL

Domain	Assessed skills[a]	Assessed areas of difficulty[a]
Listening:	Understanding of basic classroom commands and routines Single-step instructions Comprehension of simple sentences, with clear, slow speech and repetition Connection of academic vocabulary to visuals	Classroom and interpersonal conversations without repetition Academic vocabulary in isolation or with English definition Multistep instructions
Speaking:	Interpersonal greetings Basic grammatical structures in simple sentences Asking simple questions	Interpersonal and academic conversations Complex grammatical structures Small-group discussions
Reading:	Simple sentences Classroom instructions Isolated academic vocabulary with contextual support	Grade-level texts, with support Large portions of text
Writing:	Spelling of common objects Academic vocabulary of focus Simple sentences in the present tense Basic capitalization and punctuation	Simple paragraph with topic sentence and supporting details Vocabulary to permit full discussion in writing Complex verb tenses (past, conditional, etc.)

a. Assessed skills and assessed levels are based on descriptors from the Massachusetts English Language Proficiency Benchmarks and Outcomes (ELPBO).

Trang Nguyen

Grade:	8
Age:	14
Native language/Country of origin:	Vietnamese/Vietnam
Native-language proficiency:	Reads and writes at or near grade level
English proficiency:	Beginner
U.S. schooling:	Mainstreamed with ESL pull-out instruction

Domain	Assessed skills[a]	Assessed areas of difficulty[a]
Listening:	Comprehension of isolated words or phrases Recognition of interpersonal greetings Response to basic classroom commands	Comprehension of classroom conversations and lectures Questions without connection to routine
Speaking:	Pronunciation words for common objects Use of basic greetings	Use of complete sentences Interpersonal and classroom discussions
Reading:	Basic decoding of phonemes Comprehension of isolated terms with use of translation device Understanding of text structures	Simple sentences Grade-level texts
Writing:	Listing or categorizing terms Completing graphic organizers Simple sentences that have been modeled and are repetitious in structure Capitalization and end punctuation in sentences	Creation of novel sentences Correct spelling Capitalization of proper nouns

a. Assessed skills and assessed levels are based on descriptors from the Massachusetts English Language Proficiency Benchmarks and Outcomes (ELPBO).

Soan Meng

Grade:	9	
Age:	15	
Native language/Country of origin:	Khmer/Cambodia	
Native-language proficiency:	Reads at the 4th-grade level in Khmer	
English language proficiency:	Intermediate	
U.S. schooling:	Sheltered English Immersion, Grades 7 and 8; Fully mainstreamed in Grade 9	Reads/writes at the 4th-grade level in English

Domain	Assessed skills[a]	Assessed areas of difficulty[a]
Listening:	Understanding social language Understanding academic language with frequent clarification Understanding of questions about factual details and main idea	Content-area academic language and vocabulary Questions that require making inferences
Speaking:	Participation in classroom discussions using simple language Expressing opinions using simple language Informal academic presentations in small groups	Using academic vocabulary Rephrasing ideas of self or another Using academic phrases and grammar—often uses expressions such as "you know" and "that thing" to refer to specifics
Reading:	Identifies point of view in texts Understanding of text structure and use of many transitional words Comprehension of multiple verb tenses	Comprehension of multiparagraph text, without support Comprehension of literary devices Academic vocabulary
Writing:	3- to 5-paragraph composition, with support Basic organization Some supporting details Basic grammar	Organization during prewriting Using transitions Correct spelling and mechanics Recognition of own errors Varied sentence structures

a. Assessed skills and assessed levels are based on descriptors from the Massachusetts English Language Proficiency Benchmarks and Outcomes (ELPBO).

Natka Jigovic

Grade:	10	
Age:	15	
Native language/Country of origin:	Serbo-Croatian/Serbia	
Native-language proficiency:	Read at 6th- to 8th-grade level in Serbo-Croatian	
English language proficiency:	Intermediate	
U.S. schooling:	Mainstreamed with ESOL support since reaching Grade 8	Reads/writes at the 5th-grade level in English
Domain	**Assessed skills**[a]	**Assessed areas of difficulty**[a]
Listening:	Social and academic conversations (small group)	Academic and technical vocabulary across content areas
	Understanding of information when context is provided	Questions that require making inferences and abstract questions, without many contextual cues
	Understanding of questions about factual details and main idea	
Speaking:	Participation in classroom discussions expressing personal preferences	Using academic language appropriately (often struggles for a word and becomes frustrated)
	Stating and defending positions (participates in small groups yet remains quiet in the larger classroom setting)	Using pace and rhythm and pausing to affect meaning in speech
Reading:	Recognition of imagery in a text	Comprehension of multiparagraph text
	Understanding of text structure and significance (appears to use her first-language knowledge of text structure)	Comprehension of literary devices
		Uncommon or technical vocabulary
	Comprehension of multiple verb tenses	Using transitions
Writing:	3- to 5-paragraph composition, with support	Difficulty using multiple verb tenses
	Basic organization of ideas	Independent editing
	Some supporting details	Varied sentence structures—little evidence of complex structures
	Basic grammar with some complex structures	
	Correct spelling and mechanics with support in editing	

a. Assessed skills and assessed levels are based on descriptors from the Massachusetts English Language Proficiency Benchmarks and Outcomes (ELPBO).

References

Abedi, J., & Dietel, R. (2004). *Challenges in the No Child Left Behind Act for English language learners.* (CRESST Policy Brief 7.).Los Angeles: National Center for Research on Evaluation, Standards, and Student Testing (CRESST)/University of California. (Available from the University of California, Los Angeles, National Center for Research on Evaluation, Standards, and Student Testing Web site: www.cse.ucla.edu/products/policy/cresst_policy7.pdf)

Achieve, Inc. (2005, February). *Rising to the challenge: Are high school graduates prepared for college and work?* Retrieved March 29, 2008, from www.achieve.org/node/548

ACT. (2005). *Crisis at the core: Preparing all students for college and work.* Iowa City, IA: Author. Retrieved July 2, 2008, from www.act.org/research/policymakers/pdf/crisis_report.pdf

Aebersold, J., & Field, M. L. (1997). *From reader to reading teacher: Issues and strategies for second language classrooms.* New York: Cambridge University Press.

Allington, R. (2005). *What really maters for struggling readers: Designing research-based programs* (2nd ed.). Boston: Allyn & Bacon.

American Academy of Child & Adolescent Psychiatry. (1999). *Your adolescent: Emotional, behavioral, and cognitive development from early adolescence through the teen years.* New York: HarperCollins.

American Institutes for Research. (2005). *Working together: Teacher-paraeducator collaboration.* Washington, DC: Improving Outcomes for All Students K-8. Retrieved March 31, 2008, from www.k8accesscenter.org/training_resources/documents/Tchr-ParaCollaboration.pdf

American Speech-Language-Hearing Association. (2008). *Social language use (pragmatics).* Retrieved March 27, 2008, from www.asha.org/public/speech/development/Pragmatics.htm

Anderson, R. C. (1977). The notion of schemata and the educational enterprise: General discussion of the conference. In R. C. Anderson, R. J. Spiro, & W. E. Montague (Eds.), *Schooling and acquisition of knowledge* (pp. 413–431). Hillsdale, NJ: Lawrence Erlbaum.

Arau, A. (Director). (1992). *Like water for chocolate* [Motion picture]. Mexico: Miramax Films.

Arms, K. (2004). *Environmental science.* New York: Holt, Rinehart & Winston.

Aronson, E., Blaney, N., Stephin, C., Sikes, J., & Snapp, M. (1978). *The jigsaw classroom.* Beverly Hills, CA: Sage.

Asher, J. (1965). The strategy of total physical response: An application to learning Russian. *International Review of Applied Linguistics, 3,* 291–300.

Atwell, N. (1998). *In the middle: New understanding about writing, reading, and learning.* Portsmouth, NH: Boynton/Cook.

Au, K. (1993). *Literacy instruction in multicultural settings.* Belmont, CA: Wordsworth.

Au, K. (2002). Multicultural factors and the effective instruction of students from diverse backgrounds. In A. E. Farstrup & S. J. Samuels (Eds.), *What research has to say about reading instruction* (3rd ed., pp. 392–413). Newark, DE: International Reading Association.

Au, K. (2005, February). *What research tells us about improving the literacy achievement of students of diverse backgrounds.* Paper presented at the National Association for Bilingual Education, Phoenix, AZ.

Au, K. (2006). *Multicultural issues and literacy achievement.* Mahwah, NJ: Lawrence Erlbaum.

Au, K. H., & Mason, J. M. (1981). Social organizational factors in learning to read: The balance of rights hypothesis. *Reading Research Quarterly, 17*(1), 115–152.

August, D. (2002). *Transitional programs for English language learners: Contextual factors and effective programming* (Report No. 58). Baltimore: Center for Research on the Education of Students Placed at Risk.

Avi. (1984). *The fighting ground.* New York: HarperCollins.

Babbit, N. (1975). *Tuck everlasting.* New York: Square Fish.

Baddeley, A. (1990). *Human memory.* Mahwah, NJ: Lawrence Erlbaum.

Baker, C. (2006). *Foundations of bilingual education and bilingualism.* Clevedon, UK: Multilingual Matters.

Barbour, C., Barbour, N. H., & Scully, P. A. (2005). *Families, schools, and communities: Building partnerships for educating children* (3rd ed.). Upper Saddle River, NJ: Pearson.

Bartlett, F. C. (1995). *Remembering: A study in experimental and social psychology.* Cambridge, UK: Cambridge University Press. (Original work published 1932)

Beck, I., McKeown, M. G., & Kucan, L. (2002). *Bringing words to life: Robust vocabulary instruction.* New York: Guilford Press.

Beck, I., Perfetti, C., & McKeown, M. (1982). Effects of long-term vocabulary instruction on lexical access and reading comprehension. *Journal of Educational Pyschology, 74*(4), 506–521.

Bereiter, C., & Scardamalia, M. (1987). *The psychology of written composition.* Hillsdale, NJ: Laurence Erlbaum.

Berko, J. (1958). The child's learning of English morphology. *Word, 14,* 150–177. Retrieved November 1, 2007, from http://childes.psy.cmu.edu/topics/wugs/wugs.pdf

Bhatia, V. K. (1983). Simplification v. easification: The case of legal texts. *Applied Linguistics, 4,* 42–54.

Biancarosa, C., & Snow, C. E. (2006). *Reading next: A vision for action and research in middle and high school literacy—a report to Carnegie Corporation of New York* (2nd ed.). Washington, DC: Alliance for Education. Retrieved June 26, 2008, from www.all4ed.org/files/archive/publications/ReadingNext/ReadingNext.pdf

Billmeyer, R., & Barton, M. L. (1998). *Teaching reading in the content areas: If not me, then who?* Aurora, CO: McREL.

Birch, B. (2002). *English L2 reading: Getting to the bottom.* Mahwah, NJ: Lawrence Erlbaum.

Birch, B. (2006). *English L2 reading: Getting to the bottom* (2nd ed.). Mahwah, NJ: Lawrence Erlbaum.

Birdsong, D. (Ed.). (1999). *Second language acquisition and the critical period hypothesis.* Mahwah, NJ: Lawrence Erlbaum.

Blachman, B. A. (2000). Phonological awareness. In M. L. Kamil, P. B. Mosenthal, P. D. Pearson, & R. Barr (Eds.), *Handbook of reading research* (Vol. 3, pp. 483–502). Mahwah, NJ: Lawrence Erlbaum.

Bloom, P. (2000). *How children learn the meanings of words.* Boston: MIT Press.

Bomer, R. (1995). *Time for meaning: Crafting literate lives in middle & high school.* Portsmouth, NH: Heinemann.

Barlowe, A., Gerwin, D., & Bender, P. (2007). *Common sense: The rhetoric of popular democracy.* Retrieved March 31, 2008, from http://edsitement.neh.gov/view_lesson_plan.asp?id=721

Broaddus, K., & Ivey, G. (2002). Taking away the struggle to reading in the middle grades. *Middle School Journal, 34*(2), 5–11.

Brown, C. (Writer), & MacHale, D. J. (Director). (1992). The tale of the twisted claw [Televisions series episode]. In *Are you afraid of the dark?* New York: Nickelodeon.

Bush, W. S. (2003). *Understanding mathematics and culture in rural contexts* (ED 82729). Columbus, OH: Eric Clearinghouse for Science Mathematics and Environmental Education.

Canale, M. (1983). From communicative competence to communicative language pedagogy. In J. Richards & R. Schmidt (Eds.), *Language and communication* (pp. 2–27). New York: Longman.

Canale, M., & Swain, M. (1980). Theoretical bases of communicative approaches to second language teaching and testing. *Applied Linguistics, 1,* 1–47.

Carkin, S. (2005). English for academic purposes. In. E. Hinkel (Ed.), *Handbook of research in second language teaching and learning* (pp. 85–98). Mahwah, NJ: Lawrence Erlbaum.

Carrasquillo, A. L., Kucer, S., & Abrams, R. (2004). *Literacy interventions for upper elementary English language learners.* Clevedon, UK: Multilingual Matters.

Carson, J., & Nelson, G. (1994). Writing groups: Cross-cultural issues. *Journal of Second Language Writing, 3,* 17–30.

Carson, J., & Nelson, G. (1996). Chinese students' perceptions of ESL peer response group interaction. *Journal of Second Language Writing, 5,* 1–19.

Cazden, C. B. (1988). *Classroom discourse: The language of teaching and learning.* Portsmouth, NH: Heinemann.

Chalhoub-Deville, M., & Deville, C. (2005). A look back at and forward to what language testers measure. In E. Hinkel (Ed.), *Handbook of research in second language teaching and learning* (pp. 815–832). Mahwah, NJ: Lawrence Erlbaum.

Chamot, A. U., & O'Malley, J. M. (1994). *The CALLA handbook: Implementing the cognitive academic language learning approach.* Reading, MA: Addison-Wesley.

Chhuon, V., Hudley, C., & Macias, R. (2006, April). *Cambodian-American college students: Cultural values and multiple worlds.* Paper presented at American Educational Research Association, Chicago, IL.

Chomsky, N. (1965). *Aspects of the theory of syntax.* Cambridge: MIT Press.

Chomsky, N. (1972). *Language and mind.* New York: Harcourt Brace Jovanovich.

Clair, N. (2001). *Why reading is hard: Viewer's guide.* McHenry, IL: Center for Applied Linguistics/Delta Systems.

Collier, J. L., & Collier, C. (1974). *My brother Sam is dead.* New York: Simon & Schuster.

Collier, V., & Thomas, W. P. (1989). How quickly can immigrants become proficient in school English? *Journal of Educational Issues of Language Minority Students, 5,* 26–38.

Collier, V., & Thomas, W. P. (1999a). Making U.S. schools effective for English Language Learners, Part 1. *TESOL Matters, 9*(4). Retrieved July 15, 2008, from www.tesol.org/s_tesol/sec_document.asp?CID=196&DID=812

Collier, V., & Thomas, W. P. (1999b). Making U.S. schools effective for English language learners, Part 2. *TESOL Matters, 9*(5). Retrieved July 15, 2008, from www.tesol.org/s_tesol/sec_document.asp?CID=196&DID=817

Colombo, M., & Colombo, P. (2007). Blogging to improve instruction in differentiated science classrooms. *Phi Delta Kappan, 89*(1), 60–63.

Colombo, M., Jacobs, C., McMakin, D., & Shestok, C. (2007). *Teaching across difference: Perspectives of 20 middle school teachers in five urban schools.* Manuscript submitted for publication.

Cook, V. J. (1996). Competence and multi-competence. In G. Brown, K. Malmkjaer, & J. Williams (Eds.), *Performance and competence in second language acquisition* (pp. 57–99). Cambridge, UK: Cambridge University Press.

Cormier, R. (1977). *I am the cheese.* New York: Dell Laurel-Leaf, Random House.

Corson, D. (2001). *Language diversity and education.* Mahwah, NJ: Lawrence Erlbaum.

Cotone, M., Ferri, E., & Braschi, G. (Producers), Benigni, R. (Writer/Director), & Cerami, V. (Writer). (1997). *La Vita è Bella* [Motion picture]. United Kingdom: Buena Vista International.

Coxhead, A. (2000). A new academic word list. *TESOL Quarterly, 34*(2), 213–238.

Crawford, J. (2004). *Foundations of bilingual education and bilingualism* (5th ed.). Los Angeles: Bilingual Educational Services.

Cuban, L. (1993). *How teachers taught: Constancy and change in American classrooms 1890–1990.* New York: Teachers College Press.

Cummins, J. (1979). Cognitive/academic language proficiency, linguistic interdependence, the optimum age question. *Working Papers on Bilingualism, 9,* 1–43.

Cummins, J. (1981). *Bilingualism and minority-language children.* Toronto, Ontario, Canada: Ontario Institute for Studies in Education.

Cummins, J. (1984a). *Bilingualism and special education: Issues in assessment and pedagogy.* Clevedon, UK: Multilingual Matters.

Cummins, J. (1984b). Wanted: A theoretical framework for relating language proficiency to academic achievement among bilingual students. In C. Rivera (Ed.), *Language proficiency and academic achievement* (pp. 2–19). Clevedon, UK: Multilingual Matters.

Cummins, J. (2000). *Language, power, and pedagogy: Bilingual children in the crossfire.* Buffalo, NY: Multilingual Matters.

Cummins, J. (2005, September). *Teaching for cross-language transfer in dual language education: Possibilities and pitfalls.* Paper presented at the TESOL Symposium on Dual Language Education: Teaching and Learning Two Languages in the EFL Setting. Retrieved July 5, 2008, from www.achievementseminars.com/seminar_series_2005_2006/readings/tesol.turkey.pdf

Cunningham, P., Hall, D. P., & Shanks, G. (1998). *Month-by-month phonics for upper grades: A second chance for struggling readers and students learning English.* Greensboro, NC: Carson-Dellosa.

Curtiss, S. (1977). *Genie: A psycholinguistic study of a modern-day "wild child."* New York: Academic Press.

D'Ambrosio, U. (2001). What is ethnomathematics, and how can it help children in schools? *Teaching Children Mathematics, 7*(6), 308–310.

Darling-Hammond, L. (1996). What matters most: A competent teacher for every child. *Phi Delta Kappan, 77,* 193–201.

Darling-Hammond, L. (1997). The quality of teaching matters most. *Journal of Staff Development, 18*(1), 38–41.

Darling-Hammond, L. (2000). How teacher education matters. *Journal of Teacher Education, 51*(3), 166–173.

Darling-Hammond, L. (2007, October 14). High-quality standards, a curriculum based on critical thinking can enlighten our students. *San Francisco Chronicle,* p. E3. (Available from www.sfgate.com/cgi-bin/article.cgi?f=/c/a/2007/10/14/IN9GSOEUC.DTL)

Darling-Hammond, L., Holtzman, D. J., Gatlin, S. J., & Heilig, J. V. (2005). Does teacher preparation matter? Evidence about teacher certification, Teach for America, and teacher effectiveness. *Education Policy Analysis Archives, 13*(42). Retrieved February 28, 2006, from http://epaa.asu.edu/epaa/v13n42

Davies, A., & Elder, C. (2005). Validity and validation in language testing. In E. Hinkel (Ed.), *Handbook of research in second language teaching and learning* (pp. 795–814). Mahwah, NJ: Lawrence Erlbaum.

Delgado-Gaitán, C. (2001). *The power of community: Mobilizing for family and schooling.* Lanham, MD: Rowman & Littlefield.

Delgado-Gaitán, C., & Trueba, H. (1991). *Crossing cultural borders.* Bristol, PA: Falmer Press.

Delpit, L. (1995). *Other people's children: Cultural conflict in the classroom.* New York: New Press.

Díaz-Rico, L., & Weed, K. (2002). *The crosscultural, language, and academic development handbook: A complete K–12 reference guide* (2nd ed.). Boston: Allyn & Bacon.

Dycus, D. (1997). Guessing word meaning from context: Should we encourage it? *Literacy Across Cultures, 1*(2), 1–6.

Echevarria, J., Short, D., & Powers, K. (2006). School reform and standards-based education: A model for English-language learners. *Journal of Educational Research, 99*(4), 195–210.

Echevarria, J., Vogt, M., & Short, D. (2003). *Making content comprehensible for English language learners: The SIOP Model* (2nd ed.). Boston: Allyn & Bacon.

Echevarria, J., Vogt, M., & Short, D. (2007). *Making content comprehensible for English language learners: The SIOP Model* (3rd ed.). Boston: Allyn & Bacon.

Education Trust (2005). *Gaining traction, gaining ground: How some high schools accelerate learning for struggling students.* Washington, DC: Author. Retrieved March 30, 2008, from www.edtrust.org

Elbow, P. (2000). *Everyone can write: Essays toward a hopeful theory of writing and teaching writing.* New York: Oxford University Press.

Ellis, R. (1994). *The study of second language acquisition.* New York: Oxford University Press.

Epstein, J. (2001). *School, family, and community partnerships: Preparing educators and improving schools.* Boulder, CO: Westview Press.

Eskey, D. (2005). Reading in a second language. In E. Hinkel (Ed.), *Handbook of research in second language teaching and learning* (pp. 536–580). Mahwah, NJ. Lawrence Erlbaum.

FableVision Inc. (2005). Get a Clue [Computer software]. Boston: FableVision.

Farr, M. (1993). Essayist literacy and other verbal performances. *Written Communication, 10*(4), 4–38.

Fast, H. (1961). *April morning.* New York: Crown.

Flowerdew, J., & Miller, L. (2005). *Second language listening: Theory and practice.* New York: Cambridge University Press.

Forbes, E. (1943). *Johnny Tremain.* New York: Bantam Doubleday.

Fountas, I. C., & Pinnell, G. S. (1996). *Guided reading; Good first teaching for all children.* Portsmouth, NH: Heinemann.

France donates money. (2006, November 9). *DR1 Daily News* [Electronic version]. Retrieved June 26, 2008, from http://dr1.com/news/2006/dnews110906.shtml

Frayer, D., Frederick, W.C., & Klausmeier, H. J. (1969). *A schema for testing the level of cognitive mastery.* Madison: Wisconsin Center for Education Research.

García, G. E., & Pearson, P. D. (1994). Assessment and diversity. In L. Darling-Hammond (Ed.), *Review of research in education* (Vol. 20, pp. 337–391). Washington, DC: American Educational Research Association.

Gass, S. M. (1997). *Input, interaction, and the second language learner.* Mahwah, NJ: Lawrence Erlbaum.

Gay, G. (2000). *Culturally responsive teaching: Theory, research, and practice.* New York: Teachers College Press.

Geertz, C. (2000). *The interpretation of cultures.* New York: Basic Books.

Genesse, F. (Ed.). (1999). *Program alternatives for linguistically and culturally diverse students* (Educational Practice Report No. 1). Santa Cruz, CA: Center for Research on Education, Diversity & Excellence.

GI Forum v. Texas Education Agency, 87 F.Supp.2d 667, 142 Ed. Law Rep. 907 (D. TX 2000).

González, N., & Moll, L. C. (2002). Cruzando el Puente: Building bridges to funds of knowledge. *Educational Policy, 16*, 623–641.

González, N., Moll, L., & Amanti, C. (Eds.). (2005). *Funds of knowledge: Theorizing practices in households, communities, and classrooms.* Mahwah, NJ: Lawrence Erlbaum.

Good, T., & Brophy, J. (1994). *Looking in classrooms* (6th ed.). New York: HarperCollins.

Gottlieb, M. (2006). *Assessing English language learners: Bridges from language proficiency to academic achievement.* Thousand Oaks, CA: Corwin Press.

Grabe, W. (1991). Current developments in second language reading research. *TESOL Quarterly, 25*,(3), 375–396.

Graham, C. (2000). *Jazz chants: Old and new: Students book* (2nd Rev. ed.). New York: Oxford University Press.

Graham, S., & Perin, D. (2007). *Writing next: Effective strategies to improve writing of adolescents in middle and high schools—a report to Carnegie Corporation of New York.* Washington, DC: Alliance for Excellent Education.

Graves, D. (1983). *Writing: Teachers and children at work.* Portsmouth, NH: Heinemann.

Groening, M., & Brooks, J. L. (Writers), & Moore, R. (Director). (1992). A streetcar named Marge [Television series episode]. In *The Simpsons.* New York: 20th Century Fox.

Guild, P. Burke (2001). *Diversity, learning style and culture.* Retrieved July 8, 2008, from www.newhorizons.org/strategies/styles/guild.htm

Haggard, M. R. (1986). The vocabulary self-collection strategy: Using student interest and world knowledge to enhance vocabulary growth. *Journal of Reading, 26,* 203–207.

Hakuta, K. (2001). A critical period for second language acquisition. In D. B. Bailey, J. T. Bruer, F. J. Symons, & J. W. Lichtman. (2001). *Critical thinking about critical periods* (pp. 193–205). Baltimore: Paul H. Brookes.

Hall, E. T. (1976). *Beyond culture.* New York: Double Day.

Harste, J. C. (1994). Literacy as curricula conversations about knowledge, inquiry, and morality. In R. B. Ruddell, M. R. Ruddell, & H. Singer (Eds.), *Theoretical models and processes of reading* (4th ed., pp. 1220–1242). Newark, DE: International Reading Association.

Havelock-Allan, A., & Brabourne, J. (Producers), & Zeffirelli, F. (Director). (1968). *Romeo and Juliet* [Motion picture]. United States: Paramount Studios.

Hayes, C. W., Ornstein, J., & Gage, W. W. (1995). *The ABC's of languages and linguistics: A basic introduction to language science.* Lincolnwood, IL: National Textbook.

Heath, S. B. (1983). *Ways with words: Language, life, and work in communities and classrooms.* New York: Cambridge University Press.

Hedgcock, J. S. (2005). Taking stock of research and pedagogy in L2 writing. In E. Hinkel (Ed.), *Handbook of research in second language teaching and learning* (pp. 597–614). Mahwah, NJ: Lawrence Erlbaum.

Hinkel, E. (2004). *Teaching academic ESL writing: Practical techniques in vocabulary and grammar.* New York: Lawrence Erlbaum.

Howard, G. (2006). *We can't teach what we don't know: White teachers, multiracial schools.* New York: Teachers College Press.

Huerta-Macías, A. (1995). Alternative assessment: Responses to commonly asked questions. *TESOL Journal, 5,* 8–11.

Hymes, D. (1972). On communicative competence. In J. B. Pride & J. Holmes. *Sociolinguistics.* Harmondsworth, UK: Penguin Books.

Igoa, C. (1995). *The inner world of the immigrant child.* Mahwah, NJ: Lawrence Erlbaum.

Ioup, G. (2005). Age in second language development. In E. Hinkel (Ed.), *Handbook of research in second language teaching and learning* (pp. 419–436). Mahwah, NJ. Lawrence Erlbaum.

IRA/NCTE. (2007). *Affixes and root words: Teacher's guide.* Retrieved July 9, 2008, from www.readwritethink.org/lesson_images/lesson1042/teachers_guide.pdf

Ivey, G., & Broaddus, K. (2001). Just plain reading: A survey of what makes students want to read in middle school classrooms. *Reading Research Quarterly, 37*(4), 350–377.

Jacobs, W. W. (1902). *The monkey's paw.* Retrieved July 1, 2008, from http://gaslight.mtroyal.ab.ca/ mnkyspaw.htm

Jaime Escalante still preparing students for the workplace. (1998, December 23). *La Voz,* p. 1.

Johnson, J. S., & Newport, E. L. (1989). Critical period effects in second language learning; the influence of maturational state on the acquisition of English as a second language. *Cognitive Psychology, 21,* 60–99.

Jones, R. C. (2006). *Strategies for reading comprehension: Three-minute pause.* Retrieved January 29, 2008, from www.readingquest.org/strat/3mp.html

Kagan, S. (1994). *Cooperative learning.* San Clemente, CA: Kagan.

Kako, E., & Wagner, L. (2001). The semantics of syntactic structures. *Trends in Cognitive Science, 5*(3), 102–108.

Kelner, L., & Flynn, R. (2006). *A dramatic approach to reading comprehension.* Portsmouth, NH: Heinemann.

Kinsella, K. (2005, November). Teaching academic vocabulary. *Aiming High Resource.* Retrieved June 27, 2008, from www.scoe.org/aiming_high/docs/AH_kinsella2.pdf

Kluckhohn, C. (1949). *Mirror for man.* New York: McGraw-Hill.

Kluckhohn, F. R., & Strodtbeck, F. L. (1961). *Variations in value orientations.* New York: Harper & Row.

Kozol, J. (1991). *Savage inequalities.* New York: Crown.

Kozol, J. (1995). *Amazing grace: Lives of children and the conscience of a nation.* New York: Crown.

Kozol, J. (2006). *The shame of the nation. The restoration of apartheid schooling in America.* Saddleback, NJ: Three Rivers Press.

Krashen, S. (1981). *Principles and practice in second language acquisition* (English Language Teaching Series). London: Prentice Hall International.

Krashen, S. D. (1985). *The input hypothesis: Issues and implications.* New York: Longman.

Krashen, S. D., & Terrell, T. D. (1983). *The natural approach: Language acquisition in the classroom.* London: Prentice Hall Regents.

Kroll, B. (2001). Considerations for teaching an ESL/EFL writing course. In M. Celce-Murcia (Ed.), *Teaching English as a second or foreign language* (3rd ed., pp. 219–232). Boston: Heinle & Heinle.

Kunnan, A. J. (2005). Language assessment from a wider context. In E. Hinkel (Ed.), *Handbook of research in second language teaching and learning* (pp. 779–794). Mahwah, NJ: Lawrence Erlbaum.

LaBrosse, P. (2007). *Analysis of the effect of specific vocabulary instruction on high school chemistry students' knowledge and understanding.* Unpublished doctoral dissertation, University of Massachusetts Lowell.

Ladson-Billings, G. (2000). Reading between the lines and beyond the pages: A culturally relevant approach to literacy teaching. In M. A. Gallego & S. Hollingsworth (Eds.), *What counts as literacy: Challenging the school standard* (pp. 139–152). New York: Teachers College Press.

La Celle-Peterson, M. W., & Rivera, C. (1994). Is it real for all kids? A framework for equitable assessment policies for English language learners. *Harvard Educational Review, 64*(10), 55–75. Retrieved February 20, 2006, from http://ceee.gwu.edu/ Products_ELLs/IsitReal.pdf

Lau v. Nichols, 414 U.S. 56 (1974).

The leadership tide has turned on climate change. (2007, Spring). *Harvard Green Campus Initiative, 10,* 1.

Lee, S. J. (2005). *Up against whiteness: Race, school and immigrant youth.* New York: Teachers College Press.

Lenneberg, E. H. (1967). *Biological foundations of language.* New York: Wiley.

Leung, C. (2005). Classroom teacher assessment of second language development: Construct as practice. In E. Hinkel (Ed.), *Handbook of research in second language teaching and learning* (pp. 869–888). Mahwah, NJ: Lawrence Erlbaum.

Lowe, M. E. (1996). *Immigrant acts: On Asian American cultural politics.* Durham, NC: Duke University Press.

Lyman, F. T. (1981). The responsive classroom discussion: The inclusion of all students. In A. Anderson (Ed.), *Mainstreaming digest* (pp. 109–113). College Park: University of Maryland Press.

Markee, N. (2005). Conversation analysis for second language acquisition. In E. Hinkel (Ed.). *Handbook of research in second language teaching and learning* (pp. 355–374). Mahwah, NJ: Lawrence Erlbaum.

Martinelli, G. (Producer), & Luhrmann, B. (Writer/Director). (1996). *Romeo and Juliet* [Motion picture]. Los Angeles: 20th Century Fox.

Marzano, R., Pickering, D., & McTighe, J. (1993). *Assessing student outcomes: Performance assessment using the dimensions of learning model.* Alexandria, VA: Association for Supervision and Curriculum Development.

Marzano, R. J., & Kendall, J. S. (1998). *Awash in a sea of standards.* Retrieved November 19, 2007, from www.mcrel .org/PDF/Standards/5982IR_AwashInaSea.pdf

Maslow, A. (1971). *The farther reaches of human nature.* New York: Viking Press.

Massachusetts Department of Elementary and Secondary Education. (2005). *2005 MCAS Sample Student Work Grade 8 MCAS.* Retrieved July 1, 2008, from www.doe.mass.edu/mcas/student/2005/ question.asp?GradeID=8&SubjectCode=mth& QuestionTypeName=&QuestionID=3358

McKeon, D. (2005). *Research talking points: How many English language learners are there?* Washington, DC: National Education Association. Retrieved June 24, 2008, from www.nea.org/achievement/ talkingells.html

McLaughlin, B. (1990). Restructuring. *Applied Linguistics, 11,* 113–128.

Mehr, M., & Jaffee, D. (2007). *Choosing sides: The Native Americans' role in the American Revolution.* Retrieved July 9, 2008, from http://edsitement.neh.gov/view_lesson_plan.asp?id=718

Meltzer, J., & Okashige, S. (2001). Supporting adolescent literacy across the content areas. *Perspective on Policy and Practicey.* Retrieved December 31, 2007, from www.alliance.brown.edu/pubs/ perspectives/adlitcontent.pdf

Menken, K. (2008). *English learners left behind: Standardized testing as language policy.* Clevedon, UK: Multilingual Matters.

Menken, K., & Antunez, B. (2001). *An overview of the preparation and certification of teachers working with limited English proficient (LEP) students* (Report No. ED-99-CO-007). Washington, DC: National Clearinghouse for Bilingual Education. (ERIC Document Reproduction Service No. ED455231)

Mid-Continent Research for Education and Learning. (Ed.). (1999). *Including culturally and linguistically diverse students in standards-based reform: A report on McREL's Diversity Roundtable I.* Aurora, CO: Author.

Modern Language Association. (n.d.). *All languages reported to the US census in 2000.* Retrieved June 24, 2008, from www.mla.org/map_data_langlist&mode=lang_tops

Moll, L. C. (1994). Literacy research in community and classrooms: A sociocultural approach. In R. B. Ruddell, M. R. Ruddell, & Singer, H. (Eds.), *Theoretical models and processes of reading* (4th ed., pp. 179–207). Newark, DE: International Reading Association.

Moll, L. C., Amanti, C., Neff, D., & Gonzalez, N. (1992). Funds of knowledge for teaching: A qualitative approach to developing strategic connections between homes and classrooms. *Theory Into Practice, 31*(2), 132–141.

Nagy, W. E., & Scott, J. A. (2000). Vocabulary processes. In M. L. Kamil, P. B. Mosenthal, P. D. Pearson, & R. Barr (Eds.), *Handbook of reading research* (pp. 269–284). Mahwah, NJ: Lawrence Erlbaum.

Nation, I. S. P. (2001). *Learning vocabulary in another language.* Cambridge, UK: Cambridge University Press.

Nation, P., & Waring, R. (1998). Vocabulary size, text coverage, and word lists. In N. Schmitt & M. McCarthy (Eds.), *Vocabulary: Description, acquisition, and pedagogy* (pp. 6–19). New York: Cambridge University Press.

National Child Traumatic Stress Network. (2005). *Review of child and adolescent refugee mental health.* Retrieved December 5, 2007, from www.nctsnet.org/nctsn_assets/pdfs/reports/refugeereview.pdf

National Commission on Writing, College Entrance Examination Boards. (2003). *A report of National Commission on Writing in America's Schools and Colleges: The neglected "R": The need for a writing revolution.* Retrieved March 30, 2008, from www.writingcommission.org

National Commission on Writing. (2006). *Writing and school reform.* Retrieved March 30, 2008, from www.writingcommission.org

National Institute of Child Health and Human Development. (2000). *Report of the National Reading Panel. Teaching children to read: An evidence-based assessment of the scientific research literature on reading and its implications for reading instruction* (NIH Publication No. 00–4769). Washington, DC: Government Printing Office.

National Virtual Translation Center. (2007). *Languages spoken in the U.S.* Retrieved June 24, 2008, from www.nvtc.gov/lotw/months/november/USlanguages.html

Nguyen, T. A. (n.d.). *American Athenas: Women in the Revolution.* Retrieved January 19, 2008, from http://americanrevolution.org/nguyen.html

Nicolson, C. P. (2005). Is chance fair? One student's thoughts on probability. *Teaching Mathematics to Children, 12*(2), 83–88.

Nieto, S. (1999). *The light in their eyes: Creating multicultural learning communities.* New York: Teachers College press.

O'Dell, S. (1980). *Sarah Bishop.* New York: Houghton Mifflin.

Ogbu, J. (1990). Cultural model, identity, and literacy. In J. W. Stigler, R. A. Shweder, & G. Herdt (Eds.), *Cultural psychology* (pp. 520–541). Cambridge, UK: Cambridge University Press.

O'Hanlon, M. E. (2008, February 6). Turning of the tide. *The Washington Post.* Retrieved July 14, 2008, from www.brookings.edu/opinions/2003/1007iraq_ohanlon.aspx

Ohlhausen, M., & Jepsen, M. (1992). Lessons from Goldilocks: "Somebody's been choosing my books but I can make my own choices now." *New Advocate, 5*(1), 31–46.

Paine, Thomas. *Common Sense.* Philadelphia: printed. And sold by W. and T. Bradford [1776]; Bartleby.com, 1999. www.bartleby.com/133.html September 8, 2008

Pappas, T. (2002). *Math Talk.* San Carlos, CA: Wide World.

Patten, K., & Craig, D. (2007). iPods and English language learners: A great combination. *Teacher Librarian, 34*(5), 40–44.

Patterson, K. (1991). *Lyddie.* New York: Trumpet Club.

Pauk, W. (1974). *How to study in college* (2nd ed.). Boston: Houghton Mifflin.

Peregoy, S. F., & Boyle, O. F. (2004). *Reading, writing and learning in ESL: A resource book for K-12 teachers, MyLabSchool Edition* (4th ed.). Boston: Allyn & Bacon.

Persky, H. R., Daane, M. C., & Jin, Y. (2003). *The Nation's report card: Writing 2002* (NCES 2003–529). Washington, DC: U.S. Department of Education, Institute of Education Sciences, National Center for Education Statistics.

Phelan, P., Davidson, A. L., & Yu, H. C. (1998). *Adolescents' worlds: Negotiating family, peers, and school.* New York: Teachers College Press.

Phinney, M. (1991). Computer-assisted writing and writing apprehension in ESL students. In P. Dunkel (Ed.), *Computer-assisted language learning and testing: Research issues and practice* (pp. 189–204). New York: Newbury House.

Pigada, M., & Schmitt, N. (2006). Vocabulary acquisition from extensive reading: A case study [Electronic version]. *Reading in a Foreign Language, 18*(1). Retrieved January 1, 2008, from http://nflrc.hawaii.edu/rfl/April2006/pigada/pigada.html

Phinney, M., & Mathis, C. (1990). ESL student responses to writing with computers. *TESOL Newsletter, 24*(2), 30–31.

Pinker, S. (2007). *The language instinct.* New York: HarperCollins.

Poe, E. A. (1845). *The Raven.* (Available from www.poemuseum.org/selected_works/the_raven.html)

Poe, E. A., & Simon, S. (Writers), & Silverman, D. (Director). (1990). Treehouse of horror: The raven [Segment from a television series episode]. In A. Jean, J. L. Brooks, M. Groening, & S. Simon (Producers), The Simpsons. Beverly Hills, CA: Fox Broadcasting Company.

Portes, A., & Rumbaut, R. (2001). *Legacies: The story of the immigrant second generation.* Berkeley: University of California Press.

Public Education Network and National Coalition for Parent Involvement in Education. (2006). Programs of English language learners (NCLB Action Briefs). Retrieved March 29, 2008, from www.publiceducation.org/portals/nclb/lep/index.asp

Raimes, A. (1991). Out of the woods: Emerging traditions in the teaching of writing. *TESOL Quarterly, 25,* 407–430.

Ramirez, R. R., & de la Cruz, G. P. (2002). The Hispanic population in the United States: March 2002 (Current Population Reports, P20–545). Washington, DC: U.S. Census Bureau. Retrieved January 31, 2008, from www.census.gov/prod/2003pubs/p20-545.pdf

Rea-Dickins, P. (2001). Mirror, mirror on the wall: Identifying processes of classroom assessment. *Language Testing, 18,* 429–462.

Reyes, P., Scribner, J. D., & Paredes Scribner, A. (Eds.). (1999). *Lessons from high-performing Hispanic schools: Creating learning communities.* New York: Teachers College Press.

Rhawn, J. (1996). *Neuropsychiatry, neuropsychology, and clinical neuroscience.* Baltimore: Wiliams & Wilkins.

Rinaldi, A. (1986). *Time enough for drums.* New York: Random House.

Rhoder, C. (2002). Mindful reading: Strategy training that facilitates transfer. *Journal of Adolescent & Adult Literacy, 45,* 498–512.

Richard-Amato, P. (2003). *Making it happen: From interactive to participatory language teaching* (3rd ed.). White Plains, NY: Pearson ESL.

Richgels, D. G. (2001). Invented spelling, phonemic awareness, and reading and writing instruction. In S. B. Neuman & D. K. Dickson (Eds.), *Handbook of early literacy research* (pp. 142–155). New York: Guilford Press.

Rogoff, B. (2003). *The cultural nature of human development.* New York: Oxford University Press.

Rose, K. R., & Kasper, G. (2001). *Pragmatics in language teaching.* New York: Cambridge University Press.

Rose, M. (1989). *Lives on the boundary: The struggles and achievements of America's underprepared.* New York: Free Press.

Rosenblatt, L. (1978). *The reader, the text, and the poem: The transactional theory of the literary work.* Edwardsville: Southern Illinois University Press.

Rosenblatt, L. (1995). *Literature as exploration* (5th ed.). New York: Modern Language Association of America.

Rost, M. (2005). L2 listening. In E. Hinkel (Ed.), *Handbook of research in second language teaching and learning* (pp. 503–528). Mahwah, NJ: Lawrence Erlbaum.

Rost, M., & Ross, S. (1991). Learner use of strategies in interaction: Typology and teachability. *Language Learning, 41,* 235–273.

Rothstein-Fisch, C., Greenfield, P. M., & Trumbull, E. (1999). Bridging cultures with classroom strategies. *Educational Leadership, 56*(7), 64–67.

Ruddell, M. R., & Shearer, B. A. (2002). "Extraordinary," "tremendous," "exhilarating," "magnificent": Middle school at-risk students become avid word learners with the Vocabulary Self-Collection Strategy (VSS). *Journal of Adolescent & Adult Literacy, 45*(5), 352–363.

Ruddell, R. B., & Ruddell, M. R. (1994). Language acquisition and literacy processes. In R. B. Ruddell, M. R. Ruddell, & H. Singer (Eds.), *Theoretical models and processes of reading* (4th ed., pp. 83–123). Newark, DE: International Reading Association.

Russek, B. (1998.). Writing to learn mathematics. *Writing Across the Curriculum.* Retrieved March 30, 2008, from http://wac.colostate.edu/journal/vol9/russek.pdf

Salinger, J. D. (1982). *The catcher in the rye.* New York: Penguin Books. (Original work published 1951)

Sánchez, M. T. (2007). How teachers in Massachusetts experienced the passage of Question 2. *Bilingual Basics, 9*(2). Retrieved July 14, 2008, from www.tesol.org//s_tesol/sec_issue.asp?nid=3077&iid= 10029&sid=1#135

Saphier, J., & Gower, R. (1997). *The skillful teacher: Building your teaching skills.* Acton, MA: Research for Better Teaching.

Schmidt, R. (2001). Attention. In P. Robinson (Ed.), *Cognition and second language instruction* (pp. 3–33). New York: Cambridge University Press.

Selinker, L. (1991). *Rediscovering interlanguage* (Applied linguistics and language study). New York: Longman.

Seuss, Dr. (pseud.). (1957). *The cat in the hat.* New York: Random House.

Short, D. (2002). Language learning in sheltered social studies classes. *TESOL Journal,* 11(1), 18–24.

Short, D., & Fitzsimmons, S. (2007). *Double the work: Challenges and solutions to acquiring language and academic literacy for adolescent English language learners-a report to Carnegie Corporation of New York.* Washington, DC: Alliance for Excellent Education.

Skutnabb-Kangas, T. (2000). *Linguistic genocide in education—or worldwide diversity and human rights.* Mahwah, NJ: Lawrence Erlbaum.

Smiley, P., & Salsberry, T. (2007). *Effective schooling for English language learners: What elementary principals should know and do.* Larchmont, NY: Eye on Education.

Smith, R. (2003). *Zach's lie.* New York: Hyperion.

Snow, C. (2006). Cross-cutting themes and future research directions. In D. August & T. Shanahan (Eds.), *Developing literacy in second-language learners* (pp. 631–652). Mahwah, NJ: Lawrence Erlbaum.

Snow, M. A. (2004). A model of academic literacy for integrated language and content instruction. In E. Hinkel (Ed.), *Handbook of research in second language teaching and learning* (pp. 693–712). Mahwah, NJ: Lawrence Erlbaum.

Spielberg, S. (Producer/Director), & Molen, G. R., & Lustig, B. (Producers). (1993). *Schindler's List* [Motion picture]. United States: Universal.

Spindler, G. D., Spindler, L., Trueba, H., & Williams, M. (1990). Cultural process and Ethnography: An anthropological perspective. In M. D. LeCompte, W. L. Millroy, & J. Preissle (Eds.), *Handbook of qualitative research in education* (pp. 53–92). San Diego, CA: Academic Press.

Spring, J. (2000). *The intersection of cultures: Multicultural education in the United States and the global economy* (2nd ed.). Boston: McGraw-Hill.

Stahl, S. A., & Nagy, W. E. (2006). *Teaching word meanings.* Mahwah, NJ: Lawrence Erlbaum.

Swain, M. (1985). Communicative competence: Some roles of comprehensible input and comprehensible output in its development. In S. Gass & C. Madden (Eds.), *Input in second language acquisition* (pp. 235–256). New York: Newbury House.

Swain, M. (1988). Manipulating and complementing content teaching to maximize second language learning. *TESL Canada Journal,* 9(1), 68–83.

Tang, Y., Zhang, W., Chen, K., Feng, S., Shen, J., Reiman, E. M., et al. (2006). Arithmetic processing in the brain shaped by cultures. *Proceedings of the National Academy of Sciences of the United States of America, 103*(28), 10775–10780.

Tarone, E. (2005). Speaking in a second language. In E. Hinkel (Ed.), *Handbook of research in second language teaching and learning* (pp. 485–502). Mahwah, NJ: Lawrence Erlbaum.

Tatum, A. (2005). *Teaching reading to black adolescent males: Closing the achievement gap.* Portland, ME: Stenhouse.

Tatum, B. (2003). *Why are all the black kids sitting together in the cafeteria: And other conversations about race.* New York: Basic Books.

Taylor, D. (1998). *Many families, many literacies: An international declaration of principles.* Portland, ME: Heinemann.

Taylor, D. (1990). *Learning denied.* Portland, ME: Heinemann.

Teachers of English to Speakers of Other Languages. (2000). *Assessment and accountability of English for speakers of other languages (ESOL) students.* Retrieved January 5, 2008, from www.tesol.org/s_tesol/sec_document.asp?CID=32&DID=369

Teachers of English to Speakers of Other Languages. (2003, March). *Position paper on high-stakes testing for K-12 English-language learners in the United States of America.* Retrieved June 24, 2008, from www.tesol.org/s_tesol/bin.asp?CID=239&DID=375&DOC=FILE.pdf

Teachers of English to Speakers of Other Languages. (2006). *PreK-12 English language proficiency standards.* Alexandria, VA: Author.

Tharp, R. G., Estrada, P., Dalton, S., & Yamauchi, L. A. (2000). *Teaching transformed: Achieving excellence, fairness, inclusion, and harmony.* Boulder, CO: Westview Press.

Thomas, W. P., & Colier, V. (1997). *School effectiveness for language minority students* (NCBE Resource Collection Series, No. 9). Washington, DC: National Clearinghouse for Bilingual Education.

Tomlinson, C. A. (1999). *The differentiated classroom: Responding to the needs of all learners.* Alexandria, VA: Association for Supervision and Curriculum Development.

Tomlinson, C. A. (2001). *How to differentiate instruction in mixed-ability classrooms* (2nd ed.). Alexandria, VA: Association for Supervision and Curriculum Development.

Tomlinson, C. A. (2003). *Differentiation in practice: A resource guide for differentiating curriculum: Grades 5–9*. Alexandria, VA: Association for Supervision and Curriculum Development.

Tomlinson, C. A., & McTighe, J. (2006). *Integrating differentiated instruction and understanding by design*. Alexandria, VA: Association for Supervision and Curriculum Development.

Tovani, C. (2000). *I read it, but I don't get it. Comprehension strategies for adolescent readers*. Portland, ME: Stenhouse.

Tovani, C. (2004). *Do I really have to teach reading? Content comprehension, Grades 6–12*. Portland, ME: Stenhouse.

Troike, R. (1993–1994). The case for subject-matter training in ESP. *TESOL Matters*, 3, 7.

U.S. Department of Education. (2002). *Key policy letters signed by the Education Secretary or Deputy Secretary*. Retrieved January 2, 2008, from www.ed.gov/policy/elsec/guid/secletter/020724.html

U.S. Department of Education. (2005a). *Developing programs for English language learners: Charts*. Retrieved June 28, 2008, from www.ed.gov/about/offices/list/ocr/ell/charts.html

U.S. Department of Education. (2005b). *Stronger accountability: Nation's report card shows continued progress-general*. Retrieved November 4, 2007, from www.ed.gov/nclb/accountability/achieve/ report-card.html

U.S. Department of Education. (2006a). *Regulations to implement statutory provisions regarding state, local educational agency (LEA), and school accountability for the academic achievement of limited English proficient (LEP) students*. Retrieved June 24, 2008, from www.ed.gov/legislation/FedRegister/finrule/2006-3/091306a.html

U.S. Department of Education. (2006b). *The growing numbers of limited English proficient students 1994/95–2004/05*. Retrieved December 8, 2007, from www.ncela.gwu.edu/policy/states/reports/ statedata/2004LEP/GrowingLEP_0405_Nov06.pdf

U.S. Department of Education. (2007). Standards and assessments peer review guidance: Information and examples for meeting the No Child Left Behind Act of 2001. Retrieved January 3, 2008, from www.ed.gov/policy/elsec/guid/saaprguidance.doc

Villegas, A. M., & Lucas, T. (2002). *Educating culturally responsive teachers: A coherent approach*. Albany: State University of New York.

Villegas, A. M., & Lucas, T. (2002). Preparing culturally responsive teachers: Rethinking the curriculum. *Journal of Teacher Education*, 53(1), 20–43.

Vygotsky, L. S. (1978). *Mind in society*. Harvard, MA: Harvard University Press.

Ward, B. A. (1987). *Instructional grouping in the classroom* (School Improvement Research Series, No. 2). Portland, OR: Northwest Regional Educational Laboratory.

Weaver, C. (2002). *Reading process and practice* (3rd ed.). Portsmouth, NH: Heinemann.

West, M. (1953). *A general service list of English words*. London: Longman, Green.

Wiggins, G., & McTighe, J. (1998). *Understanding by design* Alexandria, VA: Association for Supervision and Curriculum Development.

Wiggins, G., & McTighe, J. (2005). *Understanding by design* (Expanded 2nd ed.). Alexandria, VA: Association for Supervision and Curriculum Development.

Wildman, D. M., & King, M. (1978–1979). Semantic, syntactic, and spatial anticipation in reading. *International Reading Association*, 14(2), 128–164.

Wilensky, M. (2005). *The elementary common sense of Thomas Paine: The famous 1776 pamphlet edited and adapted for ages 11 to adult*. Arvada, CO: 13 Stars Publishing.

Winsor, M. S. (2007). Bridging the language barrier in mathematics. *Mathematics Teacher*, 101(5), 372–277.

Zabala, D., Minnici, A., McMurrer, J., Hill, D., Bartley, A., & Jennings, J. (2007). *State high school exit exams: Working to raise test scores*. Washington, DC: Center on Education Policy. Retrieved June 28, 2008, from www.cep-dc.org

Zehler, A. M., Fleischman, H. L., Hopstock, P. J., Stephenson, T. G., Pendzick, M. L., & Sapru, S. (2003). *Descriptive study of services to LEP students and LEP students with disabilities* (Contract No. ED-00-CO-0089). Retrieved February 27, 2006, from www.ecs.org

Index

comprehensible materials in, 180–184
literacy, 188–189
for purpose, 200
rates, 199
top-down, 87–89
Realia and visuals, 173–176, 223–224
Receptive language, 31, 111
Recognizing and tapping funds of knowledge, 70–71
Reflections
of J. Hayes, 283–284
of J. Peterson, 216–218
of L. Chin, 261–263
of M. Bell, 237–239
Refugees, 60–61
Relationship with nature and fate, 56–57
Resource boxes, 184
Retelling reading strategy, 199
Revising student writing, 203–204
Revolution: America's Fight for Independence, The, 261
Richard-Amato, P., 28
Rogoff, B., 54, 56, 57
Romeo and Juliet, 127, 134, 282
Rose, M., 100
Rost, M., 80, 81

Saving Private Ryan, 58
Schema theory, 47
Schwarzenegger, Arnold, 46
Science
academic literacy and, 188–189
aligning lessons with standards in, 221–229
assessments, 149–150 (table), 219–221
biological, 112–113
classrooms, 214–215
consumer, 176
diagrams and graphic organizers in, 178
enduring understanding and, 114, 116, 129,
135–136, 145, 147
environmental, 105–106, 116, 129, 135–136
essential questions in, 129, 135–136
"finite resources" unit, 218–221
GIST strategy, 230
"growing populations, growing footprints" lesson, 224–227
informed decision making lesson, 227–229
instructional materials, 215–216
"land boundaries" lesson, 221–224
language mini lessons, 229–231
language objectives, 222–223, 225
from learning outcomes to assessment evidence in, 124 (table)
note taking for key points and summarization, 230
reading comprehension strategies, 199
realia and visuals in, 175–176, 223–224
reflections on, 216–218

resource boxes, 184
strategies for improving student writing in, 202–204
TELLiM model planning and, 208–209, 213
textbooks, 223
Second-language acquisition, 37
by adolescents, 46
affective filter and, 38
comprehensible input and, 39–41
context and, 39–41
conversational knowledge and, 26–27
first language development and, 27–28
input hypothesis and, 38–39
Krashen's theory of, 37
schema theory, 47
Self-assessment
probability and statistics unit, 240
reading comprehension, 200
Self-collection, vocabulary, 196–197
Semantics, 33
mapping, 194
Sensitive period in language development, 30, 80
Sentence combining, 205
Shadow of the Wind, The, 127
Shanks, G., 195
Sheltered English Immersion (SEI), 12–13
Sheltered Instruction Observation Protocol (SIOP), 164–165
Shock, culture, 60–61
Silent period in second language acquisition, 37
Silent Spring, 223
Simpsons, The, 177, 282
Sink-or-swim approach to teaching ELLs, 10, 14
Snow, C. E., 89, 90
Socialization and zone of proximal development, 42–43
Social structure, 57–58
Socioeconomic levels of ELLs, 7
Solis, Freddy, 3–4, 14 (table), 62–63, 66, 68 (table),
70–71, 85–86, 91, 279, 303
Sounds, language, 31
Spanish speakers, 3–4, 6–7, 58, 62–63, 77, 172
Speaking, academic, 84–86
Specially Designed Academic Instruction in English (SDAIE), 12–13
Speech, academic, 84–86
Spring, J., 53
Stahl, S. A., 189, 191, 193, 194, 195
Standardized testing, 5–6, 142–144
Standards, 142–144
English language arts, 286–296
history, 266–272
math, 241–253
science, 221–229
Statistics
graphical representations lesson, 252–253
and probability unit, 239–241

complex and sophisticated sentences, 205
connecting inquiry activities to, 202
for content-area learning, 203
content-area models and, 203
editing student, 204
essays, 295–296
product goals for, 205
reflecting on reading in, 199
revising, 203–204

strategies for improving student, 202–205
summarizing, 204
system, 90–91
teaching strategies for academic, 201–205
using computers to support, 205

Zach's Lie, 200, 293
Zafon, C. R., 134
Zone of proximal development, 42–43

About the Authors

Michaela Colombo is an assistant professor in leadership in schooling at the Graduate School of Education at the University of Massachusetts Lowell, where she supervises doctoral students and teaches Methods of Sheltered English Instruction, Diversity Issues for School Leaders, and Sociocultural Contexts of Education. Prior to joining the faculty full-time in 2004, she was the districtwide supervisor of the Bilingual/English Language Acquisition Department for the Methuen Public Schools in Massachusetts, where she worked extensively with English Language Learners (ELLs), their families, and their teachers. During her time as Department Supervisor, she implemented the Parent Partnership for Achieving Literacy (PAL) program, the central goal of which was to improve educational opportunities for ELLs by building two-way bridges between parents and mainstream teachers. She authored several articles on the PAL program, which were published by *Educational Leadership, Multicultural Perspectives*, and *Phi Delta Kappan.* Colombo holds professional certification in bilingual education and ESOL. She has taught content-area subjects to ELLs in Grades 5 through 12 and English as a second language to young children and their parents in family literacy situations and to adults in workplace literacy settings. Differentiating instruction has played an important role in her teaching, and in 2007, she published *Blogging to Improve Instruction in Differentiated Science Classrooms* with coauthor Paul Colombo. She was recently awarded a fellowship from the Asian American Institute at the University of Massachusetts–Boston to study the perspectives of successful Cambodian American high school students.

Dana Furbush works in the Language Acquisition Department for the Methuen Public Schools in Massachusetts. Within the district, she has taught English as a second language to students at all levels of English proficiency, from kindergarten to adult learners. Currently, she works as the English language development facilitator, assisting mainstream teachers of ELLs. In addition, she regularly designs and delivers professional development opportunities. Most recently, she cotaught a series of workshops to incorporate project-based learning and SMARTboard technology into the diverse, mainstream classroom. Furbush has also implemented a grant-funded ELL after-school program at the middle school level, which sought to build math knowledge through language-rich, meaningful activities and encourage the development of writing skills and interest through the writing workshop model. She has collaborated with sheltered English and mainstream teachers to design ELL rubrics and guides for mainstream teachers, to create an ESL curriculum, and to build a standards-based English language acquisition report card. As a trainer for the Massachusetts Department of Education, she trains classroom teachers in the areas of *sheltering content instruction* and *assessing speaking and listening.* She has taught courses in sheltered instruction in graduate programs in education, as an adjunct instructor, for the University of Massachusetts Lowell and Cambridge College. In Santiago, Chile, she taught English as a foreign language. She is a member of Teachers of English to Speakers of Other Languages (TESOL) and the Massachusetts Association of Teachers of Speakers of Other Languages (MATSOL).